The CAMP DAVID ACCORDS

The CAMP DAVID ACCORDS

A Testimony

Mohamed Ibrahim Kamel

KPI

London, New York and Sydney

First published in 1986 by KPI Limited
11 New Fetter Lane, London EC4P 4EE, England

Reprinted 1986

Distributed by
Routledge & Kegan Paul, Associated Book Publishers (UK) Ltd.
11 New Fetter Lane, London EC4P 4EE, England

Methuen Inc., Routledge & Kegan Paul
29 West 35th Street
New York, NY 10001, USA

Routledge & Kegan Paul
Methuen Law Book Company
44 Waterloo Road,
North Ryde, NSW 2113
Australia

Produced by Worts-Power Associates

Set in 10 on 12 pt Times
by Inforum Ltd, Portsmouth
and printed in Great Britain
by Redwood Burn Limited, Trowbridge, Wiltshire

© Mohamed Ibrahim Kamel, 1986

No part of this book may be reproduced in any form
without permission from the publisher, except for
the quotation of brief passages in criticism.

ISBN 07103–0150–2

Contents

1 Background: How I met Anwar El Sadat 1

2 Background: El Sadat President 8

3 The Peace Initiative 14

4 Ismailia (25 December 1977) 21

5 Meditations 28

6 An Understanding 41

7 Are You Afraid Of Going To Jerusalem? 47

8 Jerusalem 53

9 The Last Supper 62

10 Don't Put All Your Eggs In One Basket 72

11 The Scenario (February 1978) 78

12 Danger from Within 88

13 The European Salad 96

14 A Deadly Octopus is Born and Reared in Darkness 108

15 Personal Impressions 118

16 What About the Palestinians? 124

17 Making War While Talking Peace 132

18 An Unexpected Stab in the Back! 140

19	The Unadorned Story as seen from the Other Side	145
20	A Pause for Reflection	150
21	Towards Implementing the Scenario	155
22	Fall-Back Position	165
23	A Special Favour to Carter	175
24	Israel Rejects the Egyptian Project before it is Presented	184
25	Believe It Or Not!	190
26	Let's Topple Begin!	199
27	Inside the Ramparts of Leeds Castle	208
28	Not One Grain of Sand for Nothing	220
29	A Meeting with King Hussein	229
30	The Last Stand	239
31	The Leap to the Summit – Why?	255
32	You and I Will Make History	262
33	Fasting While Others Work	270
34	Strange Symptoms and Many Question Marks	280
35	On the Road to Camp David	294
36	The Roaring of the Lion and the Wisdom of the Monkeys	302
37	Kissinger's Curse Again	313
38	Between The Israeli Hammer and The American Anvil	326
39	Faint or Feint?	341
40	A Last Attempt Before Resigning	361
41	The Signing of the Accords, Sunday 17 September 1984	370
Appendix 1	Proposals relative to withdrawal from the West Bank and Gaza and security arrangements	383

Appendix 2   Framework fo the comprehensive peace settlement of the Middle East problem   385

Appendix 3   A framework for peace in the Middle East agreed at Camp David   390

Appendix 4   Framework for peace in the Middle East 397

Appensix 5   Framework for the conclusion of a peace treaty between Egypt and Israel   404

Selected Bibliography   407

Index   408

Chapter One

Background: How I Met Anwar El Sadat

In the early forties, I was a student at the Faculty of Law, King Fuad I University (now Cairo University). Egypt was then under British occupation. Along with a group of young people, I embraced the principles of the National Party established by Mustapha Kamel Pasha, who sought an end to the British occupation of Egypt, and to gain independence. This party had been revitalized recently by a group of young men headed by Fathy Radwan, Dr Nour-el-Din Taraf and Dr Zohair Garanna. World War II had then reached its peak and spread to North Africa. Rommel's Afrika Korps swept over the Western Desert, advancing towards Egypt in a succession of quick victories over the Allies. It was finally halted by General Montgomery at the battle of El Alamein, 120 kilometres from Alexandria.

The German invasion, whose target was the occupation of Egypt and control of the Suez Canal, provoked mixed feelings among Egyptians. Some feared that the German Nazi regime would supplant Britain in Egypt. Others were strongly in favour of it, in the hope that Egypt would be freed from British occupation and regain its independence. Several demonstrations were staged, with cries of "Forward, Rommel!"

In view of the agitated situation and the critical position of Britain and the Allies, British tanks surrounded the Royal Palace of Abdin on the night of 4 February 1942. King Farouk, who sympathized with the Germans, was compelled to dismiss Hussein Sirry Pasha and appoint to the post of Premier the Chairman of the Wafd Party, Mustapha El Nahas Pasha. This was designed to secure internal security in Egypt.

This British move aroused violent feelings, constituting as it did a gross affront to the King as symbol of the State. The events of 4 February were looked upon as a black-spot in the history of the Wafd and acted as a catalyst in intensifying the struggle to expel the British. Since Egypt was under Martial Law, clandestine nationalistic organizations began to proliferate among students and army officers.

In 1943, I, together with a group of my young relatives and some university students, set up a secret organization. This was designed to carry out operations against the British forces (whose soldiers roamed the streets of Cairo and several other Egyptian towns). The operations were modelled on the French Resistance Movement following the German occupation.[1]

The organization we established consisted of twenty-three members and a four-man directing committee, namely Hussein Tewfick, Naguib Fakhry (my cousins), Saad Kamel (a law student) and myself. Some time around the middle of 1945, Hussein Tewfick informed the board of directors that a certain Omar Abu Aly had suggested that he (Hussein) join a secret organization which, it appeared, disposed of superior resources. Hussein told him that he was already a member of another organization. They thereupon agreed to propose to their respective organizations that there should be co-operation and co-ordination between both organizations, since they were pursuing the same goal.

Our directing committee approved the proposal and instructed Hussein Tewfick and myself to meet representatives of the other organization to discuss co-operation and co-ordination between the two organizations. A few days later the meeting took place in one of the coffee shops in Opera Square. Hussein Tewfick and I met Omar Abu Aly, who introduced us to a young man accompanying him; his name was Anwar El Sadat.

Anwar El Sadat was several years older than we were. He was tall and dark, with a big moustache and a husky, deep voice. He wore eccentric clothes. He was wearing a dark grey suit, a light-coloured, red-checked waistcoat, a bright tie and white leather shoes. Our meeting lasted for close on ninety minutes. We discussed the general situation. He gave us to understand, rather vaguely, that he was a member of an organization composed of men in the armed forces. He had been an army captain but had been dismissed because he was suspected of sympathizing with the Germans. He was working at that time in contracting and transportation.

He was responsible for a change in our outlook which had never crossed our minds. Resistance to the British occupation forces was necessary and important, but ineffective. The only way we could attain our objectives effectively was through the elimination of Egyptain leaders co-operating with the British; were we to assassinate a certain number of such leaders in succession, the day would come when the British would be unable to find a single Egyptian to co-operate with them in ruling the country.

We went back to our directing committee and submitted what had transpired at the meeting. After discussion, we decided to carry out joint operations with the other organization. We likewise agreed that our activities would take in Egyptian public figures co-operating with the British.

Hussein Tewfick and I met Anwar El Sadat again in one of the popular coffee shops in El Ataba El Khadra Square called "Matathya". We informed him of our agreement to co-operate with him and his organization. He proposed the assassination of the leader of the Wafd Party, Mustapha El Nahas Pasha, for his disgraceful role in the events of 4 February. He would be killed as his car crossed Kasr el Ainy Street, the main street connecting

Background: How I Met Anwar El Sadat

Garden City, where he lived, and Mounira, the location of the Nady El Saadi (the club of the Wafd party).

We endorsed the proposal. A plan was drawn up assigning the main role to Hussein Tewfick, who had nerves of steel. Saad El Din Kamel and I, from our organization, and Sadat and Omar Abu Aly, from the other organization, would take part in the operation to cover Hussein Tewfick. Sadat's role consisted of waiting in a car he would park outside the American University in Cairo (which was near the place chosen for the attack on El Nahas Pasha). Sadat gave us a package containing two Bertha 9mm-calibre pistols, some ammunition and two British-made hand grenades.

The assassination attempt was carried out on the specified date. It failed. Hussein Tewfick was to hurl a bomb at Nahas Pasha's car to bring it to a halt as it crossed the road, and then was to shoot him. However, the driver had to speed-up to avoid a tram coming towards the car. The bomb exploded behind the car. The splinters caused some damage to the car but no one in it was hurt. The car sped quickly away. We returned to our homes and were never suspected of the assassination attempt, which was put down to persons unknown.

When Hussein Tewfick went to the place where he was to find Sadat in the car, he found no trace of either Sadat or the car.

Our activities were suspended for some months. The security forces were on the alert after the attempted assassination and stringent security measures were enforced.

On the night of 6 January 1946 (my birthday), Hussein Tewfick shot Amin Osman Pasha as he was entering the Anglo-Egyptian League Club in Adly Pasha Street. Amin Osman died shortly afterwards of his wounds.

Amin Osman, a member of the Wafd Party (and Finance Minister in Nahas' Cabinet) was known for his close and suspicious association with the British. He often made speeches and statements which were blatantly provocative of Egyptian feelings. In one such speech, he said that Egypt was tied to England in a Catholic marriage that knows no divorce . . . It was also rumoured that he had masterminded the events of 4 February.

Hussein Tewfick made his escape in the dark after an exciting adventure. Many people ran after him as he fired into the air. When his pursuers became too numerous, he threw a hand-grenade, which dispersed them without injuring anyone. He walked calmly to Ataba Square and took a tram home.

It was by a sheer coincidence that Hussein Tewfick was arrested. His father was Tewfick Pasha Ahmed, Under-Secretary of State at the Ministry of Communications. He had a reputation for being very strict in his work. He had sacked an official for misconduct. Hussein Tewfick was known to the official since he was the son of his superior. He was aware of Hussein's feelings of hatred and bitterness for the British. He had joined the Anglo-Egyptian League in an attempt to further himself through Amin Osman, its

President. As chance would have it, he met Hussein Tewfick a few days prior to the assassination in front of the headquarters of the League in Adly Street. Hussein was studying the scene of the operation to which he had been assigned. The official greeted him and exchanged a few words with him, after which Hussein departed.

After the assassination, a reward of L.E. 5,000 was offered by the government for any information leading to the killer's capture. The official went to the police and informed them that the man who had killed Amin Osman was Hussein Tewfick. It was mere guesswork.

At midnight, on the night of the assassination, officers from the political police force called on Hussein Tewfick in the villa where he lived with his family in the suburbs of Heliopolis. They searched the place and found some hidden arms and a diary. Hussein had jotted down some remarks expressing his hostility to the British, their henchmen, and the address of the Anglo-Egyptian League. They arrested him and took him away. After a lengthy interrogation he finally confessed to killing Amin Osman for political reasons. He gave the names of all the members of our organization and those of Anwar El Sadat and Omar Abu Aly.

We all, twenty-six persons, were taken into custody. All, save four confessed to being members of a clandestine organization. The four who had not confessed to such membership were Anwar El Sadat, Saad El Din Kamel, Naguib Fakhry and myself. We spent two months in the Foreigners' Prison, which was the place where political interrogations were conducted.[2] We were committed to solitary confinement and were not allowed to contact one another until the interrogations were concluded. The Public Prosecutor's Office and the political police were in charge of the investigation, and we were eventually sent to the Misr Criminal and Public Prison.[3]

My denial of any connection with the organization, and my subsequent denial of all knowledge of Sadat, were major factors in helping to clear him. With the exception of Hussein Tewfick and myself, he was unknown to the members of our organization. As to his own organization, he was known only to Omar Abu Aly. Both Hussein and Omar Abu Aly had included Sadat in their confessions. They averred that I had met him twice in their presence. My utter denial and that of Sadat strengthened his position in this case. This was particularly important as the Public Prosecutor and the political police laid great emphasis on Anwar El Sadat being primarily responsible for the assassinations committed. He was older than we were and had a record in the army. He had been pensioned off for participating with others in certain operations, among which was the attempted escape of the former Commander-in-chief of the Egyptian amry, Aziz Pasha El Masry, who was known to harbour feelings of great hostility to the British while sympathizing with the Germans.

Sadat appreciated the stand I had taken. When we were led to Misr Public Prison, we remained in solitary confinement, but were allowed to mingle for

Background: How I Met Anwar El Sadat

one hour in the morning and another in the afternoon, when we were taken to the prison courtyard for exercise and recreation. It was then that our relationship became rather close.

My father was deputy head of the Court of Appeal. He was both influential and highly popular in judicial and public prosecution circles. This gave me certain privileges. I was granted permission to receive food from my family. My mother sent enough food for me and a number of my co-defendants in the case. I shared the food equally among us. Anwar El Sadat had a great liking for good food. He often requested me to ask my mother for special dishes such as rice-and-pigeon casserole. My father was likewise able to procure for me permission for dental treatment outside the prison. Twice a week I went, under escort, to the dentist's clinic, where I met my family. Two hours later, I returned to prison laden with cigarettes and sweets. As this was forbidden, I arranged for my dental treatment days to fall on the days when a group of officers, who were Sadat's friends, were in charge. They let me in with the smuggled goods and soon allowed me to share meals with Sadat, in either of our respective cells during their shift.

In spite of the close relations between Sadat and myself in prison, he never told me anything about the group to which he belonged, nor did he reveal the names of any of its members. He did, however, mention the name of Hassan Ezzat, an air force officer, who had retired and who was Sadat's partner in the contracting business. I sometimes wondered about the truth of the matter, and whether he was really a member of such a group, or whether he was a "loner", operating on his own.

One day he came to my cell for lunch. When we had finished, he told me that some great event was to take place the following day. The event was to have a drastic effect on the case and guarantee all the defendants' acquittal, including ourselves. He said no more than that.

We were to be arraigned the following day before the magistrate. Two people in a green car attacked the court messenger, who was riding a bicycle. He had tied the original file of the case, numbering several thousand pages, to the carrier behind, and was proceeding along the highly congested Mohamed Aly Street. He was taking the file to court so it would be at the disposal of the judge when the court sat in judgment. The file had been at the judge's home for consideration before the court session. The two men tried to seize the file and carry it off in the car. The people on the street gathered around the messenger, who had yelled for help, and the men were forced to flee leaving the file behind. This was an ingenious idea. The file contained the signed confessions of Hussein Tewfick and the other defendants. Were the original text to disappear and the defendants to deny what they had previously confessed and signed, there would be no case against them and it would be impossible to secure any convictions.

The Amin Osman case, which was known as "the great political assassinations case", was a *cause célèbre*. The defendants had the services of the most prominent lawyers, who had either been retained or had volunteered for the job. Nearly all the political leaders were called to the witness-stand. Among them were the ex-Premier and leader of Wafd Party, Nahas Pasha; the ex-Premier and the then Chef de Cabinet of the King, Aly Maher Pasha; the leader of the Nationalist Party, Hafiz Ramadan; the leader of the El Kotla National Party, Makram Ebeid; ex-Premier Hussein Sirry Pasha; Hussein Heikal Pasha, speaker of the Senate House, etc. There was great sympathy among the people for the defendants. Public feeling ran high as one cabinet after another failed in the negotiations on British withdrawal from Egypt. The defendants were young people and university students, and Amin Osman had an established reputation as a traitor to his country and as a British agent. The case, and the many surprises it involved, were front-page news in all the Egyptian newspapers throughout the trials, which lasted two years.

Since great emphasis was laid on the role of Anwar El Sadat in the case, his behaviour and his sense of dramatics during the trial gained him fame and notoriety, all the more so as only four defendants were cleared of all charges; Anwar El Sadat, Saad Kamel, Naguib Fakhry and myself.

The case was certainly a milestone in his political career. He devoted several chapters to it in his book entitled *In Search of an Identity*, published while he was President of the Republic. On page 63 there is a paragraph in which he says:

> For a whole week I was indeed left alone. It was a week of tension, our minds fought a difficult battle, his trying to pin guilt onto me, mine trying to pull the case to pieces. Having thought it out thoroughly, I had come to the conclusion that Muhammed Kamel, a young cousin of Tewfik's (who is now the Foreign Secretary of Egypt) could not have made a confession. Young as he was, he should hold out, if anyone could. I tried to contact him through the warden and eventually succeeded. His response encouraged me. He was dependable, and working together, I hoped we could pull the case apart.

Footnotes

1   Palestine was under the British mandate. Zionist terrorist organizations carried out wide-scale activities against the Palestinians and the British forces stationed

in Palestine. In 1944, the terrorist Stern Gang despatched two of its men to Cairo. They assassinated Lord Moyne, who was in Cairo on a mission. They nearly succeeded in escaping, and the Egyptians would have been charged with the crime. By pure chance, an Egyptian constable happened to be present at the scene of the crime. He pursued and captured the killers, who confessed to their crime and were later sentenced and executed.

I recall that my father, who was deputy head of the Court of Appeal, had, at my request, procured for me a permit to attend the trial. I admired the courage of the defendants. They refuted the charge that their act constituted an act of terrorism, claiming that it was legitimate, as promoting the cause for the establishment of the State of Israel. Today, most Israelis deny such legitimacy to the Palestinian people and their struggle to realize their legitimate right to a Palestinian homeland. I cannot conceive of the impudence of Menahim Begin and his like, who deny the militants of the Palestine Liberation Organization the status of freedom-fighters struggling to return to their land from which they were evicted – particularly since Begin is responsible for the Deir Yassin massacre, in which hundreds of women and children were murdered. The massacre was one of the many acts of terrorism perpetrated by the Irgun Zvei Leumi and other Zionist organizations with a view to establishing the State of Israel.

2 The director of the Foreigners' Prison was an Englishman, a police commissioner living in a small villa attached to the prison garden. He had a pig, whom he called Saad Pasha after Saad Zaghloul, Egypt's celebrated national leader.

3 After the 23 July Revolution, Anwar El Sadat issued a decree for the demolition of the Misr Public Prison. He pulled down the first stones at an official ceremony:

Chapter Two

Background: El Sadat President

I graduated from the Faculty of Law in 1947, while I was still in jail. The verdict in the case was pronounced in 1948. Only after my acquittal was it possible to join the government service. I joined the Conseil d'Etat in 1949.

In July 1952, a group of military officers seized power and constituted a revolutionary council which replaced all former institutions. Among the members were Anwar El Sadat and Salah Salem, who was related to me by marriage.[1] Through this connection I was closely in touch with developments, when in 1955 relations between Salah Salem and Gamal Abdel Nasser started to deteriorate. I requested my transfer to the Ministry of Foreign Affairs for personal and public reasons. My request was agreed to and I was appointed Secretary to our Embassy in London.

After serving in London, Mexico, Montreal and Ottawa, I spent the next ten years as Egyptian Ambassador in various countries: from January 1968 I remained in Kinshassa-Zaire until October 1971; Stockholm until August 1973, and finally Bonn until December 1977. During these years Egypt in particular and the rest of the countries of the Middle East in general underwent severe trials and tribulations which occasionally assumed crisis proportions.

The 1967 War had ended catastrophically for the Arabs with Israel's occupation of the whole Egyptian Sinai Peninsula, the Golan Heights and the West Bank, including Jerusalem and the Gaza Strip – or all that then remained of Palestine.

In Egypt there reigned a feeling of frustration, coupled with a sense of bitterness and loss as the people awakened from the delusion – induced by Gamal Abdel Nasser and his propaganda machine – that the Egyptian army was the mightiest in the Middle East. The Arab world began gradually to realize the implications of the awful castastrophe and, licking its wounds, started to pull itself together. The scattered Egyptian forces were hastily reorganized and the war of attrition began. Simultaneously, the PLO, with Yasser Arafat at its head, began to be active and make itself felt, while intense Arab diplomatic efforts achieved some positive results by making a dent in the pro-Israeli bias within the Western world. Israel began to be seen in a different light: rather the devouring wolf than the role of the lamb it had perfected since it first appeared on the world scene.

On 30 September 1970, President Gamal Abdel Nasser died suddenly, affected by the bitterness of defeat, whereupon Sadat became President of the United Arab Republic.[2]

He inherited a responsibility heavily laden with problems and cares, and soon appeared to the world as nondescript in comparison with Gamal Abdel Nasser's forceful and dynamic personality. Opinions varied as to how long he would be able to stay in power: most thought not long, with the time-limit varying from a few weeks to a few months. Even Henry Kissinger, the then Presidential Adviser for National Security, expressed some such opinion, for Sadat, despite having been one of the principals who had helped to bring about the Revolution which took place on 23 July 1952, a Member of the Revolutionary Council, then Chairman of the National Assembly and finally vice-President to Nasser, had always shunned the spotlight, and was viritually unknown to anyone outside Egypt.

President Sadat soon took a series of steps that strengthened his position internally, and people began to look hopefully to the future. His first move was to eliminate what in Nasser's time were known as "power centres" – a group of powerful, autocratic men in various key positions throughout the country. These had pitted themselves against him from the very moment he became President. He succeeded in striking down the group in one fell swoop, although they included Ali Sabri, Nasser's right-hand man, who controlled the Arab Socialist Union (Egypt's only political organization); Sharawy Goma'a, Minister of Interior, who exercised similar control over all internal security; General Mohamed Fawzi, Minister of War and Mohamed Faik, Minister of Information, who presided over the radio, television and press. They were all apprehended at one stroke, brought to trial and sent to prison.

The group had been hated and feared, and Sadat's success won him a great deal of popularity among the people, who from then on pinned their hopes on him.

This first step by Sadat was followed by another: the releasing of all political prisoners, the closure of detention camps, and Sadat's declaration that Egypt would be governed by the Rule of Law. This declaration was very well received, coming as it did at a time when officials used publicly to affirm that "the Law was on vacation".

Next, Sadat embarked on a series of moves to alleviate discontent. Measures were adopted to put an end to sequestration – a revolutionary act from which a great number of people had unjustly suffered. The law of sequestration was often abused and had represented a Sword of Damocles over any who might not conform wholeheartedly to Nasser's regime. Even more important was the bringing to trial of persons accused of torturing political prisoners. The word "Democracy" began to be heard frequently.

Finally, and though motivated by difficult considerations, Sadat's expulsion of Soviet experts in July 1972 proved to be greatly popular; it particularly gratified army officers who were still smarting from their sense of defeat in 1967, and who blamed it on inadequate Soviet equipment.

Sadat had not been idle during the years he had kept himself under Nasser's shadow. He had had the time and the opportunity to get to know the people. He studied and analysed Egyptians' reaction to Nasser's performance. Silently he discovered the sources of their complaints and discontent, and he stored it all up in his memory. Nor was this all. Sadat never fooled himself: he fully realized that, whatever he achieved internally, and however strong his hold on the government became, and whatever support he got from the people, none of this would last long without tackling one particular problem – the Israeli occupation of Arab territories.

He knew full well that he could not long remain President of Egypt while Israeli forces occupied an important part of Egyptian territory, with their troops camped in full view on the East Bank of the Suez Canal, entrenched in their positions on the Bar-lev Line. This latter was presented by Israeli propaganda as an impregnable line of defence – a claim believed by the whole world, including the Arabs, the Egyptians and the Israelis themselves.

He saw quite clearly that the Egyptian people and the Arabs would never rest easy until they had regained their self-respect and their lands. He realized that he could not afford to remain inactive while the countdown was fast approaching zero: something had to be done promptly and effectively to alter the no-war/no-peace situation. He therefore began to work patiently and quietly to prepare the October War of 1973, an event that had momentous consequences. The world has never been the same since.

Following the 1973 War, the Arab nation began to breathe again, regaining some of its confidence, along with a feeling of reassurance that nothing was impossible. The Israeli giant was cut down to size. The legend of the Bar-lev Line was shown up for what it really was, and the myth of the invincible Israeli forces was destroyed. Israel's overbearing arrogance was shaken. European countries – for whom the problem was also one of life-and-death – were quick to proclaim their stand with regard to the Arab-Israeli conflict, and issued their first statement supporting the legitimacy of Palestinian rights and asserting the necessity of Israeli withdrawal from the occupied territories. Even the United States of America felt some of the tremor of the earthquake, causing it to reconsider its previous option of total support for Israeli policies. The October War also brought home the realization of the urgency of finding a comprehensive solution to the Arab-Israeli conflict which had, overnight, become a threat to the economy as well as the security of the world.

The October War along with the oil embargo represented the apogee of Arab solidarity. There seemed to be some sort of inherent co-ordination.

Egypt, together with Syria, provided the military component, while most of the oil-producing Arab states provided the economic counterpart.[3] Talk of the Arabs as the sixth world power began to gain credence in the press and, more importantly, in the conscience of the Arab nation.

There can be no doubt that Sadat played a major role in shaping this solidarity. Arab unity had been seriously disrupted in Nasser's time. It is truly ironical that the collapse of this same magnificent solidarity should have been at the hands of that same Sadat, who was to bring about its collapse in less than two years. However, that was still to come.

During the war, at the height of the Egyptian forces' triumph, President Sadat made a sagacious political move. In a speech to the People's Assembly, delivered on 16 October, he called for an international conference to be held at the United Nations for the establishment of peace in the Middle East. There was no immediate response. However, later that year a peace conference was held in Geneva under the chairmanship of the US and the USSR. It ended inconclusively but with prospects of an early reconvening, thus putting the brakes on the momentum towards a peaceful settlement that had been gained.

Then, in 1974, a youthful member of the Saudi Royal Family, recently returned from the United States where he had lived for several years, assassinated King Faisal under very strange and mysterious circumstances. A hurried secret trial was held for the assassin, and this was followed as quickly by his execution. The mystery was buried with him.

Thus the most powerful, most serious, moderate and dedicated Arab figure disappeared from the political scene – a fine figure who not only held the Arab world together through his dominance over most Arab leaders, but who had also demonstrated that he had the skill and the resolve to use that most powerful of weapons: oil.

King Faisal's murder was the signal for an attack on the recently revived solidarity of the Arab world. One might legitimately ask the classic question: who stood to gain most from Faisal's death? It is not a difficult question to answer for anyone who knows how certain organizations work in certain countries.

Relations between Egypt and the United States were practically non-existent since President Nasser severed diplomatic relations in protest at the role played by the Americans in the 1967 War. But following the October War in 1973, these relations soon revived. A year later, in fact, Henry Kissinger, then President Richard Nixon's Secretary of State, started his famous shuttle diplomacy, flying back and forth between Egypt and Israel. The first result of this was the disengagement agreement between Egypt and Israel, which President Sadat concluded without consulting with the other Arab nations, or even with Syria, Egypt's ally and partner in the 1973 War. This led to the first fissure in the Arab position.

Relations between Egypt and the United States continued to improve through Nixon's presidency. Nixon paid a State visit to Egypt, and when Gerald Ford came to power after Watergate, Sadat fostered Egyptian-American relations by developing personal and working ties with the new President. This was accompanied by a corresponding distancing from the Soviet Union.

Sadat seemed to feel that the more he attacked the Soviet Union the more he would gain American support. He therefore stepped up his attacks to a point that carried him beyond the limits which govern normal international relations – especially when one is dealing with a superpower that can help or hinder the shaping of affairs.

In 1976, Jimmy Carter was elected President and embraced the Brookings Report on the Middle East settlement.[4]

A year later, in May 1977, for the first time in the history of Israel, the Labour Party was defeated and the Likud coalition headed by Menahim Begin assumed the government of the country. Sadat had just concluded a visit to the United States and had interrupted his flight back to Egypt, stopping over in West Germany to spend a quiet day relaxing in the Black Forest.

I was Ambassador to the Federal Republic of Germany at the time and was accompanying him as he took a walk in the woods surrounding his hotel, when several reporters discovered us. One of them asked Sadat his opinion on Menahim Begin's election as Prime Minister. Sadat answered that, as far as he was concerned, there could be no difference between Begin, Rabin, Golda Meir or any other Israeli elected by the people of Israel. This might, however, have been a diplomatic answer, so I brought the subject up again at lunch, giving it as my opinion that he might perhaps have been more non-committal in his reply, particularly since Begin's party programme called for a Greater Israel to comprise all that remained of Palestine. I reminded him that Begin himself was an extremist and the terrorist responsible for the massacre of Deir Yassin. I referred to the fact that Begin was not allowed into England, where he was *persona non grata*. The result of the election would not make him change his views. I mentioned the fact that in 1954 President Kennedy (then Senator Kennedy) sent a telegram declining an invitation to the reception committee to welcome Menahim Begin as one of the liberators of Israel while on one of his fund-raising trips to the United States. The telegram read: "When I accepted to be a member of that committee, I had not known of Begin's terrorist past."[5]

I remember that Sadat answered that all Israelis were alike – a generalization which I could not accept. At the time we did not pursue the conversation any further, but Sadat's attitude and reaction remained with me for a long time.

Footnotes

1 I worked in Salah Salem's office when he was Minister of National Guidance and responsible for Sudan Affairs.
2 The name was later changed to the Arab Republic of Egypt.
3 The relationship that Sadat established with King Faisal was instrumental, since Saudi Arabia led the oil-producing states in the Gulf.
4 That report was prepared by a number of political scientists either specialized or interested in the Middle East, among whom were Zbgniev Brezinski and William Quant, who later became National Security Advisor and Assistant NSA. respectively. The report contained a study of the intricate factors at work in the Middle East conflict and purported to identify some elements that might offer a solution.
5 Alfred Lilienthal, *What Price Israel?*, 1953, p. 105.

Chapter Three

The Peace Initiative

At midnight on 9 November 1977, I went to bed and tuned to Radio Cairo as was my custom. It was broadcasting a recording of a speech delivered that day by President Sadat at the People's Assembly. A sentence in the speech attracted my attention. He said he was prepared to go any place in the world, even to the Israeli Knesset, in pursuit of peace and to spare the life of a single Egyptian soldier. The declaration surprised me somewhat but I did not give the matter much thought. Sadat often departed from the written text of his speeches, throwing out ideas and opinions as they occurred to him. The embassy, moreover, had received nothing to indicate such a train of thought.

The following day some Arab ambassadors in Bonn contacted me. They wanted to know what lay behind the statement. I told them that I had no information on the subject. It could be nothing more than a manoeuvre to embarrass the Israeli government. The latter frequently reiterated its readiness to negotiate directly with the Arab states, but had so far received no response.

But the situation developed rapidly. On 15 November, the Prime Minister of Israel, through the American embassies in Cairo and Tel-Aviv, extended a formal invitation to President Sadat to visit Jerusalem. Sadat accepted the invitation, and it was decided that the visit would begin on the evening of Saturday 19 November, the eve of Bairam. The surprise could scarcely have been greater all over the world.

This was apparent in the reaction of the German Foreign Office, which was at a loss in following the fast developing situation. Despite its impressive efficiency and competence, it lacked the background and information which would have prepared it for such an unconventional development in Arab-Israeli relations.

I rang up the Minister of Foreign Affairs, Ismail Fahmy, who was in Tunis attending an Arab Foreign Minister's conference. I was unable to reach him.

As Egypt's Ambassador in Bonn, I found myself in an awkward position. I received neither instructions nor clarifications. There was nothing I could

The Peace Initiative

say to the German Foreign Ministry; nor was I in a position to say anything to the reporters who assailed me with questions. The general atmosphere was one of complete bewilderment.

I could not conceive of any reason for such a development. All eyes were focused on Geneva where preparations for the International Peace Conference were under way. True, there were obstacles in the way of the Conference: there were likewise differences between the Arab States and Israel on various matters such as PLO representation. And the Arab states, particularly Egypt and Syria, differed among themselves. Egypt desired the separate participation of the Egyptian, Syrian and Jordanian delegations, with the inclusion of representatives of the Palestinian people in the Jordanian delegation. Syria insisted that the Arab side participated as a unified joint delegation, which would include representatives of the three States and the Palestinians.

The convening of the Geneva Conference seemed all but inevitable after the 1973 War, particularly in the wake of the United States and the Soviet Union Joint Communiqué of 1 October 1977. The joint Soviet-American communiqué consisted of a compromise agreement on a solution to the Palestinian problem and Israel's withdrawal from the occupied territories. The communiqué prepared the ground for the Geneva Conference. Israel moved heaven and earth to stir up feeling against the communiqué, claiming that it would re-open the way to Soviet influence in the Middle East following the expulsion of the Soviets by President Sadat.

President Carter, in particular, threw all his weight behind the Geneva Conference and its convening before the end of 1977.

The feeling was prevalent that the Arabs would be in a strong position at the Geneva Conference. From the time of the 1973 War to 1977, developments of an undoubtedly positive nature had taken place.

The crux of the Arab-Israeli conflict, the Palestinian question in particular, had achieved marked progress. Such progress was apparent in the recognition by the EEC of the legitimate rights of the Palestinian people, especially its right to self-determination. In 1974 the General Asembly, on whose agenda the Palestinian Question was inserted, adopted two major resolutions. The first reaffirmed the inalienable rights of the Palestinian people to self-determination without external interference and to national independence and sovereignty, and recognized the Palestinian people as a principal party in the establishment of a just and lasting peace in the Middle East. The second resolution, having considered the Palestinian people the principal party to the question of Palestine, invited the PLO to participate in the deliberations of the General Assembly on the question of Palestine in plenary meetings.[1] There was also Carter's elaboration on a homeland for the Palestinians, since his assumption of power.

For all these reasons, I could not fathom the abrupt renunciation of the Geneva Conference; nor could I understand how President Sadat could adopt a line of policy which would be oriented towards direct negotiations with Israel.

I wondered whether it was just a random thought that Sadat had included in his speech to the People's Assembly on 9 November which Begin had seized upon to invite him to Israel, thus cornering Sadat into a position where he could not decline the invitation. Several other questions came to my mind. Was there any prior understanding on the matter between Sadat and the Arab states, or at least some of them? Was it preceded by a secret understanding between Egypt and Israel? Was it planned by the United States? And were there any guarantees regarding the fulfilment of minimal Arab claims?

On the afternoon of Saturday 19 November, I learned from the radio and the news agencies that the Minister of Foreign Affairs, Ismail Fahmy, had handed in his resignation. This accentuated my concern, since he was close to Sadat. I at once suspected that Sadat's initiative had not been preceded by adequate preparation, at least as far as Ismail Fahmy was concerned – and he was a seasoned diplomat. Some hours later, the resignation of the Minister of State for Forcign Affairs, Mohamed Riad, was announced. And my suspicions were confirmed.

The Under-Secretary of State at the Ministry of Foreign Affairs, Dr Van Weil, summoned me to his office. He felt great concern over the resignations of Ismail Fahmy and Mohamed Riad. Both were known and respected by the Germans. Van Weil expressed a fear that the resignation of the two ministers might be taken as an indication of a serious division of Egyptian public opinion over Sadat's visit to Jerusalem. He dreaded lest it put the regime at risk. I gave him a guarded answer to the effect that the justifications for the resignations were unknown to me. I assured him on the stability of the internal situation and the Egyptian people's trust in Sadat. Van Weil told me that the Minister of Foreign Affairs was gravely concerned at the situation. Herr Genscher had great confidence in me, and relations between us were quite cordial. He asked to be notified of my arrival at the Foreign Ministry so that he could talk with me on the telephone from Tunis, where he was on an official visit. I did, in fact, talk to him, and was able to confirm that all was well in Egypt. He thanked me, and informed me that he was going to cut short his visit to Tunis and return immediately to Bonn.

Long before I was appointed Ambassador to Germany, it was an established custom to hold the Lesser and Greater Bairam Feast prayers in the Egyptian Embassy. The prayers were attended by the members of the Arab and Islamic diplomatic corps and other Muslims living in Bonn.

Bairam fell on 20 November, the date set for Sadat's visit to Jerusalem. In view of the violent repercussions in the Arab world provoked by Sadat's expected visit, the Foreign Ministry contacted me before the Feast. They pleaded with me to cancel the Bairam prayers in the Embassy. The security services were very apprehensive of the great risk involved in holding the prayers on that morning. I insisted on holding the prayers. Apart from patriotic and religious considerations, pride was a crucial factor. I likewise rejected the proposals put forward by the security services after I had insisted on holding the prayers in the Embassy. They wanted to have the German security services search all who came to attend the prayers before admission to the residence. Though deep down I did have fears, I called a meeting of the Embassy staff and all who worked in the residence. I requested the utmost vigilance on their part, and the inspection of any packages that might be left behind by those who came for prayers.

Certain Arab ambassadors and members of Arab embassies did not show up for prayers. Most, however, did attend the prayers, in view of our cordial mutual relations. I recall that the Imam (preacher), an Al-Azhar graduate on a study mission to Germany, referred, in the Feast sermon preceding the prayers, to the Bairam custom of sacrificing sheep and distributing meat to the poor. When he said, "God looks with favour upon slaughter this day," I shuddered. I turned to the Egyptian Councillor, our eyes met, and neither was able to suppress his laughter.

Prayers were conducted without untoward incident, much to the relief of my colleagues and myself. We went to the upper floor of the residence to watch on TV President Sadat in the Knesset. We were tense, anxious and curious.

The transmission began. We watched the arrival of President Sadat's plane and the formal reception. He shook hands with the Israeli leaders, namely Begin, Rabin, Golda Meir, and so forth. We felt as if we were in a dream glued to the TV set. We listened to Sadat's speech in the Knesset. It was an excellent speech, strong, rational and sober. Sadat laid down clearly the principles on which a just and comprehensive peace in our area should be based. I regained my equanimity.

In the evening, I was invited to the inauguration of an art exhibition by a group of Tunisian painters. This was to be followed by a reception. In spite of my utter exhaustion, I was determined to attend the reception. After the inauguration, I was surrounded by my Arab colleagues. Most of them resented the visit, and feared that it would culminate in a separate peace, especially since Sadat had not consulted any leader of the Arab world on his initiative. He had taken the risk and had presented them with a *fait accompli*.

The Arab ambassadors had feelings of affection and cordiality for me: the representatives of the states hostile to Sadat, such as Syria, Libya and Algeria, were no exception. I had felt great relief after Sadat's speech, and my morale had been boosted. I defended his initiative, pointing out that he was impelled to embark on it by Arab differences over the smallest trifles and by the fact that they were unable to reach agreement on a unified policy to face Israel at Geneva. I said that Egypt had never shirked its responsibility in the struggle against Israel or in defending the Palestinian cause. It had made enormous sacrifices in both lives and property. Most Arab states enjoyed the felicity and luxury accruing from oil, and had refrained from taking any positive steps towards solving the problem and establishing peace, while Egypt was going through difficult times economically and socially.

Egypt could no longer allow its future to hang upon the whims of Arab rulers who are reluctant to take positive stands that would help in resolving the Arab-Israeli conflict. I pointed out that the speech we had all heard involved no concessions with respect to Arab rights. He (Sadat) could not hide his head forever like an ostrich, for fear of confronting our enemy round a table in search of peace as he had already done in war. I told them that, in any case, there was no point in discussing the issue. The meeting had effectively taken place, and the *fait accompli* had become part of history. It was the duty of all Arabs to face up to the challenge of peace, and join the Sadat initiative on the basis of the principles enumerated in his speech.

Nevertheless, I spent a sleepless night. I was completely bemused. I found myself unable to make up my mind with regard to the initiative. On the one hand, the idea appeared brilliant, bold and constructive. On the other, I had apprehensions regarding such a trip into the unknown. Everything appeared to indicate that the initiative had not been preceded by the necessary preparations in addition to the fact that, in Israel, people like Menahim Begin, Shamir and Sharon were in control. They had a terrifying past, rigid ideas and publicized expansionist views. I felt that, whereas Sadat's speech had reassured me, there was absolutely nothing reassuring in Begin's response. A feeling of fear took hold of me lest this adventure dissipate the Arab strength generated by the October War, and destroy all the achievements the Arabs had accomplished in its aftermath.

Anyway, the die was cast. We had to face a new tomorrow.

On the afternoon of 22 December 1977, my wife and I took off from Frankfurt International Airport on a Misrair flight. I had to make the necessary preparations for the State visit to Cairo of the German Chancellor, Helmut Schmidt. This was to be a two-day official visit scheduled to start on 27 December. It was to be followed by an eight-day vacation in Luxor and Aswan. Mrs Schmidt had an extensive knowledge of Egyptology and was eagerly looking forward to the visit.

The flight was delayed, and we touched down at Cairo Airport at dawn on 23 December 1977. We went to the house of my brother-in-law, Ahmed Khairat Said (former deputy-minister for Foreign Affairs under Abdel Nasser). We were to stay with him until the end of the visit of the German Chancellor, after which we were to return to Bonn.

I spent that day (23 December) at home, where I received many friends and relatives. I was completely exhausted. Next day I contacted the Foreign Ministry by telephone for an appointment with the Minister of State for Foreign Affairs, Dr Boutros Ghali. I also telephoned the Office of the

President for an appointment with President Sadat. In the afternoon I went out to pay a visit to my mother in Zamalek. I returned home at half-past five. The house was full of relatives and friends, in a state of great excitement. My wife informed me that the radio and television had announced that I had been appointed Minister of Foreign Affairs to succeed the former minister, Ismail Fahmy.

Sadat had apparently taken my acceptance of the appointment for granted, and I was taken aback, especially in view of the delicate and abnormal conditions prevailing in the aftermath of the initiative. I was all the more incensed as I felt that I had been trapped, and that there was no way out. It was impossible for me, now that the appointment had been made public, to announce to the world at large that I refused the post. Nor was it possible for me to resign from a post before I had assumed it. This I could not do for personal reasons, in view of my relations with Sadat, going back more than thirty years. There were also patriotic reasons. To turn down the post, after my appointment to it had been made public, would be to add yet another resignation to the series of resignations initiated by Ismail Fahmy and followed by Mohamed Riad. To do so would create a negative impression and would be a slap in the face for Sadat. It would prejudice his moral standing, deepen doubts on the wisdom of the step he had taken, and confirm apprehensions that Egyptian public opinion was not behind its president.

To be honest, I do not know what I would have done had Sadat duly proposed to appoint me Foreign Minister. I cannot say whether I would have refused or accepted the offer. All would have depended on his explanation of the situation, his plan of action, and my assessment of the state of affairs. All that matters now is that I would have been in a position that would have made it easier for me to turn down the offer. That would have allowed him to select another person for the post without risking the public affront of three foreign ministers resigning in succession. I was all the more unhappy as my wife had qualms about the job. I sensed her disapproval, although she did not openly reject it out of consideration for my feelings; more especially on account of my poor health made worse by my indulgence in immoderate smoking. Despite doctor's orders, I have never been able to stop smoking.

The quick developments gave me no time for reflection or bitterness. Barely half an hour later the telephone began to ring. The Prime Minister, Mamdouh Salem, was on the line. He began with greetings, since I had just arrived from Germany, then went on to ask me to meet him in his office. There I was met by press and television photographers. I knew this was no more than a completion of formalities.

I had previously met Mamdouh Salem twice in my capacity as Egyptian Ambassador to Germany. I got to know him better after I joined his Cabinet. I appreciate and respect him. He is a gentleman – polite, honest and dedicated to his work. I expressed to him my irritation at not being consulted before being appointed. He told me that he appreciated my feelings, but that the situation allowed me no alternative but to accept. I learned from him that Sadat had, on various occasions, spoken of me, commending my efficiency and patriotism. He (Salem) shared these views, and wished me the best of luck.

I had barely reached home when the telephone rang. It was the Vice-President, Hosny Mubarak. He congratulated me, and requested that I accompany him the following morning by plane to Ismailia, where President Sadat was staying. I would meet the President and then, in my capacity as Minister of Foreign Affairs, would participate in the Ismailia talks at 11 a.m. President Sadat was to head the Egyptian delegation, while the Israeli delegation was to be led by Menahim Begin. I put down the receiver feeling completely at sea.

I was on the point of calling a colleague of mine at the ministry, Ahmed Maher El Sayid, when he walked into the room. I proposed to him the post of Directeur de Cabinet of the Minister of Foreign Affairs. While accepting the offer, he asked that his assumption of it be deferred for another week. He was leaving the following day for Senegal, to attend an OAU Conference. The feeling of utter loneliness that had been with me for the preceding four hours was dissipated.

Maher and I had been close friends ever since he had worked with me as First Secretary in Kinshassa. We had remained friends and time had strengthened our friendship. We thought along the same lines and thoroughly understood one another. In his own right, Maher was an extremely efficient man, and highly proficient in Arabic, English and French. He was cultured, quick-witted and able, and was dedicated to his work. He was the grandson of Ahmed Maher Pasha, the Egyptian Prime Minister who was assassinated in 1945 in the Egyptian Parliament after proclaiming that Egypt had joined the Allies against the Axis powers in World War II. The move, though unpopular at the time, had been designed to secure for Egypt the benefits accruing from the anticipated and impending victory of the Allies, and to improve Egypt's position vis-à-vis Britain with respect to Egypt's demands for the evacuation of its territory. I bagan to think about tomorrow and the many tests and responsibilities that lay ahead.

Footnote

1   The participation of the PLO in the work of the United Nations was further extended by Res. 3375 (XXX) to all efforts, deliberations and conferences on the Middle East which are held under the auspices of the United Nations, on an equal footing with other parties.

Chapter Four

Ismailia (25 December 1977)

I was having breakfast at 7 a.m. the following day when the doorbell rang. A handsome and elegant young man in civilian clothes made his appearance. He introduced himself as Captain Amr Hamdi of the ministerial police force. He had been appointed my personal security officer. I invited him to join me for breakfast.

I went down and found a Mercedes limousine, equipped with a telephone, awaiting me. In another car were four other bodyguards belonging to the security forces. We drove to Almaza Military Airport, where I met Mr Hosny Mubarak. We boarded a military helicopter which flew us to Ismailia, where we arrived at 9.30 a.m. At the Ismailia rest-house selected for the talks, I met a number of friends and colleagues who were members of the Egyptian delegation. These were the head of the Egyptian delegation to the UN, Dr Esmat Abdel Meguid; Chef de Cabinet of the Presidency, Hassan Kamel; the Minister of State for Foreign Affairs, Dr Boutros Ghali; and the Under-Secretary of State at the Foreign Ministry, Dr Ussama El Baz, who was appointed to head the Office of the Vice-President following Ismail Fahmy's resignation, while retaining his office in the Ministry.

I asked Dr Esmat Abdel Meguid to brief me on the Cairo Preparatory Peace Conference which President Sadat had convened. It was held at the Oberoi Mena House Hotel facing the Pyramids, and was attended only by Egypt, Israel and the United States. Syria, Jordan and the PLO had refused to attend the Conference, although their flags, including that of the PLO, flew at mastheads above the Mena House Hotel. Dr Abdel Meguid had barely begun when I was summoned to meet President Sadat. He was sitting in the garden, enjoying the warmth of the radiant sun. He welcomed me warmly, saying that he was unaware of my presence in Egypt, and had assumed that I was still in Germany. I reproached him for appointing me Minister of Foreign Affairs without prior consultation. I expressed my dissatisfaction at having to participate in talks that were due to take place in an hour's time. I had had no background on the meeting, not even knowledge of the agenda. He told me he had taken the liberty of appointing me without prior consultation because I was like a son to him (Sadat was nine years older than I). He had selected me because he wanted a person in whom he had full confidence. Such a person had also to be patriotic and bold. Had I known (he went on) the number of persons who were after the job, I would not regret it.

He then spoke at length of the current contradictions in the Arab states and of President Assad in particular, who had surely tried his patience. He spoke of the stance of the Soviet Union, which sought his personal downfall. It had ruined all attempts at a breakthrough of the vicious circle of the Arab-Israeli conflict. He could not maintain a policy which tied Egypt to the Arab present course, with its jealousies and struggles for leadership. Hassan Kamel then came in to inform the President of the arrival in Ismailia of the aircraft carrying the Israeli delegation, whereupon Sadat left me to meet the delegation.

When the delegation arrived, Sadat accompanied the members to the living-room, where they were offered refreshments. I remained in the garden. I sought, once more, to reconstruct the background of the talks with Esmat Abdel Meguid. However, Hassan Kamel showed up shortly afterwards to summon me to Sadat to take the oath as Minister of Foreign Affairs. He informed me that it was Sadat's intention to have Menahim Begin and some of the other members of the Israeli delegation attend the ceremony in an attempt to enhance the impression of cordiality and peace. To say I was shocked is an understatement. I requested him to tell Sadat that there was no precedent for this anywhere in the world: the Israelis had no business attending such a ceremony. Neither would I, under any circumstances, take the oath in their presence.

Hassan Kamel soon returned and said laughingly that President Sadat had accepted my point of view and had given up his idea. I accompanied Hassan Kamel to the living-room, where Sadat sat with Menahim Begin and some of his aides. The President excused himself and walked to a corner of the room. Hosny Mubarak stood at his right hand with Mamdouh Salem and Hassan Kamel at his left, while I took the oath of office. It was barely over when Menahim Begin and his aides and the Egyptians present in the room advanced towards me to shake hands and congratulate me.

Together with the other persons present, I left the room for the meeting-hall, leaving Sadat and Begin in closed session. Suddenly, and without warning, I had a strange inner feeling that I was awakening from a frightful nightmare. The anxiety and confusion that had taken possession of me some twenty hours earlier, when I first heard of my appointment, fell away from me. I had taken the oath before Sadat in a corner of a small room in the town of Ismailia, within sight and hearing of Israel's leaders, our mortal enemies: we had been fighting one another for the last thirty years. All of a sudden a feeling of confidence, strength, peace and determination came over me. It seemed to me that my presence was ordained. I had, unwillingly, become the Foreign Minister of immortal Egypt at a moment of its history that was to

Ismailia (25 December 1977)

determine its fate. The future of the Middle East, perhaps of the world, depended on the outcome of the battle for peace. The duel for a peaceful solution was to begin in a few moments. I welcomed the challenge!

The members of the Egyptian and Israeli delegations sat on either side of the negotiating table, facing one another. The talks were about to begin. Sadat and Begin, who were closeted together in the next room, were expected to appear at any moment, and they soon did so, hand in hand. Before they took their seats, Begin surprised me by announcing, his eyes gleaming with joy, that they had agreed to form two committees. The first would be a political committee, to be alternately chaired by the Egyptian and the Israeli Foreign Ministers, and would sit in Jerusalem. The second was the military committee, at which each side was to be headed by its minister for defence, and the meetings were to be held in Cairo.

I felt that Sadat and Begin had put the cart before the horse. Such a decision should result from the talks between the two delegations, rather than precede them. I was incensed at Sadat. Why agree on two committees? Was it not logical that we should first agree as to the principles upon which peace would be based? The issue was a purely political one, and were agreement to be reached upon it any number of committees, required for the implementation of the contents of such a political agreement, could be appointed.

How were we to explain to the Arab world, which was following the talks with great concern, the setting-up of an Egyptian-Israeli military committee for arrangements for withdrawal from Sinai? Would not this imply a line of policy directed towards a separate Egyptian-Israeli agreement? Any such allegations had been refuted by Sadat *ad nauseam*, and in the strongest terms. Why should Sadat accept Jerusalem as a venue for the meetings of the political committee? Had it not occurred to him that this involved implicit recognition of Israel's claim to Jerusalem as its capital? Had it not occurred to him that this would deepen Arab suspicions with regard to his peace initiative? Would it have done him any harm to insist that Tel-Aviv, rather than Jerusalem, should be the counterpart of Cairo for the committee meetings?

I was roused from such thoughts by President Sadat's deep, mellow voice opening the session. He welcomed the Israeli delegation to Ismailia. Said he: "This is my birthday, and a happy occasion for us to meet here on the soil of Egypt to end the sufferings of the two peoples. The whole world is watching this meeting and the establishment of peace. Love would thereby replace the hatred which has been ours for the past thirty years. We want to present the world with a new approach to the solution of problems among peoples. . ."

Begin answered, his voice strident. He wished the President a happy birthday, and hoped he would, like Moses, live to be a hundred and twenty. When Moses escaped, with his people, from Egypt, it took them forty years to cross Sinai, while (himself and his party) had arrived in Egypt, across Sinai, in forty minutes. Everyone recalled Sadat's visit to Jerusalem, and how heartily he was welcomed by the Israelis. Peace had become their joint responsibility. This would be achieved and the wars and sufferings would end forever.

Begin then announced that he carried with him two projects. The first was on withdrawal from Sinai, and the second on autonomy for "Judea" and "Samaria", in other words, the West Bank and Gaza. Begin then set out to explain his project for Egypt. Speaking fluent English in a harsh voice, he expatiated on it in a monotonous tone, and in absurd detail, obviously carried away by his own eloquence. What astonished me was the sheer impertinence of Begin's words; despite his attempts to make them sound simple, naïve and palatable, whereas they were, in reality, insults to our intelligence and an affront to ourselves. "When the peace agreement is signed [he said] the Egyptian army may be established on a line which will not reach beyond the Mitla and Geddi Passes." As for the rest of Sinai (more than three-quarters of its total area), this would be demilitarized. Israel would retain its military airports in Sinai, as well as the early-warning stations. The settlements between Rafah and El-Arish, and Eilat and Sharm-El-Sheikh, would remain and become civilian settlements. "This in no way prejudiced Egypt's sovereignty, Mr President. However, we have a sacred Jewish principle, namely that no civilians should be left without military protection. We shall, therefore, retain a very small force to protect such civilian settlers. We hope, Mr President, to find in you understanding for such a humane principle, in view of the afflictions the Jews have suffered at the hands of others. . ."

Things went from bad to worse. Dr Esmat Abdel Meguid interrupted Begin at one point. He pointed out that Security Council Resolution 242 stipulated withdrawal from the occupied territories, and this, so far as Egypt was concerned, implied withdrawal to the international borders between it and Palestine. Begin theatrically flew into a rage. He bombarded President Sadat with questions in quick succession, like so many bursts from a machine-gun: "Didn't you mass Egyptian army forces in Sinai in 1967? Didn't you close the Straits of Tiran? Were there not demonstrations calling for Israel to be driven into the sea? Were there not posters in Cairo calling on the Egyptian army to enter Tel-Aviv in three days? Didn't you ask the UN Emergency Forces to withdraw from Sinai?"

Sadat said "yes" to each question posed by Begin. He waited impatiently for Begin to end his flood of questions, wanting a chance to put a word in; to say, "We are sitting round the negotiating table to forget the past and establish a lasting and comprehensive peace."

However, Begin's questions were barely over when he said; "The war of 1967 was an aggression on your part. Israel was in a state of legitimate defence. Consequently, it is entitled to keep the territories it occupied while

Ismailia (25 December 1977)

defending itself against aggression." With a quick movement, he reached out for the papers before him. He picked out a book and opened it on a page he had marked with a piece of paper. He began to read passages from the book whose author, he claimed, was a legal expert on international law. The passages confirmed the right of a state to retain occupied territories if its occupation had resulted from a defensive war it had fought against its will. The principle of non-retention of other people's territories by force applied only to territories captured during a war of aggression.[1] Was this the Israeli response to Sadat's great initiative, which had caused such turmoil throughout the world and raised hopes, in the area and beyond, for the establishment of a just and lasting peace? Did Begin see nothing in the initiative, save an opportunity to conclude a business deal, securing for him all the gains, whilst we sustained all the losses?

I could hardly control myself. I stood up and walked over to President Sadat. I requested, in a whisper, that the meeting be suspended for consultation. Begin was quick to observe what I had done. He said: "That was perhaps too long, Mr President," and proposed that the meeting recess. President Sadat agreed and the meeting rose.

The Egyptian delegation moved to another room. I irritably expressed to Sadat what I thought of Menahim Begin's impertinence: he was already abusing our hospitality as hosts and our sincere desire to end the war and establish a just peace. I intimated that his approach would drag us into unending details and cause us to lose sight of our original objective. In my opinion, we should concentrate, at this meeting, on reaching agreement on the principles governing the comprehensive settlement to the Arab-Israeli conflict in all its aspects. The details could be discussed at some later period by the respective committee. There was unanimous agreement among the members of the Egyptian delegation that the Israeli project should be rejected. It involved serious infringements of Egypt's sovereignty over its territories and was a clear violation of the principles of international law. And it conflicted with Security Council Resolution 242.

The meeting was resumed. And once again we heard Begin and his over-elaborate presentation as he this time explained his second project for the future of "Judea and Samaria" and the Gaza Strip. He paused after each paragraph to praise its virtues, and pay tribute to his own great generosity and his excessive humanity. He greatly resembled a pedlar singing the praise of his wares:

With respect to "Judea and Samaria", I shall begin at the end. . .
Israel insists on its sovereignty over such territories, for they constitute the land of our forefathers. . . I shall not ask you, Mr President, to append your signature to an agreement which gives us territories you may consider Arab land. I propose we agree to leave the question of sovereignty open to discussion and in suspension. It would not be

granted to Israel, nor would it be granted to others. Let us turn now from this point to urgent and humane questions. Military rule in "Judea and Samaria" may be revoked. The army, as you must know, fights but does not rule. The Israeli authorities will be in charge of security and public order. As to the "Palestinian Arabs", they will, for the first time in history, be granted administrative self-rule after centuries of subjection to the domination of others. They will have an administrative council which will take charge of all aspects of life, such as education, health and sanitation, and so on . . . This would, in turn, allow the "Palestinian Jews" to enjoy security. . . I also suggest that the inhabitants should be entitled to choose between Israeli and Jordanian nationality, that Israelis be entitled to buy and own land in "Judea and Samaria", and that the Arabs who opt for such a nationality, should enjoy the same right. . .

When Begin had finished the presentation of his project, he added that US President Carter and Vice-President Mondale, and the British Premier, Callaghan, endorsed and praised his projects. For the record, this was not true. All they had said was that it could serve as a starting-point for negotiations.

He likewise said in the same theatrical manner that he had encountered strong opposition in his constituency, among the members of the Knesset and among his personal friends. He had, he went on, made great concessions for the realization of peace.

Sadat answered, saying that he wished to point out that Egypt had historical obligations towards the Arab world. Egypt was committed to abide by the Rabat Conference resolutions on Israeli withdrawal from the occupied territories, and the solution to the Palestinian problem on the basis of the legitimate rights of the Palestinians. To derogate from these resolutions was no easy matter. He had hoped that during the Ismailia meeting they would reach agreement on a declaration of principles between the two parties to govern the peaceful settlement. Much had been achieved by his visit to Jerusalem. However, there were clearly points of difference between the two parties. Sinai was Egyptian territory, and Egyptians should have forces there, since Israelis had forces on their territories. However, if peace were to be realized, he would not need a single Egyptian soldier there. And he would not accept any Israeli settlements or forces there. Were he to tell his people that his friend Begin wanted to retain settlements in Sinai and forces to protect them, his people would stone him. Anyway, agreement on peace would not be reached in one meeting. What really mattered was that the talks should continue. Proposals should be exchanged and the momentum maintained until a comprehensive peace was reached. The Egyptians would submit counter-proposals. When agreement had been reached on principles, the political

Ismailia (25 December 1977)

and military committees would begin work without further delay.

The second meeting was notable for the marked activity shown by the Egyptian delegation. They stood up to Begin whenever he overstepped his bounds. They based their arguments on the firm Arab stance in accordance with the principles of international law and UN resolutions.

Naturally enough, no agreement was reached on principles. The meeting broke up, and it was agreed that each side would issue its own communiqué.

On the morning of the following day, 26 December 1977, Sadat and Begin stood before reporters, representatives from news agencies and television networks. At the beginning of the news conference, Sadat announced that, "...with respect to the question of withdrawal, we have achieved some progress... As for the Palestinian problem, which we consider the crux of the matter, Egypt's stand is that, with respect to the West Bank and Gaza Strip, a Palestinian state should be established. The Israeli position is that the 'Palestinian Arabs' in 'Judea and Samaria' should enjoy self-rule. We disagreed on that. However, we have agreed to discuss this problem in a political committee..."

I was astounded at Sadat's use of Begin's artful, misleading expressions: Begin had coined the term "Palestinian Arabs" as an alternative to the "Palestinian people". At the same press conference, and in answer to a question, he had claimed: "I belong to the Palestinian people because I am a Palestinian Jew. There are Palestinian Arabs, and we want to live with them in honour, justice and equality. I have brought to the President proposals on self-rule which are the first of their kind in the history of the Palestinian Arabs".

Honour, justice and equality indeed! And all thanks to Mr Begin! I told myself that, had the Jews considered themselves nationals of the states in which they lived – and not merely Jews – there would have been no Jewish problem. And there would, consequently, have been no Palestinian problem.

As for Sadat's repetition of the words "Judea and Samaria" – I attributed that to mere naïve civility. He was unaware of their political implications, and was putting to use his knowledge of a language new to him, namely Hebrew. In his official speeches, during his visits to certain states, Sadat was fond of inserting in his speeches one or more passages in the host state's language. He did this in Germany, France and Iran.

The joint press conference was over. The world learnt that the Ismailia talks had failed, and had not furthered the cause of peace by one iota.

Footnotes

1   Begin said something to the same effect in a more devious manner during the press conference held the following day.

Chapter Five

Meditations

I spent the week that followed the Ismailia meeting in deep thought – something that was simply not possible earlier, by reason of the rapidity with which events succeeded one another. I wanted to find out where I stood on the initiative, and assess its feasibility and the kind of tactics needed to make it effective. I emerged with complete faith in the action and a belief that it could lead to a peaceful settlement.

When I reviewed the history of the Middle East since the creation of Israel particularly from the standpoint of the Arab states, it appeared to me that it was constituted by a series of missed opportunities. The Arabs had behaved like late travellers missing the train and then hurrying after it to hop on the end waggon – but by then it was too late – Israel always came out on top, greatly strengthened and having acquired even more Arab territory.

The main obstacles preventing the Arabs from seizing the opportunities offered them were their disagreements, their rhetorical slogans, their predilection for outdoing one another in talk, and their refusal to accept reality – such as referring to Israel as "the (presumed) state of Israel", despite the fact that the whole world had already recognized it as a state. Ironically the wheel had now come full circle, and it is now Israel's turn to refer to Palestine as "so-called" and, what is worse, suiting their actions to their words to the extent that Golda Meir once said, "Where is this Palestinian people?" My mind dwelt particularly on 1955, when Anthony Eden, Britain's Foreign Minister at the time, called for a round table conference on the basis of the partition resolution to settle the Arab-Israeli conflict. President Nasser straight away declared that it was an idea worth considering and that he was studying the proposal. But all hell was let loose in several of the Arab countries, especially Syria, and there was even opposition from the Palestinians themselves. Their attack was quite violent, and President Nasser had to about face and recant, under the pretext that his statement had been misinterpreted and misunderstood.

I was First Secretary at our Embassy in London at the time. I recalled that all Israel wanted was to be recognized within what were then its borders. It was even prepared, in order to win Arab recognition, to let go of some of the territories it had annexed beyond its borders as drawn by the UN partition resolution – a resolution, be it remembered, which the Arabs had rejected when it was first adopted. I felt with bitterness the irony of our situation. At that time Israel had not yet occupied the Sinai Peninsula or the West Bank: it had not yet occupied Jerusalem or the Golan Heights or the Gaza Strip – all of which were occupied in 1967. Yet again after the Summit Conference in Khartoum, the Arabs came up with their celebrated three "Nos": NO negotiations, NO reconciliation, NO recognition.

Israel was well aware of the tactical advantages of asking the Arabs for recognition, or even merely getting them to accept face-to-face negotiations. It has continued to call for either or both of these two alternatives throughout the years of its occupation, in the certainty of a negative Arab reaction. Using the Arab refusal to recognize it or negotiate with it as a screen, Israel found both the time and opportunity to pursue its expansionist policies, and bring about a new *fait accompli* in the occupied territory, making its authority felt there and building new settlements in the area, thus cutting all these territories' ties with the homeland – in short, laying hands on them, gobbling them up, digesting them and then chewing the cud at leisure! The Arab attitude had proved throughout to be ineffectual, partly because of the weakness of the nations involved, partly because of their dissension, and partly because of their indifference, or rather apathy, since they were satisfied with paying lip service to "the necessity of solving the problem" without putting their hearts into it or working towards the goal.

But the 1967 War had created a new reality, and the Palestinian question was no longer the one and only problem. Other countries were drawn into the Israeli conflict, for Israel now occupied Egyptian, Syrian and Jordanian territory, along with Palestine. The remainder of the Arab nations felt humiliated, threatened and lost: they felt they were on the waiting-list. The occupation of Jerusalem was, in itself, an act of defiance keenly felt by Arab and Islamic nations alike: Saudi Arabia, in particular, felt itself in a very critical position, being, as it was, the *primus inter pares* of the Islamic world, and Jerusalem being the city, next to Makkah, the most sacred to all Muslims.

The shock of the 1967 War and the defeat – psychological and moral as well as military – suffered by the Arabs, sparked a spirit of Arab resurrection, especially since this was coincident with the emergence of the area's vast potentialities in oil and manpower, making it a strategic and economic power to be reckoned with.

The end of the 1973 War saw the Arab world transformed. It had become a mighty giant that had awakened from its torpor and realized its own strength as soon as it had regained its self-confidence and self-esteem. Simultaneously, the image of a poor, victimized and crucified Israel was dispelled, disclosing a thief caught red-handed in the act of systematically pillaging the Arab world piecemeal while its people were sound asleep. The

Arabs were freed from all complexes and the foundations of the "NO" policy collapsed.

President Sadat's initiative should be understood from this angle. True Sadat should have attempted to prepare and plan his initiative together with the Arabs, or at least with some of the most moderate Arab countries (who, in the event, having been completely ignored, were paralyzed by the unexpectedness of his action) and then spring it on Israel and the world at Geneva – the heart of the UN – for the possibility of a Geneva Conference before the end of 1977 remained in the offing, as I have pointed out earlier.

Had he done so, he would have spared himself some minor battles with the Arab countries, but it appears that he had become very much convinced of its effectiveness – or perhaps he feared it might dissipate, stultify or leak out through the dissensions of the Arabs and their conflicting interests, and thus so weaken the effect of his bombshell that Israel and the world would no longer react to it positively.

However necessary and useful such prior preparations were, Sadat took his step without them, and the deed became a *fait accompli* and a political fact, so what could carping criticism and regret avail? The deed was done and we now had to pursue it to the end. Certainly one had to be alert and tread carefully.

What did Sadat say in Jerusalem? He unflinchingly, courageously and honestly interpreted the principles of international law and UN resolutions on the Arab-Israeli conflict. He genuinely reflected the quasi-unanimous views held by the international community – all in a very touching and eloquent call to the representatives of the Israeli people, and with the world as witness: a call for a better world, humane and just, where people might live in brotherly love and peace, joy and prosperity. He made it clear there was no other choice: the alternative was a vicious circle of instability, havoc and destruction.

And what was Begin's answer in Jerusalem? He said there that everything was negotiable, but that no party had the right to state *a priori* conditions for negotiations – as if occupation by force of arms was not an *a priori* condition and a noose about the Arabs' necks! It is a tragic irony that fate should have selected a living "fossil" by the name of Menahim Begin at this very moment to receive Sadat's offer of peace, and strangle mercilessly that beautiful hope given birth by the picture drawn by Sadat in his speech in Jerusalem.

I tried to put myself in Begin's shoes and delve into his very soul – the soul of a man who had spent his entire life fighting for the establishment of a racist Jewish state; a man who had been persecuted in his native land – Poland – and who came to Palestine to inflict the same torture on its people, shedding their blood and ousting them from their homes and country so that Jews of all nationalities from abroad might take their place; a man who, as the leader of the Hirut party, was calling for Greater Israel to be erected on what remained of dismembered Palestine; a man whom I personally beheld in Ismailia bargaining and bartering (like a petty shopkeeper), dealing with things that did not belong to him in the first place, just as if the offer of a comprehensive, just and lasting peace were a passing summer cloud!

Begin could not openly reject Sadat's initiative, which had the blessing of people everywhere and to which the world was expectantly awaiting a reply. He did not want the peace Sadat offered, since it would keep Israel with the borders it had prior to the 1967 War. He wanted to build his little empire in an age in which empires were extinct, except that the components of this empire were already within his grasp, that is "Judea and Samaria", Jerusalem, the Gaza Strip, the Golan Heights and, who could tell, maybe even Sinai or at least part of Sinai – meanwhile leaving South Lebanon for another time in the future. All he had to do was glue these parts together somehow and his empire would become a fact and a reality!

Did that naïve Egyptian hope to deprive him of his dreams just as they were about to be realized? Would Begin be prepared to lose all he had lived and fought for for the sake of a speech delivered in the Knesset? Would not Begin be thinking of some way of escaping from such an awkward position to turn the table round, manipulating it to serve his own ends? Why not turn copper into gold? Why not turn the tables on Sadat by making use of his initiative by holding on to the land and have peace at the same time? Why should he not eat the cake and have it too? All he (Begin) needed was sufficient time to confuse the issue and drain the initiative of its magnificent content by drawing Egypt into a labyrinth of detail by unending discussions on secondary matters or side-issues. In this way he might exploit Sadat's over-eagerness to see his dream of peace materialize, wheedling small advantages and concessions slowly out of him until cracks began to show in the edifice. It would then be only a matter of time before the initiative crumbled into dust. Had he not won from Sadat, at their very first meeting in Jerusalem, a promise that the October 1973 War would be the last between Egypt and Israel? And this, without any commitment on Begin's part to do anything other than keep the negotiations alive indefinitely, and thereby give himself time to gain a foothold in the occupied territory by planting more settlements there. Had he not got Sadat to agree to the meeting of the Egyptian political committee in Jerusalem? Had they not agreed at their second meeting on a military committee to discuss the pulling out of Israeli troops from Sinai before we had even begun to negotiate or lay down principles?

I tried to picture to myself what would be taking place in Begin's mind in order to achieve his ends: his first thought would no doubt be to isolate Egypt from its fellow-Arab states. The climate for such an attempt was favourable, since Sadat had embarked on his initiative without consulting with the other Arab countries beforehand, and was now a prey to their furious reaction. Now Egypt was the strongest and most important of the Arab countries, and the one most likely to pose a threat to his expansionist plans. If Egypt could be taken out of the Arab front and neutralized, none of the others would constitute any danger to speak of and would not dare to move against Israel. Furthermore, the isolation of Egypt would cut off a major source of its strength and so further weaken it.

If he could succeed in doing all this, Begin would then be able to move one stage further, and seek a partial peace with Egypt, or even a separate peace, since he had a trump card up his sleeve – Sinai.[1]

If such were not Begin's secret thoughts, how could we explain the unyielding position and the provocations inherent in the project he presented at Ismailia concerning Sinai? Sinai was not part of the Jewish patrimony, but merely the route Moses and his people had to take to get to the Promised Land. Here, of course, I am not talking of the fanatics, who believe that any land trodden by a Jew is his! The borders between Palestine and Egypt have been internationally known and defined for thousands of years; Sinai had never been the object of any claims by Jews in their prayers. It is true that Theodore Herzl, who originated the idea of a Jewish state, had, after failing to obtain from Sultan Abdel Hamid permission to establish a Jewish settlement in Palestine, attempted to obtain a similar permission from Egypt – then under British mandate – to set up Jewish settlements in the eastern part of Sinai. Even he had no eye for Sinai itself, but had hoped to use it as a springboard to Palestine when the occasion offered. His efforts, however, proved unsuccessful.

I was inclined to believe that the initiative did give us certain advantages, and might very well achieve positive results from our point of view. The main advantage was that it offered a way out of the deadlock the Arabs found themselves in by their adamant refusal of Israel's invitation to direct negotiation – which was a position the world could not understand.

Also, the time factor would operate in favour of the Arab cause, rather than against it, as had been the case prior to the initiative. For now the Israeli government was increasingly subject to pressure on all sides. The whole world endorsed the peace initiative, and everyone held on to it, looking hopefully to the establishment of peace in the Middle East. People came to a better understanding of the justice of the Arab cause as expressed by Sadat in Jerusalem. This was strengthened by a change in American public opinion, which had always been partial to Israel, while opinion in Europe and elsewhere underwent an even greater change.

Even more important – and positive, to me – was the fact that the repercussions were beginning to be felt within Israel itself. Thus the "Peace Now" movement was born with the slogan: "Peace is more important than land". There were demonstrations urging the government to seize this opportunity for peace with both hands. Those ideas gained momentum until they finally reached Begin's cabinet, so that there was a marked difference of opinion on a number of subjects, the most significant perhaps being that on the establishment of new settlements. The Israeli opposition party began to more actively oppose the settlements policy and attack the government's interpretation of Resolution 242, that it did not apply to the West Bank and Gaza Strip. This in turn had repercussions on the Jewish and Zionist organizations in the United States – organizations crucial to the survival of Israel.

There was a gathering storm of opinion that was becoming irresistible, and it was in Egypt's interest to see to it that the matter was never allowed to rest. The greatest achievement of the initiative, in my opinion, was that it created this highly favourable atmosphere for peace.

In the second place, Sadat's initiative was neither subject to bargaining nor open to concessions: the offer he made from the speaker's rostrum in the Knesset, to the Israeli people and the world, was an honest, honourable and comprehensive attempt to bring into play all the factors likely to lead to a true peace, so that to ignore or distort any of them would result in the loss of a very delicate equilibrium and bring down the whole edifice. These factors were:

1. To end Israeli occupation of all territories seized in the 1967 War.
2. To observe the basic rights of the Palestinian people and their right to self-determination, including their right to an independent state.
3. The right of all states of the Middle East to live within their borders in peace, with the necessary security measures to safeguard international borders guaranteed by the international community.
4. All countries in the area should respect the aims and principles of the United Nations Charter in their dealings with each other; to above all never resort to force; and to solve all their differences by peaceful means.
5. To bring the state of war to an end.

These principles were not of Sadat's making, neither did he reconstruct them out of a vacuum. They emanated from an honest interpretation of the provisions and spirit of international law and of the United Nations Charter as well as the resolutions adopted by both the General Assembly and Security Council. These resolutions aimed at putting an end to the Arab-Israeli conflict and thus paving the way to the establishment of a just and lasting peace in the Middle East. United Nations Resolution 242, adopted in November 1967 and accepted by all parties concerned, emphasized in its opening lines the international principle without which the world would have no sense of stability or peace, namely the inadmissibility of acquisition of territory by war. This, and only this, is the opening for peace.

Sadat's proposal, as I said earlier, was a package deal. It was an offer founded on the belief that a straight line is the shortest distance between any two points and the one most likely to succeed. Had Sadat intended by his initiative to start from a bargaining position admitting of give and take, his terms would have been totally different – he might have asked for a settlement based on the United Nations General Assembly resolution on the partitioning of Palestine into an Arab and a Jewish state with the borders as defined in 1947. But this was not what he offered. All that was required from Israel was courage and a belief in justice, to admit that it was not just to ask for oneself what was denied to others. One other thing was needed – a sense of vision and the will to take risks for peace. This requirement was all the more important. Since Israel had chosen this part of the world to establish its state, in the very heart of the Arab world – wouldn't it be wise to live there in peace and harmony, taking its members as neighbours? Wouldn't it be wiser to consider itself part of the Middle East nations rather than perpetuate its alienation and to forego its excessive dependence on the force of arms to ensure its security in exchange for true peace?

If Israel possessed foresight, the Israeli government would have seized Sadat's offer with both hands, would never have allowed this opportunity to slip through their fingers, and would never have attempted to distort this splendid moment for humanity by petty wrangling over a crumb here or a bone there.

My analysis led me to conclude that we should hold fast to the proposal as a whole, to this organic peace, and never allow Begin's government to draw us away from the main issue into a labyrinth of minor and side-issues and away from true peace.

Thus any flexibility that might be shown in negotiation should in no way involve land or sovereignty or the legal rights of the Palestinian people, but should be limited to the necessary security measures and the practical steps to be taken for co-existence and peaceful relations. For this we were ready and more than willing.

The third point that preoccupied me at the time was our relationship with the Arab countries and the Palestinian Liberation Organization.

After Sadat's visit to Jerusalem, the Arab countries were divided into three groups. The first consisted of the radical states: Syria, Iraq, Algeria, Libya, and South Yemen. The PLO joined them and they became known as the Steadfastness Front. They took an extremist, hostile view of Sadat's initiative, considering it a betrayal of the Arab cause and merely a plot by Sadat to seek a separate peace with Israel. Sadat reacted by severing diplomatic relations with them.

The second group was more favourably disposed, and was headed by Morocco – or rather by King Hassan II, who had already played a part in the secret contact that took place in September 1977, prior to Sadat's initiative, between Hassan El Tohamy (representing Sadat) and Moshe Dayan (representing the Israeli government). I found out about these contacts much later, as I shall indicate further on. In this second group with Morocco was Sudan – again, more a question of Numeiry personally – and Sultan Kabous

Meditations

of Oman, both of whom favoured the initiative.

The third group was made up of Jordan, Saudi Arabia and the Gulf states. They took a non-committed stance, and chose to await the turn of events. Normal diplomatic relations continued with this group of states.

I perceived that it would be difficult, if not impossible, for Egypt to go it alone in its quest for peace, surrounded as it was by a sea of dissensions, misgivings, doubts and mistrust as represented by the Arab world. For Egypt to disregard this and proceed along the path it had embarked upon would inevitably widen the gulf separating them and give rise to arguments and clashes that would tarnish any step Egypt might take, no matter how well-intentioned. All this would result in Egypt's total isolation, so that it would either fail in what it had set out to do, or – what would amount to the same thing – to be eventually deterred from staying the course.

For, since Egypt was seeking a comprehensive peace, it would be unable to work towards its objective while the other parties involved withheld their authorization – or their acceptance – to be spoken for on their behalf.

In fact, they denied it this right, so Egypt would eventually reach a point in the negotiations when it would find itself unable to make any move towards a comprehensive settlement. Israel would simply state that it could not negotiate the withdrawal from the Golan Heights (part of the comprehensive settlement demanded by Egypt), since Syria, the country most concerned, denied Egypt the right to enter into such a negotiation. If, despite everything, Egypt went ahead with it efforts, it was bound to run into one of two dead-ends. In the first, the initiative would peter out and fail to achieve its goal. This would put an end to Sadat's political career, as he would have proved to be no more than an adventurous gambler with a fantastic notion, who ended by losing his bet. Not only that, but he would have placed the Arab world in a worse position than it would have been in without his initiative, for it would be left a divided and splintered world – a far cry from the united Arab world (notwithstanding differences of form and procedure) that was getting ready for the Geneva Conference about to be held under United Nations auspices, presided over by the two superpowers.

The other dead-end was that Sadat cornered would be driven into a separate or partial arrangement with Israel – a far cry from the peace he had envisaged. Such an arrangement would, in fact, put paid to the chances of reaching a comprehensive peace settlement, thus giving Israel the opportunity to pursue its policy of expansion, unscrupulously endangering the stability of the area and jeopardizing its chance to escape from the vicious circle of hostility and war. Furthermore this state would, sooner or later, drive Egypt willy-nilly into embarking on yet another war, for Egypt was an integral part of the Arab world and could not forever stand apart from what was happening around it.

Thus something had to be done to get out of this impasse – some way had to be found to somehow get the Arabs to join in the peace efforts.

Camp David

I found a point of departure in the resolutions of the Arab Summit Conference held in Rabat in October 1974. These implied a peaceful settlement based on retrieving all the territories seized in the 1967 War, and observing the rights of the Palestinian people to repatriation and to self-determination – all of which Sadat included in his initiative. A further step was to prove to the Arab world our commitment to the Rabat resolutions, which Sadat had faithfully echoed in Jerusalem – save for one point, to which I shall be returning later. We had to convince the Arabs, in the process of negotiating with Israel, of the firmness of our stand and work in every possible way to regain their confidence.

It was not practical at this stage to approach the Steadfastness Front. They had adopted a very firm stand and were unlikely to be swayed. Yet two of the components of this front concerned me most: Syria, our ally in the 1973 War, and the PLO, since a solution to the Palestinian problem was the core of the entire issue. The PLO position was a highly complex one. They had been cornered and had been hustled into joining the Steadfastness Front by the unexpectedness of Sadat's initiative, yet it would not have been as difficult to try to parley with them at that particular time as with Syria. I finally decided, as a first step, to concentrate my efforts on two countries, Jordan and Saudi Arabia, both of whom, as I mentioned earlier, adopted a neutral stand with regard to the initiative, whilst both were known for their moderation. Jordan was a front-line state because of its proximity to the West Bank which King Abdullah had annexed to Jordan following the 1948 War, and also because it would have to play a role in any settlement involving the Palestinian problem. As for Saudi Arabia, it had international political and economic weight, and had down the years always enjoyed a special relationship with Egypt. Moreover, it held a prominent position in the Arab world and power to influence its members.

Furthermore, I realized that we would have to work to induce the United States to take an active part in the negotiations. Although it cannot be denied that the United States has a strong and unfair bias towards Israel, and is committed to defending and guaranteeing the latter's security, there was a difference between taking Israel's part as Israel's borders stood prior to the 1967 War, and defending Israel's occupation of territories unlawfully seized from Arab countries in the course of that war.

Again, the US has vital interests in the Arab world and the Middle East: one has only to point to the importance the United States, its European allies and Japan attach to ensuring an uninterrupted flow of oil to their respective countries. The surest guarantee of this was to ensure the stability of the area, and this could never, in my opinion, be achieved unless a just and comprehensive solution could be found to the Arab-Israeli conflict. Furthermore, the US had made several official declarations regarding the basis for any such settlement, such as the withdrawal of Israeli troops, the repatriation of the refugees and the illegality of settlements. I was counting on asking the US to adhere strictly to, and stand firmly by these declared positions and direct all its efforts to ensuring their implementation.

I also saw some truth in what Sadat was always repeating, namely that the United States held 90% of the cards, since Israel was completely dependent on it, whether for bread or for missiles. Theoretically, this should give the US the power to influence, and even pressurize Israel.

Parallel with this line of thought was a realization of the need to strike some kind of balance with regard to our deteriorating relationship with the other superpower, the Soviet Union. We had already experienced the effects of severing relations with a superpower when Nasser severed diplomatic relations with the United States following the 1967 War, and it had done us very little good. And I recalled that during the time I spent as Egypt's Ambassador in Bonn, a number of German officials had ventured statements to the effect that, "We, the Federal Republic of Germany, are a small country. We dare not antagonize either of the big powers. We have cause enough to distrust the Soviet Union and consider it our enemy, since it was the driving force behind the partition of Germany, into East and West, and since it represents the main threat to our security, yet we maintain diplomatic, economic, commercial and cultural links with it. Although we do not bend over backwards to please it, we do not anatagonize or provoke it, and we watch over our interests by direct dealing and dialogue."

This, or something very similar, was what I was frequently told, and this at a time when Sadat was vehemently, and even humiliatingly, attacking the Soviet Union. My German friends were delicately conveying the message that Egypt could not afford to have the Soviet Union as an enemy, and indeed Egypt had no strong cause to be hostile to that country, which had a long history of support for our cause, both politically and militarily, since 1956. We even fought the 1973 War with Soviet weapons. I am not claiming that our relations with the Soviet Union were ideal all along; but things being what they are, total estrangement from one superpower or the other is not good politics.

In 1972, Sadat had brought to an end the special relationship that existed between Egypt and the Soviet Union by requesting that country to recall its military and civilian experts. The Soviet Union promptly complied. What could be gained by further antagonizing and provoking them?

The truth of the matter was – as Sadat told me more than once – that he felt they were hostile to him personally from the moment he came to power. They had hoped that Ali Sabri would succeed Nasser, for Sabri had close ties with the Soviets. By that time, however, Ali Sabri was in jail, Sadat had secured his position as President, and it was time to put aside his own personal grudge.

As I saw it, our relationship with the Soviet Union should serve as a counterweight to our relationship with the US. We should make a start without further delay, albeit by degrees, to dispel the coolness and cease our

Camp David

mutual accusations and recriminations, before embarking on a pragmatic and dispassionate dialogue.

Several factors militated in favour of urgent action along these lines, some of which I list as follows:

1. The role the Soviet Union would be bound to play in any settlement of the Middle East problem, for it would be absurd to believe in the practicability of any settlement unacceptable to either of the two superpowers.
2. The Soviet Union's unwavering support for the Arab objectives: Israel's withdrawal from the occupied Arab territories; and the right of the Palestinian people to self-determination and to a state of their own.
3. To prevent the polarization of the Arab countries by the two superpowers.
4. The role played by the Soviet Union in our immediate area in Africa and the Arab world.
5. The need to minimize Soviet efforts aimed at isolating Egypt from the rest of the Arabs and so affect its internal stability.
6. To use relations with Moscow as a kind of lever to influence the United States.
7. To maintain our position as a non-aligned country and strengthen our prominent position in the movement.

I thought we might start by sending back the Egyptian Ambassador to Moscow. Sadat had recalled the Ambassador after the initiative and the unfriendly attitude taken by the Soviet Union as a result of his action.

Furthermore, I realized the need to cash in with whatever assests we already had with any and all countries.

To begin with, there had already been a marked improvement in our relations with the European community, for Europe after 1973 showed a change of attitude. It had begun to take certain initiatives and positions which revealed a better understanding of the Arab-Israeli conflict and a realization that a settlement could be brought about only if Israel withdrew from the territory it had seized in the 1967 War, and if the Palestinian people's right to self-determination and their own independent state were recognized, despite the fact of Israel's tireless attempts to neutralize the European position and prevent them from taking further initiatives. Fortunately, Europe was fully aware that its vital interests in the Middle East could only be protected throught a just and comprehensive peace which would create the stability it so surely needed. France and West Germany played a prominent part in this. Even the countries most partial to Israel, such as the Netherlands and Denmark, began to realize that it was not Israel's security that was at stake but the territorial integrity of the Arab states instead.

Meditations

All we had to do, then, was to encourage Europe to play a more positive role in assisting us.

There was also the group of non-aligned countries, among which we held a strong position from the moment of the movement's inception at Bandung in 1954, where Nasser, together with Tito and Nehru, had played so prominent a part. This group was already unreservedly won over to the Arab cause. The non-aligned countries played an active role in bringing about the United Nations resolutions stipulating that Israel withdraw from all the occupied territories, and stating the rights of the Palestinians.

If we could balance our relations with the two superpowers, this would help us activate our contacts with this group of non-aligned countries.

Neither were we without assets in Africa, for Egypt was one of the most influential supporters of the liberation movements in Africa, since it was helping the freedom fighters combat segregation and discrimination, and in the wake of the 1973 War several African countries in succession broke off diplomatic relations with Israel, and the latter's position on the continent was seriously shaken.

In brief, I came to the conclusion that our stand in any negotiations with Israel should be based on the following policies:

1. A refusal to bargain over the withdrawal of Israel from *all* occupied Arab territories (Sinai, the Golan Heights, the West Bank and the Gaza Strip), or the right of the Palestinian people to self-determination.
2. Negotiation should be limited to the necessary security measures for both parties and the relevant guarantees.
3. With regard to the Palestinian problem, we should make it clear that we were not the only Arab state concerned, and that the other parties involved must be brought into the negotiations and no final solutions reached in the absence of Jordan and the representatives of the Palestinian people.
4. To work in all possible ways to re-establish Arab solidarity.
5. The United States should take an active part in any negotiation in accordance with its declared position and statements, and should commit itself to a just settlement.
6. To halt the deterioration of our relationship with the Soviet Union and establish some kind of balance between our relations with Washington and those with Moscow.
7. To avoid being drawn into discussing secondary or fragmentary issues until we had defined our objectives in a declaration of principles.
8. To activate our contacts with regional and sub-regional groups in Africa, Asia, Europe and Latin America and with the Islamic nations. In this way Israel would have to contend with our

supporters, while we should be neutralizing its own.
9. To emphasize the fact that we do not reject peace, but that it is the Israelis who are seeking to destroy Sadat's initiative by refusing to respond and co-operate.
10. To encourage and enhance the international repercussions of Sadat's initiative, which changed world opinion and even opinion inside Israel; and to pursue it, as an investment, to its final goal: that of forcing Israel to give way to the demands we considered essential for the establishment of peace.

I derived some confidence from these pointers, and decided to adopt them as my guidelines in any future course of action. I perceived, that, if they were to be followed, we should be left with one of two alternatives: either Sadat's initiative would succeed in achieving a just and comprehensive peace in every meaning of the word – or should it fail, because the Israelis refused to give up the land they had seized by force, Israel would be forced to reveal its true face and would assume the responsibility for the failure to achieve peace, with all the consequences this would entail.

I overlooked then a factor I had not taken into consideration which was undermining the initiative and working for its destruction. This unknown factor – the last thing that could have occurred to me – was Sadat himself. His bouts of enthusiams, his precipitate action and his exaggerated concern to succeed were bound to defeat his own objectives. He had fallen victim to stimulants that few could fail to succumb to, all stemming from his initiative: the hopes that millions pinned on peace; the fierceness of attacks from brother Arabs; the inflexibility and perfidy of Begin; his straying from the Arab fold; and, finally, the fact that he seemed to be mesmerized by the deceitful American mirage he was vainly pursuing.

Footnote

1   *Vide* Weizman, *The Battle for Peace*, p. 190

Chapter Six

An Understanding

In the days following the Ismailia meeting I attempted to organize the work in my office at the Foreign Ministry. I took some administrative decisions and held a meeting with the Minister of State for Foreign Affairs, Dr Boutros Ghali, whom I knew slightly and had met socially. We enjoyed working together though we did differ about certain subjects and our concepts of the right way to fulfil our jobs. He was a well-read and very able professor of international law, with extensive international contacts in his field. His approach to problems was academic and largely theoretical. However, he was of a flexible dispostion in ordinary conversation, and was humorous and gay. We met every day in my office, if only for a few minutes. We engaged in smalltalk and exchanged information to relieve ourselves from tension and exhaustion. I held meetings with the senior officers at the Ministry, selecting a group to handle the talks, namely Ussama El Baz, Ahmed Maher El Sayid, Abdel Raouf Al Ridi and Nabil El Araby.

I recall also during these days that the United States Ambassador, Herman Eilts, spoke to me over the telephone to ask whether he might visit me in an hour's time. I agreed. The moment he arrived, and before sitting down, he said that he had just left Sadat, who had wanted us to meet and become acquainted. Sadat had informed him that I was "one of his boys" – which I did not relish. Even less to my liking was the American Ambassador's repetition of his words to me, and I immediately replied: "We were in prison together. I was never anyone's boy, and never will be." Eilts apologized, saying he meant no harm. I said I only wished to put things right from the start. Thus began a working relationship which soon ripened into friendship. Eilts was an experienced diplomat of high calibre: he was highly intelligent, knowledgeable, and expressed himself with great precision. His diplomatic career was spent in the Middle East, where he served in Iran and Iraq, and was Ambassador to Saudi Arabia before being appointed Ambassador to Egypt. Diplomatic relations between Egypt and the United States had been broken off in 1967, seven years before his appointment. When I met him, he had already been three years in Egypt, where he had established strong relationships, and had attended the first and second disengagement talks, initiated by Kissinger, between Egypt and Israel.

On 2 January 1978, I travelled to Aswan to meet President Sadat, who had gone there straight after the conclusion of the Ismailia talks on 26 December 1977. We were expecting President Carter on 4 January. He was to hold a meeting with Sadat on his way back to Washington from a State visit to India.

On the afternoon of the following day, I went to Sadat's rest-house near the Aswan Dam: this was a modest villa set on a hill, with a lovely view overlooking the Nile, the fields, and date- and dom-palms. It was surrounded by a beautiful garden full of tropical plants. Sadat was meeting with a French military delegation on a visit to Egypt. I joined the meeting, until it came to an end. The President then conducted me to a gazebo in the garden. The gazebo was covered by bougainvillaea in full blossom.

After we had seated ourselves, he spoke, in a relaxed manner and at length, of the reasons that had prompted him to seize the initiative and to go to Jerusalem. He had lost all hope of reaching a common stand that would enable the Arabs to attend the Geneva Conference. He elaborated on the October War of 1973, indicating how he had prepared for the war with President Assad and King Feisal, whom he had informed of his intention to conduct the war without fixing any date. He spoke bitterly of his partner in the war, El Assad, who had deceived him. Assad had entered the war in the belief that it would not last more that forty-eight hours – sufficient time for the Syrian army to recover the Golan. Israel would have been surprised by the war, and would have been occupied with fighting on the Egyptian front. He would have called for a ceasefire through the Soviet Union, thus solving this problem with respect to the restitution of the Golan, regardless of what happened to Egypt, his war partner. The Soviet Union had connived at this with Assad. Most of the losses sustained by the Egyptian army occurred during the attack it launched to ease the pressure on the Syrian army when the Israeli army launched a counter-attack against Syria.

He spoke of the difficult conditions he had inherited from Nasser. The Soviet Union was employing all its means to frustrate and destroy him. It had tried to have Ali Sabri succeed Nasser in the Presidency. He, Sadat, had achieved nothing during the three visits he made to the Soviet Union, which had been prevaricating when it had offered to provide him with arms to replace his losses in the October War.

He said that the 1973 War had prepared and paved the road to peace. With their honour restored, the Arabs had regained faith in themselves. Israel had realized the fallacy of the myth of the invincibility of the Israeli army, and its theory of secure borders. He had called for an international peace conference when the Egyptian army was at the height of victory. It was time for Egypt to enjoy peace after thirty years of human and economic sacrifices. Experience had taught him that the Arabs could not agree on a united stand with which they could go to the Geneva Conference; months

An Understanding

elapsed without their agreement on matters of procedure, and he wondered how it would have been when matters of substance came up for discussion.

Sadat referred to the efforts Carter had exerted, without success, to convene the conference. President Carter had finally written to him, saying regretfully that he had exhausted every effort to convene the Conference, and almost despaired of its ever being held. He had sent an answer to Carter, intimating that he was contemplating a "bold action" to break the stalemate. What the bold action was to be had not yet crystallized in his mind. He had thought of several things, such as inviting the five permanent members of the Security Council to meet in Jerusalem to end the war and establish peace among the concerned parties or offer the necessary security guarantees. He had given up the idea, fearing that the Soviet Union or China would refuse to attend out of frustration, or would adopt unconstructive positions.

It had suddenly occurred to him to visit Israel, meet the Israelis in a direct confrontation and propose peace to them. He recalled that the Romanian President Ceaucescu had on several occasions proposed direct negotiations with Israel as an important step in breaking the vicious circle to which the Arabs had committed themselves from the outset. He had thereupon visited Ceaucescu to enquire as to Begin's personality, and whether he was "a strong man" capable of realizing peace. When Ceaucesccu confirmed this, he had resolved to go to Jerusalem and carry out his initiative.

Sadat compared his own personality with that of Gamal Abdel Nasser. The latter thrived on tension, cared nothing for the joys of life and did not appreciate the blessings God had bestowed upon him. He was suspicious of everyone, including his assistants. His motto was to suspect people until he was proved wrong. Sadat hated tension, and could think only in a quiet atmosphere. This explained his love of the countryside and the fact that he lived outside Cairo at the Barrage or other quiet areas, areas with natural beauty, thanking God for all His blessings. His principle, unlike that of Nasser, was to have faith in people until such faith was shown to have been misplaced.

He went on to say that, in the course of his visit to Jerusalem, he had agreed with Begin to allow the presence of an Israeli military mission in Cairo to handle contacts between the two countries. The venue was, in fact, to be Cairo, and he requested that I should consider the subject as confidential.

He then spoke of the members of the National Security Council, of which I would henceforth be a member. He commended the members individually, indicating the virtues of each.

It was now my turn to speak, and I informed him, laughingly, that there was an exception to every rule. I had hoped he would make an exception of Menahim Begin in applying his principle of placing faith in people until this was proved to be misplaced. I told him that I had been watching Begin closely at the Ismailia meetings in an attempt to sort out his personality, mind and methods. I was firmly convinced that he was a treacherous snake and a liar who falsified history and facts. I had been watching Sadat himself during the meetings, and had observed his considerate and courteous treatment of Begin as though the latter was a gentleman. In my opinion, such treatment was wasted on Begin, who even tried shamelessly to exploit it. My impression was that he was trying to change the course of Sadat's initiative in the hope of driving us into a separate settlement with Israel and sowing dissension between the Arab states and ourselves as well as between us and the Palestinians. I expressed the opinion that, whatever the shortcomings of the Arabs, they were part of us as we were part of them, and that they constituted the *espace vitale* for Egypt. Consequently, I went on, Begin should be handled warily, without any trust, otherwise we would drift along and be entangled in his nets, heading us into blind alleys. I put before him in detail my thoughts as detailed in the preceding chapter, and the approach that should be adopted so as to capitalize on the positive effects of the initiative on world opinion.

Sadat expressed his unqualified approval of everything I had said. He intimated that he harboured no doubts as to the success of his initiative or the attainment of its goal. During our conversation, I referred to the fact that I should have preferred it if Sadat had not approved Begin's proposal on the composition of a military committee to be chaired by the defence ministers of both countries to consider withdrawal from Sinai. That, I said, was premature and would arouse the worst suspicions in the Arab states, namely, that it would all end in a separate settlement with Israel.

Sadat told me that he could not tie Egypt's destiny to the Arab states' positions, suspicions, and inability to take decisions. Egypt had borne the brunt of the sacrifices, and was in no condition to maintain such a situation for an unspecified period of time.

I told him that I fully understood all that. I was, first and foremost, an Egyptian. However, a separate solution, were we to slide into one, would realize nothing worthwhile for us. The lasting, comprehensive peace put forward in his initiative should be achieved, otherwise the region would remain a vortex of tension and instability. This would not benefit Egypt, since events would, sooner or later, force it into another war. I was therefore of the opinion that withdrawal from Sinai should be suspended until we reached a declaration of principles with Israel. Such a declaration would affirm Israel's recognition of the right of the Palestinian people to self-determination, and the former's commitment to withdraw from the occupied territories in accordance with Security Council Resolution 242. Here, I was primarily concerned to obtain Israel's commitment to withdraw from the West Bank and Gaza. In my opinion, withdrawal from the Golan or Sinai was no big problem. Were we to succeed in securing a declaration of principles, to be recorded, say, at the UN, the venue of the meetings should be changed from Jerusalem or Cairo, to Geneva or New York. This would allow the participation of the other parties in the talks. Were we to achieve this, and were the other Arab parties to hesitate to join our peace course, that would be their responsibility. We should then be free to set about implementing Israeli withdrawal from Sinai while following up our commitment to put into effect the declaration of principles. I told Sadat bluntly that these were the only bases on which I could continue to work with him.

To this, President Sadat agreed, saying that he, in turn, held the same views. A feeling of great relief swept over me.

Before leaving, I informed Sadat that, following the Ismailia meeting, Begin had made several statements before the Knesset and elsewhere in Israel to the effect that the Egyptian Foreign Office was obstructing the peace efforts. These statements implied that our Foreign Ministry's stand was contrary to Sadat's stand in the talks. I said I would make a statement pointing out that Egypt was speaking with one voice, and that trends in the Egyptian delegation to the talks were neither divergent nor conflicting. Sadat cried: "No, don't do that! Let him bark like a dog. Give no thought to such trifles."

A year later, I was struck by a passage in the book entitled *The Year of the Dove* by the Israeli journalist Eitan Haber. In the chapter on the Ismailia talks, Haber says:

> Sadat asked Begin to spend a few minutes alone with him. Half apologetically, he explained to the Israeli Prime Minister that it was his advisers from the Foreign Ministry who had insisted that he not yield an inch on the matter of self-determination for the Palestinian people. [1]

I went with President Sadat to Aswan Airport the following day to meet President Carter, who was on his way back from India to Washington. Carter's visit was designed to give a push to the Egyptian-Israeli talks following the failure of the Ismailia talks, and to demonstrate that the US was intent on a peaceful settlement of the Arab-Israeli conflict, and boost Sadat's morale. The most important result of this visit was Carter's declaration at Aswan Airport, before he boarded the aircraft to return to the US, a declaration setting forth the American position. The most important part of the declaration, which came to be known as "The Aswan Formula", was paragraph 3 on the Palestinian issue. It was stipulated that there should be a solution to the Palestinian problem in all its aspects. The solution should include a recognition of the legitimate rights of the Palestinian people and enable the Palestinians to participate in the determination of their own future.

The formula was mainly distinguished by the crystallization of the US stand on the subject of the rights of the Palestinian people. This stand had fluctuated to and fro ever since Carter become President. For our part, Ministry experts considered that the formula represented the minimum

Egypt could accept, leading eventually to the realization of the right of the Palestinian people to self-determination.

During Carter's short visit to Aswan, I met Cyrus Vance for the first time. We had a ten-minute chat, and I was very favourably impressed by his personality, for I felt that he was a man of integrity. His words were clear and devoid of ambiguity, and discussion with him was easy. The coming days confirmed my impression, and I still retain feelings of cordiality and friendship for him.

Footnote

1 Eitan Haber, *The Year of the Dove*, 1979, p. 136.

Chapter Seven

Are You Afraid Of Going To Jerusalem?

On 31 December 1977, the US Ambassador, Herman Eilts, called on me and presented me with a New Year gift: Israel's proposals for the agenda of the meetings of the Political Committee. It had been agreed that the Committee should convene in Jerusalem in mid-January. The Israeli proposals consisted of the following points:

1. The situation of the Israeli settlements east of the Arish and Ras Muhammad line (the settlements Israel established in Sinai after its occupation in 1967).
2. The principles of the peace treaty on "Judea and Samaria" and the Gaza Strip on the basis of the autonomy project (submitted by Begin in Ismailia).
3. The points to be included in the Peace Treaty.

The following day, 1 January 1978, we sent Israel our draft agenda for the Political Committee, through the US Embassy. This consisted of the following items:

1. Termination of Israeli occupation of Arab territories occupied since 1967.
2. The conclusion of a just settlement to the Palestinian problem in all its aspects on the basis of the right to self-determination through negotiations in which Jordan, Israel and the representatives of the Palestinian people would participate along with Egypt.
3. Guaranteeing the territorial integrity and political independence of all the states in the area through measures to be agreed upon by the parties on a reciprocal basis.

A close look at the proposals of the two sides shows the chasm dividing them. More important, it underlines the approach and objective each was seeking.

Camp David

We naturally rejected the Israeli proposals while the Israelis, in their turn, rejected ours. Draft agendas continued to pass to and fro between the two parties through the United States embassies in Cairo and Tel-Aviv. They included amendments in form and formulation, without changes in the substance.

At this juncture, the US intervened and presented a draft agenda for the meetings of the Political Committee, which the American Ambassador submitted directly to President Sadat on 14 January 1978. Sadat accepted the agenda without discussion. Israel started a row and was slow to accept it, alleging that it had been submitted to Egypt before being submitted to Israel, and that it did not give the West Bank its Hebrew name of "Judea and Samaria". Finally it accepted the draft when the US Secretary of State, Cyrus Vance, threatened not to participate in the meetings of the Political Committee unless Israel announced its acceptance of the draft.

Sadat did not send the American agenda to me, nor did he talk to me about it. However, I was surprised early the following morning, 15 January, by an invitation to attend a meeting of the National Security Council to be held in Sadat's house in Giza at 10 a.m. of the same day, but no reference was made as to the purpose of the meeting.

The National Security Council was chaired by the President of the Republic, Sadat. Its members were composed of the Vice-President, Mr Hosny Mubarak, the Premier, Mr Mamdouh Salem; the Speaker of the National Assembly, Mr Sayed Marei; the Secretary-General of the Arab Socialist Union, Dr Mustapha Khalil; the Defence Minister, Lieutenant-General El Gamassy; the Minister of the Interior Mr Nabawy Ismail; the Head of Intelligence, Mr Kamal Hassan Aly; and myself in my capacity as Foreign Minister; with Mr Hassan El Tohamy in an ex-officio capacity which I could not then and cannot still define.

Of the members of the Council, I knew Mr Mubarak, whom I met while he was on a visit to the Federal Republic of Germany when I was Ambassador there. I also knew Mr Salem and Mr Marei, whom I met once during the visit of the German Foreign Minister, Herr Genscher, to Egypt some years previously. As for Dr Mustapha Khalil, our acquaintance went back to 1945, when we were both members of the Royal Rowing Club.

With regard to my colleagues, the ministers, I knew them by sight from their pictures in the newspapers and magazines, as I had not yet attended any meeting of the cabinet. When I went into the meeting-hall (the dining-room in Sadat's house), all the members were present. Sadat followed me immediately and sat at the head of the table. He looked glum and appeared tense. He opened the meeting with a short address. Presenting me to the members, he announced the purpose of the meeting, namely the departure of the Egyptian delegation to start on the meetings of the Political Committee. The delegation was to leave that same afternoon for Jerusalem. I was taken aback and asked Sadat on what basis was I to leave. He replied that it would be on the basis of the American agenda he had received from the American Ambassador the previous day. I said I had not seen it and must make an adequate study of it before I left. Sadat flew into a rage and shouted, "Are you afraid of going to Jerusalem?" I answered sharply that he knew quite well that I feared nothing and nobody. A profound silence settled suddenly on the room, and I felt the eyes of those present on me, as they stared at me in consternation and amazement as though I were some strange creature from outer space. They were wondering how anyone could dare to address Sadat in such a tone and so unceremoniously and unhesitatingly. They were all the more astonished when they heard Sadat resume in an extremely quiet and gentle voice, "I have called you, Muhammad, and the National Security council, to discuss the subject." The eyes again swivelled to me, only this time they were accompanied with a smile, and they no longer looked at me with that condescending look older members have for newcomers.

Sadat read out the items on the American agenda, consisting of three points, namely:

1 A declaration of principles to govern the negotiations on the realization of a comprehensive, peaceful settlement in the Middle East.
2 Guideline for the negotiations on matters pertaining to the West Bank and the Gaza Strip.
3 The items of a peace treaty between Israel and its neighbours according to the principles set forth in Security Council Resolution 242.

The discussion became heated when I said I would discuss in the Political Committee item 1 of the agenda only. I said that item 2 pertained to the Palestinians, the owners of the land and the party concerned. We had not been delegated by them to consider this subject. Like the rest of the Arab states, we had only a general commitment to solve the Palestinian problem. In my opinion, the item as such should not be on the agenda because it was covered by the principle of withdrawal from the occupied territories, which we would be discussing under item 1. As to item 3, this, in turn, depended on the principles of any comprehensive peace, if and when agreement would be reached on such principles.

President Sadat was summoned to the telephone, and left the meeting-hall. I recall that I went up to Mr Mubarak to speak to him on a certain matter. He told me then, "Muhammad Bey, I am pleased with your stand. The Israelis should be approached with the greatest caution." I was happy to hear his observation, because I felt alone in the council, which I was attending for the first time, and most of whose members were either silent observers or spoke of subsidiary matters unrelated to the main point.

Camp David

Sadat returned, elated, saying he had spoken to President Carter by telephone. Carter had informed him that the American delegation, headed by the Secretary of State, Cyrus Vance, would arrive in Jerusalem the following day, 16 January, and would participate in the talks of the Political Committee along with the Egyptian and Israeli sides. It would appear that Sadat's tension that day was due to his uncertainty as to Vance's participation in the meetings of the Political Committee. He requested me then to leave to prepare for my departure in the afternoon. I reiterated what I had previously affirmed that I would not tackle more than item 1 on the agenda, unless agreement was reached on principles. He agreed.

It may be pertinent at this point to refer to the climate Israel had created prior to the departure of the Egyptian delegation for Jerusalem.

Successive statements were made by Israeli leaders such as Begin, Weizman, Dayan and Sharon, after the Ismailia meetings, that Resolution 242 did not apply to the West Bank and Gaza and Israel's claim to a right to establish settlements there, as a result of which the Egyptian press launched an attack on the policy of the Israeli government, and that the latter's short-sighted policy, if maintained, would abort all chances for peace created by Anwar El Sadat's initiative. Mustapha Amin, the well-known editor, compared Menahim Begin to Shylock in Shakespeare's *The Merchant of Venice*, which made Begin violently angry.

While preparations were diligently under way for the meetings of the Political Committee in Jerusalem, grave reports, which were soon confirmed, came in. Israel was establishing new settlements in Sinai. The atmosphere became electrified, tension rose and Sadat awoke from his beautiful dream. He had been full of confidence and optimism that his search for peace would succeed, and that its implications would not be lost on Israel, which would be quick to grasp such a great opportunity. Instead, Israel was building new settlements to consolidate its illegitimate occupation on the land. In an interview with *October* magazine, Sadat said that it seemed that Israel had failed or had refused to understand that he had offered it, in his visit to Jerusalem, more than it had ever dreamt of since its establishment, viz, the recognition and the legitimization of its existence by the Arab states and peaceful co-existence with its neighbours.

Sadat declared that he would not allow a single settlement to remain on the Egyptian soil of Sinai. If Begin wished to burn the settlements before their evacuation, he was free to do so. Menahim Begin flew into a rage, and answered Sadat saying that only Nero burnt cities. Sadat replied that he had not said "burnt" but "ploughed", two words that could easily be confused in Arabic. I cannot conceive of any difference between "burnt" and "ploughed" if by that was meant the dismantling of the settlements, which is a legitimate demand, unless the Israelis chose to offer them to us. In truth, Sadat had some justification for what he was saying, since Israel had previously destroyed everything and had ploughed up the roads when it was forced by Eisenhower to withdraw from Sinai in 1958.

I cannot leave the account of the establishment of new settlements without further elaboration. It was designed, purely and simply, to create a new bargaining card. This "noble" idea had occurred to the Agriculture Minister, Ariel Sharon, when the Israelis realized, in Ismailia, that the Egyptians were insisting on the dismantling of the Israeli settlements. He had proposed the idea to Moshe Dayan, who had endorsed it. It was soon approved by the Israeli cabinet, which entrusted a committee, chaired by Sharon, to plan and implement a project to step up the building of Israeli settlements in Sinai without further delay before the meeting of the Political Committee.

Since the purpose was not to establish settlers in the new settlements but merely to create a new bargaining card in the form of a dummy project, the affair was confined to transporting some stones, placing some old buses and beat-up water trucks in position, digging shelters and anything else to give the appearance of building new settlements at little cost. In brief, the idea was a revival of the age when precious stones, gold and ivory was bartered for alcohol, bead necklaces and cheap mirrors. This was an insult, and I could not well see what more Shylock could have done than Begin, had he lived in our age. Weizman, who was the Israeli Defence Minister at the time, wrote of this cheap trick of which he did not approve saying:

> And now we were to adopt the guise in which the most venomous of anti-Semites have always depicted the Jews: crafty petty traders, slyly cashing in on every available opportunity, and reneging on their undertakings whenever it was profitable. [1]

I had not overlooked the possibility that such methods might be used. I have explained my opinion with regard to Begin's stand on the negotiations in the previous chapter of this book. However, I should like to point out to the reader that such methods were not confined to "exchanging new lamps for old". More was intended, namely the exchange of the whole of Sinai if need be, with the neutralization of Egypt and the swallowing up of the West Bank and Gaza.

To return to Weizman's book:

> But those like me, who had followed events from an inside vantage-point and from a close acquaintance with Menahim Begin, knew that he had not changed. I have not the slightest doubt that renouncing the Sinai was highly painful for Begin. However, behind the willingness to give up the peninsula was the true Menahim Begin, alive and active. He must have decided to reach a compromise with the Egyptians in the south as a way of perpetuating some form of Israeli rule over Judea and Samaria. Whereas the Egyptians saw the Sinai agreement

Camp David

as the model for similar undertakings with Jordan and Syria over the West Bank and the Golan Heights, Begin saw it as the precise opposite. As far as he was concerned, the withdrawal from Sinai would be the end of the story. [2]

Are such the implications of the Hebrew word "Shalom"? Was this the corresponding alternative to a sincere offer of peace, one that would embrace the area as a whole, with all those living in it, be they Arabs, Israelis, Muslims, Christians or Jews? Was this the peace which was to destroy fear, remove tension, put an end to bloodshed, save money, and revive and rekindle the hopes of thousands of uprooted refugees? Was this the peace in which all were to co-exist to build up prosperity and live their lives in security? Was this the peace which was to go beyond the bounds of the region, and affect the world as a whole? Was this the peace which was to set the precedent and example for how to settle conflicts among states and peoples in Asia, Africa and Latin America? Was this attitude fair? Was it intelligent?

I see it only as a destruction of ideals, a dissipation of hope, and a sowing of the seeds of evil. Nevertheless, Begin was awarded the Nobel Peace Prize jointly with Anwar El Sadat.

Footnotes:

1   Weizman, *The Battle of Peace*, p. 146.
2   Weizman, *The Battle of Peace*, p. 190.

Chapter Eight

Jerusalem

At 3.30 a.m. on 15 January 1978, a private Egyptian aircraft took off from Cairo Airport, on its way to Israel, carrying the Egyptian delegation to the meetings of the Political Committee.

When we arrived at Ben Gourion Airport, we were met by the Foreign Minister, Moshe Dayan, and some of his aides. Dayan accompanied me to a platform which was surrounded by a certain number of journalists and television reporters. He made a brief speech welcoming the Egyptian delegation, and expressed the hope that the work of the Political Committee would be crowned with success. He then invited me to the microphone and I made the speech we had prepared for the occasion. We had come to Jerusalem with open hearts and minds and a sincere intention of building together a just and lasting peace. We looked forward to joint work designed to achieve clear-cut and definite results. I mentioned that there were basic facts to be confronted with courage and foresight. These facts were that peace could not be established while the lands were occupied or while the national rights of the Palestinian people, and particularly their right to self-determination, were denied. A lasting peace could not be established unless the peoples of our region strove to create conditions conducive to living together peacefully and securely.

The sun was about to set when the motorcade carrying the Egyptian delegation set out for Jerusalem. Our arrival at night had prevented us from being flown there by helicopter. I rode in the company of Moshe Dayan. The distance that separates Ben Gourion Airport from Jerusalem is about an hour by car. We spoke little of the object of our visit, save expressing our hopes for the success of the meeting. We both knew deep inside that our objectives were diametrically opposed. Night fell and silence prevailed, except for the noise of the engine and the voice of Dayan, who from time to time pointed out some landmark as it glided past. As for me, I was in another world, I was back in 1954 when I visited Jerusalem for the first time as a member of the Egyptian delegation headed by the then Information Minister and Member of the Revolutionary Council, Major Salah Salem. The delegation had visited Saudi Arabia, Yemen, Lebanon and Iraq before going on to Jordan in an attempt to prevent those states from acceding to the Baghdad Pact. The US and Great Britain were seeking to establish the pact among the states in the area, so that it might form a line of defence against the Soviet Union. Our policy then was to steer clear of alliances; we did not consider that the Soviet Union constituted a direct threat to the Arab world. The obvious, present, crushing danger was Israel, which existed in our midst and seized every opportunity to jump down and cut off a slice of Arab territory. The programme of the visit included a visit to Arab Jerusalem by the delegation. We had then travelled from Amman to Jerusalem by car, crossing the desert, which stretched to the outskirts of Jerusalem.

I remembered that Jerusalem had taken possession of me at first sight and remained in my heart ever since. As the car moved swiftly through the night, I saw in my mind's eye its beautiful pastel-coloured hills, its olive and palm trees, old historical buildings, churches, mosques, shops and narrow, winding streets. I remembered the strange feeling of sanctity I felt. How we halted at the Asqa Mosque, where a large crowd consisting of the inhabitants of Jerusalem were waiting to welcome the Egyptian delegation. At their head were religious scholars, imams and city officers. I wandered then from the delegation and proceeded alone and on foot until I came to the Dome of the Rock built on the spot from which our Prophet Muhammad (peace rest with him) set off on his midnight journey to the seven heavens. The rock was colossal. To one side was an opening, leading to a cave inside it which seemed to be five metres long and wide, and was dimly lit. In one corner was a sign marking the Qibla, in the direction of which all Muslims pray. My breast heaved with emotions I had never before experienced. Without thinking, I found myself addressing God in a heartfelt and genuine prayer. On the other side and behind the walls of the Old City of Jerusalem stretched the New City of Jerusalem, built by the Israelis who, until 1967, had awaited the opportunity to jump on it and encompass it. Even then, I recalled the days of the Crusaders who came from afar and occupied Jerusalem in the tenth century. They ruled it for nearly a hundred years but it was finally liberated by Salah El Din El Ayouby, who restored it to the Arabs; we had kept possession of the city ever since. King Feisal was martyred for Jerusalem, for he had announced to the world his hope to pray in the El Asqa Mosque before dying.

I was roused from my thoughts by the voice of Dayan, who had drawn my attention to the fact that we were entering the city. We passed through districts with new buildings and wide streets, until we reached the Jerusalem Hilton, which had been selected to lodge the Egyptian and American delegations to the Political Committee, instead of the King David Hotel, which the Israelis had at first proposed, until it was discovered that it did not have enough rooms to lodge the members of the delegations. One should mention that the King David Hotel had been the scene of a big terrorist operation in which more than twenty officers had lost their lives. The Irgun

Zvei Leumi Organization, under the leadership of Menahim Begin, had blown up the Hotel when Palestine was under the British mandate.

The manager of the hotel conducted me to the suite assigned for me. It was spacious, and had elegant modern furniture. There were green plants and flowers everywhere. On one side of the wall was a large table on which reposed a huge construction of various fruits, oranges, apricots, strawberries, peaches, custard-apples and apples, etc. Near the table was a bar stocked with different kinds of drinks. The suite consisted of three bedrooms, of which I occupied one. The Head of my Office, Ambassador Ahmed Maher, occupied the second, and Major Amr Hamdy the third.

The members of the delegation soon came to my suite, after leaving their luggage in their rooms. Egyptian security men inspected the suite inch by inch to test for bugging or recording equipment. They left us after advising us, as an extra precaution, to talk only when the radio was on, to make it more difficult for listeners if there were any.

We sat around a table and had dinner. We then switched on the radio to the Voice of Israel, which was broadcasting Arab music, and proceeded to talk and exchange jokes gaily to ease the fatigue of the long day. The music soon ceased and the announcer read a news bulletin in Arabic. The first item of news concerned the arrival in Jerusalem of the Egyptian delegation on the Political Committee. The second reported Menahim Begin as saying to a delegation of Dutch Jews visiting Jerusalem that President Sadat had indicated to him that the leaders of the PLO were agents of the Soviet Union. I was furious! What could be the reason for broadcasting such talk? And why was it tied in with the arrival of the Egyptian delegation for negotiations with Israel? Its only significance could be to sow dissension between Egypt and the Palestinians. What could be more damaging than that? Why should the Egyptian President accuse the PLO, the sole representative of the Palestinian people, of being agents of the Soviet Union?

The two items of news, namely the arrival of the Egyptian delegation and Begin's allegations with respect to Sadat's accusation of the PLO leaders, headed the news bulletins every half hour on Radio Israel.

I was not greatly surprised at this. It was logical as far as Israeli tactics were concerned. It was clear to all of us that these tactics were meant to raise obstacles, to torpedo the talks of the Political Committee.

Later I received a coded cable from President Sadat, who had apparently considered my airport speech violent, and was now asking me to control myself, refrain from outbursts and show patience in the negotiations. As to the statements Begin had made before the meetings of the Political Committee, Cairo was of the opinion that they should be ignored for the moment and that Cairo would assume the task of answering them if need be, and had already raised the matter with the Defence Minister, Weizman.

At 10 a.m. the following day, 16 January, the Political Committee held its inaugural session, in which the three delegations participated. It was attended

Camp David

by numerous journalists and correspondents of various news agencies and television networks.

I read out my statement, which indicated that the goal of the meetings was a comprehensive – rather than a separate – peace, based on complete withdrawal from all Arab territories occupied since 1967, including Jerusalem, and guaranteeing the basic right of the Palestinian people and their right to self-determination.

Moshe Dayan's statement, for its part, indicated that the task of the Political Committee would be to bring about peace agreements between Israel and its neighbours, laying down the principles for a just solution with regard to the "Palestinian Arabs" and securing agreement on a peace accord between Egypt and Israel, with concessions by both parties.

Cyrus Vance then made his statement, focusing on the following points:

> There should be an Israeli withdrawal from territories occupied in 1967 and agreement on secure and recognized borders within the framework of natural and peaceful relations in pursuance of UN Security Council Resolutions 242 and 338.
>
> A solution should be found to the Palestinian problem in all its aspects; such a solution should recognize the legitimate rights of the Palestinian people, and should enable it to participate in determining its future.

With that, the inaugural session came to an end. It was followed by a brief reception for the members of the delegations. The first closed session then took place under the chairmanship of Dayan. Israel submitted its peace treaty, differing only slightly from that presented by Begin in Ismailia. We submitted our own project, based on the same lines as the declaration of principles governing the settlement.

I took the floor, and declared that the agenda of the Political Committee meeting was the American agenda, drafted in English. There was, I said, no reason why the words "Judea and Samaria" should be used. I likewise referred to the fact that the Committee was being convened within the context of the Cairo preparatory meeting with the aim of preparing the ground for a comprehensive settlement. [1]

Dayan suggested setting up working committees for each point of the settlement. I proposed that the question be postponed until the conclusion of discussions on the Declaration of Principles: Withdrawal and Self-Determination, and that the meeting be adjourned for consideration of the projects submitted.

Dayan then invited the Egyptian delegation to lunch at the King David Hotel. No reference was made during lunch to the topics under discussion. Before the end of the meal, Dayan leaned towards me and suggested holding a joint press conference after lunch to be attended by the heads of the three delegations. I replied that I did not believe it would be wise to do so: it would be better to put off the press conference until the meetings of the Political Committee were concluded. There was nothing we could say to the newspapermen. We could only reaffirm our already stated positions, which involved nothing new. The holding of such a conference now might be harmful to the work of the Committee.

Dayan, however, insisted on his proposal, saying that the agenda of the meetings of the Committee contained nothing that pledged the participants to secrecy. Each was entitled to express his views in full freedom to the press. I told him I would not take part in the conference. He replied that, in that case, the conference would be held by Vance and himself. I said he was free to act as he pleased. However, when he proposed the idea to Vance, the latter, in his turn, voiced his opposition to it, and for the same reasons as mine. In the event, Dayan held a one-man press conference. He made statements that offered nothing positive to the climate of the committee meetings, declaring that it would be better for the peace initiative to fail than for Israel to abandon the components of its security, and went on to assert further that Israel could not negotiate with a gun pointed at its head.

I could not see who was pointing the gun at whom. We, for our part, sought peace based on justice and restitution of rights in return for security for all parties. The gun was the Israeli government's insistence on illegitimately occupying territory. That gun was pointed at us and at peace.

Dayan was a cunning fox. His manner of speech was not, like Begin's, rigid and unyielding. Dayan approached things indirectly, so that listeners were almost convinced of his flexibility and reasonableness. In reality, he sought to expand the area controlled by Israel, and he set about this by applying the principle of the iron fist in a velvet glove. He was the originator of the theory of open bridges between Israel and the Arabs in the West Bank and Gaza. Following the occupation of Sinai he was of the opinion that the Bar-lev Line should not be drawn on the edge of the Canal but that it should be drawn ten miles from the Canal to reduce the direct provocation that would result from the presence of Israeli soldiers within sight and hearing of the Egyptians on the west bank of the canal. He also formed the theory of the suspension of sovereignty for the West Bank and Gaza, without laying immediate claim to them as Begin had wanted. He wished to make use of the time to bring about changes in the occupied land that would culminate in a de facto annexation. He kept his voice low, and gave the impression of calm. He spoke through a mask, his face wreathed in a perpetual smile – the result of operations on his one-eyed face. Although his personality was characterized by modesty, he liked to be in the limelight. He longed to have his pictures, stories and interviews dominate the news. He had gained immense popularity both inside and outside Israel following the 1967 War, as the hero of Israel's astonishing victory in 1967. As a result of the 1973 War, however, Dayan's reputation began to wane somewhat. He was among those who were held responsible for what befell Israel then. His defection from the Labour Party and participation in Begin's cabinet had further weakened his standing with the Israelis. He made every effort to reassert himself and regain the esteem he had once enjoyed in Israeli and world opinion.

It is my belief that his obsession with fame and his desire to steal the limelight took on new dimensions with the growing power of the mass media in our time. This power has become the scourge of the age especially where public figures are concerned. Many have fallen prey to the disease. Sadat was soon, in his turn, to become one of its chronic victims, as I shall show later in the course of this book.

After lunch I returned to my hotel suite, where I found a cable from Mr Mubarak which read as follows:

> The President has followed the inaugural session, and congratulates you on its success and your address. He hopes you will maintain your calm, and that your speech be deliberate and controlled. Should a difficulty arise, you could ask to consult Cairo and so gain time to think it over. We should immediately be notified to consider the matter. Any request for information may be sent at any time round the clock, and you will receive the answer with the utmost dispatch. The President wishes you every success.

This astonished me since my calm had not deserted me.

In the afternoon, the leader of the Israeli side on the Military Committee and Minister of Defence, Ezer Weizman, paid me a visit. He intimated that this was a courtesy call, since I was Israel's guest. The visit was in no way connected with the work of the Political Committee. I welcomed him and told him that President Sadat had confidence in him, and that we were relying on his good judgment and influence with Prime Minister Begin to convince the latter to adopt a position appropriate to President Sadat's goal. Weizman replied that he was working to that end, but that we had to take into consideration the importance of security to Israel and both Begin's internal problems and the fact that he lacked Sadat's strong position within Egypt. I told him that we fully understood the importance of security, which we also needed. Security was not brought about by the annexation of land. He was a military man, and could understand that. There were diverse other means to achieve mutual security for both parties. As for Begin's internal problems, it was naturally no secret to him that we had our own problems in the Arab world. Problems do not rule out the necessity of facing up to them courageously as Sadat had done.

My impression of Weizman was that he was open and tended to discuss matters frankly. He had the smiling face and gay disposition found in many pilots. He had lived in Egypt for several years during World War II, when he served in the British Royal Air Force. I felt that he had taken Sadat's initiative seriously, and realized that, in order to secure peace with Egypt, Israel would have to pay a price and make concessions. I had no way of course of estimating how far he would go along this line for he was a member of the Hirut Party which called for a Greater Israel.

Whatever the personality of Weizman or others, I was at pains, from start to finish, to exercise the greatest reserve and preserve formality in my contacts with Israeli figures. I never allowed any of them to address me by my first name, nor did I address any of them by other than rank and title.

After Weizman left, Cyrus Vance paid me a visit. We spoke of approaches to the talks. I told him we looked forward, from the start, to his taking an active and positive part in the search for a clear Declaration of Principles, a comprehensive settlement and a self-determination for the Palestinians. I reaffirmed our position on what had been raised by Dayan during the morning session, i.e. our non-approval of the establishment of sub-committees to consider the items of the agenda before we had reached agreement on Principles. I likewise affirmed to him our rejection of Begin's project. I told him I did not approve of his proposal that the latter should be considered as a starting-point for the talks. To his question as to whether we would accept a period of time on the West Bank and in Gaza, I replied that we had no objection, but that such a period had to be fixed from the outset and end with the exercise by the Palestinian people of their right to self-determination. Moreover, other parties had to participate in considering the matter.

Vance intended to spend two days in Jerusalem, during which he would participate in the committee meetings. He would then leave for Washington, where he had other engagements. He requested that the committee meeting be continued after his departure, and I replied that everything depended on the result achieved.

The following day, 17 January, Vance shuttled between the headquarters of the two delegations in the hotel in an attempt to ascertain whether points of agreement could be found and to define the areas of disagreement. I was of the opinion that such an approach was ineffective and would divert us from the essential confrontation of the subject. Was Israel willing to withdraw from the occupied territories in return for peace backed by security measures and guarantees or not? And I told him so.

A banquet was to be hosted by the Israeli Prime Minister at 8 p.m. that evening in honour of the Egyptian and American delegations. Yet Begin requested that I meet him at his office in the Knesset at 6 p.m.

Dr Boutros Ghali and Ambassador Ahmed Maher accompanied me on this meeting. We drove to the Knesset, where we were welcomed by Menahim Begin, who had with him Moshe Dayan and General Tamir, who was a member of the Military Committee. Begin began by saying that he had feelings of friendship and love for President Sadat. He had been impressed by the spirit of cordiality with which he had welcomed him in Ismailia. He pointed out that, on his return from Ismailia, he had been the object of a fierce attack directed at the peace proposals he had put forward, and that some of his closest friends had taken part in the onslaught. The project (he went on) he had submitted at Ismailia included retention of the settlements in El Arish and Rafah, and the need to defend such settlements. It was evident that differences existed. But then, said he, negotiations naturally start with differences, which should be expressed dispassionately. He had been surprised and hurt after his return from Egypt, because Egypt gave the impression that he, Begin, was provoking a crisis. Yet in Ismailia President Sadat had accepted the discussion of the settlements and other topics in committee. Begin intimated that, had he intended to bargain, he would have submitted a project on the division of Sinai between Egypt and Israel, especially since the 1967 War had been a war of defence and would result in territorial adjustments. He had, however (his words!), been generous, and had not asked for this . . . As for the autonomy project he had put forward, it was the humane compromise for the inhabitants of "Judea and Samaria". The Arab Palestinian inhabitants desired self-rule, which they would acquire for the first time in history. The Jewish Palestinian inhabitants, on the other hand, desired security. His project fulfilled the hopes of both parties!

Begin went on to say that differences between friends were understandable. However, he had been surprised by President Sadat, who had created a crisis over the settlements, as though it were a new Israeli claim with which he was unacquainted. This was all the more surprising since this was not the President's reaction at Ismailia!

He informed us that he disliked diatribes. He had been deeply offended by Mustapha Amin's article in which he had compared Begin with Shylock. This was to him the height of anti-Semitic insults. Again, the President's interview to the *October* magazine likewise involved an attack on his honour. President Sadat, he added, had perhaps been too precipitate, and had sought to hurry things along. It was not, however, desirable to precipitate matters, since they had ample time at their disposal to reach an understanding on all matters. He trusted that I would inform President Sadat of what he had just explained to me so as to avoid misunderstanding. I replied that he, Begin, might look upon settlements as a humane solution to a problem, as he put it, however we, as well as the whole world, considered it an example of encroachment on the land of others, and it consolidated the illegitimate occupation of parts of our territories. It constituted a violation of our sovereignty, and was not open to discussion. If he was surprised and hurt by President Sadat's interview with *October* magazine, we were greatly shocked when confirmed reports reached us on Israel's establishment of new settlements in Sinai while we were making preparations for the convening of the Political Committee. Israel was establishing settlements instead of proceeding to dismantle existing ones. Such methods would realize neither understanding nor peace.

Jerusalem

Begin replied, saying, "If such was your point of view regarding settlements, why do we not discuss this in the Political Committee?" I answered that we would not do that because the task of the Political Committee was to discuss general principles, including total withdrawal. As to the settlements, they represented no more than a part of the implementation of that principle, as did the forces, the airports, the warning stations and all the other installations violating our sovereignty. The logical place to consider the matter was in the Military Committee. As to what Mustapha Amin had written, he was expressing his personal opinion. However, I would affirm to him that we were not anti-Semitic, for the simple reason that we are semites. Moreover, we look upon the Jews as "People of the Book", recognizing their Prophet, Moses, in the same way as we recognize Jesus and the Prophet Muhammad.

I then asked him how he explained the statement with which Radio Israel welcomed us, namely Sadat's informing him (Begin) that the PLO leaders were Soviet agents. Was he aware of its significance and the repetition of it every half-hour by Radio Israel?

He was somewhat taken aback at this, and said, "Those were the President's very words." I told him I had my own doubts on the subject and, even it they were, there were certain conversations that should under the circumstances not be disclosed. Begin replied that he had not ordered it broadcast: he had mentioned it to some Congressmen, who had spread it about until the radio got hold of it.

The meeting was over, and we agreed on the need to eschew exchanges of statements, and take all measures conducive to the creation of an atmosphere of calm. Such an atmosphere would enable the Political Committee to achieve the desired results.

We returned to the hotel. The time was past seven. In the hotel I found a cable from Mr Mubarak awaiting me. The cable read as follows:

> The President agrees to all the measures you have taken. He deems your analysis and evaluation excellent. He recommends insistence on the Declaration of Principles and says to inform Vance that Presidents Carter and Sadat have agreed on the Declaration of Principles as the basic issue.

Footnotes:

1   I had wanted the venue changed to Cairo for a very cogent reason. Should the meeting succeed in achieving a Declaration of Principles, other Arab parties might be induced to take part in the talks. It would be diffficult, if not impossible, for such states to go to Jerusalem.

Chaper Nine

The Last Supper

At eight o'clock sharp I proceeded with some members of the Egyptian delegation to the Festival Hall on the first floor of the hotel, where the banquet was to be held. I felt quite fresh, for I had taken a hot shower and changed my clothes. I was quite relaxed following my talk with Begin and the agreement we had reached on eschewing any statements that might affect the atmosphere of the committee meetings. President Sadat's cable, too, had given a boost to my morale. I felt rested and looked forward to spending a couple of hours seeing new faces and putting aside work and getting out of the four walls we had been shut up in ever since our arrival in Jerusalem.

And, in fact, the party was a gay one, with everyone looking forward optimistically to the success of the talks that could lead to peace. Over a hundred men and women had been invited to the banquet, and these included politicians from both the government and the opposition; and writers, journalists, judges and several foreign consuls-general accredited in Jerusalem, besides the American delegation and the editors-in-chief of the Egyptian newspapers. I spoke with many guests, including the leader of the Israeli opposition, Shimon Perez. Shortly afterwards, we were summoned to dinner and took our places. I went to the main table headed by the Israeli Prime Minister, Menahim Begin, and seated myself at his right, where I had been assigned. Vance sat on his left. To my right was the wife of Moshe Dayan, and next to her the Vice-Premier, Ygal Yadin.

From time to time I engaged in smalltalk with Begin, Moshe Dayan's wife and Yadin, who was an archeologist and insisted on speaking in Arabic. One dish followed another, but before the meal had ended, the doors were suddenly thrown open and an army of photographers, newsmen and television network representatives made their appearance. There were far too many of them, and Begin turned proudly to me, saying: "The whole world has come to see us, Mr Minister." He took a small piece of paper from his pocket and showed it to me: there were some words jotted down on it in Hebrew. "That is my speech," said he. I laughingly responded, "I hope it won't create any new problems for us," to which he replied: "Of course not– who wants problems?"

The Last Supper

Begin then began his speech, and within a few minutes, the atmosphere of gaiety and relaxation that had prevailed prior to his address evaporated and in its place reigned sorrow and distress, wafting the guests to Dante's Inferno. He gave an account of the history of the Jews from its beginning. He described their misfortune down the ages. He spoke of their sufferings and persecution starting with Pharaoh and ending with Hitler. As he read on, his face became distended like a turkey's wattle. The sound of his own voice filled him with ecstasy, making him oblivious of time and place. He referred to my airport address upon the arrival of our delegation, and to my opening speech to the inaugural session of the Political Committee as though it was the most grievous thing the Jews had suffered: how dared that person who had come from Egypt ask them to redivide their capital, Jerusalem, after it had been unified? Would I agree to his going to Cairo to ask that it be divided? How dared I ask for their withdrawal to the pre-1967 borders? Did I forget that they were defending their lives and those of their children against our aggression? Worst of all, was I asking for the Palestinian Arabs' right to self-determination? And why was I doing this? To establish a terrorist state on their (the Israelis) doorstep, so that it could massacre women and children? The Arabs, he ranted on, exercised their right to self-determination in twenty-one states, and now wished to establish a new state, by means of the right to self-determination, and so ruin their (the Israelis) future. The Minister (myself) was a young man and was unaware that Hitler used the right to self-determination in the thirties to annex to Germany territories belonging to Czechoslovakia and other states. I say "No" loudly and clearly to the division of Jerusalem (he went on) – "NO" to the withdrawal to the 1967 borders, and "NO" to the right to self-determination to terrorists . . .

His monotonous, irritating voice rang in my ears and almost paralyzed my thinking. I was completely bewildered. Why, less than three hours before, this very same person, in the flesh, had asked that both of us should desist from polemics to enable the Political Committee to embark on its search for peace without let or hindrance! I had agreed with him on that, and we had pledged ourselves to do so in the presence of witnessess from both his side and mine! What was I to do? Should I withdraw from the banquet? Should I stand up and return his rudeness? Remind him of what the Israelis were doing to the Palestinian people? Should I remind him that his own hands were stained with the blood of the women and children he had massacred at Deir Yassin?

I became aware that he was ending his speech, as he called upon the Egyptian Foreign Minister to deliver his address. I tore up the sheet of paper on which I had written the short address I was to deliver on this occasion. I rose slowly, with my nerves well in control, and began to speak calmly. I thanked the Israeli government for the warm welcome it had accorded to the Egyptian delegation. When we had accepted the invitation to attend the dinner party we had hoped to while away a pleasant hour or two free of tension after a long and difficult day's work. Such at least, I repeated, was our hope. The Prime Minister of Israel, however, had chosen otherwise. That (I went on) he was perfectly entitled to do. I went on to say that I did not believe the banquet was the appropriate place to answer him. All I wished to say was that the principles I had defined in my speech at the inaugural session of the Political Committee – which the Israeli Premier had rejected – formed the sole basis on which a just and lasting peace could be established. As for my answer to what he had just been saying, I intended to reserve it for the meeting of the Political Committee the next day, since that was the proper forum for it.

I sat down without either drinking a toast to peace or shaking hands with him. A profound silence prevailed in the room for a few moments, followed by a burst of applause and some commotion. Begin was somewhat disconcerted and hurried to the microphone to call upon the American Secretary of State to deliver his address. Then I felt Begin's hands on my shoulders. I turned and saw surprise and concern on his face. He told me he had not intended any harm. I did not answer him and turned my face away.

Vance delivered his address, but hardly anyone paid any attention and the dinner came to an end. I rose and walked quickly towards the lift to go to my room, whereupon I was surrounded by several foreign newsmen, who wanted to know whether we were going to break off the talks. I told them to go and ask our host, Begin.

In my suite were assembled the members of the delegation and the editors-in-chief of the Egyptian newspapers, who were seething with anger at Begin, but were, they admitted, soothed by my even and balanced response. Shortly afterwards I received a visit from Vance, who expressed profound regret at Begin's behaviour, telling me that if it was any comfort to me, Begin had treated him in a similar manner on a previous occasion in Washington.

It was after three o'clock when the last guests left, and I sat alone and smoked until I was out of cigarettes. I tried to sleep but was unable to do so. Ahmed Maher rose at six in the morning and came to my room. Together we had breakfast. I borrowed a cigarette from him. I then went to bed and slept until 9.30.

At ten we held another meeting with the members of the American delegation, headed by Vance, who presented a draft of an American Declaration of Principles. We did not, however, approve it, because it fell far short of what Carter had declared in Aswan. Vance said he realized that, but that Israeli opposition would lead to failure to secure a Declaration of Principles. I informed him that Egypt was not interested in just any declaration that could be entitled "A Declaration of Principles". We insisted on a clear declaration fulfilling its purposes and encouraging other Arab parties to adopt a positive attitude towards the initiative. We insisted that the declaration should stipulate a withdrawal, and a solution to the Palestinian problem in all its aspects, on the basis of the right to self-determination. We would not accept ambiguous formulas. At this moment, Atherton (Assistant Secretary of State for the Middle East) suggested that Egypt should propose a project on the West Bank and the Gaza Strip as a counter-project to Begin's scheme for administrative self-rule. This we rejected, since we were not authorized by the Palestinians to do so. The only key in our opinion, to move in that direction was a clear and straightforward Declaration of Principles. Whereupon the meeting broke up. Vance said he would contact us again, and we again met the American delegation an hour later.

Vance indicated that he had made some amendments to his draft Declaration of Principles, and wanted to know whether we accepted the text of President Carter's declaration in Aswan, with the addition that participation in self-determination would be through negotiations. He added that the American concept of the legitimate rights of the Palestinians was political, public and economic rights, and asked if we agreed to this. As to withdrawal and boundaries, which the American project combined in one article, a thing to which we had objected, would we accept reference to them as two separate items?

The first item was the withdrawal of forces from territories occupied since 1967. The second item was that boundaries between all the countries in the area would be secure and recognized.

We embarked on a discussion of this until lunch time. Vance indicated that he would invite us to dine with him at seven to continue the debate, and to this we agreed.

I was tired and exhausted. I had a quick lunch and went to bed, requesting not to be awakened before six-thirty to prepare myself for Vance's dinner at seven. I was dead to the world when I felt a hand shaking me violently, and heard a voice telling me to wake up. I failed to respond, however, this went on until I was finally awake, though my mind was still asleep. I beheld a stranger, whom I had never seen before, standing beside my bed. I had no way of knowing how he had reached my bedroom. I asked him who he was, and he replied that he was the Chief of the Egyptian Communications Team which had accompanied the delegation to Jerusalem. He bore an urgent cable from President Sadat. He had been trying, to no avail, to wake me up for the last half-hour, and he asked my pardon for having had to do this.

I attempted to read the cable more than once, but nothing registered. I got out of bed and washed my face with cold water. I then re-read the cable. It contained President Sadat's instructions for my immediate return, with the Egyptian delegation, to Cairo after it became clear that Israel was seeking to put forward partial solutions. Dayan's statements on the need to make concessional agreements, and Begin's speech at the banquet, showed the futility of the Committee's continuing its work.

Camp David

In the cable, the President requested me to explain that the instructions for our return did not indicate that the talks were being broken off, but was merely a summons. Also, I was to meet Vance and explain the situation to him, and inform him that the President wished to see him in Cairo.

There was nothing I would have wanted more than to leave Jerusalem and return to Cairo. However, I realized at once the gravity of this sudden decision, taken without prior consultation with me. This would have the effect of playing directly into the hands of Menahim Begin, and make it appear that we were not serious in our search for peace, otherwise what reason could there be for breaking off talks in the Political Committee when it had hardly begun? Moreover, I realized that for the delegation to withdraw without warning would constitute an affront to the American Secretary of State, Cyprus Vance, who had left Washington and his work there to participate in the attempt to reach a solution and who was straining every nerve to achieve this, and whose attitude showed an understanding of our viewpoint.

I put on my dressing-gown and hurried to the communications-room, where I asked to contact President Sadat. I failed, however, to locate him, and contacted the Vice-President Mr Mubarak, to whom I explained my viewpoint. He informed me that the decision had been taken in the National Security Council, and was irreversible. I suggested that he propose to the President that I return alone, leaving the delegation behind to proceed at Vance's dinner and see how it would end. I added that it might be important to continue the meetings of the Political Committee as the Israeli cabinet was studying the American proposals. Begin would otherwise capitalize on the breaking of the talks and make us responsible for it. While it would be in our interest that the recall of the delegation should appear to be the result of Israel's intransigent attitude which, one could be sure, would be announced following the Israeli cabinet meeting. The Israelis would, in consequence, bear the responsibility for the failure of the talks.

The Vice-President promised to pass this on and to contact me again. Twenty minutes later, he did so informing me that the decision stood and the information media had got wind of it: Cairo Radio was even then broadcasting the official Egyptian communiqué on the reasons for recalling the Egyptian delegation from Jerusalem. He had issued instructions for the departure of two Egyptian aircraft from Cairo to carry the delegation back. He concluded by wishing me every success.

I returned to my room and held a meeting with the members of the delegation to consider the situation. In the meantime I received a cable from President Sadat telling me to meet the Israeli Prime Minister before my return to Egypt to explain to him the reasons for the recall of the Egyptian delegation. I was to make it clear to him that this did not constitute a rupture of the talks, but it was merely a temporary recall for further consideration of the situation.

The Last Supper

Just then Vance broke into the room. I was still in my pyjamas. He appeared disturbed and saddened. He enquired of the truth of the reported recall of the delegation to Cairo, and I confirmed it to him, inviting him to be seated. I offered him a Scotch and he thanked me. "Why? Why? Why?" he kept asking. I replied that I was asking myself the same question, but that I first wished to affirm to him our special consideration for his sincere efforts and for his understanding of our position. I had reported on this to the President on a day-to-day basis, and I intimated that he was no doubt aware of the President's dependence on the United States, President Carter and himself for the attainment of peace. The President himself had instructed me to meet him and explain to him the reasons for the recall of the Egyptian delegation. This in no way was meant to affect him personally. The President saw a real danger in Begin's methods, which were designed to induce us to bargain and draw us into side-issues, the results of which could only be negative. I referred to the statement broadcast by the Israeli Radio at the time of the Egyptian delegation's arrival in Jerusalem, purporting that President Sadat had informed Begin that the PLO leadership were communist agents. I spoke of the press conference that had been held the day before by the Israeli Foreign Minister, Moshe Dayan (which we had both refused to take part in, since it was pointless to do so, before the Committee meetings had concluded). I referred to what Dayan had announced on the need to have the settlement based on territorial concessions. I told him that he had himself heard Begin's speech less than three hours after Begin had agreed to abstain from making any statement likely to impede the work of the Committee.

For all these reasons, I went on, the President saw the need for a pause, following which the talks would resume on a constructive basis. I told him that President Sadat had invited him to Cairo so that he, Sadat, could explain the matter and consult with him regarding it.

Vance replied that there was no doubt that Begin had not been tactful. He could have helped to create a more favourable climate for the talks. Vance said it was his intention to travel to Egypt to meet President Sadat. He stated that he believed he had come close to securing Israeli agreement to a text on the Palestinian problem that might have been acceptable to us, He would have preferred to have been given another twenty-four hours to attempt to influence Begin, through his ego and building him up as the one man capable of achieving peace and being remembered in history for this achievement. He was of the opinion that matters were going to be clarified one way or the other within the next twenty-four hours. He would then be able to meet Sadat with a balanced assessment of the situation, showing what was possible and what was not. Sadat would be able to make his decision accordingly. He added that he feared that the decision to recall the Egyptian delegation would have a negative effect on American public opinion, which might believe such a summons hasty and insufficiently justified. He felt obliged to inform the press that he was on the point of realizing some progress, that the talks were useful, and that he regretted Egypt's decision.

Vance was summoned to the telephone to speak to President Carter. Upon his return, he informed me that Carter was greatly concerned over the decision to recall the Egyptian delegation to Cairo. Carter would be telephoning President Sadat to find out what could be done. Vance also informed me that Begin had contacted him to enquire as to the reason for the withdrawal of the Egyptian delegation. I informed Vance that I had instructions from President Sadat to meet Begin before I returned to Cairo. He said he would get in touch with me after my meeting with the Israeli Premier and before my departure.

At 8.30 p.m. I proceeded to the office of the Israeli Prime Minister, accompanied by Ambassador Ahmed Maher. A large crowd had gathered in front of the building in which the Israeli Premier's office was situated, and their faces showed concern. The news of the recall of the Egyptian delegation to Cairo had become common knowledge. When we entered the building, we were assailed with questions as to what had happened. Would the talks be broken off? Had the peace efforts failed?

The interview between Begin and myself lasted for nearly two hours, with Moshe Dayan attending the last part of it. I began by explaining in very clear and straightforward terms all that I felt with respect to the Israeli statements, behaviour and position with regard to the peace initiative. I concluded that such a method could only lead to the loss of an historical opportunity to realize comprehensive peace.

Begin replied that he had done nothing he had not indicated from the outset. Sadat had come to Jerusalem asking them to withdraw to the pre-1967 borders and recognize the rights to the Palestinians. He, Begin, had answered him in his answering speech that he would not do so, but that everything was negotiable. In Ismailia, Begin had submitted his peace project. Sadat had not approved the project, and had presented projects we had promised to consider. "Why should Sadat be incensed at my objecting to the American project's failure to call the West Bank 'Judea and Samaria'? We had agreed in Ismailia that each party would use whatever name it wanted. President Sadat himself used the words 'Judea and Samaria' at the press conference in Ismailia, so why should he be incensed now?" After Ismailia, Sadat had threatened another war if Israel did not agree to his demands before October 1978 (the date of the expiry of the period of service of the United Nations Emergency Force II). Sadat had said, "I have to wait until October. The Arabs could unite and another October could take place," which meant (Begin went on), he was directly threatening us with aggression and holocaust. How could he do so when we were negotiating peace? He had promised me (Begin) that the 1973 War would be the last war between Egypt and Israel.

"You," continued Begin, "consider yourselves to have been victorious in

The Last Supper

the October War. We, for our part, do not like to boast. We say that the first days of the war we encountered many difficulties and suffered many losses. But at the end we were able to drive back those who had attacked us on two fronts. Then along comes Sadat threatening war. We do not fear threats. Sadat told *October* magazine that he had given us everything, while I gave him nothing. Was this nothing [pointing to a huge map of Sinai on the wall]? Sadat said in his interview that the Jews are shrewd merchants. I am a militant, not a merchant. Dayan, Weizman and Sharon are likewise militants representing our people, who elected us and expect us to look after their interests.

"And then you came to Jerusalem as a guest and hurt our feelings by asking us to leave our heart, Jerusalem. This is our capital, which was divided. We liberated it in 1967 and took a democratic decision to have it restored to us. We never heard of a state anywhere in the world say that its capital could be divided. You ask us to leave the Golan so that it may again become a gun pointed at our heads. You ask us to give up Judea and Samaria, the cradle of our civilization and history. I had to answer you with a political speech, and my opportunity came with the dinner-party. This is common practice everywhere. And now President Sadat comes along and calls off the talks in the middle, and recalls you to Cairo . . . We shall not divide Jerusalem, and shall not return to the 1967 borders. That was what President Sadat heard from me in the Knesset, and that was what I put to him in Ismailia. However, we are ready to go on negotiating with you."

Begin concluded his words by asking me whether I thought the record of that meeting should be published in full. I replied that I was going to meet the President and would report to him what he (Begin) had said. He persisted, saying that if we did not want to publish anything about the meeting, then they (the Israelis) would not do so either. I told him he was free to either publish or not to publish the record, and that I would report his words to the President. Whereupon Begin turned to Dayan for his opinion. Dayan affirmed his belief that it should not be published. However, he said, Minister Kamel would naturally be making a statement to the press when he would be asked about what transpired at this meeting. Begin suggested: "Why should we not say that you gave me the reasons for your recall, and I expressed my regret at your departure, and that we both were prepared to resume the talks at some future date?" I replied that I had no objection to this, since my recall did not necessarily imply a break in the negotiations, but rather consultation before taking a further step. Dayan announced that he agreed to this. We should not, he said, forget, that there was a third party effectively participating in the talks, namely the United States. Vance had decided to remain in Jerusalem until the following day, even if there was nothing for him to do. He would meet Begin the following morning because he wanted to keep the door open for the talks to continue. It was important that we made no statements which would create problems for the third party to the talks.

To this we agreed. I was not interested in what should or should not be published about the meeting. All I was concerned with now was that I had made sure of Menahim Begin's targets and was aware of his methods. He sought to gain time through negotiations, without giving anything away. It was upon such a basis that we should determine our own position and tactics.

It was nearly 11 p.m. when we returned to the hotel, where the lobby was full of newspaper and radio correspondents who assailed us with questions. I said only that I was going back to Egypt to consult with Sadat about the following step.

While we were getting ready to leave, Vance appeared in my room, and I informed him of the substance of our meeting. He again expressed his regret at Begin's hard line. He intimated that the process required time and perseverance. He was going to Cairo to meet President Sadat in two days' time, on his way back to Washington.

I waited for him to leave so I could quit the hotel. He became aware of this, and said he would see me off to the airport. I responded that this would be impossible, since the airport was an hour's journey from Jerusalem, and it would mean that he would get back to Jerusalem around 3 a.m. after a long and tiring day. He replied that he was aware of this, but wished to demonstrate that the decision to recall the Egyptian delegation in no way affected him. He was concerned to get it across to people that his feelings towards Egypt and myself were unchanged.

I thanked Vance and told him that his visit had served just that purpose. He answered that in that case, he would accompany me to the car so that the crowd of reporters in the lobby would see for themselves.

I again rode with Dayan as we travelled to Ben Gourion airport. We talked for sometime, and he informed me that he was sorry for Begin's speech at the dinner. He believed it was the direct cause of the Egyptian delegation's recall. Begin, he went on, was a sincere man, but could not resist seizing any opportunity to explain Jewish history and his own point of view. Our conversation then came to an end and each of us was occupied with his own thoughts.

The plane was not awaiting us at the airport – it had left carrying the Egyptian technicians who had been attached to the delegation, and was to return for us. This took over an hour, which we spent at the airport cafeteria, which served us sandwiches. I sat at a small table with Dayan and Boutros Ghali, but took no part in the conversation as I was deep in my own thoughts. Dayan was speaking of his contacts with, and knowledge of, the many Palestinians amongst whom he had grown up. He was a "Sabra", or Palestinian-born Jew, who had not emigrated to Palestine. I heard him tell Boutros Ghali that the Gaza Strip was of no importance to them whatever. It was small in area and inhabited by four hundred thousand Palestinian refugees. It had no economic resources. There was nothing in it but snakes, rocks, poverty and wretchedness. If that made matters any easier, they (the Israelis) were prepared to give it up if we pledged ourselves not to allow it to become a base for terrorist action against Israel!

I did not attach much importance to what he said until some months later, when certain pro-Israeli American Congressmen raised the point with our Embassy in Washington. The idea was that a partial solution for the Palestinian problem might lie in Gaza as a first step. Later, but for only a little while, Sadat embraced this idea. I was amazed at Israel's ability to infiltrate ideas, which seemed apparently attractive yet could have far-reaching complications.

Chapter Ten

Don't Put All Your Eggs In One Basket

Returning from Jerusalem, I reached home at 5 a.m., surprised to find lights on in the house at such an early hour. The reason for this soon became clear: my wife was getting ready to go to the airport to fly to Germany and arrange for our personal belongings, which we had left behind when we had gone to Egypt for the visit by Chancellor Schmidt the previous December, to be shipped back. After greeting each other, she left for the airport while I went to bed. I fell into a deep sleep, but was awakened by the persistent ringing of the telephone line to the President. I raised the receiver. The speaker, one of the Presidency chamberlains, informed me that the President was expecting me at eleven at the Barrage rest-house (an hour away from Cairo). In my irritation at being wakened, I asked him to tell the President I would go and see him when I had managed to get some sleep, and would be unable to meet him before 1 p.m., whereupon I then hung up.

I reached the Barrage rest-house at 1.30 p.m., and found the President sitting in the sun in the garden with Mr Hosny Mubarak and the Prime Minister, Mr Mamdouh Salem. They welcomed me warmly, and I gave them an account of my trip to Jerusalem. I then asked the President why he had summoned me, adding that it was a sensitive matter to Vance, and Begin would undoubtedly make the most of it. He replied that it had to do with the behaviour and statements of Begin and Dayan. When Dayan had stated, at the inaugural meeting of the Political Committee, that both sides would have to make concessions, he (Sadat) had been concerned lest I be manipulated into making such concessions! I assured him there was no call for such fears, since I was neither entitled nor inclined to give up anything, and was in close contact with him in every step I took at all times.

He informed me that President Carter had spoken to him on the telephone the day he had decided to recall the Egyptian delegation. Carter had pressed for the resumption of the meetings of the Political Commitee as soon as possible, but he had refused. However (Sadat continued) he agreed, for Carter's sake, to the meeting of the Military Committee!

I failed to see the point in so doing, and drew his attention to the fact that this would confirm Arab doubts that all he sought was the restitution of Sinai

Don't Put All Your Eggs In One Basket

rather than a comprehensive solution. Sadat answered that this was not his intention: he cared nothing for what the Arabs said, and his action had been aimed solely at pleasing his friend Carter. He invited me to attend the wedding of the son of Osman Ahmed Osman at 8.30 that evening, but I declined, saying I was very tired and in urgent need of rest. However, he insisted, intimating that the event would be going on all night, so that I could get as much sleep as I wanted and still go to the wedding at midnight.

In the event I did attend the wedding in Osman Ahmed Osman's residence close to the Pyramids. It was swarming with notables and personalities. Osman Ahmed Osman received me and conducted me to the main table around which sat the President and his wife; the Prime Minister, Mr Mamdouh Salem; the Speaker of the People's Assembly, Sayed Marei and Mrs Marei, and Osman Ahmed Osman himself. When I reached the table, Sadat stood up to welcome me and invite me to be seated between himself and Mrs Sadat, who was longing to hear what had happened in Jerusalem. Raising his voice, Sadat then asked me: "What do you say to our appointing a foreign affairs adviser to you?" He went on to point out that the former Foreign Minister, Mr Ismail Fahmy, had for several days been pestering him, through third parties, seeking to obtain the post of Adviser on Foreign Affairs to the President of the Republic. Some of those sitting at the table made biting remarks at Ismail Fahmy's expense. I answered Sadat forcefully: "Why not?" We had (I went on) reached a sensitive stage requiring the mobilization of all of our expertise. Ismail Fahmy had great experience, which we could put to good use. Furthermore, we were always on the best of terms and I should be glad to co-operate with him. My words, however, were coolly received.

The following day I proceeded to the airport to meet Vance upon his arrival from Israel. I accompanied him to the Barrage rest-house to meet the President. Sadat explained to Vance his reasons for summoning the delegation back to Cairo from Jerusalem. He thanked Vance for the part he had played in the talks which I had reported to him, saying that the reason behind his decision was Israeli intransigence, which showed no response to the constructive climate created by his visit to Jerusalem. The Israelis continued to raise obstacles which aimed at destroying such a climate. He (Sadat) had sought to ensure an active and continuing American role in the talks in every possible way. That role was not to be confined to negative mediation, and his intention was to make the US a full partner in the talks. Israel's real aims had been revealed by her insistence on retaining the settlements in Sinai and her claims to sovereignty over the West Bank and Gaza. He believed that, faced with such a revelation, it was the responsibility of the US to pressurize Israel into changing its stand. Vance submitted to President Sadat the American project on a Declaration of Principles, and passed on to him President Carter's invitation to visit Camp David on 4

Camp David

February 1978. Sadat accepted the invitation, which appeared to give him much pleasure.

Despite my appreciation of the importance of the American role and US participation in the talks, I felt that Sadat over-estimated what the US could do. I feared that to lay such a burden on the US would result in a slowing-down of international action designed to bring pressure to bear on Israel. We had had to struggle for years before we were able to achieve sensible results in that direction. On the other hand, it was clear that the US sought to monopolize the situation in order to reach an American solution to the conflict.

I felt that there was a certain danger in isolating the Middle East issue in any way from international participation and interest. The issue would otherwise be concentrated in the hands of the US, who would become the sole arbiter between the Arabs and Israel. An event that occurred at this time confirmed my fears. Our Embassy in New Delhi informed us that the US had been urging the government of India to recognize – and exchange diplomatic representation with – Israel. Now, India was one of the main pillars of support for Arab rights and of condemnation of Israeli aggression on our territory. India had refused to comply. However, American efforts had their own implications.

It so happened that Atherton paid me a visit just then, and I mentioned American efforts aimed at inducing India to recognize Israel. He denied their existence out of hand. However, I informed him that I was certain such efforts had been exerted. He promised to verify the matter and to give me an answer. Sure enough, he called on me the following day with confirmation of the American efforts, which he justified on the ground that the US believed that Israel's relief at ending its isolation in the international arena – India's recognition being a step in that direction – would have a positive effect on its hard-line policy, and thus lead to greater flexibility in the Israeli attitude.

My reply to this was that I felt it would have been more appropriate for the US to have kept us informed of such efforts, rather than proceed with them behind our backs. Moreover, I continued, such efforts had been proven ineffective and even dangerous in the past. Nothing showed this better than the US' constant emphasis on the fact that its supply of sophisticated weapons to Israel would give the latter a feeling of security and hence promote greater flexibility on its part. What invariably happened (I went on) was the exact contrary. As its arsenals were filled with American weaponry, Israel became increasingly arrogant and intransigent. Furthermore, it used such weapons in new aggressions and further consolidation of its occupation of Arab territories.

It was certain that the US was exerting similar efforts with the African states, who had severed their relations with Israel following the 1973 War. Their action was based on the fact that Israel had occupied Egyptian territory: Egypt was an African state and a member of the OAU, and now

Don't Put All Your Eggs In One Basket

that Egypt had entered into direct negotiations with Israel, the African states would see no obstacle to re-establishing relations with Israel. In fact, the only thing standing in the way was the fact that the African states sought the support of the Arab oil states in dealing with their economic crises in the aftermath of the rise in oil prices. This was compounded by the ever increasing Israeli collaboration with the racist regime in South Africa.

Moreover, it was no secret that the US was exerting pressure – sometimes rather crude pressure – upon the EEC, to induce it to abstain from taking any initiatives or positions aimed at the settlement of the Arab-Israeli conflict. The EEC initiatives were predicated by the vital interests of such states in the stability of the Middle East area, which could only be brought about by securing a comprehensive peace in the region, while the Americans claimed that such initiatives by the EEC affected the American on-going efforts for peace.

And what of the non-aligned group that strongly and positively supported the Arab position? The group found itself in an extremely difficult and embarrassing situation as a result of the divisions among its Arab members as regards the confrontation with Israel, in the wake of Sadat's visit to Jerusalem.

The effects of the Egyptian initiative on the Arab position, the non-aligned states and the international situation in general, are highlighted in President Tito's letter to President Sadat on 29 January 1978:

> However, bearing in mind the fact that undoubtedly the interests of Egypt, Syria and the Palestinian people, in the conflict with Israel, are mutually most closely linked and that they are, so to speak, inseparable, we feared from the very outset that a separate action by Egypt would cause great misunderstanding and difficult disputes among the Arab countries, as well as diverse reactions among non-aligned countries, unfortunately these apprehension of ours, have proved to be correct.

The letter continued:

> The present situation in inter-Arab relations is arousing our concern, especially because of the division which had occurred among the Arab countries. I am profoundly convinced that such a division causes multiple damage not only to the mutual relations, but the overall Arab position and the position of the Palestinians, who have found themselves in an exceptionally complex and difficult situation.
>
> Such a state at the same time is detrimental also to the non-aligned movement, and, I am convinced, also to the interest of the international community at large, both of which have for years unselfishly supported the justified struggle of the Arab countries and PLO.

Camp David

> I believe that Israel will look upon the present division among the Arab countries as a great advantage and that it will display even greater intransigence and lack of readiness for the conclusion of peace agreements which would be acceptable to all directly involved Arab countries and PLO as the only legitimate representative of the Palestinian people. Regrettably, I do not see in Israel today any far-sighted statesmen to whom peace, friendship and good neighbourly relations with Arab countries and peoples would be more important than greed for annexing Arab territories and imposing unacceptable conditions based on Israel's temporary and transitory military supremacy in the Middle East.

In brief, we were in a difficult position full of contradictions. We sought to have the United States bring all its weight and its assumedly strong influence to bear upon Israel in the peace talks. Meanwhile, we wanted to maintain the international position, which was generally favourable to the Arab cause. And we tried to prevent the erosion, freezing or weakening of such a position which would result form reliance and dependence on the United States alone in reaching a solution.

There was also the fear that international support would erode since Egypt, the most important Arab country, had taken matters into its own hands and had entered into direct negotiations with Israel. One had also to take into account the weariness and boredom with the Arab–Israeli conflict, which has preoccupied the world and has filled the files of the United Nations for thirty years.

We had to work with determination to save the Arab situation from the divisions which had torn it apart, in an attempt to achieve a minimum level of solidarity. We had to deal with the states of the "Steadfastness Front", exploit the capacities of the Arab states which had supported the initiative, and attract those which took a neutral or negative stand while awaiting developments.

We had to prevent the progressive collapse of our relations with the Eastern block in general and the Soviet Union in particular. A certain modicum of understanding with the Soviet Union would protect us from the perils which would result from alienating it, and would enable us to benefit from its potentials. We had to prepare for the day when the initiative would be declared dead as a result of Israeli intransigence and American abandonment, when we would look around us and find nobody to help us.

This was no simple or easy matter with President Sadat. He had been disillusioned with the Soviet Union and exasperated by the Arabs, and he was imbued with the idea that his initiative could not fail, that the theory of the two superpowers was basically wrong. There was only one great power in the world, namely the United States of America, and it alone was capable of realizing the objective of his initiative – the realization of a just and

Don't Put All Your Eggs In One Basket

comprehensive peace in the Middle East region. Sadat refused to recognize the importance of any efforts not directed at the United States.

Yet the Ministry of Foreign Affairs was directing every effort in all directions. Many of its efforts were successful, while others failed.

Chapter Eleven

The Scenario (February 1978)

Preparations went ahead for President Sadat's visit to the United States, scheduled for 4 February 1978. It was decided that we should begin our journey with a visit to King Hassan in Rabat. It was likewise decided that Sadat should also pay visits to the United Kingdom, the Federal Republic of Germany, Rumania, France and Italy (including the Holy See) on his way back from the United States.

The flight to Morocco took over five hours. The aircraft had set out on a lengthy, zigzag course to avoid flying over Libya for reasons of security. It was feared that Colonel Gadaffi would have few qualms about highjacking the plane, or even shooting it down. King Hassan received President Sadat at Rabat airport, and accompanied him to one of the guest palaces outside town. I went with the other members of the delegation to the Sheraton Hotel, where we were accommodated. We only saw Sadat the following day, for he had bilateral meetings with King Hassan. As for the other members of the delegation, we were invited to dinner at the palace of one of the King's advisers.

The Moroccan Foreign Minister, Ahmed Bou Setta, and a number of ministers and royal advisers attended the banquet. It was a lovely evening, with an uninterrupted flow of appetizing food and drink with a distinctly Moroccan flavour. After dinner, there were Berber dances and songs by a Berber troupe.

At dinner, we laid great emphasis in our conversation with Minister Bou Setta and his aides on utilizing Moroccan efforts as a bridge to the other Arab states. King Hassan had special ties with the other Arab monarchies, especially with the Royal Kingdom of Saudi Arabia and the Hashemite Kingdom of Jordan. We stressed the great importance of these two states and the need to win them over to the peace initiative.

The internal situation aside, my short visit to Morocco left a beautiful and romantic impression on me, for it is a country that has succeeded in retaining its own personality and traditions in most things, while keeping pace with modern methods and developments.

As for King Hassan, he is, to my mind, undoubtedly an intelligent man, but he gives me the impression of being rather too self-conscious. This could hardly be otherwise considering the halo of sanctity surrounding him as a descendant of the Prophet Muhammad.

King Hassan is the son of Muhammad V, who was greatly loved by the Moroccan people both for his struggle to secure Morocco's independence and for his sufferings for that cause until his death. His self-consciousness was, perhaps engendered by the fact that any Moroccan he met, whether young or old, knelt in humility and veneration to kiss his hand. My attention was drawn to a strange scene. In the corridors and gardens of the Royal Palace, groups of Moroccans in embroidered costumes sat at no great distance from one another. Their job was to jump to their feet, cheer the King, praise and extol his virtues, and wish him long life whenever he passed by!

King Hassan was an enthusiastic supporter of Sadat's initiative. At that time, I was unaware of his part in the preparation of that initiative. In September 1977 and later, the King had arranged a number of secret meetings at his palace between Hassan El Tohamy and Moshe Dayan. Sadat had always evaded the question, constantly repeating that what inspired his initiative was the letter President Carter addressed to him, in which he (Carter) told of the frustration he felt as a result of his efforts to convene the Geneva Peace Conference.

Sadat said nothing definite about his talks with the King. I recall, as we were leaving the Royal Palace to the airport, King Hassan asked that I ride with them in the car. He spoke of his relations with his Foreign Minister, Ahmed Bou Setta. He confided all his secrets to him, hiding nothing, whether big or small. Such confidence should exist between the ruler and his foreign ministers, in particular. He advised Sadat to do the same with me for he had – as he put it – heard good reports of me.

Would to God Sadat had followed his advice! We would have avoided many pitfalls resulting from his actions taken on the spur of the moment on the basis of ideas that had just occurred to him, without prior consultation or consideration.

En route for the US, I sat with Ahmed Maher in the aircraft reviewing the situation. It was amply clear to us – following the Ismailia and Jerusalem experiences – that maintaining direct negotiations with Israel would achieve nothing, but would give rise only to numerous difficulties and lead to negative results. It was evident that Israel sought to gain time to confuse the issue with respect to the initiative, i.e. to consolidate the estrangement of Egypt from the Arab states, and entrench itself even further in the occupied Arab territories. There were many indications to this effect, beginning with the self-rule project, patterned on those the colonialists imposed on the peoples they colonized in the nineteenth century. Numerous official Israeli statements were issued to the effect that Israel would not give up its policy of establishing settlements in the West Bank, Gaza, Sinai and the Golan, but intended to proceed with the consolidation of existing Israeli settlements and the establishment of new ones in such areas. Moreover, at this point Begin introduced an innovation: he announced that Security Council Resolution 242 did not apply to the West Bank and Gaza!

Such a situation was not only impertinent, but conflicted with Israeli commitments with regard to the Resolution. No Israeli official had hitherto dared to make such a statement!

Moreover, to pursue the negotiations with Israel in the light of its conduct and statements within sight and hearing of the Arab states and the Palestinian people was impossible, and could neither be justified nor explained. To do so would inevitably affect Egypt's moral standing, confirm the worst doubts as to its intentions, confirm its separation from the Arab states, and isolate Egypt – as Israel had always intended – from such states.

Sadat had begun to realize that his sanguine hopes for a favourable Israeli response to his initiative had been unduly optimistic. He believed that the United States was alone capable of extricating him from the fix he was in, and that it would do this by progressing from its position as a negative mediator between Israel and Egypt to take up a positive stand in an effort to move Israel from its unyielding and intransigent position.

With these considerations in mind Maher prepared a strongly worded memorandum on the position that should be adopted by President Sadat during his separate bilateral talks with President Carter. It described the dangers inherent in continuing them under such circumstances, unless the United States pledged itself to take action which would impel Israel to adopt more positive attitudes – the memorandum went on – President Sadat would announce the termination of talks with Israel in both the Political and Military Committees, and the situation would return to what it had been prior to the initiative. It would be evident to the world at large who wanted peace and who sought to undermine it. Israel alone would bear the responsibility for wasting the historical opportunity provided by the initiative.

I had begun to feel somewhat concerned with respect to Sadat's personality. I had observed, over a period of time and in my continuous contacts with him following my appointment as Foreign Minister, that this was not consistent. At times he was simple and modest while at others he was complex and austere. He would be calm and then flare up angrily without any apparent justification. Sometimes his thinking could be clear and logical when he would discourse at ease, at other times he would be incapable of speaking or pointing out what he wanted or stating his point of view, or he would digress into side issues. At times, he preserved an open mind and could absorb fully what he read or heard – while at others he was indolent and indifferent, and neither heard nor absorbed anything, whatever the importance of the topic submitted.

I could think of no explanation for this, but attributed it to the heavy responsibilities he had borne ever since assuming power on the death of

The Scenario

President Nasser. I was thinking of all this as I took the memorandum to his private sitting-room in the aircraft. Sayed Marei, who was a member of the delegation, sat with him. Our talk was on general matters, and had not to do with politics. I then handed him the memorandum, which he read attentively. He appeared very pleased with it: then he gave it back to me. I told him I had another copy of it, and hoped he would carry the memorandum with him when he met Carter. He would have it within reach during the meeting, and if the need arose, would be able to refer to it. He looked at me in astonishment, saying he had read it and absorbed its contents. I replied that I was aware of this, but there could be no harm in taking it with him. I claimed that many of the great statesmen, such as Churchill, De Gaulle and Schmidt, were in the habit of doing so, and that such a custom was generally followed.

Pressing a button, Sadat summoned his private secretary, Fawzi Abdel Hafiz, and handed him the memorandum, requesting Fawzi to let him have it when on his way to the meeting with President Carter.

At Washington Airport, we were met by the American Vice-President, Walter Mondale, and the Secretary of State Cyrus Vance. President Sadat went directly to Camp David where President Carter was waiting for him. I went with the other members of the delegation to Washington.

The following day we received an invitation to go to Camp David for a joint meeting of the American and Egyptian delegations. When we arrived there, Presidents Carter and Sadat were still closeted together. We sat with the members of the American delegation, and were offered drinks. We then introduced ourselves to one another, after which we engaged in informal conversation. Nearly an hour later, we were called to the hall assigned to the meetings of the joint delegations. The American side consisted of President Jimmy Carter, Vice-President Mondale, the Secretary of State Cyrus Vance, the National Security Adviser to the President, Brezinski, the Assistant Secretary of State for the Middle East, Roy Atherton, the American Ambassador to Egypt, Herman Eilts, George Saunders and other aides.

The Egyptian side was headed by President Sadat. Members included the Speaker of the National Assembly, Sayed Marei, myself, the Minister of State for Foreign Affairs, Dr Boutros Ghali, our Ambassador in Washington, Dr Ashraf Ghorbal and my Directeur de Cabinet, Ambassador Ahmed Maher.

President Carter opened the meeting, saying that now he had separately met President Sadat and heard his explanations and his analysis of the situation, he decided to pass on his understanding of what President Sadat had been telling him, so that the matter would be clear to all. It was a rare occasion to know what had taken place at the private talks between the two presidents. Moreover, it was astonishing that the American President should reveal what had transpired between himself and President Sadat at a private meeting. I soon discovered, however, President Carter's reasons for so doing. It was what Menahim Begin, the Israeli Prime Minister, had done after his separate meeting with President Carter in December 1977, when he submitted to the latter his (Begin's) project on withdrawal from Sinai and autonomy for the West Bank and Gaza. Carter had indicated to him that these were quite satisfactory. Upon his return to Israel, Begin put both projects before the Israeli cabinet, which had made several amendments to them at a meeting lasting seven hours. The projects emerged different from those that had been originally submitted to President Carter. Then, in Ismailia, Begin had presented the two projects to Sadat, affirming that they had been commended and endorsed by President Carter and the British Prime Minister James Callaghan. Begin then announced this to the media.

Carter feared a repetition of what Begin had done: Sadat might claim that he (Carter) had committed himself to something or other at the private meeting, either on purpose or as the result of a misunderstanding. Carter deemed it fit therefore to inform the two delegations of what had passed between himself and Sadat, and so have both delegations as witnesses.

For over half an hour, President Carter explained calmly and in clear terms what took place between President Sadat and himself in their separate meeting. I admired his capacity for clear presentation. He concluded by informing us that President Sadat had assured him that the Arabs, including Saudi Arabia, the Egyptian people and the other friends of the US were indignant at the US. They were disappointed because they felt that Israel's intransigent attitude would not have been possible without US military and economic aid to Israel. President Sadat had informed him that he could not pursue the talks with Israel in the Military and Political Committees. He had decided to make an announcement to that effect at the International Press Club the following Monday.

I exchanged glances with Ahmed Maher. We both realized that the President had had before him the memorandum I had submitted to him on the plane during the first meeting with President Carter.

Vance exclaimed: "It would be a catastrophic statement, which people would likely interpret as a halt in the progress towards peace. This could have grave repercussions, and I trust it will be possible to abstain from issuing such a statement, and that we should, rather, work together and seek to reach agreement on targets and how to implement them."

Mondale, for his part, opined: "You are aware that your Jerusalem visit has had a great impact. In forty-eight hours you became the most important statesmen and a prophet of peace. An incredible change has taken place. It is of the utmost importance, if Israeli policy is to change, that people should continue to hold such an opinion of you. They should keep on asking Israel what it has accomplished in return. You should not allow the Israeli government the chance to exonerate itself from the people's accusations.

The Scenario

You should not give Begin the chance to manoeuvre you into a position in which he would be able to say he no longer had to do anything.

"I recall [Mondale continued] Begin's toast, which went against all convention, during the meetings of the Political Committee in Jerusalem. It was lacking in taste and quite out of tune with the new spirit.

"Pressure is mounting because Begin is not doing anything. The Jews here [i.e., in the US] do not like settlements. They told me so. However, a day later [the one following the recall of the Egyptian delegation from Jerusalem], I heard differently. The best way to alter Israel's position is to exert pressure on Begin to move and show some progress. Were you to state that you would not engage in talks, they [i.e., the Israelis] will say that the Egyptians are not serious, and use this as a pretext not to move."

Carter then said: "I know from experience how frustrating Israelis can be . . . However, it is my sincere belief that the Israelis are nearer to accepting the idea of giving up territory. They are doing so reluctantly, because if they thought they could do this without losing the support of the United States public opinion, they would not withdraw. When President Sadat went to Jerusalem, they were caught off balance and were unprepared. However, I can now understand the concern felt when your delegation walked out from the Political Committee, for there was a general feeling that President Sadat was in the wrong, especially since Begin had up till then been the object of a fierce attack. I also understand why Egypt withdrew its delegation, although public opinion harbours doubts whether this was Begin's fault entirely.

"I do not wish to deceive you, neither do I intend to shirk my responsibilities, yet without you and without popular support I cannot force Israel to change its position in the short or long term. With you, I shall be able to exert pressure on them to modify their position. There is a growing feeling among American Jews that Begin and his government are obstructing the peace process by their insistence on the settlements. Were there to be a confrontation between Begin and myself, the American Jews would find it difficult not to stand by Begin. I am trying to win over leading figures in Congress and the Jewish leaders. I want them to put pressure on Begin to induce him to abandon his settlements plan and agree to a five-year transitional period in the West Bank.

"But if President Sadat decides to terminate the negotiations, Begin will say, 'We were willing, but Sadat was not', and the argument that you want peace while they do not will sound rather hollow.

"Next week, Congress will begin to consider the Panama Treaty. To be frank, I have not yet secured the necessary votes, and if Congress were to reject the treaty, this would constitute a great blow to my leadership. We could then have a situation which could lead to a military clash with Panama. Many of those who endorse the treaty are staunch supporters of Israel, and if the termination of negotiations gives rise to a crisis in the Middle East, I shall be in a very difficult position . . .

"I hope you will give me the opportunity to explain to you American public opinion and the problems I am facing. We could then think the matter over together and then set our targets, draw up a timetable and decide on the best means of securing public support. We would consider what would be most likely to induce the Israelis to be more flexible. I shall indeed be sorry if your visit to me were to result in even more difficult problems than the ones we already face . . ."

At this point Brezinski intervened saying: "I have an observation to make. If you were to announce such a decision, the American reaction would be to consider this meeting a failure, and this by itself would benefit the Israelis, since they would declare that Egypt does not want to come to an understanding. For this reason, I suggest that your announcement on your readiness to pursue the talks be combined with a strong affirmation of your position on the settlements and on the applicability of Resolution 242 to all the territories. This would secure you considerable support and place you in a better position when negotiations are resumed."

Here I interjected: "President Sadat's reluctance to resume negotiations stems from the fact that they would lead to the re-occurrence of what happened at the meetings of the Political Committee in Jerusalem.

"The President, I believe, has no objection to continuing the talks provided this sort of thing doesn't happen again. I personally believe that we could devise a formula expressing our readiness to pursue the negotiations provided the talks are postponed for a later date. During this period, the United States could play a positive role by narrowing differences, and at the same time reaching agreement with Israel on some points that could serve as a starting point for the negotiations. This would naturally depend upon Israel's readiness to adopt positive positions."

Brezinski then said: "I concur in this view – Kamel's idea is worthy of consideration, that is to say an expression of readiness to negotiate, while the role of the United States would be to create conditions conducive to the success of the negotiations."

President Carter continued: "I believe Kamel's answer to Brezinski is in line with my own view. I, personally, will not return to the negotiating table if the first item on the agenda concerns the settlements and their retention. I am of the opinion that we could devise a formula whereby the United States would assume the responsibility and influence Israel through pressure of public opinion."

At this point President Sadat put in: "I have heard what my American friends have said. I am of the view that we have reached a point which makes it incumbent upon the United States to make its position clear to the Israelis. That position could be based on certain agreed principles: no encroachment on sovereignty or territory as well as respect for Israel's security. The Israelis are entitled to a feeling of security and to special relations with the United

The Scenario

States . . . I do not object to the continuation of talks. As I have just been saying to President Carter, it did not take me more than five minutes to agree with Begin on the composition of the two committees. He made the suggestion on his arrival in Ismailia and I immediately gave my approval . . . When you invited me, I welcomed the invitation. I wanted to present the case clearly. My primary cause for concern, as I have indicated to Eilts and Atherton, was the fact that the Egyptian and Arab peoples have been disappointed by the United States. Begin is exploiting United States support in every possible way. He makes false claims, such as when he informed European leaders that he has United States support for his proposals. I was beginning to wonder whether we should ever be presented with an American position.

"Does the United States not feel that the time has come to do so? It would save a great deal of time!

"It is Begin's obstinacy that created difficulties for me and for you. As far as I am concerned, there is nothing to prevent the establishment of peace. It could be done in a week!"

To this Carter replied: "The answer is yes. In my opinion, it is time the United States adopted a definite stand to be put forward to both parties . . . as President Sadat indicated in Aswan, there are no differences of opinion between us. Nonetheless, I believe that were the United States to make a proposal after this meeting, it would look as though it were an Egyptian-American proposal, and would, for that reason, be rejected by the United States Jewish community. The Arab world reacted in a very similar manner when I submitted a working paper following my meeting with Dayan, describing it as an American-Israeli paper. So I must meet Begin. I shall invite him over, and at the end of his visit we shall promptly set forth what we consider to be the appropriate American position, and then state it publicly and gain support for it. You will, I feel, be satisfied with what we shall submit. I shall have differences with Begin. What matters is that public opinion will believe that we had consulted with both parties prior to making our position known.

"In brief, my answer to your question, then, is yes. It is time and we want prompt action. We could agree without delay on a timetable, for we are all of the view that it is time we produced the project."

To this Sadat replied: "I agree on that." [1]

Ways and means of breathing life into the American project were then discussed. Initial agreement was reached on the following scenario prepared by Brezinski in the light of the discussions:

1. Egypt would declare its stand on the application of Resolution 242 to all occupied territories, and its categorical rejection of settlements.
2. The United States would express its support for the Egyptian stand.

3 After the meeting between Carter and Begin, Egypt would submit a project on the West Bank and Gaza.
4 After Israeli refusal on the Egyptian project, the United States would submit its own project; and
5 The United States would inform Egypt of the American project for consideration before it was submitted.

The third point gave rise to much discussion, since Egypt's established stance was non-submission of any project on the West Bank and Gaza in the absence of the Palestinians – the main party concerned – and without its authorization. The Egyptian position would be confined to achieving a Declaration of Principles for a solution to the Palestinian problem based on the right of the Palestinian people to self-determination. However, the American side continued to stress that an Israeli project on the West Bank and Gaza had been presented, namely Begin's autonomy project, while there was no corresponding Egyptian project. In view of the fact that the United States was required to submit an American project, it would be appropriate that it should have before it an Egyptian project to counter the Israeli project. The American side requested that the Egyptian project on the West Bank and Gaza should include the maximum Arab demands, so that they (the United States side) might be able to submit a compromise which, they let it be understood, would be closer to the Egyptian, rather than the Israeli position.

Sadat was very pleased at the conclusion of the meeting. The hope he had constantly entertained had been realized. The United States had taken a positive stand on the trilateral talks, or what Sadat called the role of the full partner. As for myself, I was satisfied that the United States had pledged itself to influence Israel in changing its position. This would allow us to suspend direct talks with Israel and spare us the odious techniques employed by Begin in the conduct of such talks. It gave us time, which we could then use to tackle the fragmented Arab situation as best we could, win over supporters for the Egyptian position, and try to dispel whatever suspicions as to Egypt's intentions.

Moreover, this was the first time I had met President Carter, whom I observed closely. The impression he gave me was most encouraging. He appeared honestly convinced that Israeli withdrawal under Resolution 242 included all territories, and that the settlement should include recognition of the Palestinian people and their "right to participate in determining their own future". In addition, he took a firm stand in condemning the settlements which, in my opinion, constituted both the key and the instrument of Israeli expansion. It was likewise clear that he had no confidence in Menahim Begin, and that his faith in Israeli policies had been shaken. He described negotiations with the Israelis as "frustrating".

He referred to two incidents, the first of which had occurred in September

1977. At a meeting between him and Moshe Dayan in New York, Dayan had pledged not to establish new settlements other than six of a military nature, whose inhabitants would be increased. But despite such a promise, the Israelis established thirteen new settlements.

The second incident occurred when Begin claimed Carter's approval for the project he submitted in Ismailia. The project he had shown Carter was quite different from the one submitted at Ismailia. Carter pointed out that the project Begin had presented to him included a five-year transitional period during which Jordan, Israel and perhaps Egypt would participate in the administration. Upon the expiry of the said period, the resident Palestinians would have the right to determine their own future. Moreover, Begin had promised him that Israel would not claim sovereignty over territories lying beyond the 1967 borders.

To sum up, my first impression was an optimistic one, especially since Carter was the first American President to call for the right of the Palestinians to a national homeland. He had also declared that respect of human rights was fundamental to his policies. Despite my awareness of the strong Israeli influence on the United States, I imagined at the time that Carter, as President of the world's most powerful state, would be able to stand up to any pressure, particularly since the matter related to the United States' vital interests in the Middle East. He was not being asked to forsake the United States commitment to the security of Israel, but to guarantee it through the establishment of a just and comprehensive peace in the area.

However, men are of varying mettle: Carter had not Eisenhower's strength, just as Sadat had not Nasser's. The strength of both Carter and Sadat was more apparent than real. They spoke of noble principles, but these were not ingrained in their souls.

Footnote

1 These are not quotations but translations of the exchange drawn from my notes in Arabic.

Chapter Twelve

Danger from Within

The following day, Sadat returned to Washington. He stayed at Blair House. He had a crowded schedule, including meetings with congressmen and senators, and various political and economic personalities. I attended some of these meetings and interviews. Sadat was generally successful and won much sympathy and support for his views and the sincerity of his intention with regard to peace.

The day was 7 February, and I was in Blair House. I walked into a room and saw the Speaker of the National Assembly and member of the Egyptian delegation, Engineer Sayed Marei, sitting beside Dr Ashraf Ghorbal, the Egyptian Ambassador in Washington, who seemed to be paying a great deal of attention to something he was writing. I asked Ghorbal casually what he was writing with such great concentration. Engineer Sayed Marei answered that he was preparing a memorandum on the meeting between himself and President Carter's Adviser on National Security, Brezinski, which Ashraf Ghorbal had attended. They had met to lay down the bases for the agreement on the Egyptian-American strategy for the following weeks. I did not answer Sayed Marei, but reproached the Ambassador for agreeing to take part in such an interview without prior consultation with me. He was well aware that Sayed Marei had no business discussing such matters. Ashraf answered that Sayed Marei had asked him if he might attend the meeting, whose purpose he ignored. Whereupon Sayed Marei retorted that he had no intention of encroaching upon my sphere of competence. I shot back that I did not interfere in other people's work, and did not like them to interfere in mine. His interference complicated matters with respect to a process which was complicated enough in itself.

When I came to read the initial agreement reached by Sayed Marei and Brezinski, I was furious. It was entitled: "A Strategy for the coming weeks", and stipulated the following:

A STRATEGY FOR THE COMING WEEKS

    1   A declaration of principles must be reached as soon as possible so as to widen the scope of present negotiations through the

inclusion of Jordan, representatives of the Palestine people, Syria and Lebanon with a view to concluding a comprehensive settlement to the Middle East conflict.
2. Reaching of an agreement on Sinai which would include specifically provision for the withdrawal of Israeli settlements in application of the respect of the sovereignty and territorial integrity of Egypt.
3. The US role now is to modify the Israeli position regarding the above. Other Sinai issues, including the demilitarized zones and other matters, would be handled directly by Egypt and Israel.
4. The Sinai agreement must be reached as soon as possible. Its principles, agreed upon by Egypt and Israel, will be announced but its signature will take place at a later date to be agreed upon following the Declaration of Principles. This agreement will not constitute a separate agreement.
5. After Premier Begin's coming visit to Washington, Egypt will present a paper containing its views of the principles for settling other aspects relating to the Palestinian problem, the West Bank, Gaza and Jerusalem.
6. It is expected that the US will, in the light of the Israeli and Egyptian papers concerning the West Bank and Gaza, present its own views and proposals on how to achieve a just solution for the West Bank and Gaza.
7. As to the West Bank the Egyptian paper will provide:
   a) a transitional period, the duration of which will be fixed by the parties concerned, and which will end by the exercise of the right to self-determination.
   b) Egypt believes that following the adoption of the Declaration of Principles and reaching agreement on the Sinai, the representatives of the Palestinian people and Jordan will participate with the UN and Israel in negotiations concerning the West Bank.
8. Gaza will be subject to the same negotiations between Egypt, the representatives of the Palestinian people, Israel and the UN.
9. Syria could on its part enter into similar negotiations on the Golan.
10. Saudi Arabia will participate with Egypt, Jordan, the representatives of the Palestinian people and the UN on the future of Jerusalem.
11. All these negotiations are to deal with the issues of withdrawal from all territories as well as the issues of mutual security between Israel and its Arab neighbours.

In the evening, I called on President Sadat in his bedroom at Blair House. Engineer Sayed Marei was with him. I informed the President, in the latter's presence, of the understanding he (Marei) had reached on matters of great importance. I handed him the copy of the paper they had prepared between them. He had done so without prior consultation or co-ordination with me. I pointed out that if each member of the delegation were to conduct himself in such a manner, we would indeed be faced with a strange situation. We would forfeit the respect of the American side. It would seem as though we were proceeding senselessly and aimlessly. I pointed out that I did not approve of what had been agreed between Engineer Sayed Marei and Brezinski, since this conflicted with the line we were following. And I explained to him how I saw the understanding they had reached, as summarized in the following points:

1. Priority should be given to agreement on a clear and precise Declaration of Principles which would make it possible for Arab states to support Egypt in its efforts to achieve a comprehensive settlement. Within the context of such a Declaration it would be possible – as he [Sadat] had more than once indicated – to proceed towards an agreement on Sinai which should become part of a comprehensive settlement.
2. What Brezinsky and Marei proposed was reaching an agreement on Sinai and the declaration of its principles before agreement on a Declaration of Principles for the comprehensive settlement. This would create a situation in which the Egyptian people, Israel and the United States would exert pressure on the Egyptian government to speed up its signing irrespective of the other aspects on the problem. Moreover he himself [Sadat] was constantly announcing that any agreement which did not include a settlement of the Palestinian problem – the crux and basis of the problem – would be marginal and would fail to secure stability and peace.
3. The paper alluded to, in dealing with the West Bank and Gaza, separated them in such a manner as to afford Israel the opportunity to claim that representatives of the residents in either of them should participate in the negotiations on each of them. This went beyond what Israel was at present demanding, and ruled out participation of those Palestinians living abroad. It is true that President Sadat had suggested that negotiations on Gaza could start with Egypt, Israel, the representatives of the Palestinian people and the United Nations, while Jordan would negotiate with the representatives of the Palestinian people, Israel and the United Nations on the West Bank. However, it was clear that the matter was related only to security measures. As for the political future it was envisaged that the West Bank and the Gaza Strip should be considered as a political Palestinian entity.
4. When the American side asked us to present a paper on how we

visualized the settlement of the West Bank and Gaza Strip issue, they clearly stated that we should submit a project which would include the maximum Arab demands in order to enable them to present on such a basis a compromise solution which they clearly indicated would be closer to the Egyptian rather than the Israeli position.

5. The Egyptian paper on the West Bank and Gaza was not supposed to include such details as those set forth in the paper prepared in accordance with the understanding reached between Engineer Marei and Mr Brezinski.

Sadat approved of my observations and said to Engineer Marei: "Let him be, Sayed, so that his work is not messed up."

I then handed him a paper prepared by Ahmed Maher containing a precise and honest summary of what had been dealt with at the Camp David session between himself and President Carter, and the subsequent meeting between the two delegations. The paper noted that President Sadat would be discussing it with President Carter, while I would be talking to Secretary of State Vance on the same subject. It contained the following points:

1. Egypt's understanding of the strategy for the coming weeks agreed upon between President Carter and President Sadat and between the two delegations, is the following:
   (a) An American declaration will be published on Wednesday 8 February reiterating the US position as to the settlements and Resolution 242 and its applicability to all fronts. It will also state the determination of the US to play an active role, and the desire of Egypt to see the process of peace continue.
   (b) Mr Alfred Atherton will be sent to the region to pursue efforts to bridge the gap between Egypt and Israel regarding the Declaration of Principles. Mr Atherton will also be consulting with the Jordanians and the Saudis to seek ways to engage new Arab countries in the peace process.
   (c) Premier Begin will be asked to visit Washington by the end of February, or the beginning of March. During the visit, the US will express forcefully to him its views on the settlements, on Resolution 242, and on the necessity to resolve the Palestinian question in all its aspects.
   (d) After the visit of Premier Begin to Washington, Egypt will present to the US a paper containing its views on the settlement of the Palestinian problem. As agreed upon in Camp David, this paper will contain the maximum demands concerning the West Bank (including Jerusalem) and Gaza. It will address itself generally to the need of ensuring mutual security. It could also state that Egypt is ready to exert its

influence to establish an official and declared link between Jordan and the West Bank and Gaza. Egypt and the US will explore the possibilities that this paper be a joint Egyptian-Jordanian proposal.
(e) After the expected refusal by Israel of the Egyptian paper on the West Bank and Gaza, the US will present its own views and proposals. It is hoped that the US will consult with Egypt before formally presenting its proposals to the parties concerned.

2 *Egypt expects*:
(a) That this course of action will not delay serious efforts to reach an agreement on the Declaration of Principles as soon as possible.
(b) That the US will convince Israel to abandon its claim to keeping Israeli settlements and airports in Sinai.
(c) That the US will help reaching an agreement on Sinai as soon as possible. This agreement is based on the respect of Egypt's sovereignty and territorial integrity and will be signed at a later date in the light of the progress on the other fronts or in the light of the refusal by an Arab party to negotiate despite the agreement on the Declaration of Principles.
(d) That the US will respond favourably to the request of Egypt to buy American arms.

I now return to the paper prepared by Engineer Sayed Marei and the Adviser on National Security to the US President, Mr Brezinski, entitled "Strategy for the coming weeks".

The content of this paper, upon closer examination, shows clearly that it was geared towards a separate solution between Egypt and Israel, though this is thinly veiled in phraseology and generalities. Now neither Engineer Sayed Marei nor Mr Brezinski can be said to be naïve, and there can be no doubt that a separate settlement was implicitly or explicitly implied whichever way one reads the paper.

This aroused my concern for two reasons: first, the paper cast suspicion and doubt on the American side's compliance with the obligations it had pledged to fulfil with regard to the scenario agreed during the Camp David meetings. Brezinski had been the author of this scenario, so how was it possible for him, while preparing the "strategy", to overlook everything he had thought up in the scenario, when the ink was hardly dry? Did not this imply that, were the Egyptians to make any concessions or show any signs of weakness, the American side would be quick to exploit the situation in order to reach an easy and speedy solution, regardless of the consequences to Egypt and the Arab world? The American side would then hail it as a step towards a comprehensive settlement, to be followed by further steps, as had been done by Kissinger. To me this was a trial balloon in an attempt to crush Egypt's determination. From an American standpoint, in view of its special relations with Israel, on the one hand, and its priorities as a big power on the other, that was to be expected. We should therefore be vigilant and firm, stick to our positions while at the same time fostering them with international support. It was clear that Sadat's firm stand, when he threatened to break off negotiations with Israel, had forced the Americans to promise some move, however limited, in the scenario.

Secondly, and of far greater concern, was the spirit with which Engineer Sayed Marei had approached his meetings with Brezinski. This was a dangerous phenomenon which left me defenceless and for which there was no cure. Engineer Sayed Marei was firmly convinced of the danger of a prolonged Israeli occupation of Sinai in view of the fact that it had assumed the appearance of colonial settlement. Numerous settlements had been established in Rafah, Arish and other parts of Sinai. His fears had been increased by Israel's announcement, after the Ismailia meeting, that it intended to step up the establishment of settlements in Sinai. He had, in truth, made no attempt to conceal his views, and had expressed them in the National Security Council prior to the departure of the Egyptian delegation to the Political Committee for Jerusalem. He had reiterated them to me. This did not mean he felt no concern for the fate of all the other Arab parties who had been the victims of Israeli aggression, but simply that Egypt had the greater priority. Were Egypt to lose Sinai as a result of the overgrowth of Israeli settlements, the future effectiveness of Egypt – the most powerful Arab country – to support the determined Arab stand on other aspects of the problem would be impaired.

I was and still am of a different opinion. I believe that Egypt's future in this part of the world lies in a comprehensive settlement of the Arab-Israeli conflict as well as peace and security in the area. Egypt's prestige and prosperity can only be fully realized in an Arab world in which solidarity and co-operation prevail. The Arab world has great potentials and constitutes Egypt's *espace vitale*. If, on the other hand, Egypt were to drift into a separate solution it would end by succumbing to inescapable moral, spiritual and material decay. It would become one of those countries which are faceless, of no relevance or consequence. It would become a cog in the giant United States wheel, which would exploit and manipulate it in accordance with its own desires. Egypt was not cast for such a role.

The danger lay not only in Sayed Marei's individual view. True, he was the Speaker of the People's Assembly, and was well placed to influence Sadat by virtue of his personality and the fact that he was Sadat's close friend and was related to him by marriage. The danger lay in the fact that his view reflected that of a large section of Egyptian public opinion for one reason or another. Mohamed Hassanein Heikal, the wellknown political writer, analyzed the causes of such phenomena in his book *The Talk of the Initiative* as follows:

Egypt's Arabism is a scientific fact, Egypt's Arab interests are a second scientific fact, and Egypt's Arab security is a third scientific fact. However, we have agreed that political facts were sometimes the opposite of scientific facts. And one of the political facts in Egypt – and this is a matter we must concede – is that Egypt's Arab affiliation has not yet become sufficiently rooted among the Egyptian masses for numerous reasons, which I have indicated in a previous series of talks. I have said that Egypt was the oldest state in the world. This creates confusion with respect to the concept of the State and that of the Nation. I have said that Egyptian political thought and action have considered Egypt's Arab affiliation as a matter which is taken for granted. As a consequence, nobody has exerted a sufficient effort to trace it to its roots. I have said that the unity of Arab security is not sufficiently clear to the Egyptian mind, and the same goes for the unity of Arab interest. All this adds up to the fact that the Arab concept in Egypt is exposed and vulnerable to calls of the nature of "Egypt only" . . . or "Egypt first", and the like. All are calls which are easily propagated and may successfully be relied upon – in some instances – to delay the necessary interaction between the people on the two banks of the river and the nation from the Ocean to the Gulf.[1]

The exaggerated optimism of Sadat's speeches and statements, affirming that peace was close at hand, helped to promote this view by publicizing an end to wars and their woes, and the deaths of fathers, mothers and sons. They indicated that the doors of prosperity were open wide, with the paradise of affluence just around the corner. This constituted an additional problem for me: efforts needed to be exerted to equate and balance the influence of some of Sadat's entourage or close connections by presenting the other view, not my own personal view, but rather one supported by studies and analyses by the departments of the Foreign Ministry. I considered dealing with this obtrusion by stepping up my contacts with Sadat to immunize him to the best of my ability. This, however, was no easy matter. My work involved heavy responsibilities. Moreover, the task of warner-preacher was neither easy nor pleasant. Sadat, too, was hard to reach, being constantly on the move from the Barrage rest-house to that of Ismailia, King Mariut and so on . . . To cap it all, I had neither a private plane nor the time to fly.

On 8 February 1978 the visit ended and the White House issued a tolerable communiqué which affirmed the following:

1   That Security Council Resolution 242 was applicable on all fronts.
2   That the Palestinian issue should be solved in all its aspects and that the solution should include the recognition of the legitimate right of the Palestinian people, enabling it to participate in

determining its destiny [The Aswan Formula].
3   That settlements constituted a violation of International Law and were illegitimate; and that the planting of new settlements was considered to be inconsistent with efforts being exerted for peace.

A press release on the meetings between Presidents Carter and Sadat at Camp David from 3-5 February, indicated interest in continuing the talks begun some months past. President Carter pledged to undertake a positive role in the search for peace, and to intensify his efforts to guarantee progress in the following weeks. The press release also referred to agreement reached between the two Presidents on the return to the Middle East of Assistant Secretary of State Atherton in the near future, to carry on the efforts to achieve an agreement on a Declaration of Principles.

The White House communiqué and the press release were issued in implementaiton of items (a) and (b) of the previously agreed upon scenario.

On 10 February, Cyrus Vance held a press conference during which he launched a strong attack on the Israeli policy of settlements, in which he declared:

". . . We have said that all these settlements are contrary to international law and for this reason they should not exist." He also stated that: "The territories in the West Bank and Gaza should become the homeland of the Palestinians while being tied to Jordan."

Israel was furious. The Israeli cabinet met and issued a statement attacking the idea of a homeland for the Palestinians which would lead to "a Palestinian state ruled by terrorist organizations" threatening the destruction of Israel. With respect to the settlements, the statement indicated that the Israeli government insisted that, "It did not conflict with international law, and was, and would always be, legitimate and necessary."

Moshe Dayan hurried to the US to assess Sadat's achievements during his visit, and to spur on the American-Jewish Organization to greater zeal in practising its "benign pressures" on the American administration.

Footnote

1   H. Heikal *The Talk of the Initiative*, p.93.

Chapter Thirteen

The European Salad

On the plane from Washington to London – our first stop in a tour of seven countries – Sadat was pleased, proud and optimistic about the results of his visit to the United States. I, for my part, was also satisfied, feeling that I had gained new knowledge since I was glad to have met the American group in charge of the Middle East issue and felt I could deal with them. The discussions had likewise confirmed to me the power of Jewish influence. The visit had also shown that we had gained some ground within the United States itself, which had previously been denied to us. A large segment of American public opinion began to better understand the facts underlying the Arab-Israeli conflict. They now had a clearer idea of the justice and reasonableness of the Arab claims, which had hitherto been clouded by a thick smoke-screen of propaganda put out by Israel and the Jewish organizations. I considered this a good start which should be followed up and developed with care.

At 10 a.m. the following day we touched down at Heathrow Airport near London, where we were met by the British Prime Minister, Mr Callaghan, and the Foreign Minister, Dr David Owen. The talks were held at the airport, and while President Sadat was closeted with Mr Callaghan, I had a meeting with David Owen, who was young and personable. However, after we had discoursed for fifteen minutes, I became quite exasperated with him, since all what he had to say centred around the Israeli settlements and the need to reach a formula securing Israel's retention of the Sinai settlements in one form or another. To this I replied by a simple "why?", whereupon he began beating about the bush. I finally realized that he feared that any dismantling of the Israeli settlements in Sinai might constitute a precedent for a similar dismantling in the West Bank and Gaza, which would be difficult to effect in practice and it would involve inhumane treatment to individuals.

I felt that such logic reflected racial discrimination, for, surely, the same applied to the Palestinians, the rightful owners of the land. I gave him to understand that the British should be the last to speak of such matters, as his country bore the prime responsibility for the tragedy that had befallen the

Palestinian people since the Balfour Declaration and as a result of the devious policy applied during the British Mandate over Palestine.

From London we travelled to Hamburg, where Chancellor Schmidt was staying (Hamburg is the Chancellor's home town), to attend the International Socialist Conference being held there.

Germany had only recently regained its equilibrium with regard to the Middle East. Israel had exploited Germany's "guilt complex" to obtain from it billions of dollars as compensation for the victims of Nazism under Hitler, although at that time, strangely enough, the State of Israel was not yet in existence as it was only established in 1948. Germany played an active role in the EEC in the search for a comprehensive peace in the Middle East that would achieve stability in the area and guarantee to it a continued flow of oil which was vital to both its industy and its trade with the rich oil states. Moreover, the Federal Republic of Germany was among the most sincere supporters of the Palestinian people's right to self-determination since it hoped that the people of the Democratic Republic of Germany would one day exercise its own right to self-determination. President Sadat and Chancellor Helmut Schmidt met together, while Foreign Minister Genscher and I did the same. Relations between Genscher and myself were characterized by friendship and cordiality going back to the days when I occupied the post of Egyptian Ambassador to Bonn. I briefed him on the developments that had taken place since the Ismailia meeting and that of the Political Committee in Jerusalem. I spoke to him of what had happened during our visit to the US although I naturally refrained from any reference to the subject of the scenario.

From Hamburg we flew to Munich, capital of Bavaria. President Sadat left for the beautiful village of Berchtesgarten in the Alps for a day's rest, while we remained in Munich until he rejoined us the following day, when we all left for Salzburg. I recalled an incident that had occurred two years earlier. President Sadat had been on a State visit to Germany and the programme had included a visit to Bavaria. We had travelled from Bonn to Munich by private train under tight security arrangements, with aircraft, helicopters and a police escort the whole way to Munich. A formal reception awaited us at the railway station in Munich, where an honour guard of the Bavarian police stood to attention while Bavarian tunes were played. The Prime Minister of Bavaria stepped forward, shook hands with President Sadat and introduced to him prominent figures, among them the mayor. He then accompanied Sadat to his car and they rode together to the Bavarian Prime Minister's office, where a formal reception awaited him.

The programme included also a visit to the mayor in the magnificent municipal palace of Munich. Two speeches had been prepared for Sadat for each of the two occasions. At the President's request, the first paragraphs in both speeches were drafted in German. The President's private secretary, Fawzi Abdel Hafiz, was in charge of the President's papers, spectacles and pipe. As the Prime Minister concluded his speech welcoming the President he invited him to the rostrum. The President stepped forward, followed by his private secretary, who handed him his glasses and the speech he was to deliver. Following the applause, an expectant silence descended upon the chamber. The Chief of German Protocol stood beside me, and suddenly we heard Sadat's deep resonant voice begin his adddress with the phrase "Lieber Herr Burgermeister" (Dear Mr Mayor). The Chief of Protocol looked at me in alarm. However, there was nothing we could do, and Sadat continued with his speech, concluding it without realizing that there was anything amiss. There was polite applause. Fawzi Abdel Hafiz had handed to the President – who was lost in one of his moments of distraction – the wrong speech.

In Salzburg, we were met at the airport by Chancellor Kreisky. We were taken to a historical palace where the talks were scheduled to take place. The Palace was offered in the eighteenth century by the Cardinal of Salzburg to his mistress, who had given him seven daughters. President Sadat met separately with Kreisky, while I talked with the Foreign Minister Bahr who made no attempt to conceal his pessimism as to the success of the initiative. His sympathy with the Palestinian problem and the PLO was evident and frank, and was based on his conviction of the justice of their claims and his appreciation of their painful human tragedy. That satisfied me and a relationship based on mutual sympathy and understanding was established between us. Kreisky, who was himself a Jew, took a clearsighted view of and a firm stand on the Palestinian problem, criticizing Israel's rigid and obdurate attitude. Prior to the outbreak of the October War, and in the aftermath of a Palestinian commando operation in Austria, he had closed a reception camp for Jews emigrating from the USSR in transit to Israel. The Jewish emigrés had been accommodated in the camp pending processing for their eventual transfer to Israel to supplant the Palestinians Israel had uprooted and expelled. Golda Meir, Prime Minister of Israel at the time, had protested vigorously against the closure, but Kreisky had refused to be swayed.

Kreisky attacked the policy being adopted by Begin, who was dragging his feet on the peace initiative and was attempting to sidetrack it by insisting on retaining the lands of the Palestinians. Kreisky had arranged a meeting between President Sadat and the leader of the Israel Labour party, Shimon Perez, who had travelled from Hamburg, where he was heading the Israeli delegation to the Socialist International Conference, to meet Sadat. Kreisky had been President of the Socialist International for five years until he was succeeded by the former Chancellor of the Federal Republic of Germany, Willy Brandt. He had made several visits to the Arab states and Israel as the head of a delegation of the Socialist International in an attempt to resolve the Arab-Israeli conflict.

Following his meeting with Sadat, lasting over two hours, Perez asked to see me. He began by expressing his admiration for President Sadat, his courage and his aspirations to peace. He soon turned to the settlements and, as though to win my good will, informed me that he did not approve of the establishment of new settlements in Sinai. To this I replied that their settlements in Sinai, whether old or new, were of no great concern to me since they were, in any case destined to disappear. What did concern me, I went on, were the new settlements established in the West Bank and Gaza. He enquired in astonishment what there was in that to take exception to: Israelis were entitled to settle any place, since the settlements were of a civilian nature and were inhabited by Jews who worked hard for a living. I affirmed that this was admissible in a land without owners, however that land was the property of the Palestinian people. He wished to know, then, with whom he could talk on that issue. I said I was here to talk with him, and that I hoped he would seek an end to the establishment of settlements on Palestinian soil until this had been negotiated with the representatives of the Palestinian people, who would decide whether to approve or reject the establishment of settlements . . .

The officer in charge of my security entered at this point to inform me that I would have to leave as President Sadat was setting off for the airport. I stood up and hurriedly shook hands with Perez, who was staring at me in consternation. I only understood the reason for this some months later: Perez was taken aback because a Minister of Sadat's (myself) was following a line contrary to what Sadat had conveyed to him barely twenty minutes before.

The flight to Romania was difficult and exhausting. After covering nearly half the distance, the aircraft was informed that it would be unable to land at Bucharest airport due to high winds and poor visibility. After consultation with President Sadat, it was decided that the aircraft should travel to Paris where we should stop overnight and resume our voyage in the morning. When we were half-way to France, however, the plane received another message to the effect that it would be able to land at an airport 120 kilometres from Bucharest. The aircraft thereupon changed course again and we alighted at the airport indicated. This turned out to be a military aerodrome, and we were received by its Commander and the Chief of Romanian Protocol. We seated ourselves in the cars that had been prepared for us, but they were too few and our retinue had to go in two buses. Sadat took numerous aides with him on his travel who together with retinue and guards, numbered over a hundred persons. This gave rise to various minor problems wherever he went. The motorcade moved very slowly, since there was thick mist and the ground was covered by snow.

We reached Bucharest at midnight and proceeded to the guest-house, where we found Ceaucescu and his aides awaiting us. He had been greatly concerned by our delayed arrival. President Sadat repaired to his suite, while we proceeded to the dining-hall for a luxurious dinner. Ceaucescu had a special standing with Sadat, who considered himself indebted to him for the steps which led to the initiative: in reply to Sadat's question as to whether Begin was a strong man, capable of taking a decision on peace, Ceaucescu had answered in the affirmative. I recall that President Tito had sent a letter to President Sadat in which he drew his attention to the harm done to the Arab camp and the rigidity of the Israeli stance, and had pointed out that Israel had previously sought the annexation of territory. We had prepared the President's answer to Tito. However, Sadat put off signing it, though I pressed him to sign. I indicated to him that President Tito's wrath had already been sufficiently kindled, and that we ought to refrain from adding insult to injury by delaying to answer his letter, especially since Tito represented one of the strongest pillars of support for the Arab cause. In this he had proved himself staunch and positive, and his attitude was based on a firm conviction. Anyway, Sadat eventually signed the leter, saying, "You're right: President Tito is jealous because I resorted to Ceaucescu instead of to him!"

Sadat and Ceaucescu engaged in bilateral negotiations, my share in the latter consisting in my talks with the Foreign Minister. These were dull and protracted, with the Foreign Minister being careful not to go beyond reiterating the declared Romanian policy with regard to the Arab-Israeli conflict. This was a policy of support for the Arab position on withdrawal from all territories and the legitimate rights of the Palestinians. Presidents Sadat and Ceaucescu, however, were alone entitled to approach the issue, and I felt that the reason for his attitude was that he was bent on abstaining from expressing any view condemning or endorsing either party, as this was the prerogative of the two Presidents. I bethought myself of some of the attitudes adopted by several of our prominent figures, ministers or ambassadors, who preferred to simply repeat what they were told or what they heard without weighing it up for themselves, as though the leader's words or thoughts were sacrosanct. Consequently, our conversation turned to Egyptian-Romanian bilateral relations in all fields. Romania enjoyed brisk trade and industrial relations with us. Such a conversation, however, did not appeal to me, for I had then neither the data nor the inclination to do so.

A joint communiqué was issued at the conclusion of the Egyptian-Romanian talks, stating the Romanian position with regard to a peaceful settlement and Romania's resolution to exert efforts in the search for such a settlement and the realization of peace . . .

What pleased me was President Ceaucescu's specifying that Israeli-Egyptian talks should culminate in a Geneva Peace Conference, and the fact that the two sides endorsed the call by the United Nations Secretary General Kurt Waldheim for the convening of a preliminary meeting of the parties concerned in New York. I believed that the Conference represented an outlet – should the talks either succeed or fail – enabling the other Arab states to participate, in the presence of the two superpowers, under the

The European Salad

auspices of the United Nations. However, President Sadat still felt nostalgic for the Cairo preparatory conference, which was his brainchild.

On the following day, we flew from Bucharest to Paris. Snow covered the buildings and trees, mantling the city in a beautiful stark whiteness dappled with green. President Sadat stayed at the Marigny Palace, at one time the property of the Rothchilds; while we were lodged in the Crillon Hotel. My suite overlooked the Place de la Concorde.

President Giscard d'Estaing invited President Sadat to dinner, and this was followed by talks. Our Ambassador in Paris, Hafiz Ismail, invited me to dine at his Residence. He had invited the Secretary-General of the Foreign Ministry and the officers in charge of Egypt and the Middle East. The French Foreign Minister, M. de Guiringeau, was then in New York to attend the Contact Group on Namibia. [1]

Ambassador Hafiz Ismail had originally been an army officer and was appointed Under-Secretary at the Foreign Office in 1961, when I was Consul-General in Montreal. Later, he was appointed Minister of State for Foreign Affairs and was then elected by President Sadat to fill the post of National Security Adviser to the President. He had travelled to Washington to meet President Nixon's National Security Adviser Henry Kissinger in an attempt to sound out the American position on the Arab-Israeli conflict. This was before the 1973 October War, when our relations with the US were still severed. Ahmed Maher had worked with him as a National Security Adviser and he occupied the post of Counsellor to our Embassy in Paris when Hafiz Ismail was Ambassador. Hafiz Ismail was severe in appearance and was clearly a military man. He had an all-embracing strategic outlook and was precise and highly disciplined. Despite his stern exterior, he was gentle and fun-loving when not engaged in work. I had – and still cherish – feelings of cordiality towards him as well as appreciation and respect.

We talked at dinner of President Sadat's initiative and subsequent developments. The French side was not sanguine, but were actually pessimistically inclined in view of the rigid nature of Begin's government and they ruled out the possibility of any Israeli concessions compatible with the comprehensive and lasting peace we were seeking. Moreover, the rifts and fissures the initiative had sparked off in the Arab world gave France cause for great concern and embarrassment in view of its extensive dealings with an area containing great wealth and much potential. French policies towards the Middle East had drastically changed since President de Gaulle had assumed power.

France was favourably inclined towards the Arab cause, a fact which in turn made the Arab countries receptive to France's economic interests.

We then turned to Africa and the success achieved by the USSR in Angola and Ethiopia after it had lost its base in Somalia, and discussed the tension in the Horn of Africa.

President Sadat had been incensed at the success of the Soviet penetration in Africa, which had received its essential impetus as a result of Soviet support for the African liberation movements and its vigorous attack on racial policies, to which the Africans were extremely sensitive. President Sadat adopted a line of policy which consisted in dogging the Soviet Union in Africa and supporting shaky regimes moving in the Western orbit. He even went to the length of intervention in the internal affairs of such states, providing them with armaments and weapons and, in some instances, with Egyptian military advisers. In so doing, Sadat paid no heed to the internal difficulties of such states, inherent in the prevailing corruption, injustice, hunger and disease.

I had several arguments with Sadat over his policy, pointing out that such a policy would tarnish our image in Africa to the detriment of the special position we occupied and the great respect in which Egypt was held in the African continent. Egypt's standing had been the fruit of stable and persistent support for the African liberation movements and combating racial discrimination in Africa. My efforts in this respect, however, were to no avail. Without bothering to inform me, Sadat took decisions and steps which were implemented by organs of the state other than the Foreign Office. I understood, at some later period, that he sought, through such policy, to win the support of the West in general and of the USA in particular, for his initiative and his policies in general. Labouring under the delusion that he would consolidate his standing with the West, Sadat sought to be acknowledged the West's policeman in Africa. The West's arsenals would be opened to him and provide him with all the arms he needed to carry out such a task. President Sadat was the decisive factor in impelling Syiad Barre to flee the inferno of the Soviet Union and enter the paradise of the West. Sadat furnished Barre with some Soviet weapons the price of which Saudi Arabia had paid to Egypt. Syiad Barre aspired to create a Greater Somalia through the annexation of certain Ethiopian and Kenyan territories. He sought to capitalize on Mengistu's coup d'état in Ethiopia and rashly invaded the Ogaden in an attempt to annex it to Somalia. He appeared to have been labouring under the misconception that his renunciation of the Soviet Union and its eviction from its base in Somalia entitled him to receive considerable aid and weaponary to support his expansionist aspirations. However, matters proved not to be that simple.

Syiad Barre had not taken into account certain fundamental factors. One of the OAU's principles is respect for existing boundaries, and the position adopted by Syiad Barre was a subject of great concern to many African countries. Barre, furthermore, aspired to annex a part of Kenya, thus casting shadows on his credentials with the Western powers. Accordingly, they made any supply of arms to Syiad Barre conditional upon his pledge for the territorial integrity of his neighbours. He, however, refused to accept such conditions. I attempted, but without success, to persuade the Foreign Minister to issue a declaration denying any Somali designs to annex territory. I understood from him that such a declaration would constitute a betrayal of popular aspirations, including those of the inhabitants of Ogaden province, and would lead to the downfall of Syiad Barre and his regime.

The Secretary-General of the French Foreign Ministry indicated that Foreign Minister Guiringeau had requested him to inform me that President Carter was sending an envoy on 13 February (the following day) to Addis Ababa, who would be delivering a letter to President Mengistu to the effect that the latter had entered on a decisive stage which was very nearly the point of no return. He (Mengistu) had either to choose between military aid from the Eastern bloc – in which case it would be difficult for the US to maintain for much longer its policy of wait-and-see – or follow a more reasonable policy. In the latter case, it would be possible for the US to take positive action. The Secretary-General of the French Foreign Ministry also informed me that the five Western states had decided to refer the problem of the Horn of Africa to the Security Council. This, however, would require Syiad Barre to make a declaration denying that he had any territorial designs, even if such a declaration were to be accompanied by a request for self-determination for the Ogaden. Were such a declaration to be issued, the five states would be willing to go immediately to the Security Council, with a demand for an end to intervention and the despatch of arms to the region. Were the matter to be submitted to the Security Council without such a statement being proclaimed, no results would be reached. Somalia seemed cast as an aggressor, since its forces had crossed the borders, thus enabling the Soviets to claim that they were contributing to the defence of Ethiopia which had fallen victim to aggression.

When the guests had left, I remained with Ambassador Hafiz Ismail for quite a while, and we discussed various matters connected with the current situation. I found his advice and viewpoints extremely valuable. He had previously been our Ambassador in Moscow and he expressed his willingness to support me in urging Sadat to agree to the return of the Egyptian Ambassador to Moscow.

The following day, Ambassador Hafiz Ismail and I went to the Marigny Palace and attended part of Sadat's meeting with the delegation of leaders of European Jewry, headed by the President of the World Jewish Council, Nahum Goldmann. The latter saw things differently from Begin, and he feared that Begin's rigid and provocative attitude might, in time, culminate in Israel's losing the sympathy of world opinion and, in particular, USA public opinion. Each member of the delegation in turn commended President Sadat's courage, and his hopes for peace. They hinted that they would like to make massive investments in Egypt. They kept advising him not to lose patience, and to give Menahim Begin time for the latter's attitude to gradually become more flexible. Any concession Begin might make as a result, they said, would be willingly accepted by the Israeli people, but they would not accept them from anyone other than Begin.

Camp David

I left President Sadat in Paris, while he was preparing to go to the Vatican, where he was scheduled to have an audience with the Pope. He was also to have talks with the Italian government. I travelled to Bonn to take official leave and to say goodbye to my friends, since my term of duty had come to an end. I was, moreover, in need of an urgent medical examination. There I met President Walter Scheel, who was Foreign Minister when I was posted to Bonn in August 1973. I was very glad to see him, as he is an able, engaging personality with a great sense of humour and joie de vivre. We spoke of the difficulties besetting the negotiations following the Ismailia and Jerusalem experience. Scheel was of the opinion that intensive efforts would be required, since the Israeli government was not prepared to adopt a constructive attitude just then. He believed this should be met with firm insistence on stands based on principle. He expressed satisfaction at President Sadat's attempts to win over American opinion, as this would enable President Carter to take up the position he (Scheel) believed Carter wished to adopt. Scheel hoped other Arab states would join the talks if agreement were reached on the Declaration of Principles that were to govern the settlement. He expressed his belief that Soviet participation would be essential at some point in the search of a settlement.

When I met Chancellor Schmidt, he indicated that the peace sought by President Sadat enjoyed the support of world opinion. In order for this to continue, it was vital to show that Egypt's policy was a stable one, both as to its targets and its approaches.

Schmidt affirmed that Shimon Perez had given him the impression that the matter of airfields in Sinai could be solved: Israel would gradually withdraw from the airfields in the course of a transitional period. As for the settlements, Perez believed that it would be difficult for Begin to change his stance. The Chancellor desired to know my opinion regarding the feasibility of an agreement on the Egyptian-Israeli territorial exchanges he (Schmidt) had previously proposed to Sadat in Hamburg. Israel would retain the area of the settlements in Rafah, while Egypt would be given in exchange a part of the Negev. I answered that this would be unacceptable for several reasons, including the fact that Egypt's borders had remained unchanged for thousands of years and could not be altered. Israel did not own the territories it offered to exchange: such territories constituted Palestinian land occupied by Israel and were not covered by the resolution on the partition of Palestine. We could not, and were not entitled to haggle over such territories with Israel. Consequently the question of retention of settlements or territorial exchange did not arise.

Schmidt went on to say that when he had met President Giscard d'Estaing, he had sensed the latter's pessimism and his reservations with respect not only to Egyptian-Israeli relations, but also with respect to Egypt's relations with those Arab states making up the "Steadfastness Front". I intimated that we attached much importance to the German and European efforts to promote a just and comprehensive peace. He affirmed to me those countries' readiness to do so, in particular, to ensure that the Americans steered a steady course, for they had recently noted certain fluctuations in American policy, and they saw the need for a more stable approach. He added that they were of the opinion that Sadat's Washington visit had emphasized this aspect. In Germany (he continued) some fifteen years earlier, and ever since the meeting between Chancellor Erhard and Ben-Gurion, there had been a feeling of sympathy towards Israel as a result of Germany's guilt complex. Although this feeling had not completely disappeared, it was, he said, on the wane.

The Minister of State at the Foreign Ministry, Van Weil, who had attended the meeting, said the reports from their embassy in Israel indicated that Israel did not set much store by Atherton's coming tour of the Middle East, but placed the greatest emphasis on Begin's impending visit to Washington. He added that the Secretary-General of the Israeli Prime Ministry had informed him that the settlements were marginal and of no great importance to them. Chancellor Schmidt indicated his disbelief in such a statement, particularly since Shimon Perez had led him to understand that the topic had special significance for Begin personally.

Chancellor Schmidt enquired about the latest developments in the relations between Sudan and Libya. Sudan had agreed to resume its relations with Libya several days after our departure for the US and Sadat had been incensed at the news.

I answered that Sudan was beset by conflicts and surrounding régimes which sought to destabilize it, and that President Numeiry was intent on avoiding the trouble the Soviet Union could create for him through its exploitation of Libya. I affirmed the strength of our relations with Sudan, and the inadmissibility of its being affected by anything, as it was based on the interests vital to both states.

I then met the German Foreign Minister, Hans Dietrich Genscher, who was Minister of the Interior when I first arrived in Germany. Our relationship went back to the moment of my arrival in Bonn, for I sought to do away with the restrictions on the granting of entrance visas to Arabs in general and Egyptians in particular, as well as prevent the rough, sometimes even brutal treatment of Arabs entering Germany, such as thorough inspection and detainment pending completion of procedures for other travellers arriving on the same aircraft. Such conditions had originated in the aftermath of the Munich incident during the holding of the 1972 Olympic Games in Munich.

Genscher informed me that Germany sought to make use of its relations with Israel to induce the latter to adopt positive attitudes. He had advised his colleagues, the European Foreign Ministers, whom he had met the previous day in Copenhagen, to adopt a similar position. He added, that, in Copenhagen the Nine had felt that it would not be useful, at the present time, to issue a new communiqué on the Middle East, especially since their views were known, declared and established. However, they decided to make use of all diplomatic means available to them vis-à-vis Israel and the Arab states in support of Egypt's peace efforts.

Genscher added that he had been in New York a few days earlier, where he had gained the impression that President Sadat's visit to Washington had made a considerable impact on American public opinion and in the decision-making centres in the Administration and Congress, where they were aware of the fact that they had a role to play. He hoped, he went on, that they would now adopt more forthcoming positions than they had hitherto. He informed me of his meeting with Dayan, in which he had pointed out to the latter that the stability of the Middle East, and consequently the stability of Israel, could be brought about only through the stability of all the states surrounding it. This would not be possible as long as the Palestinians lived in camps, and that therefore the solution of the Palestinian problem and the establishment of a Palestinian state connected with Jordan, was ultimately in Israel's interest.

Genscher concluded by affirming that the German stand on the issue was based on moral principles and European interests, in view of the inter-relation of the two areas. He said he was convinced of the firmness of the Egyptian stand and that Egypt's insistence on the principles of a just and comprehensive solution would have positive effects on the Arab attitude and on the peace-seeking process. We than talked of the situation in Africa, and Genscher mentioned Somalia, expressing the hope that we might urge it to make a gesture of reassurance to Kenya by announcing that Somalia harboured no ambitions with regard to Kenyan territory. Germany believed that Soviet expansion in the African continent should be halted. Syiad Barre's position on the invasion of the Ogaden would enable the Soviet Union to claim that it (the Soviet Union) was contributing to the defence of Ethiopa as a victim of aggression.

While I was with Genscher, he received news, based on a report by Reuter's News Agency, to the effect that an Egyptian plane carrying weapons to Somalia had been forced to land in Kenya, and had been seized by the authorities there. I said that I had no information on the subject. I affirmed that our aid to Somalia was confined to within the latter's borders, and that we were opposed to any expansionist aims it might have. I added that it was important that Somalia should feel that it had someone's support after it had freed itself from Soviet influence, especially since it felt it had been abandoned by the West.

When I was in Germany, it was reported that two Palestinians had assassinated the Egyptian writer, Youssef El Sibai, in Cyprus. He had gone to Cyprus at the head of the Egyptian delegation to attend the meetings of the Afro-Asian Solidarity Conference which was meeting in Cyprus. I was greatly moved by the incident and had hardly recovered from the shock when I was stunned by news of serious and disturbing developments. An Egyptian aircraft carrying an Egyptian commando force had arrived at Larnaka airport in Cyprus. The task of the force was the kidnapping of Youssef El Sibai's killers, who were to be brought back to Cairo to stand trial. The operation ended in a horrible, traumatic disaster involving the deaths of twenty young men of the Egyptian commando force at the airport, not, however, at the hands of the Palestinians, but at those of Cypriot forces in defence of the sovereignty of Cyprus, which had been violated.

Sadat enjoyed acting, and he imagined he saw an opportunity to emulate the Israeli raid on Entebbe, overlooking the fact that whereas he was an amateur, the Israelis were professionals. I shall be elaborating further on this tragedy and its consequences at a later stage in this book.

Footnote:

1 The Contact Group on Namibia is composed of the United States, United Kingdom, France, Federal Republic of Germany and Canada.

Chapter Fourteen

A Deadly Octopus Is Born and Reared in Darkness

Before proceeding with the narrative on the experiences I have gone through, it may perhaps be in order to deal with a point in the preceding chapter which has, in all probability, not passed unnoticed by the reader. In describing President Sadat's European tour following his visit to Washington, I made no mention of the "in camera" meetings he had with the British Prime Minister, Callaghan, Chancellor Schmidt, Chancellor Kreisky, the Leader of the Israeli Labour Party, Shimon Perez, President Ceaucescu and, finally, President Giscard d'Estaing.

Truth to tell, closed political meetings at and below Summit level have become symptomatic of the age. There is no doubt that they have often proved useful. They engender a calm atmosphere conducive to confidence and trust. The process thereby promotes an easy and smooth discussion of views, which could lead to agreement or non-agreement on the subejct under discussion or on some of its points.

Talks at such closed meetings, however, are neither personal nor the private property of either party, but relate to a topic because of which one party sought a meeting with another to execute a political task. The process is thereby looked upon as complementary to other activities related to the topic, and thereby should be added to the other results attained, and should then be submitted to the organ – or organs – in charge of implementing the general political line, so as to enable that organ or organs to take them into consideration in devising or amending the plans of action and adequate measures of implementation. Thus, everything taking place at such meetings should be faithfully confined to paper and filed, so that they may become a readily available point of reference for subsequent talks.

This must not be taken to imply that what takes place in closed talks should be made known to the public, what I meant was that the contents of these conversations be assigned various degrees of secrecy and the people entitled to the information or parts thereof should be predetermined in accordance with their status in the hierarchy and the roles that would be assigned to them, each being given the exact amount of information necessary for the accomplishment of his task.

This was not the case with President Sadat, save on very rare occasions. He usually had some appointment or other following the closed meetings, a speech to deliver, or a lunch or dinner, or else he would repair immediately to his room to catch up on his sleep. There was hence a time-lag between the bilateral meetings and my conferring with him. Of course, I did not leave him in peace, but instead pursued him with questions and enquiries on matters raised at the bilateral meeting. Yet his accounts would, for the most part, remain incomplete and be of a general nature, or they would focus on a single aspect that may have appealed to him or attracted his attention, to the neglect of everything else. In time, I came to feel he either did not wish to commit himself by informing me or others of what transpired at such meetings, or else that he purely and simply forgot parts of them. I was reminded of his secretive, cautious and inscrutable nature when we were in the prison together. Circumstances then, though, were very different. My ignorance of the purport of the meetings was the cause of great inconvenience and – in some instances – embarrassment to me. However, it was no easy matter for me to persist in pressing for information. I assumed that Sadat abided by our plans and targets in the course of such meetings.

I must crave the reader's indulgence in further elaborating this point, since this will enable him to understand the many contradictions and enigmas associated with the peace process until its culmination in the Tripartite Camp David Conference in September 1978. Time, successive events, observation and experience have convinced me that the long chain of Sadat's bilateral meetings was such an important factor in the erosion and deterioration of Sadat's position, that when he crossed the threshold of Camp David he was naked and bankrupt and had forfeited all manoeuvrability. One slip of the tongue after another behind the closed doors, entailing concessions, excesses and pledges in one meeting after the other, had tied his hands, so that he lost all the ground he had gained. The outcome was that he was obliged to put his signature to the document spelling out the bankruptcy of his initiative.

To explain myself further I have to turn back to 1977. I recall, for example, what Sadat had announced at various interviews, what he had written in his book *In Search of an Identity*, and what he himself told me, that the idea of the initiative had occurred to him for the first time upon his receipt of a letter from President Carter informing him of the developments and the difficulties of convening the Geneva Conference. Sadat had replied that he was contemplating a bold action. The idea had crystallized in his mind after his meeting with President Ceaucescu, who had affirmed to him that Menahim Begin was "a strong man" and "desired peace". President Sadat had reached his decision to go to Jerusalem during his flight from Bucharest to Iran.

Was this true? I really cannot tell. I was struck by a passage in Golda Meir's book, *My Life*,[1] in which she relates that at the beginning of 1972 the

Camp David

Deputy Foreign Minister of Romania, under the pretext of visiting his colleagues at the Israeli Foreign Ministry, had asked to see her alone. He had informed her that President Ceaucescu had instructed him to tell her that he had an extremely important message to convey to her in person, and that the message related to the talks he had recently with President Sadat while he was on a visit to Cairo. He therefore addressed an invitation to her to visit Bucharest, either secretly or publicly – whichever she thought best.

Golda Meir writes that she travelled to Bucharest and held two meetings with Ceaucescu lasting fourteen hours. He informed her that, "He understood from Sadat himself that the Egyptian leader was ready to meet with an Israeli, maybe with me, maybe not; maybe the meeting would be on slightly lower level than the Heads of State. But a meeting of some sort could take place." [2]

Golda Meir says that Ceaucescu showed as much enthusiasm for the idea as she herself, and had not the least doubt that he was delivering to her a historical and sincere message. They had then got down to details. Ceasucescu proposed that his Deputy Foreign Minister should contact Golda Meir personally through her Political Secretary, Simha Dinitz, who had accompanied her to Romania. Golda Meir writes [3] that she waited and waited after her return to Israel, but to no avail. The subject was not followed up. She believed Ceaucescu could not speak to her on the subject because he could not confess – even to her – that Sadat had fooled him.

Following my appointment as Foreign Minister, I undertook – after the Ismailia meeting and prior to my departure for Jerusalem – to attend the meeting of the Political Committee to study the two disengagement agreements concluded between Egypt and Israel, the first on 18 January 1974, and the second on 4 September 1975. I had a strong feeling that in the two agreeements, particularly the second, entitled "The Second Sinai", lay the seeds of Sadat's initiative in 1977.

I was not particularly interested in studying the provisions and dangerous appendices of the agreements. I wanted to visualize the background against which these agreements were concluded. In my opinion they were born of the bilateral talks which took place at that time between President Sadat and Dr Henry Kissinger. Unfortunately, however, I found no trace of any records or papers in the archives of the Foreign Ministry or elsewhere.

I had read Matti Golan's book, *The Secret Conversations of Henry Kissinger*, [4] published in 1976. The book had given me cause for great concern and doubts as to Sadat's negotiating capacity. Nothing confirmed the facts mentioned by the said writer, and I ascribed some of what he had to say to that writer's ill intentions. However, when I later came to read William Quandt's book, *Decade of Decisions*, on US policy on the Arab-Israeli conflict from 1967 to 1976, I became convinced of the truth of some of the things Matti Golan had alluded to in his book, and my impression of Sadat's poor negotiating qualities was confirmed. In the first place, Quandt's book was supported by documents, papers and references, and in the second, Quandt himself was an authority on American policy in the Middle East. He is a Professor of Political Science at the University of Pennsylvania, and a member of the Brookings Institute, and played a part in drawing up the Institute's paper on the Middle East issue. He is likewise a member of the US National Security Council, and had been a witness to Kissinger's negotiations. He was also a member of the American delegation to the talks which followed the initiative, culminating in Camp David. I came to know him through the talks, and I am convinced of his integrity and greatly respect him.

In resuming the subject with which this chapter deals, I shall be referring to several passages in Quandt's book touching on the talks between Kissinger and President Sadat.

UN Resolution 338 had been passed on 22 October 1973. The first paragraph provided for a ceasefire in an immediate end to military operations, with each party remaining in the positions it actually held on that date. However, the Israeli side, *despite Israel's acceptance* of the Security Council resolution, continued to advance to new positions in violation of the said resolution. By so doing, Israel succeeded in almost completely surrounding the Egyptian Third Army Corps. As a result, the Security Council passed Resolution 339 on the afternoon of 23 October calling for an immediate end to engagements and the return of the forces to the positions they occupied on 22 October at the time of the enforcement of the ceasefire. Nonetheless Israel disregarded the second resolution as well. President Sadat called upon the US and the Soviet Union to send forces to control Israeli violations of the ceasefire lines. The Soviet Union addressed a letter to the US informing it of the Israeli forces' violations of the ceasefire. The letter added that, unless the Israeli forces returned to their positions, and unless the US approved undertaking joint Soviet-American action in implementation of the said resolution, the Soviet Union would take appropriate unilateral steps.

On 25 October 1973, a third resolution was passed by the Security Council, namely Resolution 340, calling for total compliance with the ceasefire and a return ot the 22 October lines.

To go back to Quandt's book. He describes the first meeting between Kissinger and President Sadat, on 7 November 1977, in the following terms:

> He met President Sadat for the first time . . . In private talks that day, Kissinger began to develop a genuine admiration for the Egyptian leader. The turning-point came in discussing the issue of the 22 October lines. Kissinger was in an awkward position for he knew that the Israelis could not easily be pressured and yet he felt that Sadat was right that Israeli forces should not be allowed to keep the Third Army Corps at their mercy. [5]

Camp David

Kissinger submitted to Sadat the Israeli government's proposal indicating its intention to respect the ceasefire. It would allow the Third Army Corps to receive supplies of non-military materials under the control of the United Nations and Israeli forces. It would likewise permit the City of Suez to be supplied with food, water and medicines on the same conditions. In return, there would be an exchange of prisoners and the naval blockade of Bab-El-Mandeb would be lifted. As for the 22 October lines, it would be possible to discuss them within the context of an agreement on the disengagement of forces.

Quandt goes on to say:

Sadat was prepared to accept most of these points, although he was still anxious for Israel to pull back to the 22 October lines. Kissinger replied that if Egypt insists, he would agree to persuade the Israelis, but he offered his opinion that it might be just as easy, although it would take more time, to work a substantial disengagement of forces that would bypass the issue of the 22 October lines. Meanwhile, arrangements could be made to re-supply the Third Army Corps. To Kissinger's surprise Sadat agreed with this line of argument.

Quandt says that Kissinger sent Joseph Sisco and Harold Saunders to Israel to work out the details of the agreement. He also says that when the Israeli Prime Minister, Golda Meir, heard that Sadat had accepted the waiving of a return to the 22 October lines, she had described this as "a fantastic achievement".

Another example is provided by Quandt, when he writes:

On 13 January, the Israelis handed Kissinger a map of the proposed disengagement line and authorised him to show it to Sadat which he did on the second day. Sadat had already accepted, in his first talk with Kissinger, the idea of force limitations in three zones, and had promised to work for the end of the oil embargo once an agreement is reached. Now he also indicated that he would accept Israeli forces west of the passes, but he had trouble with the extent of force limits. To overcome Sadat's reservations Kissinger suggested that the United States might take the responsibility for preparing the limitation of forces. Perhaps it would be easier for Sadat to accept an American plan than an Israeli one. And instead of publicly announcing the limits in the formal documents, they could be deferred in letters exchanged by Sadat and Nixon. In addition, Sadat's private assurances on Israeli cargoes transiting the Canal could be handled in a secret memo of understanding. Sadat agreed. [6]

Quandt goes on to describe what took place. The reader in general, and

Egyptian and Arab readers, in particular, cannot but feel bitterness, pain, shame, anger and contempt while perusing, through the pages, the intransigent – not to say immoral – Israeli stands on the one hand, Sadat's over-generous attitude on the other, and finally Kissinger's questionable manipulations. He (Kissinger) exploited both Egypt and Israel in a Machiavellian fashion to implement the strategy of the United States.

Quandt writes:

> Negotiations continued for several days, with Israel offering deeper withdrawals in return for a substantial reduction of Egyptian armoured strength. On 26 November, Yariv suggested that Israel would even withdraw east of the passes if Egypt would reduce its level of armour in Sinai to token strength. Egypt showed interest in the proposal, but insisted on mutual force reduction; then, on 29 November, Gamassy discovered that Yariv had gone back to his original proposal that both sides should withdraw from territory gained in the war. This reversal of position angered the Egyptians and led to the breakdown of the talks.
>
> Kissinger has been charged with responsibility for aborting this promising experiment in direct Egyptian-Israeli negotiations. There is some truth in the charge. Kissinger felt that the talks were proceeding too rapidly. He was beginning to think of the Syrian front, and feared that if Egypt and Israel reached a disengagement agreement before Geneva, Assad would insist on the same, and this might mean indefinite delay in convening the Geneva Conference. Then, too, Kissinger wanted to demonstrate that a United States' rule was essential for sustained diplomatic progress. Perhaps Egypt and Israel could reach agreement without his help, but would the same be true when it came to Syria, the Palestinians, or even a second Egyptian step? He doubted it. If the oil boycott was to be lifted, it would also be in return for American success in promoting agreement. And if Soviet prestige was to remain low, the USA must remain in control of the negotiations. Kissinger therefore advised the Israelis to slow down at kilometre 101 and to reserve their position on disengagement until Geneva. To some observers this seemed to be cynical, but it fitted into Kissinger's broader diplomatic scheme. And it should be added that Israel did not resist this piece of advice. [7]

One of the ironic passages in Quandt's book that is worth consideration is his description of the talks between Kissinger and President Hafiz El Assad. On 14 December, Kissinger had his first meeting with him. Quandt writes:

> Kissinger found Assad to be intelligent, tough, personable, and possessed of a sense of humour. He was also the least conciliatory of

Camp David

all the Arab leaders Kissinger had met to date. Assad implied that he did not object to the convening of the Geneva Conference on 21 December, but Syria would not attend unless a disengagement of forces agreement was reached first. And disengagement should involve the entire Golan Heights. Neither was he prepared to yield to Kissinger's pleas to turn over a list of Israeli prisoners of war. After six and a half hours of talks with Assad, Kissinger left for Israel empty handed. [8]

In following up the talks between Kissinger and Assad, one cannot but admire President Assad, who achieved the maximum possible. However, as indicated by Quandt:

An improbable but genuine personal relationship was begining to develop between these two very different men. [9]

Reading this, I could not but feel sorry that Syria had not participated in Sadat's initiative, and I thought fleetingly of what the negotiations would have been like had Assad been in charge and not Sadat.

There can be no doubt that the disengagement talks constituted a useful experience for the Israelis. They analyzed Sadat's personality, put it to the test, and discovered the keys to his character. Their mouths watered for more concessions to swell their pockets – and why not?

The Disengagement Agreement signed on 18 January 1974 was a pressing necessity imposed by the urgency and dangers represented by the confusion of the Egyptian and Israeli military lines and the interlocking of the Israeli and Egyptian forces west of the Canal, it was difficult to control the ceasefire in case of any provocative act or an unintentional mistake, and in view of the besieged position of the Third Army Corps.

As a result of Israeli violation of the ceasefire imposed by the Security Council resolution and its spillover onto the 22 November positions, the Egyptian Third Army Corps had been surrounded.

As for the second Disengagement Agreement, there was neither need nor cause for its conclusion. It was entitled "The Second Disengagement Agreement" in an attempt at deceit and camouflage. The first agreement defused the dangerous situation resulting from the interlocking of the forces at the time of its conclusion. Its result had been to effectively separate the two forces, and allowed for the freeing and disarming of the forces. A buffer-zone separated the forces of the two parties under the supervision of the UN. This was followed by the signing of a similar disengagement agreement between the Israeli and Syrian forces on 31 May 1977.

If a third disengagement agreement had to be concluded at all, it should have been done with Jordan as requested by King Hussein. However, this would have not given Kissinger an easy triumph, and would have tarnished the lustre of Kissinger's apparently mythical reputation. He therefore turned away from it. It had likewise been rejected by Israel [10]. The natural and logical thing to do after the Egyptian and Syrian Disengagement Agreements was to proceed to the Peace Conference in Geneva in pursuit of a comprehensive settlement for the Arab-Israeli conflict.

This was not to Israel's liking and it was not what Kissinger wanted for numerous reasons, perhaps mostly to deprive the Soviet Union of the opportunity to contribute to the efforts being exerted towards reaching a settlement.

Kissinger found what he had been looking for in President Sadat, Head of the Egyptian State, the centre of gravity on the Arab side. Kissinger's dealings with him during the discussions of the Disengagement Agreement had whetted his appetite for more transactions. He therefore proceeded to conclude a new agreement between Egypt and Israel. This is not the place to elaborate on the provisions of the Second Sinai Agreement, which was signed on 4 September 1975 in Geneva. However, I should like to clarify one point, namely that this agreement is not exclusively military but also has its political aspects. Egypt pledged itself to abstain from the use of military force to solve the Arab-Israeli conflict, which would be solved by peaceful means. Egypt would not use force or threaten to use force. This means giving up the legitimate Arab right to resort to force in order to liberate Arab territory from Israeli occupation. It was, in effect, a commitment in practical terms to end the state of war. I shall not speak of its provisions, concerning the two-way passage of Israeli goods through the Suez Canal, which undermines an important Arab weapon, namely the Arab boycott of Israel. And I shall likewise make no comment on the last article of the agreement, which includes the strange provision that the period of duration of the agreement was indefinite and would only be determined if supplemented by another agreement. I shall also overlook President Sadat's oral commitments, such as ending the boycott of certain foreign firms dealing with Israel and toning down the propaganda and media with respect to Israel, etc.

The real disaster was inherent in the three secret agreements between the US and Israel which were concluded simultaneously with this agreement. They were considered appendices to the agreement and include manifold American commitments where Israel had bound the United States to the following:

1. The United States and Israel are committed to consult each other on the date of the meetings of the Geneva Conference.
2. The United States pledges itself to maintain its commitment on non-recognition of the PLO unless the latter recognized Israel and Resolutions 242 and 338. The United States commits itself to co-ordinate its stands and strategy at the Geneva Conference with

Camp David

   Israel on this point as well as the participation of any other state in the Conference.
3. The United States commits itself to veto in the Security Council any attempt to amend Security Council Resolutions 242 and 338 or the bases and conditions on which the Conference was established.
4. The American Administration is committed to submit every year to Congress requests for approval of military and economic assistance to Israel.
5. The United States pledges itself to fulfil all Israel's needs in military equipment, and defence and energy requirements as well as all its economic requirements.
6. The United States agrees with Israel that any future agreement concluded between Egypt and Israel shall be a final peace agreement.
7. The US pledges itself to reject any attempt at presenting proposals it and Israel consider harmful to Israeli interests, and to seek, at the same time, to prevent any efforts by others to do so.
8. The American government affirms that Egypt's obligations under the Egyptian-Israeli agreement (The Second Sinai Agreement) are not dependent on any action or developments between any other Arab state and Israel. [11]

The secrecy of these agreements – between the USA and Israel – did not extend to Egypt. The last paragraph of the third agreement stipulates that:

> The US government has notified the Israeli government that it had procured Egypt's approval on the contents of the above mentioned agreement.

In other words, Sadat had been acquainted with and approved of the above mentioned provisions of this agreement.

Israel obtained all this from Egypt and the US in return for Israeli withdrawal from some few other kilometres to the heights east of the Gedi and Mitla passes in Sinai. Furthermore, Israel realized some success in the fulfilment of one of its coveted objectives, namely sowing the seeds of dissension and division within the Arab camp. The agreement shook Arab confidence in Egypt. And, Egypt and Syria, the comrades in arms of the 1973 October War, broke up with each other.

Footnotes:

1. Golda Meir, *My Life*, London, 1975, p. 386.
2. Ibid.
3. It is worthy of note in this regard that Golda Meir's book was published in 1975, before the initiative.
4. Matti Golan, *The Secret Conversations of Henry Kissinger*, New York, Quadrangle Books, 1976.
5. William B. Quandt, *Decade of Decisions*, University of California Press, p. 216.
6. Ibid., p. 226.
7. Ibid., pp. 219–220.
8. Ibid., p.222.
9. Ibid. p.233.
10. Mahmoud Riad, p. 489. Mahmoud Riad says in his *Memoirs* (p.504) that Kissinger was unable to fulfil his promise to King Hussein with respect to a disengagement agreement on the Jordanian front similar to those concluded with Egypt and Syria. Israel refused to do this and insisted on the Memo of Understanding Kissinger had granted Israel in 1972, which makes it incumbent upon the US to discuss any political initiative with Israel before going ahead with it.
11. *New York Times*, 17–18 September 1975.

Chapter Fifteen

Personal Impressions

It cannot be denied that President Sadat's character was a unique one and many a psychoanalyst will be induced to study it in the years to come. Though not myself a psychoanalyst, I have deemed it useful to give my own personal opinion on it, particularly in view of the previous chapter both for the sake of continuity and in order to shed light on the President's past and subsequent actions. It pains me to embark upon this task.

In the first place Anwar El Sadat was a man who had great faith in his own personal good fortune. This is not to be wondered at, since he had had some dangerous experiences and prevailed over the most formidable dangers. He came of modest stock, and his early life was one of hardship. He was later to join a group of officers, who engaged in a successful revolution. Sadat, as a member of their Revolutionary Council, was to see them all disappear one by one, while he alone remained, together with their leader, Gamal Abdel Nasser. Such were the circumstances under which he was successively appointed Secretary-General of the Islamic Conference Organization, Speaker of the People's Assembly and Vice-President. Gamal Abdel Nasser died suddenly at an early age, and Sadat found himself the President of Egypt. A power struggle later developed between him and Nasser's ex-protégés, who were in full sway over the country out of which he emerged victorious. When he asked the Soviet Union to withdraw their experts from Egypt, this was accomplished without any difficulty. Later still he entered a war with Israel, and succeeded in crossing the impregnable Bar-lev Line within a few hours. The phrase he very often repeated, to the effect that he was "naturally inclined to be optimistic", is, perhaps, a reflection of his faith in his good fortune. His faith in his good fortune has perhaps developed in him a tendency to adventurism and a proclivity for gambling.

On the other hand, Sadat was by nature romantic with a vivid imagination. He was a lover of nature and was inclined to solitude – perhaps as a result of the years spent in solitary confinement. He spent lengthy and frequent periods away from Cairo at one of the many government rest-houses, separated from his family, whom he visited from time to time. His meetings over, he would sit alone, in the shade or out in the sun, undisturbed by anyone, with his secretariat, guards and servants at a distance. It was at such moments that his imagination would roam unrestrained far and wide. His experience of life had shown him that nothing was impossible, and it was at such times that he would ponder new roles of greatness and fame for himself in one sphere of life or another.

In this respect, Sadat reminded me of a movie I once saw a long time ago entitled "The Secret Life of Walter Mitty" starring Danny Kaye. Thus was Sadat sometimes. He pictured himself as a war hero, a prophet of peace or even as a simple fellah (Egyptian peasant). At other times he saw in himself a clan chief, a czar, a paragon of democracy or even Omar Ebn El Khattab, Saladin or Richard the Lion Heart.

I wonder whether it was not also the Egyptian people's assessment of him. I once heard an anecdote – our people's favourite form of expression – to the effect that President Sadat (known for his fondness for dress and uniform on every conceivable occasion), on hearing of the outbreak of a fire, during the 18 and 19 January 1977 incidents, at once flew back to Cairo from Aswan. When he arrived there, he asked his Interior Minister the location of the fire, and received the proud reply that the fire had been completely extinguished and everything was under control! Whereupon Sadat cried: "What a pity! It would have been a splendid opportunity to wear my uniform of commander-in-chief of the fire brigade!"

Sadat, however, was not a milkman (like Walter Mitty), but a head of state. He should have been preoccupied with his country's manifold problems. As he sat alone, he could not afford to let his thoughts roam from the realm of fancy to that of reality or vice versa.

I believe that while he was enacting these fantasy roles he made his decision to visit Jerusalem. Sadat himself has said that he neither consulted nor told anyone about it prior to his public announcement of it.

Sadat, too, was inclined to be excessively courteous and open-handed, this being a characteristic of the East and perhaps too of village-dwellers, as he so often liked to say. It is nothing out of the ordinary in the countries of the East for guests to drop in on an unprepared host, whereupon the solitary goat or sheep in his possession will be offered for a meal. In the same way, were some guest to admire a horse or a watch, the host would insist upon making him a present of them. This system, of course, works both ways, since the person enjoying a meal or receiving the gift would ensure that both were returned at the first opportunity. However, while this is possible at the personal level and within the bounds of one's personal possessions, it cannot be so where business is concerned.

Sadat, moreover, developed a taste for listening to praises of his qualities and genius at all times. If Henry Kissinger came along and confided to him that he had now met someone who was more than a match for him in strategy, this was sure to go to his head. He, in turn, lavished abundant praise upon others, and this is reflected in the friendship he bestowed upon people at his first encounter with them. He talked of his friend Ceaucescu, and of his friends Nixon, Ford, Carter, Giscard d'Estaing and Kreisky, topping them all with his friendship for Begin. Once such a title was bestowed upon an individual, Sadat persuaded himself it was true, embracing that person as a true friend and accordingly treated him as such, revealing to him his innermost self, thereby affording all those who wished to deceive him the opportunity to do so. He likewise accommodated any party he conferred with, in order to gain their confidence and sympathy, or showed flexibility and made concessions he considered of no great importance, so as to win over the interlocutor. Thus, if the party was the United States he would attack the Soviets; if Morocco, he would attack Algeria; with radicals, he would be against reactionaries, and so on. I wonder whether Begin's report of Sadat's saying that the Palestine Liberation Organization was an agent of the Soviet Union, was true or not.

He, furthermore, became enamoured with the sound of his own voice and with the contemplation of pictures of himself. Granting interviews and making statements became his favourite pastime. Consequently, newspapers, news agencies, and radio and television networks – particularly American and Israeli – assigned permanent correspondents in Egypt. These became itinerant and travelled, with their equipment, with the President from Aswan to Alexandria to Ismailia to the Nile Barrage. If he visited Fayoum for Friday prayers, they would lie in wait for him at the door of the mosque: he had only to inaugurate a project, plant a tree in the desert, attend a fishermen's meeting or celebrate Teachers' or Engineers' Day for them to be there, bombarding him with questions on the Arabs, the Soviet Union, the Palestine Liberation Organization, the situation in Chad and so forth.

His ever-increasing public appearances and the torrent of his quasi-daily statements triggered the interest and concern of friends and foes alike in an attempt at ascertaining what would be his next step.

Another hobby-horse was the holding of joint press conferences following his meetings with heads of state. He later enlarged the circle to include others with foreign ministers and less important officials. A meeting with the President and a photograph with him were among the major events marking any visit to Egypt. Subsequently, too, his meetings took in non-political figures and he extended audiences to men of letters and artists and such figures as Elizabeth Taylor and Julio Iglesias. Priorities as to who deserved to be met were rather confused: the ambassador of a major European state once informed me of his embarrassment and surprise when his minister of state for foreign affairs – who had come on an official visit to Cairo and who among other things intended to meet the President – could not be granted an appointment in view of the President's busy work-schedule. The following day the minister saw the President's picture in the papers together with the French Algerian-born singer Enrico Macias taken in the garden of the Barrage rest-house singing the song he had composed for the Hero of Peace.

His upbringing, and circumstances,[1] the time available for his education and his secret activities while he was an army officer, deprived him of the opportunity to acquire the amount of knowledge necessary for the development of his political character. In his childhood he had read and memorized the Koran and this gave him a command of the Arabic language and enabled him to quote the Holy Book during his talks and speeches. Moreover, he possessed a considerable and diversified store of general knowledge as well as superficial fragments of culture. The sources of his knowledge were derived from his readings in modern Egyptian history, and biographies and articles written on a few political figures whom he admired, such as Ahmad Orabi, Moustafa Kamal, Ataturk and Hitler. The lengthy periods he spent in jail gave him the opportunity to read some books not of his choosing, most of them being detective stories or romance novels. He likewise had access to a variety of magazines in prison, such as *Readers' Digest*, *Look*, and Egyptian periodicals. Other sources of knowledge took the form of films, particularly American ones, dealing with historical romances, cowboy lore and crime fiction. He would often refer to these sources of "Knowledge and Learning" in his public speeches and film interviews. When, for example, he was speaking on human rights, he would expound his point by indicating that, ". . . as one sees in American films, a police officer, upon arresting a person, reminds the latter of his rights and of the possibility of abstaining from making statements in the absence of a lawyer. . ."[2]

In his defence of the law on ethics, Sadat pointed out that such a law was not of his making, but that a similar one existed in the United States. In a film he had recently seen (he said) Clark Gable, a married man, was engaged in an amorous liaison with Carole Lombard. This constituted a violation of the US law on ethics and thereby entitled the judge to fire him from his government job or cancel his contract with the company in which he was employed.[3]

Other sources of knowledge were reports he read on various topics after becoming a member of the Revolutionary Command Council and Speaker of the People's Assembly and following the assumption of other functions up to his accession to the Presidency.

Neither was Sadat sufficiently well-versed in the political sciences or law to be capable of engaging in political negotiations alone or without prior preparations. Often he lacked the necessary technical background to sense the implications of certain terms and expressions such as "the right of sovereignty", "termination of war" or "self-determination". This often made it difficult for him to respond confidently to his adversary's arguments. He would fear not to agree with a given interpretation to avoid the embarrassment of answering lest he appear unfamiliar with the terminology used by his interlocutor, who would assume through Sadat's silence that there could be no differences of opinion.

Finally, I felt that he never completely rid himself of the mentality,

Camp David

methods and techniques commonly associated with a member of an underground organization secretly scheming to carry out a plot either for the assassination of a traitor, or for the overthrow of a regime. This trait continued to largely dominate his character, even after he became President.

In my review of Sadat's character, I have not in any way sought to defame or slander him, but have merely wished to demonstrate the impact which the negative aspects of his character had on the course of the peace initiative. I do not believe, in fact, that a President needs to be highly cultured, scholarly, a brilliant lawyer or a formidable negotiator. The responsibilities of the President of Egypt are manifold and the problems he has to consider unending; whether they relate to liberating the occupied territories, the establishment of peace, the raising of living standards, finding solutions to housing, education or the reclamation of desert land . . . and so on. It is not humanly possible to perform all these duties all at the same time without assistance, this is exactly what Sadat used to do, and is reproached for having taken decisions alone and for having confronted problems without consulting his ministers, advisers or experts although the entire state set-up was at his disposal and willing to co-operate fully with him.

Anwar El Sadat has many attitudes and could draw on a worthy patriotic past. He might have been capable of accomplishing many lasting achievements could he only be persuaded that the era of the individual had come to an end and that the age of the computer had dawned.

I recall that my excellent Foreign Ministry staff and myself worked ceaselessly, leaving nothing to chance. We systematically provided the President with information on developments and submitted reports to him. I can attest that no meeting took place between him and any foreign official – whether I attended or not – without my supplying him with a comprehensive report on the matter at hand. I often gave him oral briefings in person, or even over the phone if the President was not in Cairo. Unfortunately, enough time was not always at his disposal. He would content himself with a quick glance at these reports, or at other times simple dispense with them altogether, relying on his flair.

Yet to complete the picture, I have to acknowledge that when he *did* read any report provided by the Foreign Ministry, he invariably showed approval and admiration. And, at such times he would bear in mind the recommendations contained in the report, disregarding them on very rare occasions. He had personal confidence in me. When discussing or reviewing an issue with him he was patient and understanding. He likewise showed consideration and was always considerate towards me even when I argued with him. However, his impatience and enthusiasm for success were more than he could control, so that he would set out on a course without my knowledge, in the hope of accomplishing the objective he had set for himself without too much delay. Maybe he sensed that his days were counted.

Footnotes

1 See *In Search of our Identity*.
2 *Al Ahram*, 24 April 1979.
3 *Al Ahram*, 10 March 1980.

Chapter Sixteen

What about the Palestinians?

Upon my return from the Federal Republic of Germany on 23 February 1978, I contacted President Sadat at his residence in Ismailia and he asked me to go and meet him the following morning. He sat with Prime Minister Mamdouh Salem in one of the rest-house rooms, wearing an Arab wool cloak. Conversation centred on the assassination of Youssef El Sibai and the subsequent tragedy at Larnaka Airport. I strongly condemned the dispatch of Egyptian commandos to Cyprus to abduct Sibai's assassins and bring them to Egypt. I pointed out that, regardless of the success or failure of the operation, it constituted a violation of another state's sovereignty and was unworthy of Egypt's position and reputation within the international community. Moreover, I added, Cyprus was a friendly state and the least we should have done was to come to an understanding with it before embarking upon such an operation. The situation was made even worse by its subsequent failure and the poignant tragedy that ensured. Sadat let me talk on, but interrupted me suddenly, shouting: "Should we have allowed them to go on killing us while we looked on?" I answered that the operation had resulted in the loss of eighteen officers and an aircraft as well as the deterioration of our relations with Cyprus. The world at large had also condemned the operation. I added that the question was a very serious one, and that an immediate investigation had to be conducted in order to identify who was responsible for it. To this Sadat replied furiously: "I ordered it!"

I explained that I shared his feelings over the murder of Youssef El Sibai and the other victims of the operation, and advised him to exercise self-restraint as the situation was a delicate one and Egypt could well be spared the problems created by this action. I added that we were all liable to such assassination attempts, and that if our reactions were not calm and collected, we would be led into side issues we could well do without.

A few days later I sent in a report in which I suggested the need to reinforce co-ordination among the planning authorities in the field of national security. I likewise proposed to set up a permanent National Security Council Sub-Committee to include experts from all administrations involved. The sub-committee would number representatives from the For-

What about the Palestinians?

eign Ministry, the Interior Ministry and the War Ministry. The Foreign Ministry would be in charge of this sub-committee, which would convene whenever an emergency arose to draw up studies and make alternative proposals on questions affecting Egypt's national security for submission to the President.

The proposal, however, got lost in the flurry of events and no decision was made on it. The Larnaka tragedy led to a serious development, causing us to adopt an embarrassing position with regard to the Palestinian question making it, naturally, extremely convenient for Israel. The slaughter of the Egyptian commandos was a veritable national tragedy arousing both the grief and wrath of the Egyptian people. Questions began to be asked as to whether the operation was worthwhile and who was responsible for it. It was therefore necessary to absorb national resentment and to direct it elsewhere. A scapegoat was soon found in the Palestinian nationality of Youssef El Sibai's assassins.

The Egytian media launched a violent campaign against the Palestine Liberation Organization and against Palestinians wherever they were to be found, and they were accused of criminal ingratitude. They had repaid Egypt's sacrifices and the four wars it had engaged in on their behalf by killing its sons. Of course, no one paid the slightest attention to the statement issued by the PLO following Sibai's murder, in which it strongly condemned the incident. Neither did anyone look into the results of the investigation to determine whether the perpetrators had committed the crime on their own account or at some other party's instigation. If the latter, who was the party? Where was it located? Was it Arab or Israeli? And who had a direct interest in the matter? No one wished to be reminded of the fact that the Egyptian commandos had not been slaughtered by Palestinians, since it was the Cypriot soldiers at the airport who had shot them while repelling the sudden invasion. The People's Assembly took part in the hate campaign against those Palestinians residing in Egypt, issuing decrees depriving them of the privileges they had been granted ever since they were evicted from Palestine.

It was in vain that I strove to deflect the torrent. I tried to caution Sadat against it and pointed to the dangers inherent in such a position with regard to his peace initiative. I believed that such a stance seriously undermined Egypt's negotiating position and played into Israel's hands. However, the only step I was able to take after the storm had subsided was to freeze the measures taken against the Palestinians in Egypt. It was difficult to annul these measures altogether, as to do so would have been to acknowledge their injustice.

Everybody agreed that the comprehensive peace Sadat sought to achieve by embarking upon his initiative would be unattainable unless a solution were to be found to the Palestinian problem. Such a solution constituted the backbone of the peace initiative, and if such a solution was not found, the initiative was doomed. Consequently, the Palestinian factor in achieving a comprehensive peace was vital. Since this was so, how could Sadat, who had volunteered and appointed himself the advocate of the Palestinian cause, choose to slight, antagonize, ignore or reject those he was supposed to be defending?

On hearing President Sadat's speech in the Knesset, I noted that he avoided any reference to the Palestine Liberation Organization as the sole legitimate representative of the Palestinian people in accordance with the decisions taken by the Arab Summit Conference in Rabat in 1974. I did not, however, attach undue importance to this, since the organization's status was a *fait accompli* at both the Arab and international level. On reading Moshe Dayan's book my attention was drawn to the following excerpt relating to the conversation that took place between Boutros Ghali and Dayan as they drove from Ben-Gurion airport to Jerusalem during Sadat's visit in November 1977: "We also touched upon the PLO in our talk. I suggested to him that it would be well if Sadat did not demand that Israel negotiate with that organization. If he did, he would receive a vigorous rejection. Ghali promised to tell this to his President and indeed, when Sadat addressed the Knesset the next day, he made no mention of the PLO."[1]

If it is true that Dayan's words were the motive behind the omission of the PLO in the speech before the Knesset, it is indeed a strange and difficult thing to understand for a number of reasons:

1) Egypt's permanent and declared public policy from Gamal Abdel Nasser's time and after consisted in supporting all liberation movements everywhere, more especially the Palestine Liberation Organization. Sadat himself was among the most fervent of those who held that the organization should be vested with the status of sole legitimate representatives of the Palestinian people. Egypt had thrown its full weight behind the Arab states for this purpose.

2) If Sadat had intended his speech to accommodate Israel's position, he could have abstained from referring to the necessity for Israel to withdraw fully from all the occupied territory or the need for it to recognize the legitimate rights of the Palestinian people. Israel had already rejected both points prior to and following the speech. It could have adopted the same position on the PLO and have refused to negotiate with it.

3) With regard to who should represent the Palestinian people, the option before the Rabat Summit Conference lay between King Hussein and the PLO. The choice of the heads of state and government as to who should become the sole legitimate representative of the Palestinian people fell unanimously upon the PLO, and King Hussein finally decided to conform to their decision. The omission of the PLO in the speech to the Knesset if

What about the Palestinians?

deliberate, would result in the confusion of the political leadership of the Palestinian people and make of it a figure without a head or a cause without advocates. This, of course, was in line with Israel's aim of selecting its Palestinian interlocutors before engaging in negotiations with them.

There was, indeed, something odd in Sadat's refusal, during the Rabat Conference, to allow King Hussein (half of whose kingdom is made up of people of Palestinian origin) a role in representing the Palestinians by agreeing to the PLO becoming the sole legitimate representative of the Palestinian people[2] compared to his latter exclusion of the PLO and agreement that Jordan should be involved in negotiations under the Camp David accords.

To go back to the Palestine Liberation Organization, I should like to mention that while in Bonn I entertained good relations with the Organization's representative in West Germany, Abdallah El-Afrangy. The latter was a sober young man, devoted to his mission, which he was engaged in carrying out under trying conditions in view of Germany's sensitivity with regard to anything related to Jews or Israel. He kept me informed of the difficult situation in which the Organization found itself, and of its internal and external problems. It is my personal belief that the PLO was over hasty in deciding to join the Steadfastness Front and take part in its Tripoli conference following the peace initiative. Though members of the Steadfastness front, such as Syria, Algeria and Libya, could afford to take such a decision, the PLO's position was more delicate. The PLO is not a state with resources and capabilities of its own, but to a great extent depends on the Arab states in its struggle to liberate Palestine. This situation, therefore, required that it maintain a difficult balance in its relations with Arab states, and that it refrain from aligning itself with one side against the other so as not to impair its freedom of action. In saying this, I do not mean to imply that the PLO should have lined up behind President Sadat's initiative or have agreed to attend the Cairo Preparatory Conference. This would, in itself, have been difficult if not impossible, for the President had surprised the PLO with his sudden visit to Jerusalem without even reaching a prior understanding with them on that score. For the PLO to have welcomed the initiative would have been neither better nor worse than its hasty adhesion to the rejectionist front. It would, I believe, have been possible for the PLO to have adopted a more cautious and flexible position by refraining from severing relations with any party until matters had crystallized and until the development of a dialogue had enabled it to determine its options with regard to each and every Arab state.

Be that as it may, I stubbornly strove to maintain links with the PLO and tried to persuade the President to do the same. I would, for instance, tell him that any break between Egypt and the Organization would be greatly detrimental to the Palestinian question and would signal Egypt's reluctance to find a solution to the problem. It would deprive us of the justification to carry on with the initiative. I therefore steadily supplied him with statements made by the moderate members of the Organization, and prevailed upon him to recall Gamal El Sorani, the PLO representative in Egypt, so as to preserve a channel of communication between ourselves and the Organization's political leadership. I also instructed our Ambassador in Jordan to maintain his contacts with all Palestinian mayors, sheikhs and prominent figures on the West Bank, and to assure them of Egypt's integrity and loyalty in the search for a solution to their problem. He was likewise to dispel any doubts with regard to any likelihood of Egypt's concluding any unilateral agreement with Israel.

In my talks with the US Secretary of State, Cyrus Vance, and his aides, I had invariably been at pains to stress the need for PLO participation in any settlement, and to point to the fact that the leadership was prepared to obtain the rights of the Palestinian people through peaceful means if that were possible. I stressed the legitimacy of their resistance-like activities against Israel so long as the latter continued to occupy their land by force. I likewise observed that the Israelis should be the last to qualify the Palestine struggle as terrorism, since it was they who had introduced it to the Middle East, led by their Prime Minister, who had a price of ten thousand pounds sterling on his head, offered by the British government to whoever captured him and delivered him up on account of his terrorist activities. I should like to add that our continuous diplomatic endeavour succeeded in overcoming Israel's attempts to persuade all states harbouring a PLO representation office to withdraw their recognition of the Organization and close such offices.

Roy Atherton arrived in Egypt towards the end of February 1978 to begin his diplomatic shuttle between Egypt and Israel as agreed at Camp David in an attempt to reach agreement on a declaration of principles. I attended the meeting that took place between Atherton and President Sadat in Ismailia. No significant developments had occurred since our recent visit to the US, save a decision by the Israeli Cabinet issued following Atherton's arrival in the Middle East stating Israel's intention to pursue its policy of building new settlements and expanding existing ones. Sadat again explained to Atherton on this occasion that Menahim Begin had not responded to the spirit of his initiative, and he pointed out that Begin was creating difficulties on every occasion, and had ventured to distort facts and statements made by him. Sadat considered sending a private letter to Begin through Atherton during the latter's visit to Israel, and he entrusted me with the task of drafting it on the basis of points raised in his discussions with Atherton. A reference to the contents of this letter affords a useful indication of the hopes, ambitions and optimism of the President with regard to the beneficial results that would flow from his initiative.

What about the Palestinians?

The President expressed pleasure at the outset that the letter was being delivered to Begin by Mr Atherton, who was deploying his good offices on behalf of the US to assist the two parties achieve a comprehensive peace in conformity with Sadat's concept, namely, the need to create appropriate conditions for the establishment of good neighbourly relations with all its implications, requiring that no party would violate another's territory, sovereignty, honour or dignity.

Sadat also expressed concern at the course events were taking, which did not accord with the spirit of his visit to Jerusalem. Agreement on crucial issues had not been achieved, and instead differences still subsisted as to wording and formulation; he noted that had agreement been reached on fundamental issues such as withdrawal, the Palestinian question and security of the parties, any difficulties of formulation would be facilitated.

The President likewise voiced regret at finding himself in the same situation that existed before his trip to Jerusalem as a result of the futile concepts sprung by Israel in the political and military committees. He indicated that he approved of the continuation of the Atherton mission and the resumption of the meetings of the political and military committees in principle, provided they did not destroy the hopes for peace to which the world aspired.

Sadat also approved Israel's need for security, but it has to be agreed that this was not to be secured at the expense of territory and sovereignty. With regard to the Palestinian question, which he had hitherto stressed as the crux of the problem, Sadat requested Israel to refrain from raising it in connection with territory or sovereignty. He asked the Israelis, too, not to deny the legitimate rights of the Palestinian people. He endorsed Israel's need for security and, to that end, expressed readiness to participate in any force which might be formed for that purpose in Gaza (comprising Israel, the Palestinians and the United Nations) during the transitional period prior to self-determination. With regard to the West Bank, he considered that the United Nations should assume responsibility there, as agreed with King Hussein at the beginning. An agreement could later be reached on a quadripartite arrangement, including the United Nations, Israel, King Hussein and the Palestinians, that would secure Israel's security during the transitional period on the West Bank.

Sadat observed that the Steadfastness Front states and the Soviet Union were actively attempting to abort his initiative, but he had so far been able to resist this. He stressed his resolve not to abandon his initiative and emphasized that terrorist activities, such as the Youssef El Sibai assassination, would not shake his determination to achieve peace. However, he added, Menahim Begin, by his adoption of inflexible positions, supplied the rejectionists with ammunition with which to counter his peace initiative.

Sadat pointed out that Israel's thinking was still, unhappily, directed to acquisition of strategic advantages and to the annexation of territory

Camp David

belonging to other parties. Sadat declared that territory could not be conceded. He was prepared to grant Israel all the other concomitants of peace provided this did not impair territory or sovereignty. He had already demonstrated this by his trip to Jerusalem, by inviting Begin to Ismailia, and by agreeing to hold direct contacts with the Israelis at the Cairo Preparatory Conference and in the political and military committees.

Atherton soon returned with Begin's reply to Sadat's letter. The letter was dated 5 March, and I here quote some excerpts from it in order to shed light on Begin's thinking and his ways with Sadat:

> Permit me to pass on to other issues essential to our dialogue. You complain that "we are still unfortunately dealing with 'wording' ". All of us remain engaged in this exercise because, Mr President, your advisers propose to us "wording" which has only one meaning: that the Government of Israel give a commitment of withdrawal to the lines preceding the Six Day War of defence. This is an old concept going back to the autumn of 1967. As I said to you in Ismailia, Israel is not committed under Resolution 242 to such a withdrawal, nor is it required to agree to such a pre-condition. In May and June 1967, we were threatened, Mr President, with the destruction of our independence and, indeed, of our people. I remember well when we last met, that you yourself recalled the slogan of those days: "Throw them into the sea". Israel defended itself.
>
> As you know, it is the great rule of international law that in the wake of the use of the inherent right of national self-defence, territorial changes do take place in peace treaties. Were it otherwise, the whole map of Europe and the Far East should be changed immediately.
>
> In your letter, you continue to espouse the formation, after an interim period, of a Palestinian state in Judea, Samaria and the Gaza Strip. Mr President, I have to say again, as I explained in Ismailia: such a state, in whatever form, would constitute a mortal danger to Israel. An interval of a few transient years will not eliminate the peril. No nation lives on borrowed time. The mortal danger must not be created.
>
> In its proposals to you, the Government of Israel introduced a new approach and concept. We stand by our suggestion for a complete administrative autonomy for the Palestinian Arabs living in Judea, Samaria and the Gaza Strip, while security be assured for the Palestinian Jews. On hearing this from me in Ismailia, your reaction, and again I remember your words vividly, was: "It is a step forward." Such a step can hardly, therefore, be characterized as "old" or as a "step backward".
>
> I am gratified to read in your letter of your wish to go on with the

peace-making effort and that you are not against the resumption of the talks within the framework of the political and military committees which we agreed to establish during our good talks in Ismailia. I, therefore, suggest directly to you, Mr President, that the negotiations be renewed...

I was not surprised by the contents of Begin's letter nor did I attach much importance to it. I was under the impression that we were in a relatively comfortable position since agreement had been reached during our recent visit to the United States that the latter would take on the responsibility of inducing Israel to change its rigid stance. I therefore gave myself entirely to exploit the breathing-space to put our house in order and seek reconciliation with our Arab brothers.

Footnotes

1   Moshe Dayan, *Breakthrough*, p. 78.
2   Mahmoud Riad's *Memoirs*, p. 492.

Chapter Seventeen

Making War While Talking Peace

Activities at the Foreign Ministry were at a peak at the beginning of March 1978 in preparation for the Arab League Council meetings during the second half of the month. The Council was convening in one of its regular ordinary sessions to discuss several items relating to the League Budget and other administrative issues. The meeting was supposed to he held at the level of Arab ambassadors accredited to the League.

The matter was all the more significant to me as it was the first Arab League Council meeting to take place following Sadat's visit to Jerusalem. It followed that depending on who was present or absent at the meetings, the level of representation had important connotations.

It is true that attendance was not necessarily associated with the position of states vis-à-vis the Egyptian stand, since the Arab League was an independent entity, and its location in Cairo, by virtue of its Charter, by no means implied that attendance of its meetings was tantamount to approval of Egypt's policy.

There was a possibility that the Steadfastness Front states – Syria, Algeria, Libya, South Yemen, Iraq with the PLO (also a working member) would boycott the meeting. More serious was the possibility that the Front would exercise pressure over a number of non-committed states on the initiative to boycott the meetings.

It was, therefore, considered important to act rapidly by exerting intense efforts to maintain the meeting at ministerial level rather than ambassadorial level and by securing the participation of the greatest possible number of Arab League member states, both for the sake of appearances and to provide myself with the opportunity, in my own country, to introduce myself to the Arab ministers as the new Foreign Minister of Egypt. My purpose was to assure them of the integrity of Egypt's position and of its honest sincerity in striving for a comprehensive settlement of the Arab-Israeli conflict. I also wished to refute rumours circulated by some quarters that we were seeking a partial solution or a separate agreement with Israel. My main concern was to engage in a dialogue in the hope of finding a way to preserve the Arab front from total collapse, which could negatively affect our position in the negotiations with Israel, particularly in view of the violent and obstinate attitude adopted by the Steadfastness Front and the PLO with regard to the initiative.

I could not claim an extensive knowledge of Arab affairs or any prior acquaintance with Arab Foreign Ministers, some of whom I had met during my diplomatic assignments abroad when they had paid visits to the countries to which I was accredited. My instinct led me to seek the assistance of Mr Mahmoud Riad, who had been closely following the Arab-Israeli conflict from the outset. He had been a member of the Egyptian delegation to the 1949 Rhodes Negotiations which gave birth to the Egyptian-Israeli armistice agreement, later followed by similar agreements between Israel and Syria, Jordan and Lebanon. He had been Foreign Minister of Egypt for seven consecutive years, and was subsequently elected Secretary-General of the Arab League in 1972. Mahmoud Riad was a serious person of vast experience, highly respected and esteemed by everyone. He was, moreover, an authority on Arab affairs and enjoyed close relations with Arab kings and heads of state, as well as their foreign ministers.

Riad was of the opinion that the initiative undertaken by Sadat would not succeed in achieving a comprehensive settlement to the Arab-Israeli conflict, for two reasons:

1. That Israel had no intention of returning the occupied Arab territories in pursuance of its expansionist policies.
2. That the initiative had created fissures in the Arab front, affecting the Arab solidarity which had peaked during and after the 1973 War.

The disengagement agreements concluded between Egypt and Israel had, Riad observed, sown the seeds of this division. He deemed, however, that since the initiative had already been undertaken, it had to be treated as a *fait accompli*. His (Riad's) prime concern at the moment was, therefore, to preserve the Arab front from disintegration and maintain some measure of solidarity among Arab states to serve as a shield should the initiative fail. Neither did he wish to see Egypt isolated by the Arabs nor isolating itself from them. As a result, he fully responded to my plan for the deployment of his good offices to convene the Arab League Council at ministerial level.

King Hassan II of Morocco, on the other hand, enthusiastically supported Sadat's initiative, and exerted considerable efforts in that direction.

Meanwhile, an incident occurred that had grave consequences, further complicating the situation between Egypt, Syria and the PLO. On 11 March, a group of Palestinian commandos undertook a daring operation by managing to land, using rubber boats, on the Israeli coast near Haifa, and seize a bus, which they drove in the direction of Tel-Aviv where they were met by Israeli forces. An engagement between the two parties ensued, in which

Camp David

most of the commandos and thirty-five Israelis were killed while others were wounded. Most of the casualties were caused when the bus exploded upon being attacked by the Israelis.

We naturally expected an Israeli response. On 12 March the Egyptian Foreign Ministry issued the following statement:

> The incident that occurred yesterday in Israel provides new evidence that the Egyptian position, represented by President Sadat's peace initiative, is sound. It is necessary to find a comprehensive peaceful settlement to the Middle East problem. Peace in the area will be impossible to achieve unless a settlement for all the aspects of the Palestinian problem is reached and the Palestinian people are enabled to exercise their legitimate right to self-determination. The policy which refuses to recognize the legitimate Arab rights has hitherto been responsible for introducing violence and loss of life to the area during the past thirty years. President Sadat's initiative seeks to find a way out of this situation by its endorsement of right and justice.

The Israeli retaliation came late in the night of 14 March in the form of a comprehensive and devastating attack against South Lebanon that could in no way be compared to the commando operation that was Israel's pretext for perpetrating this aggression. The latter was carried out in such a way as to openly reveal Israel's expansionist designs to annex South Lebanon and seize the sources of the Litani river. More than thirty thousand Israeli troops drawn from Israel's ground, sea and air forces, launched a large-scale invasion of South Lebanon to hunt down the Palestinian commandos and liquidate their bases. The Israelis made use of devastating weapons produced in the United States that indiscriminately claimed the lives of men, women and children, whether these were Lebanese, Palestinian commandoes or refugees driven from their homeland. The invasion caused ruin and destruction wherever the troops set foot, and more than ninety peaceful villages were uprooted. The wretched refugees fled, carrying their wounded and children, in the direction of Beirut. There were over one hundred thousand of them.[1]

Israel was assisted in its invasion of South Lebanon by a fifth column in the form of Lebanon's Phalangist Militia headed by dissident Major Saad Haddad, an Israeli agent who shared its racial fanaticism. However, the aggression was met on the part of PLO fighters and the Lebanese national forces with unparalleled courage, and hundreds of the attacking troops were killed and wounded and a considerable quantity of Israeli arms and ammunition was destroyed. The Israeli invasion ultimately failed to achieve its fundamental objective, namely the extermination of the Palestinian resistance.

The day following the invasion I telephoned President Sadat at his

Barrage rest-house in order to place before him the statement I had prepared on the incident, but found him still asleep. I later placed several widely spaced calls, but to no avail, so I decided to issue the statement without consulting the President. The situation was an extremely embarrassing one, especially for Egypt in its relations with the Arab world, constituting as it did a violation by Israel's armed forces of Lebanon's sovereignty by attacking Lebanese territory, overrunning its villages, uprooting its inhabitants and carrying out a systematic genocide operation against the Palestinians – all without the least reaction on our part.

At 1.30 p.m. Sadat contacted me at the Ministry and asked me drowsily why I had called him several times. I replied that the matter concerned the Israeli attack against Lebanon, whereupon he laughingly enquired: "Did they teach them a lesson?" I could not believe my ears, and queried: "What did you say?" He responded with: "Have they punished them yet?" The blood rushed to my head as I answered: "Quite the contrary – it is the Palestinians who have taught the Israelis a lesson." I then undertook to brief him on the latest information that had reached me concerning the brave resistance put up by the Palestinians and the Lebanese national forces in countering the Israeli attack. It appeared, I said, that they had been expecting Israeli retaliation and had duly organized themselves. The President listened to me with some surprise and when I informed him of the statement I had issued, he replied: "You did well."

Although I understood Sadat's feelings up to a certain point, I did not approve of them. He bore a grudge against the PLO for having joined the rejectionist front and for its attacks on him. It is also my opinion that he considered the commando operation in Israel as directed against his initiative and aimed at warning off any country who might wish to join it, especially Jordan. To my mind, however, the matter went far beyond the desire for revenge.

Later, when Ezer Weizman's book *The Battle for Peace* was published in 1981, I read the following excerpt:

> A few minutes after the first Israeli tank crossed the border into Southern Lebanon, the telephone rang in the office of Eleizer Rimon, the head of our delegation in Cairo. The late hour notwithstanding, Rimon was instructed by headquarters in Tel-Aviv to contact the head of the Egyptian Intelligence, General Shawkat, with an important message. It was not easy: the Egyptian soldier on duty was afraid to call up his general at such an unusual hour. Finally, he was persuaded to do so by Rimon's urgency.
>
> "A short time ago," Rimon notified Shawkat, "our forces began a limited operation along the Lebanese border to dislodge the terrorist bases from the area. I hope this limited operation will not disrupt talks between our two countries."

This was the substance of the message – the first of its kind – conveyed to Egypt's Chief of Military Intelligence after its text had been agreed between Begin, Dayan and myself.[2]

My memory flew back three years to the telephone conversation between myself and Sadat at the time of the Israeli attack before and I now understood the secret that lay behind his untroubled, bantering tone as he enquired about the "lesson" the Palestinians had received. Before going to sleep he had received a message to the effect that Israel intended to undertake a "limited operation" on its borders with Lebanon. And I now understood the reason for his surprise when I acquainted him with the details of the operation and he discovered upon awakening that the "limited" Israeli operation had taken the form of an army of thirty thousand troops reinforced with planes, tanks and naval craft.

If the Palestinian commando operation and consequent Israeli attack on South Lebanon were embarrassing to Egypt, it was even more directly embarrassing to Syria. Syria had been militarily involved in Lebanon after the outbreak of the civil war there between the National Forces and the Phalangists. The war had threatened Lebanon's territorial integrity, exposing it to division and disintegration. The Syrian army had succeeded in controlling the situation in 1976, after having engaged in fierce battles with both sides. On 25 November the Extraordinary Arab Summit Conference held in Cairo endorsed the Syrian military presence in Lebanon as part of the Arab Security Force set up by the Conference. The other decisions asked for the adoption of the necessary safeguards to bring about a ceasefire in Lebanon, protect the Palestinian Resistance, ensure that Lebanon would not be divided in any way, and prevent all intervention in its internal affairs.

However, the Syrian army in Lebanon constituted the backbone of the Arab Security Forces as the participation of troops from North Yemen, South Yemen, Sudan, the United Arab Emirates and Libya was merely nominal.

There can be no doubt that the Israeli army's invasion of South Lebanon, when more than twenty thousand Syrian troops were present but did not lift a finger to deter it, instead seeking by every means to avoid a confrontation, constituted a great embarrassment to Syria. For however sound and sensible the Syrian position may have been in avoiding a battle with the Israeli army – a battle for which the Syrians had determined neither the time nor the place – and however correct it had been for the Syrians not to engage in a conflict that had resulted from a Palestinian commando operation carried out at random, Syria's position and appearance in the eyes of Arab public opinion were embarrassing, particularly in view of its rejection of the peace initiative and its active role in the Steadfastness Front.

Sadat made no attempt at deeper consideration of the situation resulting from the Israeli invasion of Lebanon, nor did he ask his advisers for a thorough examination of its various aspects, so as to adopt counter measures, commensurate with the grave situation created by the Israeli invasion, to protect Arab interests, in general, and those of Egypt in particular. Rather, he gave free rein to his feelings and instructed his Information Minister and the newspaper editors to launch an intensive campaign against Syria and its claim to Steadfastness and castigating the failure of its army to confront the Israeli invasion that had violated Lebanon's sovereignty. The campaign was also designed to point to the fact that Syria had failed to meet its commitments in defence of the Palestinian Resistance, which Syria claimed to protect, and laid heavy emphasis on Syria's unenviable record during the Tel El Zaatar slaughter of the Palestinians.

It was in vain that I attempted to persuade Sadat to stem the torrential campaign. I feared that Syria, under pressure from embarrassment and defamation, would undertake to engage the Israeli forces, which would have had serious and unforeseeable repercussions not only throughout the Middle East, but also at the international level. One of the consequences of such a situation, were it to arise, would be the liquidation of the initiative. I furthermore told Sadat that the situation reminded me of what had happened in May 1967, when some Arab states, notably Syria and Jordan, had attacked statements made by President Nasser, in which he had declared his readiness to go to war with Israel. They had accused him of making such statements while enjoying the protection of the the United Nations Forces which stood as a buffer between Egypt and Israel, along Egypt's frontiers and the Gaza Strip, inducing him to demand their withdrawal. This was used by Israel as a pretext for waging the 1967 War, which led to the occupation of the Arab territories – a situation which is still with us.

I also told Sadat that our position should be based on a declaration of our solidarity with Lebanon, Syria and the PLO. I likewise pointed out that there had to be strong condemnation of the Israeli aggression, especially since it had been perpetrated to further emphasize the division and bitterness resulting from the initiative, and because, sooner or later, we will have to revert to our Arab world, whether in war or peace, and irrespective of whether the initiative succeeded or failed. How were we, I added, to carry through demands made by him in his Jerusalem speech with regard to Israel's withdrawal from the Golan, and the solution of the Palestinian question, if differences between ourselves and both Syria and the PLO remained unresolved?

Moreover, I warned, the campaign we were waging against Syria from that particular angle would reflect upon us, for we too, according to the Joint Arab Defence Charter, were pledged to rush to the rescue of Lebanon or of any Arab state that was a Charter member, if such a state were exposed to any external aggression.

Sadat, however, once more let his feelings and instincts, prevail over his good sense.

Camp David

The third party to be embarrassed by the outcome of the Israeli aggression on Lebanon was the United States itself. In the first place, the United States had repeatedly assured many Arab capitals that it would not allow any Israeli attack against Lebanon. Secondly, Israel had, in the course of its air attacks on Lebanon, employed US weapons such as Phantoms and cluster bombs, contravening the terms of the 1952 agreement between the two countries, according to which the said weapons were to be supplied to Israel only after the latter had pledged to use them only in self defence. In April 1978, the US State Department officially stressed that:

> Israeli forces have used the cluster bombs against civilians during their invasion of South Lebanon thereby violating United States laws. Moreover, the agreement according to which the weapons have been delivered to Israel stipulates that they should be used only in the event of a large-scale war against military and not civilian targets.

The United States also realized the dangers inherent in the development of fighting between Israeli and Syrian forces on Lebanese territory and the complications such a situation could entail internationally, particularly where the Soviet Union was concerned. The State Department therefore rapidly issued an official statement calling upon Israel to withdraw from South Lebanon and for the adoption of security measures to ensure that no attacks on the part of the PLO would be undertaken against Israel from Lebanese territory in the future.

Sadat, in turn, realized the gravity of the situation in Lebanon, when it dawned on him that if a solution were not speedily found, the peace talks would definitely come to an end. He asked that an urgent message be prepared for President Carter urging him to intervene and take serious action to bring about the withdrawal of Israeli forces from Lebanon. I delivered the message to the American Ambassador on 17 March, and I would like to quote a few excerpts:

> I should like, in the spirit of friendship that requires absolute frankness, to point out to you that this withdrawal should take place immediately. The Israelis should be made to understand that the present situation, resulting from their massive attack and their continued occupation of large areas of Southern Lebanon, is fraught with grave dangers and creates mounting tensions which might harm the peace process to which we are both firmly committed. Israel should realize that its actions, which are clearly out of all proportion to the bus incident which I publicly deplored, provided arguments to those who hold that the government of Israel is not sincere in its desire to meet our resolve to reach a just, lasting and comprehensive peace. . .

As to the problem of security, which I have already fully recognized, I think it could be partially met by stationing either the Lebanese or UN forces on the borders between Israel and Lebanon. But this should, in my opinion, be linked with the acceptance by Israel of at least your formulation on the solution to the Palestinian problem in all its aspects, this in fact, is the only way of ensuring durable security and of preventing frustrated Palestinians from continuing to be impelled along the path of violence.

I think we have a real chance to turn these regrettable incidents into an opportunity to push our efforts towards peace. But the first order of the day should be a withdrawal, to take place as early as possible, followed immediately by steps in the direction I have indicated.

The United States submitted a draft resolution to the Security Council which was adopted as Resolution No. 425 of 19 March, calling upon Israel to immediately cease its military action against the territorial integrity of Lebanon and withdraw its forces therefrom. It also called for the stationing of United Nations forces in the South of Lebanon that would act on behalf of the Lebanese government.

Israel was, as usual, reluctant to implement the withdrawal as stipulated in the resolution, and it adopted the same position as with the flood of resolutions taken against it over a thirty-year span. Israel acted as if only one UN resolution was acceptable, namely the one dividing Palestine into a Palestinian and a Jewish state. It speedily implemented this resolution, establishing its state, and promptly applied itself to the execution of the following step in its expansionist scheme by engulfing large parts of the territories allocated to the Palestinian state under the resolution.

In 1967 it occupied the rest of those territories, namely of the West Bank and Gaza Strip, and was now seeking to consecrate its occupation and impose a *fait accompli* in order to create the appropriate conditions for their annexation. The Palestinian people, along with the United Nations, could go to the devil for all Israel cared.

Footnotes

1   Moshe Dayan, *Breakthrough*, p. 122.
2   Ezer Weizman, *The Battle for Peace*, p. 274.

Chapter Eighteen

An Unexpected Stab in the Back!

It was in this turbulent atmosphere that the Arab delegations began arriving in Cairo to attend the meeting of the Arab League Council on 27 March 1978. The meeting was attended by representatives from all the Arab states except Syria, Libya, Algeria and South Yemen, who boycotted it in protest against President Sadat's visit to Jerusalem. The PLO was among those participating and this gave me great satisfaction. Fourteen foreign ministers participated, which was in itself of considerable significance.

I spoke during the meeting, and referred to the tremendous impact of President Sadat's peace initiative on world public opinion. Signs of widespread understanding and of sympathy for the Arab cause had become apparent, I said, particularly in the United States, which had long been misled on the facts of the case by Israeli propaganda, and I referred to the differences that had arisen between the governments of Israel and the US as a result of Irsael's refusal to accept a comprehensive peace. I told them that the effect of the visit had a great impact within Israel itself, and I furthermore stressed Egypt's commitment to the establishment of a comprehensive peace based upon Israel's withdrawal from all the occupied Arab territories and on the legitimate right of the Palestinian people to self-determination.

Mahmoud Riad, the Arab League Secretary-General, also passed the situation under review underlining the need to restore Arab solidarity, especially following Israel's refusal to respond to our demand for a comprehensive peace and the widespread offensive it had launched against South Lebanon. He proposed a concerted Arab action to hold an Arab summit conference to confront Israeli provocations.

A decision was taken during the meeting to approve Kuwaiti Foreign Minister Sheikh El Sabbah's proposal to appoint a committee with the task of ironing out existing differences between Egypt and the Arab states rejecting the initiative. The Arab Solidarity Committee was formed, under the chairmanship of Sudanese President Gaafar El Numeiry, which included the Secretary-General of the Arab League and the Foreign Ministers of Saudi Arabia, Kuwait, Jordan, the United Arab Emirates and North Yemen. The Arab League Council likewise decided to hold an Arab summit

An Unexpected Stab in the Back!

conference at the earliest possible opportunity.

The true value of this meeting was that it afforded the opportunity for unofficial contacts with the Arab foreign ministers and for a general appraisal of the situation. Upon his arrival, I visited Prince Saud El Faisal, the Foreign Minister of Saudi Arabia, in his suite at the Hilton Hotel. The meeting lasted over three hours. The Foreign Minister struck me as being charming and enjoying a remarkable intelligence combined with a superb cultural background. Although this was my first meeting with him, I felt – perhaps because of the admiration I had for his father, the late King Faisal – as if I had known him long before. I had followed his statements in the international press prior to my assumption of office, and admired their moderation, logic and consistency.

I introduced myself to him and undertook to talk to him with complete frankness. Touching on the initiative, I affirmed my faith in President Sadat's intention to attain a comprehensive peace and my conviction that the conclusion of a partial or separate peace with Israel was out of the question. I added that under the circumstances, this could not be envisaged and I pointed out that this had been my condition for accepting the post of Foreign Minister. Had the matter been otherwise, I assured him, I should have immediately resigned. I likewise stressed the great importance of Saudi assistance in bolstering the President's position. Saudi Arabia had immense resources and could wield much influence in the US. Besides, I emphasized, his country was seeking to put an end to the dissensions threatening the Arab cause as a result of the peace initiative. Discussions between us unfolded easily and naturally and, when I took my leave of him, we agreed to keep constantly in touch so as to co-ordinate our positions as far as possible. I felt that a true relationship based on frankness, understanding and mutual confidence had developed between us.

An hour later I met Prince Saud El Faisal again, along with other Arab Foreign Ministers and the League Secretary-General at an informal dinner given by Sheikh Sabbah, the Foreign Minister of Kuwait. Lengthy discussions between myself and those present again took place, extending into the early hours of the morning. Sheikh Sabbah assumed the role of prosecutor-general and spoke against the initiative, whilst I pleaded for it, in the guise of defendant. The general atmosphere, however, was open, friendly and fraternal. The questioning to which I had been subjected had afforded me the opportunity to ascertain the positive aspects of the initiative and to dispel any doubts that may have arisen concerning it. It was, I maintained, impossible to conclude that the initiative had been a failure up to this point, since the Egyptian position on the establishment of a comprehensive peace was firm and consistent, and developments and reactions – even within Israel – were in favour of it. I believe my review was accepted by most of those present. It is probable that my handling of the meetings of the political committee in Jerusalem had been appreciated in some Arab circles.

Camp David

At the Arab League Council meetings the following day, Prince Saud El Faisal expressed a wish to meet President Sadat, and I promised to arrange an appointment for him. Returning to my office, I at once contacted the President and informed him of Prince Saud's request. He replied that he was not feeling well and was, besides, engaged. To this I responded that I could not undertake to apologize to the Prince on his behalf, since this was not in our interest, the President agreed to meet him on the afternoon of the following day (28 March), at the Barrage rest-house, and asked me to be there.

At noon the next day, as I sat in my office, together with the Foreign Under-Secretary, Ambassador Ahmed Othman, and my Chief of Cabinet, Ambassador Ahmed Maher, to whom I was relating, in a happy and optimistic mood, the discussions that had taken place with the foreign ministers when suddenly the direct line rang. President Sadat, at the other end, wanted to know how things had gone with the Arab foreign ministers. I replied that it had all gone off well, adding that I had sent him a memorandum on the subject, He replied: "By the way, Mohamed, Ezer Weizman cabled me (through the Israeli mission), asking if he could come to Cairo, and I replied in the affirmative."

In utter amazement, I shot back: "How could you agree, while the Arab foreign ministers were meeting here and the Israeli army is spreading death and destruction in Lebanon?" I particularly remember the conversation that followed:

Sadat: He must have some important message to convey.
Myself: Why doesn't he send it through the American Embassy or the Israeli station?
Sadat: What do we stand to lose by allowing him to come and listen to what he [Weizman] has to say? No one need know of his coming to Egypt.
Myself: (in a rising temper): We have a lot to lose: he has deliberately chosen to visit Egypt now, when the Arab foreign ministers are convening here, in an obvious attempt to ruin all chances of an Arab rapproachment with Egypt. If you insist on not cancelling his visit, then his arrival must be made public. My dealings with people are based on confidence, and I am not prepared to destroy the reputation I have built up and maintained all my life.
Sadat: (angrily) Of course I shall announce his arrival; I never deal under-handedly, and I fear no one.

As I once more sought temporarily to persuade him to cancel the visit or at least postpone it, Sadat replied: "You don't understand. Weizman is my friend." At this I exploded with: "You appear to forget he's a member of the

An Unexpected Stab in the Back!

Hirut Party. I have before me now statements made by Weizman a few days ago to an American television network to the effect that he is in total agreement with Menahim Begin's line. Yet you still say he's your friend! May God damn him and his father too!"

Before he slammed the receiver down, I heard him mutter in anger: "All right, Mohamed effendi, all right!"

In the car taking us to the Barrage rest-house I conversed with Prince Saud El Faisal. I had regained my calm and was in two minds as to whether I should inform him of Weizman's visit. I finally decided against doing so, in the hope that I could succeed in persuading the President to cancel the visit and avoid a furore.

A few moments after we had entered one of the rest-house reception-rooms, we were joined by President Sadat. After greeting us, he lapsed into one of his silences, seemingly distracted. Finally, addressing the Prince: "I am happy that you have at last met Mohamed Kamel. I hope your relationship will be one of fraternal co-operation." To this the Prince replied that this was already the case, and he looked forward to a close relationship with me. I spoke in similar vein, and the ensuing silence was broken by the Prince, who conveyed to President Sadat the greetings and best wishes of King Khaled and Prince Fahd respectively. Sadat, in turn, asked him to convey his best wishes to them, and ventured to enquire about sundry other princes, among them Prince Sultan and Prince Turk. . . Prince Saud assured him of their well-being. For the third time there was a pause, which was broken when I undertook to review, in summary form, the developments that had occurred during the Council meeting, interspersing my account with some amusing incidents that had occurred. When I had done, there was another silence, which was broken by the President suddenly turning to the Prince to inform him that Weizman, Israel's Defence Minister, had asked him to come to Cairo for an audience with him (Sadat), and that he (Sadat) had accepted. The President went on to say that Weizman was the only person in the Israeli team with whom he could communicate. Sadat added that he believed Weizman carried news of some change in Israel's intransigent position, and he would listen to what he had to say and then decide on the action to be taken in the light of this meeting.

The Prince stared at me in utter amazement, but without vouchsafing a single comment. Sadat continued to speak, expressing his confidence in the success of his initiative, despite the obstacles being raised by Begin as a result of his (Begin's) inflexible mentality and expansionist ambitions. Begin, said Sadat, would be compelled to retreat in the face of international pressures, particularly those exercised by the United States and those from within Israel itself. Once again, the President asked the Prince to convey his greetings and best wishes to King Khaled and members of the Royal Family, whereupon the meeting came to an end.

Prince Faisal kept firing questions at me on our way back, and these seemed to be aimed impartially at both of us. Why, he wanted to know, was Sadat doing this, and at this particular juncture, when the Arab foreign ministers were in Cairo? Why was he not providing an opportunity for the restoration of the Arab solidarity they were all doing their utmost to salvage? And if there was, indeed, anything to be gained by receiving Weizman, was this opportune while the Israeli army was invading Lebanon? And so on and so forth... I assured him that I agreed with him entirely, and that I had informed Sadat of what I thought. I told him of the altercation between us over the phone. Sadat, I further assured him, had intended no harm, perhaps deeming that nothing would be lost by such a meeting. It was, I said, even possible that he hoped to persuade Weizman to withdraw his forces from Lebanon or get him to modify Israel's position, etc... Before we reached the Hilton Hotel, Prince Faisal asked me whether I thought he should cable King Khaled and request him to send President Sadat an urgent message asking him to refrain from receiving Weizman in Cairo. I at once gave him my whole-hearted approval, while promising him that I, for my part, would again raise the subject with the President.

In the evening, I gave a dinner in honour of the Arab foreign ministers, ambassadors and Arab League officials, on the occasion of the conclusion of the Arab League council meetings, at which I spoke, after I had laughingly asked their leave to deliver my address in colloquial Egyptian dialect, and so avoid making any grammatical blunders before an audience made up of the masters of the Arabic classical language. It was a short and succinct speech in which I stressed anew Egypt's determination to bring about a total Israeli withdrawal from all the occupied Arab territories and the restitution of the legitimate rights of the Palestinian people. I likewise underscored our keen interest in the maintenance of Arab solidarity, pointing out that Egypt welcomed all efforts aimed at eliminating any misunderstanding that may have arisen between Egypt and its sister Arab states.

The Arab foreign ministers began leaving for home the following morning, 29 March, and the arrival of the Israeli Defence Minister was announced the same evening.

Two days later, President Sadat called me on the telephone and informed me that Weizman had told him nothing new during their meeting and that he (Sadat) had requested him just before he left to inform Menahim Begin that he (Sadat) had received no positive reply from him concerning the peace initiative. The President also informed him that Egypt was not seeking a separate or partial agreement but a comprehensive peace based upon Israel's complete withdrawal from the occupied Arab territories.

I had no reason to disbelieve Sadat.

Chapter Nineteen

The Unadorned Story As Seen From The Other Side

Three years elapsed before I had any certain knowledge of the Sadat-Weizman meetings on 30 and 31 March. I had had only Sadat's version to go on. In 1981 a friend sent me a copy of Weizman's book, *The Battle for Peace*, published in March that year.

How I wished Weizman had not written this book, or had, at least, omitted to refer to the discussion that had taken place between himself and the President in the course of the said visit! How I wished that the book had not fallen into my hands, and that I had not read it! The book aroused in me feelings of bitterness, for I felt I had been deceived, nay, stabbed in the back, I felt bitter that the sincere and honest efforts that I, together with my colleagues, had exerted, at the expense of our nerves and health, to provide Sadat, or, more precisely, to provide our country and cause, with what we believed was a stronger negotiating position to ensure the success of the initiative had gone with the wind.

After reading Weizman's book, I recalled George Orwell's *Animal Farm*, and was reminded of the character of Comrade Napoleon, the pig, and that of Boxer, the horse. I trust my modesty will not be impaired if I say that I consider myself more intelligent – and less innocent – than Boxer. It was, perhaps, my perusal of Weizman's book that induced me to start recording my experiences: hence this book.

At the outset, I should like to confess that I cannot be definite as to which of the two following versions is correct: Sadat had informed me that Weizman had contacted him and requested to come to Cairo, while Weizman, in his book, says the opposite, namely, that it was Sadat who sent for him. This means that one of them was not telling the truth. As for what passed at the meeting, which was indubitably of a very serious nature, nothing had been conveyed to me other than that recorded at the end of the last chapter, namely that Sadat had informed Weizman that he was not seeking a partial or separate settlement. Consequently, the version as recounted by Weizman in his book on the subject is the only other version available to us, but I cannot vouch for its authenticity.

Wrote Weizman:

> A coded cable transmitted by our Zahava station in Cairo rekindled the flame. My colleagues at GHQ at the Defence Ministry saw no prospect of the peace talks being renewed as long as our forces were engaged in active operations in Lebanon, but the top secret cable confounded all our predictions: the Egyptian president was asking me to come and meet him on 30 March 1978.[1]

Weizman expressed his great satisfaction at receiving the cable and immediately passed it on to Prime Minister Begin who, in turn, convoked the Israeli cabinet for consultations on the matter. Weizman goes on to say:

> At the time of Sadat's coded cable to me, Cairo was packed with Arab foreign ministers gathering for an Arab League conference. An invitation to Israel's defence minister, while Israeli forces were stationed on Lebanese soil, was an open challenge to the Arab world.

Weizman added that he informed the Israeli cabinet of the delicacy of the matter, and that the Egyptians had demanded (in their cable) that no announcement be made prior to the visit. Weizman furthermore asked for a cabinet briefing as to the points he should raise with the Egyptians, and Begin's reply was: "The Defence Minister should say there is no party in Israel that will consent to dismantle the settlements. What you Egyptians want is total withdrawal and the establishment of a Palestinian state. Tell them: 'Both are unacceptable. Are you prepared to adopt any other terms?'" Weizman also says that the Minister of Trade and Industry, Yigal Horowitz, declared during the meeting:

> Ezer has been invited to Cairo, because they imagine him to be closest to them. He should tell Sadat to find a formula which does not take us back to the 1967 borders. . . after the Prime Minister's visit to the United States, and with Carter taking sides with Egypt, Sadat's mood is sky-high, and his eyes are in the clouds. His self-confidence will grow unless someone restores him to sanity.

Finally, the Israeli cabinet gave its approval to Weizman's departure for Cairo, provided he was accompanied by Aharon Barak, the cabinet's legal adviser.

Weizman notes that television cameras were there to receive him at the airport and again upon his arrival at Sadat's retreat, indicating the President's intent to pursue his peace efforts despite the embarrassing position in which he and his country found themselves as a result of the Israeli military offensive against Lebanon. He remarks that the President shook hands with him warmly, saying:

I welcome the Defence Minister and rejoice at his arrival. You should
know there was opposition to your coming here. King Khaled of Saudi
Arabia was against your doing so, and my own Foreign Minister was
also against it. But I wanted to see you.

Weizman later says that he sensed the difficulties with which the President was surrounded, arising both from the Arab states' attitude and on the domestic front. Opposition parties had begun to step up their attacks against the peace talks, and there had been some attempts by students to stage protest demonstrations against them. Weizman adds that the most serious opposition, as far as both Sadat and Israel were concerned, was that deriving from the Egyptian Foreign Ministry. The Israelis had taken stock of this attitude ever since the Ismailia meeting, where the Foreign Ministry men demonstrated "inflexibility" by insisting that no peace could be achieved unless a solution was sought to the Palestinian problem.

Weizman subsequently proceeds to recount the discussions that took place between himself and the President as they sat under a sycamore at the Barrage rest-house. He writes that:

Summarizing my conversation with Sadat put me in a better mood.
Like us, the Egyptian President was not interested in a Palestinian
state. He was willing to leave our West Bank settlements in place: he
would substitute for Hussein should the king refuse to take part in the
negotiations. I was gratified to have had Aharon Barak listening in on
our conversation. Without his testimony, no one in Israel would
believe me.

Weizman also notes that the Secretary-General of the ruling party, Dr Mustapha Khalil, Dr Boutros Ghali and Gamassy visited him later that evening at the El Tahera Palace where he was staying, and he goes on:

Professor Barak and War Minister Gamassy conducted a fruitful
exchange. They withdrew for a long conversation in the course of
which Gamassy proposed secret talks between our two countries to be
held in Egypt, Israel or anywhere else. If the sides so desired the
Americans could be brought in, he said. The aim of the talks would be
to work out the details of the arrangements for the West Bank and
Gaza and of the bilateral relations between Israel and Egypt. On the
conclusion of the talks, two documents would be initialled – in secret.
   The document detailing the arrangements in the West Bank and Gaza
would include a declaration of intent. From an Egyptian viewpoint,
there would have to be an Israeli proclamation of willingness to
withdraw from the West Bank and Gaza – other than those points our
forces would continue to occupy for security reasons, such as our

Camp David

settlements along the Jordan River, or on the tops of the mountain ridges. Sadat would then announce that Israel and Egypt had agreed on a Declaration of Intent and go on to invite the confrontation states to enter into negotiations on a bilateral basis. He would wait a few weeks, after that, he would sign a peace agreement with Israel with regard to the Sinai. If Jordan came into the picture, Hussein would handle Judea, Samaria and Gaza. If Hussein refused to take part in the negotiations, Sadat would enter in his place and sign an agreement to cover the West Bank and Gaza.

Under the agreement, the existing settlements would remain. Settlement would be permitted to continue on private land purchased by Jews. A solution was also to be sought for state lands, which would be made available for Jews to buy. The Israeli army would be stationed in agreed upon bases, such as those along the Jordan, in the settlements and at other points. Should there be any PLO activity in the West Bank and Gaza, the Israeli army would have a free hand to take care of the terrorists. The settlements in the Sinai could remain under Egyptian sovereignty. The inhabitants would become Egyptian citizens and could not enjoy the protection of the Israeli army.

Weizman observes on that occasion that he had reason to rejoice, and says he intended to stress, in his report to the Israeli cabinet, that immense progress had been achieved. The following morning, 31 March, as he was preparing to leave for Israel, Weizman received an urgent telephone call from General Gamassy, summoning him to the Barrage to meet President Sadat. When he saw Sadat, Weizman noted his extreme tenseness as he told him:

> After Carter's meeting with Begin, Carter asked me if I insisted on a Palestinian state. I gave the matter a great deal of thought, and my cogitations lead me to make the far-reaching proposal I put forward yesterday. After meeting with you, I had a meeting last night with Palestinian representatives from Gaza. They did not accept my ideas. They want self-determination. At this juncture, Palestinian support is important to us. In view of their opposition, I cannot say that my plan of yesterday is in force.
>
> We have a problem, I know my limitations, and I will not propose anything I am unable to carry out. But when I make an offer, I stick to it. Now, in view of the opposition of the Palestinians, I don't know if I can stick to it. Therefore I return to the position existing prior to yesterday: Begin must display flexibiltiy; I don't demand a Palestinian state – only a link with Jordan. A link with Jordan implies that there is no Palestinian state. That was my view before the peace initiative. That is my view now. There will be a plebiscite. . .

At this point, Weizman interrupted him, saying:

> A plebiscite is unacceptable to us. Let us go back to our talk of yesterday and my proposal that we conclude a peace treaty as the first stage. You are a courageous man. You expelled the Russians, you launched the peace initiative, and you should have the courage to bring it to a conclusion.

Weizman comments on the event and indicates that the sudden change in President's stand was extremely deplorable and justified his critics' accusations of his instability and retreating from the fulfilment of pledges previously made.

President Sadat appeared to be assuming a new role, that of the dual personality of Dr Jekyll and Mr Hyde – but was it only a part he assumed?

If there is one thing I regret, it is that Weizman did not reveal this discussion immediately upon the termination of his visit, instead of recording it three years later in his book. I would then have resigned my post as Foreign Minister, and he would have spared me the long hours, days and months of suffering I endured up to the Camp David conference.

Footnotes

1   E. Weizman, *The Battle for Peace*, p. 289.

Chapter Twenty

A Pause for Reflection

Events were developing at such a fast pace, that the time had come for a pause for reflection. I felt that the developments in the situation from Sadat's visit to Jerusalem until Israel's invasion of Southern Lebanon needed to be assessed in order and put into their proper perspective and that there was need to draw guidelines for our strategy in the days ahead in the light of this assessment. I therefore, together with a number of collaborators, applied myself to this task. On 18 March 1978 I submitted to Sadat a memorandum entitled "Observations on the current political situation".

The memo contained in its introductory part a description of certain manifestations prevailing in the area among which were:

1. Israeli intransigence together with attempts to waylay the positive effects of the Egyptian peace initiative culminating in the invasion of Lebanon.
2. The differences in the Arab world highlighted by fierce press campaigns allowing Israel to entrench itself deeper in its positions and thus discouraging the United States from exerting necessary pressure on Israel.
3. The feeling among many Afro-Asian countries of Egypt's increased dependence on the United States, and that Egypt sometimes adopts positions on certain issues which cause smaller countries concern (the conflict with Libya; the Somali-Ethiopian conflict; the situation in Chad; the incident in Larnarka, etc.).
4. The provocative tone of the Egyptian media and sometimes wavering attitudes towards certain issues.

The memo proceeded to suggest that we should be acting in the following domains:

- The internal situation.
- Arab unity.
- Diversification of our international relations.

A Pause for Reflection

On the internal situation it was stressed that the government should be more vigilant in satisfying the basic needs of the people and that a frank dialogue between government and people should be established.

On Arab unity, the memo underlined the following:

1 Though Egypt, with its potential, is in a position to exert influence, Arab solidarity would enhance that position even more, the Arab world being Egypt's *espace vitale*. Accordingly, we should strive to uphold Arab unity if only at present at the lowest common denominator. It was noted that Egypt should always maintain its leading role in the Arab world without arousing too many susceptibilities.
2 The polarization within the Arab world engenders many dangers, chiefly that it would open the doors wide to foreign intervention particularly that of the superpowers and would allow those forces that seek Egypt's isolation from its natural allies to succeed.
3 It would seem advisable to gradually restore Arab unity using the good offices of moderate Arab countries with a view of re-establishing diplomatic relations with those countries, with whom relations were severed.
4 It is to be noted that the differences we have with the Arab states arise from differences in approach and not in the objectives.
5 That Syria-Libya and the Palestinians are important allies whose security is closely linked to ours and can constitute through co-operation and co-ordination a force to be contended with. But several factors should be taken into consideration:

SYRIA

It should be realized that Syria needs the support of Egypt whether in war or peace but is constrained by:

- The pressure of the Ba'ath Party in Iraq.
- Its involvement in Lebanon.
- The pressure of certain Palestinian elements.
- The fear of military takeover.
- The fear that Egypt would leave it to face Israel alone.

In view of the fact that Sadat's initiative is widely accepted, time has come to enter into exploratory talks towards restoring relations.

LIBYA

Libya and Sudan represent the national extension of Egypt. The integration of the three countries where human resources, wealth and agricultural land abound would create a formidable new power. In view of the presence of a large Egyptian community in Libya, notwithstanding the severance of relations, it might be deemed appropriate to explore the possibility of opening a diplomatic office as a first step towards improvement of relations. The contacts could be undertaken through the Sudan or directly with the Libyan representative of the Arab League.

It is not in our interest to leave Libya exposed to Soviet influence. Furthermore it should be noted that Libya is seeking to obtain technical expertise from other sources (Jordan and Turkey). It is possible to find a formula making it possible to co-exist with Gadaffi.

THE PALESTINIANS

The Palestinian problem is part and parcel of Egypt's national security, while Israel would remain Egypt's main foe even were a peaceful settlement reached. The consolidation of Palestinian positions becomes therefore a national duty. Desperate actions on the part of the Palestinians as a result of their feelings of despair and frustration should not in any way influence our attitude towards them. Our determination to support the PLO should act as a counter balance to Israel's adamant refusal for the right of self-determination to the Palestinians.

6 Egypt has contributed immensely to the welfare of the Arab nation, yet that contribution should not be presented as having been made grudgingly, for that would entail both resentment on the part of the Arabs and abhorrence by the Egyptians of anything Arab. The net result would be the isolation of Egypt from the area of its immediate concern in a world symphonized by big military and political groupings and at a time when Egypt is in dire need of the full support of the Arab nation to enable it to face confidently the challenge of peace.

On the diversification of our international relations, the memo defined the objectives of diversification in the following:

– Avoiding polarization.
– Increasing the circle of international support for our positions thereby isolating Israel.
– Gaining new international grounds in addition to those previously obtained.
 And to this end it was incumbent upon us to:
1 Establish a balance in the relations with the two superpowers.
 In this regard it was imperative to introduce some warmth in our relations with the Soviet Bloc, especially since the Soviet Union has

expressed an interest in reactivating Soviet-Egyptian relations. We should respond positively to this *démarche* in view of:
- The eventual role that the Soviet Union would be playing in any settlement of the Middle East problem.
- The past support of the Soviet Union for Arab positions, militarily and politically.
- The presence of the Soviet Union in Africa and the Arab world.
- To act as a deterrent to Soviet attempts at isolating Egypt in the Arab world and to interfere in its domestic affairs.
- To use the improvement of relations with the Soviet Union as leverage with the United States.

The first step would be the return of the Egyptian Ambassador to Moscow.

2   EGYPT AND AFRICA

The African continent has always been a dominant factor in the elaboration of Egyptian foreign policy. Yet in recent years Egypt's prominent position in Africa has suffered a setback in favour of Algeria and Libya. It is still not too late to restore our position to its former prominence. It would be opportune to restate our adherence to certain principles to which African states are particularly attached, i.e.

- Respect for existing international borders and rejection of secessionist movements.
- Strict adherence to non-intervention in the internal affairs of African states while underlining our readiness to offer our good offices in the settlement of disputes should they be requested.
- Combating apartheid and racial discrimination and support for the liberation movements in Southern Africa.
- Consolidation of Afro-Arab co-operation.
- Resistance to all foreign interventions in Africa.

3   EGYPT AND THE NON-ALIGNED MOVEMENT

As a result of the restoration of the balance in our relations with the two superpowers, Egypt's position within the non-aligned movement would be enhanced, yet that should be supplemented by extensive contacts and visits to the various members of the movement in Africa, Asia and Latin America.

4   EGYPT AND EUROPE

Although the Egyptian policy has achieved substantial success in Western Europe, that policy requires a sustained follow-up, first to ensure the economic involvement of Western Europe through increased investments and technical co-operation, and second to make use of Western Europe's political clout as a back step to American efforts in search of peace in the Middle East.

The memo concluded by stressing once more that despite all our sincere efforts towards the establishment of a just and lasting peace, Israel was still maintaining an intransigent posture which was acting as a stumbling-block to all the peace efforts. There was a need, therefore, for Egypt to move on all fronts as indicated in the memo. Only thus would Egypt possess the necessary strength to confront Israel, which experience has shown will listen to the voice of reason only if it is faced with corresponding strength.

Chapter Twenty One

Towards Implementing The Scenario

When President Sadat returned from his visit to the United States in February 1978, Washington began the first steps towards implementing the initial phases of the scenario agreed upon between the Egyptian and American sides at Camp David. President Jimmy Carter invited the Israeli Prime Minister to visit Washington. The visit was timed to take place at the beginning of March, but events in Lebanon caused it to be put off until 21 March. In inviting Begin, President Carter set out to influence the Israeli Premier and urge him to transform Israel's negative attitude into a more positive one so as to allow a resumption of direct negotiations between Egypt and Israel. Egypt, as I have earlier pointed out, had adopted a firm position during the Camp David talks, and had emphasized that it would on no account resume negotiations with Israel unless the latter came forward with a more positive attitude, and the United States had pledged to do what it could to that effect.

There can be no doubt that the American side – and in particular President Carter and his Secretary of State, Cyrus Vance – exerted sincere efforts to bring about a change in the Israeli position. In their talks with Israel's Prime Minister and Foreign Minister, the Americans adhered to the principles inherent in the White House statement issued on 8 February, following President Sadat's visit. This statement called for the implementation of Resolution 242 and indicated that its withdrawal provisions applied to all fronts. In so doing, the administration's purpose was to stress that Resolution 242 called for withdrawal not only from the Sinai and Golan Heights, but also from the West Bank and Gaza – a move the Begin government sought to evade by every means. In its statement, the American administration likewise pointed out that it was committed to the search for an overall solution to the Palestinian problem based upon ensuring the legitimate rights of the Palestinian people. It also called for the Palestinians to participate in the determination of their own future along the lines of the Carter formula, better known as the "Aswan Formula". In conclusion, the statement indicated the illegality of the settlements in the occupied territories and considered them an obstacle to peace.

Camp David

I have earlier referred to Secretary of State Vance's attack on the settlements (10 February), and the fact that he had called for their removal at a press conference. President Carter, too, took some steps that aroused Israel's ire: meeting the leaders of Jewish organizations in the United States, and acquainting them with the intransigence of the Israeli position and the obstacles Israel was raising with regard to the peace process. In so doing, he won over these leaders and convinced them that Israel was deliberately seeking to thwart the opportunity for peace created by the Sadat peace initiative. He also spoke to the Senate and Congress Foreign Relations Committees, winning the sympathy of many senators and congressmen. In his book[1] Dayan says:

> The most important event that afternoon, however, would be the President's appearance before the first of the committees. What would he say, and how would he say it? We were very apprehensive. And we soon felt we had good cause to be. Shortly after we left the White House, the information apparatus of the State Department and the White House went into high gear. Our position was presented adversely, with Israel shown as obdurate and recalcitrant, rejecting proposals that could bring about peace. The American press tended to follow the US government's view, and even Israel's friends in the House and the Senate, Jews and non-Jews, supported the President in his praise of Sadat and criticism of Israel. Relations between Carter and Begin were very strained.

The endeavours of Vance and Dayan to reach a Declaration of Principles on the Palestinian question had failed.

In April 1978, Dayan returned to Washington again at the invitation of Cyrus Vance for talks on the future of the West Bank and Gaza – or, in other words, the future of the Palestinian people. The position adopted by Irsael was that it was prepared to implement the autonomy project brought to Ismailia by Begin which Egypt had rejected. The United States considered the project a convenient starting-point for preliminary negotiations. The Israeli project called for a five-year transitional period, during which Palestinian administrative autonomy would be established under Israel's political and military authority, and under which no party was entitled to claim sovereignty over the West Bank and the Gaza Strip.

It is clear that Israel was demanding the suspension of the sovereignty issue during the transitional period, both for lack of any legal grounds to that claim and to create a *fait accompli* on the ground which would make negotiations on security irrelevant.

On the other hand, it was possible for Jordan to claim sovereignty over these territories on the grounds that they were part of it since it annexed them in 1948. If any party had the right to dispute Jordanian sovereignty over them, it was the Palestinians themselves. Israel had no right whatsoever. Jordanian sovereignty over the West Bank would in no way detract from Israel's sovereignty over the territories it annexed outside those specified for it in the United Nations General Assembly Resolution of 1947 that created the Jewish state. Therefore the undisputed right to sovereignty over the West Bank and Gaza belonged to the Palestinians by virtue of the aforementioned resolution, which allotted them this territory by the same instrument which set up the Jewish state.

Thus the suspension of the sovereignty issue during the five-year transitional period was designed to give Israel the time to stengthen its grip on the West Bank and Gaza as a prelude to their prospective annexation.

Let me again return to the talks that took place between the American Secretary of State and the Israeli Foreign Minister in connection with the future of the West Bank and Gaza. Vance sought vainly for a clear-cut answer on this from Dayan, who evaded the issue by indicating that any reply at present was premature, and that any party could raise it in five years' time.[2]

Israel's covert intentions, however, were not lost on the intelligent Vance, and he concluded the talks by addressing two questions to the Israeli government:

1 Was Israel prepared to pledge that the sovereignty issue would be discussed at the end of the five-year transitional period? And...
2 if so, how would Israel envisage dealing with it?

The Israeli government put off its reply for weeks on end, before finally giving its answer on 18 June 1978. The reply – if it can be considered as such – affirmed that after a local administrative government in "Judea", "Samaria" and Gaza had been in being for five years, the Israeli government would agree to consider the nature of future relations with any party wishing to raise the issue. The reply further stated that any agreement had to be reached through negotiations between the parties themselves, with the participation of the representatives of the territory elected according to the local system of government.

Even the United States, Israel's sympathetic friend, failed to understand the Israeli reply, which some United States' officials considered "no reply at all".

President Sadat was happy and sanguine as the tension rose between the United States and Israel, for it was undoubtedly the result of his successful negotiations in the United States. We at the Foreign Ministry viewed the Israeli-American differences with cautious and wary satisfaction. We were not blind to the fact that the battle for peace would be a long one. Neither were we unaware of the Zionist influence in the United States and Israel's ability to overcome any differences with America, particularly in view of

Camp David

President Carter's need of the Jewish lobby's support for the Panama Treaty and his energy programme, both of which were meeting with strong opposition. Moreover, the Congress elections of November 1978 were imminent, and Israel was an old hand at exploiting those events through its Jewish organizations.

Again, the Israeli-American differences caused another important factor to come into play in our favour, in that it gave us more time to enhance our negotiating position. We could continue to eschew direct bilateral negotiations with Israel, leaving the United States to pressure Israel into changing its attitude, while we made it clear that the door to peace remained open.

Meanwhile, President Carter, for his part, appeared to be moving to implement the scenario agreed upon at Camp David in February between Egypt and the United States.

If Washington intended to come up with new ideas for a settlement, then Egypt had to start co-ordinating its activities with the US to ensure that such ideas were suited to the Egyptian position before they assumed final form.

Dr Ghorbal, our ambassador in Washington, sent us a nine-point paper containing American preliminary views on a prospective paper that could form a basis for a United States project to be presented after Egypt had put forward its project on the West Bank and Gaza, as agreed at Camp David in February.

When Atherton arrived in Cairo on 20 April I met him and Eilts at the Ministry and he read out to me the nine points. I told him that, although they contained some positive aspects, the points had been formulated with Begin's Autonomy Project, as presented at Ismailia, in the background. I informed him that we completely rejected the Begin project, adding that the ideas contained in the nine points were far removed from anything we could accept, nor did they measure up to our expectations with regard to a United States project. Atherton replied that the paper on the West Bank and Gaza which Egypt had presented to the United States in March when he had last visited Cairo – was, from the American viewpoint, a satisfactory basis for negotiations of a very general character. But it was not sufficiently detailed, notably as regards the security aspects.

The aforementioned Egyptian project had called for an Israeli withdrawal from the West Bank and Gaza and for the enforcement of safeguards guaranteeing the security of all parties. However they (the Americans) had drawn largely on the Begin project, which was rich in details.

Atherton urged us to come forward with a more detailed project, especially concerning security safeguards. I informed him that we would give the matter consideration, but added that I wished to stress two essential points, which were:

1 That the essence of any American project should not be based upon a compromise or middle way between an Egyptian and an Israeli

Towards Implementing The Scenario

project, and they should totally rule out any mixture of the two projects, since this would only lead to failure. I also indicated that any American project should be based on the United States' officially declared positions at the United Nations, notably:
- The application of the withdrawal provision of Resolution 242 to all the occupied territories, with the exception of some minor modifications of the demarcation line in the West Bank.
- A reaffirmation of America's non-recognition of the Israeli decision to annex Jerusalem.
- Adherence to General Assembly Resolution 194 relating to the right of return and compensation of refugees of the 1948 War, which the US had voted in favour of over the years.
- The settlement of all aspects of the Palestinian problem on the basis of the legitimate rights of the Palestinian people, including their right to self-determination according to the formula announced by President Carter in January 1978.
- The American position on the illegality of the Israeli settlements established on occupied territories should be underlined.

This meant that the United States project, when presented, should reflect previous pledges by the United States as a big power that respected its declared position.

2 The United States should discuss its project with Egypt before presenting it.

Atherton replied that the first point was logical and difficult to reject. As to the second point, he promised that the project would be shown to us before it was presented.

President Sadat fixed an appointment for Atherton in Hordaga, on the Red Sea, for the afternoon of 22 April. Sadat was staying at one of the bungalows of the Sheraton Hotel. I left for Hordaga by air in the early morning in the company of Ambassadors Ussama El Baz and Ahmed Maher.

I went to see the President at 9 a.m. Vice-President Mubarak was with him. The President seemed relaxed and receptive, and I seized the opportunity to suggest to him that he approve the appointment of Mr Mohamed Riad, former Minister of State for Foreign Affairs, to the post of Assistant Secretary-General of the Arab League (Sadat considered him as having resigned from his former post when Riad displayed reluctance to accompany him to Jerusalem on November 1977 following the resignation of Ismail Fahmy, the Foreign Minister). The Secretary-General, Mr Mahmoud Riad, had asked me to speak to the President. The term of office of Sayid Nofal,[3] the Assistant Secretary-General, was due to expire soon, and the Secretary-

General did not wish to renew his term of office. After a moment's hesitation, Sadat agreed. I then put before the President the nine points Atherton had conveyed to me and was to submit to him at their meeting. I let him have my initial reaction to them. I told him that in my opinion the American project should hold to the declared American positions on the various aspects of the Middle East problem. I impressed on him the need to make the point to Atherton that the United States should consult with us prior to the presentation of any project. I likewise handed him a memo containing our comments on the nine points.

I strolled down to the beach. It was a bright and sunny day, with a fresh breeze. Total silence reigned here, broken only by the sound of the wavelets lapping at the sand in an endless, mystic threnody. The sea stretched away as far as the eye could see, a beautiful carpet of blue, sprinkled with fishing-boats. I took off coat, tie and shoes and walked along the edge of the beach, where the waves pressed forward to kiss the sands, retreating only to return again and again, never-ending, eternally indifferent to the misery and strife in this vale of tears.

For the first time since I assumed the post of Foreign Minister, I was overwhelmed with joy and happiness, a world away from papers, discussions, telephones and meetings. I went back in memory to the past, with its weave of bitter and sweet. And here was I, free for the nonce, enjoying my liberty, untrammelled by the grave responsibilities thrust upon me that were not of my own choosing. They had come to dominate my thoughts, these responsibilities, devouring all my time, feeding on my health and shattering my nerves. . .

Two hours slid by, and I became conscious of time only when I was summoned to attend the meeting between Atherton and the President.

The meeting was attended by Atherton, and the US Ambassador, Eilts, on the American side, and by Ambassadors Ussama El Baz and Ahmed Maher on the Egyptian side. Atherton advanced the American points successively. President Sadat would then comment on each, and after consulting with me would, perhaps, tell Atherton to delete this point or that, or that such and such a text or formula be amended.

Atherton explained that the nine points were no more than a general, preliminary conception. They had put them to us to get our reaction. Their main objective was to determine clearly the future of the West Bank and Gaza following the five-year transitional period which Israel was seeking to side track.

And so the meeting proceeded, in a pleasant and constructive atmosphere, and when it drew to a close, Sadat addressed to Atherton the importance of first submitting any American project to us for consultation and co-ordination before its final presentation, making it quite clear to him that it would be preferable for the United States to abstain from submitting any project whatsoever rather than submit one which might harm the Arab

Towards Implementing The Scenario

cause, place us in an embarrassing position and affect the United States position in the Arab world generally. Atherton promised to submit all projects to us, and he agreed with the President on the damage that could be done by submitting any project which failed to take into account the basic requirements needed in any solution to the Arab-Israeli conflict.

Upon our return to Cairo, I charged three of the Egyptian working group, namely Ambassadors Ussama El Baz, Abdel Raouf Al Ridi (Director of the Foreign Ministry's Planning Department) and Ahmed Maher El Sayid, to meet with Mr Atherton and his asides to discuss in detail the technical and legal aspects and the formulae relating to the points discussed at Hordaga between the US envoy Atherton and the President. Accordingly, the two groups held two meetings on 23 and 24 April. The Egyptian side had, right from the start of the meeting, laid great stress on the technical nature of the discussion, so that we might not be bound by any results that might be reached. The discussions were friendly and the Egyptian team succeeded in putting over its views to the Americans most of the time. The Americans promised to take our observations and comments into consideration when preparing their projects. And a memorandum was submitted to the President on the topics both sides had dealt with.

On 23 April, President Sadat sent President Carter a letter via Atherton as he returned to Washington. In the letter, President Sadat indicated that:

> I had a very extensive talk with Ambassador Atherton on which he will fully report to you. He has acquainted us with the points reflecting the general line of your government's thoughts on the West Bank and Gaza. I would like to tell you, in the spirit of frankness and friendship prevailing between us, that such an American proposal would complicate matters for us and have negative reflections in the Arab world. Instead of contributing to enlarge the scope of negotiations and encouraged other parties to join in and abandon their attitude of wait and see, it would encourage countries like Saudi Arabia to take a negative attitude and would give ammunition to those who try to sabotage our peace efforts.
>
> Since I understand from Ambassador Atherton that these ideas reflect the fact that the only plan officially tabled is the Begin plan for self rule, I have allowed him to present at the appropriate time to the Israeli side our proposals on the West Bank and Gaza submitted to the US on 6 March 1978. This would perhaps be more appropriately done after the time limit for Congress to object to the arms package has elapsed and after Mr Begin's visit to the United States.
>
> I recognize that our proposals are of a general nature, but you realize that they cannot be more specific as this is the limit of our mandate, since we are not the only Arab party involved in the solution of the Palestinian problem.

Camp David

I think that they will however be sufficient to allow the United
States to work out a compromise plan in conformity with your public
stand on the question, and in particular your Aswan statement.

Egypt and the United States agreed to defer the submission of United States' proposals on the settlement issue to the end of May: there were two major reasons for putting it off. The first was that, by then, Begin's visit to the United States, on the occasion of the thirtieth anniversary of the establishment of the State of Israel would have been completed. Begin was counting on exploiting the emotional atmosphere surrounding such an occasion within the American Jewish community to consolidate his position, which had been shaken among Jewish groups and organizations in the United States. (The American Administration had succeeded in portraying him as the stumbling-block standing in the face of the success of President Sadat's initiative, as I have already explained.) Begin planned to take advantage of favourable atmosphere to pressure the United States administration into overcoming the differences that had arisen between them.

The second reason was to allow some time to elapse in case Congress objected to the United States arms deal with the Saudi Arabia and Egypt.[4]

However, after Atherton's return to Washington and before April was out, there were reports of developments giving us cause for grave concern. These clearly demonstrated the vulnerability of the American administration vis-à-vis the Zionist lobby in the United States.

As I indicated earlier, differences existed between Carter and Begin on many issues. Among them was the scope of application of Resolution 242, which led the United States administration to address their questionnaire to the Israeli government regarding the future of the West Bank and Gaza at the end of the five-year transitional period.

But it seemed that President Carter was seized with alarm at the prospect of Menahim Begin's visit to the United States. Just as Begin arrived in New York and even before he was to meet him at a party held at the White House on that occasion, to which 1200 rabbis and Jewish Readers had been invited, Carter made a statement which was published in the *New York Times* on 30 April 1978. He was quoted as saying: ". . . that the Middle East problem would be solved without the establishment of an independent Palestinian state on the West Bank. The future of the West Bank will be based on the project prepared by Begin granting self-rule to the Palestinian Arabs. A lasting settlement to the Middle East problem [he added] would not require complete withdrawal from the occupied territories," and "that the most important consideration in his policy was – and would continue to be – Israel's security above everything else".

Such statements meant that the United States President was yielding to Israeli pressures at the expense of the Arab rights. It certainly conflicted with recorded American positions since the 1967 War on the settlement of the Arab-Israeli conflict.

The danger of such statements was that Begin would put them on record and later use them against Carter. He would endow them with his own interpretations. Moreover, such statements were at variance with the scenario[5] agreed between Egypt and the United States in Camp David in February 1978. Such statements were more likely to encourage Israel to entrench itself in its former position than to induce a change of heart.

If further proof of Carter's irresoluteness and wavering were needed, those statements provided it. He was caught between his desire to maintain his image as the strong man of principle calling for justice and human rights and the political exigencies of his re-election.

I immediately summoned United States Ambassador Eilts and asked for the full text of the statements published by the *New York Times* and attributed by that paper to President Carter. I demanded clarification of their content. I reaffirmed that Egypt's irreversible position was that the crux of the Middle East problem was to be found in the Palestinian question. Egypt absolutely rejected Begin's autonomy project, which was designed to perpetuate Israeli domination of the West Bank and Gaza. Egypt was of the opinion that the project clearly reflected the expansionist policies of Begin's government and its violation of all principles of international law. The solution of the Palestinian question required complete Israeli withdrawal from all Arab territories occupied in 1967, with the Palestinian people exercising their legitimate right to self-determination.

I informed Ambassador Eilts that Carter's statements indicated that the United States was reneging on their previous proclaimed positions. I likewise told him that such statements ran counter to the scenario which had been agreed upon at Camp David. I pointed out to him that it would be impossible for us to resume negotiations with Israel in view of Carter's statements, which would make Israel even more intransigent. I received the impression from my meeting with Eilts that he was not at all pleased with Carter's statements.

Eilts met me the following day and informed me that the statements attributed to President Carter did not indicate a change in the American position as set forth in the communiqué issued by the White House on 8 February at the end of President Sadat's visit to Washington. He also specifically stressed that the United States did not consider Begin's autonomy project for the West Bank and Gaza a proper basis for a settlement. It did not provide the Palestinian people with the opportunity to participate in determining their future. I told Ambassador Eilts that the Egyptian government would consider the United States clarifications and assurances as conveyed by him and would accordingly decide whether these were sufficient.

I put the matter to President Sadat and suggested that we prepare a

Camp David

strongly worded letter from him to President Carter in this respect. However, he told me that the assurances given by the United States Ambassador to me were sufficient and that there was no need to escalate the matter.

As far as I was concerned, I considered these statements an indication that President Carter could not be entirely relied upon. His statements appeared to reflect the general outlook of American thinking with regard to the settlement of the Middle East problem. I decided to bear this in mind in future.

Footnotes

1 Moshe Dayan, *Breakthrough*, p. 128.
2 Moshe Dayan, *Breakthrough*, p. 133.
3 President Sadat later appointed Sayid Nofal Secretary-General of the League of Islamic Peoples he had thought fit to establish. The Arab states had decided to move Arab League headquarters from Cairo to Tunis in the wake of the Camp David Agreements.
4 The deal included the sale of Phantom F15 aircraft to Saudi Arabia and fifty Phantom F5 aircraft to Egypt, the latter being obsolete models incapable of standing up to modern sophisticated planes. However, President Sadat was interested in pushing the deal through: it would establish the principle of US provision of arms to Egypt. Needless to say, Israel did its level best to prevent the conclusion of the transaction, though its efforts ended in failure.
5 See Chapter XI of this book.

Chapter Twenty Two

Fall-Back Position

Meanwhile, the working party, composed of Ambassadors Ussama El Baz, Nabil El Araby, Director of the Department for Legal Affairs at the Foreign Ministry, Abdel Raouf Al Ridi, Director of the Department of Planning, and Ahmed Maher, completed the project on the West Bank and Gaza Strip. The project was based on the idea suggested by President Sadat in an interview with the *New York Times*. It centred around bringing the West Bank under the administration of Jordan – not as part of Jordan as was the case before 1967 – and the restoration of Egyptian administration to the Gaza Strip (as had been the case prior to 1967) after Israeli withdrawal from both the Bank and the Strip.

Despite my previous reservations about going no further into the Palestinian issue than determining the principles, I was satisfied with the project because it circumvented Israeli arguments on the Palestinian people's right to self-determination. This was a legitimate and inalienable right for the Palestinians which Israel had no ability to grant or deny. When Israeli withdrawal from the West Bank and Gaza was completed, in implementation of Resolution 242, which stipulated the non-admissibility of acquiring territories by force, the Palestinians' control over their future, that is, their self-determination, would become an internal Arab matter. It would be resolved exclusively within an Arab context.

King Hussein had expressed his views at the Arab Summit in Rabat in 1974 on the recognition of the PLO as a legitimate representative of the Palestinian people, but that it should not be the sole representative, in view of the fact that half of Jordan's population was of Palestinian origin. Jordan should be allowed to participate in any international activity or negotiations relative to the implementation of Security Council Resolutions 242 and 338.

King Hussein had stated that "he would work for the accomplishment of an Israeli withdrawal from all the occupied Arab territories, and primarily Jerusalem". As for the West Bank, he pledged that once it was liberated, Jordan would leave its inhabitants the choice of determining the future they wanted in full freedom under neutral international supervision. King

Camp David

Hussein added that discussion of the future of the West Bank was unjustified until it had been freed from the Israeli occupation.[1]

At the beginning of May, I delivered a copy of the project[2] to United States Ambassador Eilts for him to pass on to his government for consideration. It would then be discussed when I went to the United States at the end of that month to attend the Special Session on Disarmament to be held by the United Nations General Assembly in New York.

At about the same time an event took place to which I feel bound to refer, because it shows the simplistic way Sadat dealt with highly complex and dangerous matters.

In the early morning of 3 May I received a telephone call from the Minister for Electricity and Energy to the effect that he would be calling for me in an hour's time, we were to proceed together in his car to Shubra El Kheima to hear the speech President Sadat was delivering on the occasion of Labour Day.

I agreed to this. On the way to the place where the festivities were to be held, the Minister said he wished to broach some urgent business with me. So saying, he opened his briefcase, took out a file and handed it to me. The subject, he confided, concerned the conclusion of an agrement between Egypt and Austria. Under the agreement, Egypt would receive nuclear waste from nuclear reactors in Austria. Egypt would keep and store this waste on its territory. The Minister informed me that there were lime dunes in the area west of the Canal which were appropriate for such a purpose. Egypt, he went on, would acquire valuable technical experience from this operation, which could be of great use to us when we established nuclear reactors in Egypt to meet our energy needs. The urgency stemmed from the fact that other states were doing everything in their power to procure the nuclear waste from Austria. Among such states was Iran. The Shah had offered Austria large sums of money to that end, but Chancellor Kreisky preferred – in view of his friendship with President Anwar El Sadat – to give the material to Egypt free of charge. Austria, he added, would even make a donation of one million Austrian schillings (approximately 50,000 US dollars) to Egypt as a contribution to the establishment of a new hospital. The Minister of Electricity and Energy added that he had put the matter to President Sadat after his recent return from Austria. President Sadat had shown great enthusiasm, had approved the project and had asked him (the Minister) to see to its implementation. He therefore requested me to delegate to him authority, in my quality of Foreign Minister, to sign the agreement with Austria without further delay, lest we lose the deal.

Two days later I met President Sadat. I had various matters to discuss with him. Vice-President Mubarak was present at the meeting. He was then staying at King Mariut in the Western Desert in an area celebrated since the time of the Ancient Egyptians for its dry, refreshing climate. The climate itself being a cure for many chest diseases. Sadat was sojourning in a small rest-house with a beautiful garden, leased by the Egyptian government from its Greek owner.

I raised the subject concerning the nuclear waste with Sadat. I discovered that the Minister had placed the matter before him and that he had, in effect, approved it in principle. I told Sadat I was no expert on such matters. However, I was aware that all Western states faced the problems of storing nuclear waste, and would be greatly relieved to rid themselves of it. Many European peoples, while admitting the need to increase their sources of energy, strongly opposed the establishment of nuclear reactors on their territories. Demonstrations had been staged against the building of nuclear power stations. The whole matter, I told Sadat, was debatable. Nothing required us to expose Egypt's beautiful climate, a God-given gift, to the risk of pollution and the resultant complications. Whatever the technical benefits of the project claimed by the Minister of Electricity, it no doubt would have serious side-effects, which could overshadow any benefits. I pointed out that the Canal area selected by the Minister for the storage of such material was within range of an Israeli attack. Furthermore, the storage of such material might affect navigation in the Canal and the environment of the whole area. Nor could I predict the popular reaction to the idea of Egypt becoming a storehouse for the nuclear waste of a rich state. I concluded by saying I thought we should refrain from taking any steps in that direction before a more thorough study had been carried out. A committee should be created, made up of representatives of the Ministries of Foreign Affairs, Defence, Health, Agriculture, Industry and Irrigation.

The President heard me out, and then said:

Add to the committee you propose the Academy of Technical Research and the Suez Canal Authority. Seek an understanding with Mr Mamdouh Salem, the Prime Minister, on setting up this committee, and then follow up its work. All this is conditional upon the whole business being treated as highly confidential.

I then showed the President a copy of the letter I had sent to Kurt Waldheim, the United Nations Secretary-General, on the serious consequences of the illegal Israeli practices in the occupied Egyptian territories in violation of Egypt's territorial integrity and its permanent sovereignty over its natural resources. Over and above the appropriation of the oil extracted from the occupied territories in Sinai, Israel had recently begun large-scale oil-drilling operations in Eygptian soil and territorial waters. Its impudence was such that it had even drawn an imaginary line down the middle of the Gulf of Suez – which lies entirely inside Egyptian territorial waters – and now considered the Eastern part of the Gulf as falling within its territorial waters in view of its occupation of Sinai! It was preventing Egyptian, and foreign oil companies working in Egypt, from engaging in any activities in

Camp David

the eastern half of the Gulf, and from crossing the said imaginary line. As a result their work was affected and production suffered. The letter concluded by requesting the Secretary-General to inscribe Egypt's complaint against Israeli violation on the agenda of the General Assembly.

I also showed the President a copy of the letter I sent to United States Secretary of State, Cyrus Vance, on the same subject. It demanded that United States' companies undertaking oil drilling and exploration in our occupied territories and territorial waters on behalf of Israel be warned and held fully responsible for such illegal operations.

I had already spoken to the President on that subject which the Egyptian Oil Minister had raised with me. Sadat had then advised that we do not raise the subject just then, lest it affects the talks with Israel. However, I decided as a protective measure to despatch these letters. The President expressed satisfaction at my action and said he would claim compensation from Israel for each drop of oil it appropriated from Sinai and its territorial waters once a settlement was reached.

I then brought up the subject for which I had requested the meeting, namely the opportunity of a visit by me to Saudi Arabia for talks with responsible officials there. I had on several occasions broached the subject with him, but he had always put me off, asking me to defer my visit until a later date. This time I insisted, explaining that the main object of the visit was to persuade Saudi Arabia to take a clearer and more positive stand towards the Egyptian peace efforts. I explained that I would ask the Saudis for a firm declaration of support for the initiative as well as the intensification of their contacts with the United States with a view to pressurizing Israel into adopting positive stands. Saudi Arabia should likewise urge the Hashemite Kingdom of Jordan to participate in the peace efforts. I referred to a statement made in its time by the Saudi Oil Minister, Zaki El Yamany, indicating that Saudi Arabia would cut down oil production and end its support for the US dollar if the aircraft deal did not go through Congress. I hinted that it would be useful to persuade Saudi Arabia to pursue a similar line in endorsing Egypt's peace effort.

At the end, Sadat agreed to the visit, but suggested it be postponed until the Israeli forces had pulled out of Lebanon. I retorted laughingly that were I to do this, the visit would never take place! So he agreed that I should visit Saudi Arabia before my departure for New York to attend the Special Session on Disarmament at the end of May.

I suggested to him once again that he agree to the return of the Egyptian Ambassador to Moscow. He preferred that the matter be placed in abeyance for the time being, but concurred in my suggestion on the reactivation of our stagnating relations with the other East European states. Those ministers heading technical departments such as Industry, Electricity, etc. would accept the invitations already extended to them.

On 7 May, President Gaafar El Numeiry of Sudan arrived in Egypt following a visit to Syria in his capacity as chairman of the Arab Solidarity Committee. President Sadat received him at the King Mariut rest-house. I attended the meeting. President Numeiry gave an account of his Damascus visit and his talks with Syria's President Hafiz El Assad. He disclosed that he (Numeiry) had proposed that he mediate for the resumption of diplomatic relations between Egypt and Syria. He had likewise proposed that Assad agree to take part in an Arab summit conference which would review the present situation and strive for the restoration of Arab solidarity. President Assad had told him he had no objection to either proposal provided President Sadat announced the failure of the peace initiative and the suspension of bilateral contacts with Israel.

Sadat reaffirmed what he had previously indicated – before Numeiry's visit to Damascus – that he was ready to respond to the efforts the Arab Solidarity Committee was exerting for the resumption of diplomatic relations with the states of the Rejectionist Front. Furthermore, he was prepared to participate in an Arab summit conference provided there were adequate preparations for it. However, he (Sadat) could not announce the failure of the initiative for the simple reason that he was convinced of its success. This was becoming increasingly apparent in the change that was taking place in world opinion, which was now more inclined to support the Arab cause. Israel, as a result, was becoming increasingly isolated within the international community.

With respect to announcing the suspension of Egyptian-Israeli bilateral contacts, Sadat indicated that the Egyptian-Israeli talks were virtually suspended in both the political and military committees. However, he could not formally announce the suspension of the talks, since to do so would enable Israel to capitalize on the situation by portraying the initiative as a tactical manoeuvre rather than a genuine offer of peace. The result would be that all the progress made by the initiative in winning over world opinion would be lost.

President Sadat added that, despite this, and in order to allow President Numeiry a better chance to restore Arab solidarity, he (Sadat) pledged himself to ensure that no Israeli-Egyptian talks would be held in either Israel or Egypt. If the need arose for a meeting between Egyptian and Israeli foreign ministers, he would see to it that this took place in a third state, such as Romania.

President Numeiry left shortly afterwards to round off his visits to other Arab states attempting to restore Arab solidarity, in pursuance of the task he had assumed.

On 24 May I flew to Jeddah in Sadat's private Mystère. I was accompanied by Ambassador Ahmed Maher and some of my office staff. We were received at Jeddah airport by the Saudi Foreign Minister, Prince Saud El Faisal, and senior officers at the Foreign Office. The Prince accompanied me to the guest-house. In renewing my acquaintance with the Prince, it was as though I was meeting a brother and an old friend, and I somehow sensed that he felt the same way about me.

After lunch, which we took in the guest-house, I received a call from the Prince to inform me that, to spare me the trouble of going over to the Foreign Ministry, he would himself come to the guest-house to see me.

Prince Saud El Faisal arrived at 4 p.m. My meeting with him lasted for over two hours, and was attended by Ambassador Ahmed Maher. I explained to him the developments since our encounter in Cairo in March. The Prince's main concern was seeking ways and means of stemming the further deterioration of the Arab front and restoring Arab solidarity as soon as possible. This, from the Saudi viewpoint, meant taking steps to put an end to the differences induced by Sadat's initiative. Egypt and Syria, being front-line states, particularly needed to iron out their differences. This would pave the way for an Arab summit which would agree on a plan of action based on the decisions of the 1974 Rabat Summit. The Prince alluded to the fact that the Rabat decisions had not ruled out a peaceful settlement with Israel, provided the latter agreed to withdraw from the occupied Arab territories and recognized the Palestinian people's legitimate right to self-determination.

The Prince said it had become clear to them in Saudi Arabia, as a result of their contacts with the Arab states and President Numeiry's contacts as chairman of the Arab Solidarity Committee, that the obstacle standing in the way of Arab conciliation and the convening of an Arab summit conference was the insistence of the states of the Rejectionist Front, especially Syria, that the convening of the conference should be preceded by a declaration by President Sadat to the effect that the initiative had foundered and pledging himself to terminate Egyptian-Israeli contacts.

Saud El Faisal was convinced that Sadat's initiative would not succeed due to the inflexibility of Israel. He therefore thought it was time for the President to announce the termination of contacts with Israel, rather than proclaim the failure of his initiative as Syria wished. The Prince expressed the belief that the world would understand Egypt's position and the fact that the breaking-off of Egyptian and Israeli contacts resulted from Israeli rejection of a just and comprehensive peace.

The Prince said that once such an announcement was made, the way would be clear for Arab reconciliation and a summit. We would fall back on the Rabat decisions which, as he had pointed out, did not rule out a peaceful settlement.

I replied that I was no less aware than he of the primary importance of eliminating Arab differences and ensuring unity in the Arab ranks to face up to the situation. I referred to the fact that Sadat had announced his readiness to resume diplomatic relations with the Arab states and take part in an Arab summit conference at any time or place. I felt, however, that any statement on breaking-off contacts with Israel would do more harm than good. I

Fall-Back Position

expatiated on the initiative's positive aspects, and alluded to the demonstrations in Israel and the petition three hundred Israeli officers and men from the services had handed to the Israeli Premier indicating their preference for peace to the occupation of other people's land. This, I suggested to him, was a matter of some significance. I likewise referred to the transformation in public opinion throughout the world, especially in the United States. This was reflected in the position of the US government, which had pushed through the aircraft deal concluded with Saudi Arabia and Egypt despite fierce opposition by Israel and the Israeli lobby in the United States.

In effect, contacts between Egypt and Israel had been frozen since Egypt had withdrawn its delegation from the political committee in Jerusalem. Weizman's visit to Cairo had been a mistake that would not be repeated.

Our position at present consisted in refraining from engaging in any negotiations with Israel, as agreed in Washington, until the latter modified its negative attitude. We had thrown upon the United States the burden of inducing Israel into being more forthcoming, and the United States had accepted the task. As a result, the American government undertook to address to the Israeli government some preliminary questions as to the future of the West Bank and Gaza after the termination of the five-year transitional period. This had been done the previous April, placing the Israeli government in a dilemma. No reply had, so far, been received from Israel.

In view of all this, I considered it appropriate to await the Israeli reply, which would be one of two things: either positive, on the future of the Palestinian people, and their right to self-determination, in which case there could be no objection to a resumption of negotiations, with the participation of other Arab states, or (and most probably) negative, which would furnish a pretext for not resuming negotiations with Israel.

I assured him, moreover, that negotiations with Israel would not be resumed in the future, as I had succeeded in convincing President Sadat (this is what I believed at the time). Recent statements by the President were in this vein, stressing as they did that there would be no resumption of negotiations unless Israel relinquished the territories and its claims of sovereignty over them. Once Israel had declared its readiness to do so, negotiations would be restricted to issues on the security of the parties, good neighbourly relations and peace, to which no Arab country could object.

In conclusion, I agreed with him totally that Egyptian-Israeli negotiations had to be halted, unless Israel adopted a positive attitude – a remote possibility – of which there had hitherto been no sign. Egypt, I said, should return to a unified Arab position. The only differences concerned the timing of Egypt's return, and I considered that this should take place when we had been assured that both the people and government of the US were convinced that their protégé, Israel, had refused a just and comprehensive peace and sought to thwart President Sadat's initiative. I laid special emphasis on the United States in that respect, since it constituted Israel's only significant pillar of support, and if it were to decide to withdraw its backing for Israel's illegal occupation of another's territory and Israel's denial of a people's rights, a radical transformation would ensue which would gradually sap Israel's resistance to peace claims. When that point was reached, we could announce the breaking-off of negotiations with Israel without being accused of lack of seriousness in our pursuit of peace. Nobody would be in a position to ask us to continue negotiating with a party that was arrogantly and obdurately proclaiming its intention to retain territory it had forcefully occupied against all accepted norms of international law and behaviour – a party, moreover, which was trying to get us to grant it security and peace while it proceeded to exploit our land and humiliate our people under our very noses with our consent and with complete impunity.

At this juncture, the Saudi role was to prepare for the moment we would announce the termination of negotiations with Israel by paving the way as of now for the restoration of normal Arab relations, and the preparation for an Arab summit in which joint action would be decided on whether at an international conference or by the adoption of a new resolution in the Security Council.

Prince Saud El Faisal wanted to know how much time I thought was needed before the halt to the negotiations was announced, and I replied that, in my view, not more than two or three months, at the utmost, would be necessary. The Prince showed understanding and acceptance of my assessment of the situation, assuring me that he would pursue his contacts personally with the Arab states in his capacity as Foreign Minister and a Member of the Arab Solidarity Committee headed by President Numeiry, so as to clear the way for the holding of an Arab summit conference once Egypt had announced the termination of negotiations with Israel. He asked me to keep in touch with him for consultation and co-ordination prior to the announcement of the Egyptian decision, so that King Khaled and Crown Prince Fahd could make the necessary contacts with the Arab kings and heads of state. Prince Saud El Faisal described the contacts to be undertaken by the King and Crown Prince as the Saudi Kingdom's "heavy artillery".

Our discussions also covered the form of the summit: whether an enlarged or a restricted conference was to be envisaged, confined to the confrontation states, the PLO and Saudi Arabia, together with a few other countries. We left this issue to be decided in the light of further developments. Our discussions likewise dealt with the importance of the Saudi role, in view of its special relationship with the United States. Saudi Arabia could influence the United States into putting pressure on Israel. At this point our meeting ended, and Prince Faisal left. He rang me later to inform me that an appointment had been fixed for me to meet Prince Fahd at 7.00 that evening, and he would stop by and accompany me. I concluded that, after our

Fall-Back Position

meeting, he had met with Prince Fahd and had reported to him the tenor of our discussion.

My meeting with Prince Fahd lasted for approximately half an hour, and was attended by a number of Saudi officials. The discussion centred mainly on the futility of negotiating with Israel, since it was evident that the Israeli government had refused to respond to President Sadat's initiative. The Prince advised that it was useless to continue holding talks that would only result in increased suspicion and Arab disruption, and he added that it was imperative for Arabs to confront Israel as one. Therefore, he observed, Arab differences had to be resolved and an Arab summit held for that purpose. He stressed Saudi Arabia's preparedness to exert every possible effort in that direction. He also underlined the wisdom of Saudi Arabia's oil policy.

In the evening, Prince Saud El Faisal gave a dinner in my honour, attended by senior Saudi officials and Arab ambassadors, some of whom were from the Rejectionist Front, but who had accepted the Saudi Foreign Minister's invitation as a gesture of courtesy to him.

The following day I returned to Cairo, pleased and optimistic at what had been agreed between myself and Prince Saud El Faisal. The course we were to pursue should Israel refuse to accept a comprehensive peace settlement became clearer, which to me was very encouraging.

I met President Sadat to report to him on the visit to Saudi Arabia. He expressed satisfaction at the fact that I had been able to put off the Arab demand to end negotiations with Israel. He did not, however comment on, or show interest in, the scenario that had been agreed upon with the Foreign Minister of Saudi Arabia.

When I returned to my office that day, I found in my papers a secret memorandum that had been prepared by Ambassador Ussama El Baz on an incident that had taken place during my absence. The memo read as follows:

1. General Gamassy sent a cable to Weizman a few days ago enquiring as to the course of action to be followed regarding the members of the Israeli military group that had remained in Cairo since the halt in the military committee meetings. (The persons in question had been staying at El Tahera palace, and had been recently moved to a villa close to Gianaclis airport.)
2. Weizman had at once seized on this opportunity, and in his reply to General Gamassy proposed to come to Egypt accompanied by Barak [the Attorney-General] to discuss this matter as well as other questions related to the peaceful settlement.
3. A reply was sent back the same day (yesterday), Thursday 25 May, as follows:
    a. The Israeli military group has nothing more to do at present, and we have allowed it to remain out of courtesy.

Camp David

    b No purpose is served by holding meetings so long as there are no new developments in the situation. By any new developments we mean specific ideas that may overcome the present stalemate. This requires a fundamenal change in the Israeli position. Meetings, at present, in the absence of new developments would be more harmful than beneficial. If the purpose of the meetings is still of an exploratory nature we are well beyond this stage. Israel is aware of what we may or may not accept. I see no need for a meeting when there is nothing new.
    c In case there is something new, General Gamassy is prepared to meet Weizman publicly in a third country.

I recalled Weizman's last visit to Cairo during the meeting of the Arab League Council of Ministers, and I could not help but wonder whether Weizman's request to come to Cairo this time, while I was in Saudi Arabia, was a coincidence or a deliberate action on the part of Irsael which followed our every move towards Arab reconciliation and sought to counteract it.

Footnotes

1 *Memoirs of Mahmoud Riad*, p. 493 (Arabic text – unauthorized translation).
2 The text of the project may be found in an appendix, see p. 383.

Chapter Twenty Three

A Special Favour To Carter

On 27 May I flew to New York to attend the General Assembly's special session on Disarmament, which was being held at the request of the group of non-aligned countries.

The speech I delivered before the Assembly, as it referred to Israel, ran as follows:

> Although we consider the nuclear-free weapons zone in Latin America a model to be followed in the creation of similar zones elsewhere and a major step towards disarmament, the situation in Africa and the Middle East is totally different and would not permit us to follow such an example.
>
> The similarity of goals, in the case of South Africa and Israel, both of whom pursue aggressive policies defying international will and seriously violating the UN Charter and international law, renders any collusion between them in the nuclear field a direct threat to the peace and security of those two regions as well as to the world at large.
>
> We have consistently sought – together with fellow-African states – to implement the Declaration for the Creation of Non-Nuclear Africa, but despite the assistance received from the international community in this respect, the persistent attempts by the racist regime in South Africa to acquire nuclear weapons to reinforce its aggressive racist policy have prevented us from enforcing the Declaration in practice.
>
> Events in the Middle East, an area with a distinctive strategic location, are closely connected with the maintenance of international peace and security. Egypt is intensely aware of this fact, and has accordingly directed its policy to the establishment of stability in the region by bringing about just conditions to spare it the confrontations between the various powers. It does this because it believes that any such confrontation would lead the world to the brink of a third world war. It cannot be doubted that the wars the region has endured as a result of Israel's expansionist plans will bring the international

community to realize the great benefits to be gained by providing the conditions for a just and durable peace in the region, thereby transforming it entirely into a zone of peace. Hence the Iranian-Egyptian intiative four years ago calling for the transformation of the Middle East into a nuclear-free zone, purported to offer a positive contribution to disarmament efforts and sought to maintain international peace and security.

Both Iran and ourselves have persevered and have sought to accomplish this objective, which conforms to the desires of the states of the region, and which has received international support. However, whenever, in the course of the past four years, the issue has been raised at successive General Assembly sessions, Israel alone has voted against its unanimous acceptance. And Israel still refuses to adhere to the treaty on the non-proliferation of nuclear weapons, and refuses to subject its nuclear activities to a system of safeguards under the supervision of the International Atomic Energy Agency.

Allow me, Mr Chairman, to announce from this forum that Egypt seeks to keep the Middle East a nuclear-weapon-free zone. Should Israel, together with South Africa, attempt to impede this and thus realize its aspirations, the international community, as represented at the United Nations, is bound to adopt the necessary measures, in conformity with the UN Charter and in accordance with the spirit and letter of Security Council Resolution 255 of 1968, to ensure that no threat is posed to international peace and security through the implementation of such irresponsible acts.

Both the representatives of Arab states at the United Nations and those of Israel were closely watching the stand being taken by Egypt at the special session on Disarmament with a view to ascertaining its intentions. While the Arab representatives regarded the reference to Israel in Egypt's statement with satisfaction, Israel's UN representative, General Chaim Herzog, was greatly angered. It would appear that he had been expecting Egypt to refrain from attacking Israel from the UN forum in view of the peace talks that had begun and which dated from President Sadat's visit to Jerusalem. We had, moreover, touched a sensitive chord in Israel, by alluding to the close ties existing between it and South Africa, since this was the main reason that had prevented Israel from restoring its position in Africa after all the African states – with the exception of Malawi – had severed relations with it after the 1973 War.

During my stay in New York, I met with a number of foreign ministers who had come to attend the special session of disarmament. Our conversation centred on the current state of the talks between Egypt and Israel and possibilities for their success or failure. I also met Kurt Waldheim, the United Nations Secretary-General. Ever since I assumed office as Foreign

A Special Favour To Carter

Minister, I had been anxious that the United Nations should play a role in any settlement with Israel. Any such settlement would have to be based on the resolutions of the General Assembly and the Security Council.

I had also sought to sustain interest in the United Nations Secretary-General's proposal to convene an international conference in the Middle East to prepare for the Geneva Conference. I was mainly interested in the convening of such a conference to afford an opportunity to any Arab state wishing to join the talks to do so. It would be useful if our own bilateral talks with Israel failed. My discussions with the Secretary-General likewise dealt with Israel's exploitation of natural resources in Sinai and the same issue of Israel's withdrawal from Lebanon. Waldheim expressed intense irritation at the base and dilatory tactics being employed by Israel in its attempt to bypass implementation of Security Council Resolution 425 providing for its withdrawal from Lebanon.

I met, too, with the Cypriot President, Kyprianou, who was staying at the same hotel as myself. Egypt had severed its diplomatic relations with Cyprus in the wake of the Larnaka airport episode, and President Sadat adopted a hard line towards Cyprus for its refusal to extradite the assassins of Youssef El Sibai to Egypt. Indeed, Sadat had even condoned calling the Cypriot President "the Leader of the Greek Cypriots", thereby inferring the division of Cyprus into two countries. This was inconsistent with Egypt's declared position recognizing the unity of that country. Kyprianou expressed deep regret at the bloody incident which had led to a breakdown of the good relations that had existed between our two countries. The Cypriot President explained to me the difficulty involved in extraditing Sibai's murderers, for to do so would infringe the sovereignty of Cyprus, upon whose territory the assassination had occurred. He told me he was prepared to find a way to hand them over to Egypt a little later, when matters had calmed down. I, for my part, had been opposed to President Sadat's demand that the Sibai assassins be extradited, tried and executed in Egypt. I was anxious not to arouse feelings of hostility between Egyptians and Palestinians, which prosecution of the Sibai murderers would renew. I wished to end this tragic chapter of Egyptian-Palestinian relations, which only benefited Israel, and which adversely affected our position in the talks designed to resolve the Palestinian question – the core of the Arab-Israeli conflict. So, during my meeting with President Kyprianou, I made no reference to our demand for extradition of the culprits, insisting only that Cyprus carry out the sentence pronounced against them as soon as possible. We agreed to work to calm the situation between our two nations as a prelude to restoring diplomatic relations.

On 2 June I met Secretary of State Cyrus Vance over a working lunch at his suite in the Plaza Hotel. Attending with me were our Permanent Representative at the United Nations, Dr Esmat Abdel Meguid, our Ambassador in Washington, Dr Ashraf Ghorbal and Ambassador Ahmed Maher. The

American side was represented by the US delegate to the United Nations, Andrew Young, Ambassador Alfred Atherton, and Vance's assistant for the Middle East, Mr Saunders. Our conversation centred mainly on the Egyptian project for the West Bank and Gaza Strip. We had presented them in May with a copy of the project, providing for the withdrawal of Israel and the placing of the West Bank under Jordanian – and the Gaza Strip under Egyptian – supervision. Vance showed interest in our project and approved it in principle, but wanted certain points to be clarified. Their main comments centred around the absence of sufficient detail with regard to security measures, and Vance asked me to give due consideration to this aspect, since Israel invariably made this the pretext for turning down any project. I promised to do so on my return to Cairo.

Vance observed that they were still awaiting Israel's reply to the questionnaire addressed to them by the US on the West Bank and Gaza. He added that he did not expect a positive response, and said he intended to pay a visit to the Middle East area after the Israeli reply had been received. If this reply was positive, a new round of direct talks could be initiated between Egypt and Israel, but if it was not, the Egyptian project would be put forward later and the American ideas and proposals would be submitted. To this I agreed, while indicating that it was not enough for the US alone to consider the Israeli replies as positive – we, too, had to view them in the same light. I stressed that, unless the replies were truly positive and not merely a tricky formulation that gave the impression that Israel had altered its position, we would not agree to resume direct negotiations with the Jewish state.

President Sadat had taken certain measures and imposed certain laws restricting liberties in Egypt, and these had been presented for approval in a referendum on 22 May 1978, under the pretext of protecting the internal front and ensuring social stability. The measures included the elimination of certain elements from old parties who, it was claimed, had corrupted political life in Egypt. The socialist public prosecutor had also been instructed to look into the cases of several Egyptian journalists who had attacked Sadat's policy, and the Egyptian authorities expelled certain foreign correspondents who had engaged in similar attacks. These actions had an adverse effect on European and American public opinion and were strongly criticized by their media as a reneging on the democratic course Sadat was claiming to pursue. They also regarded it as an indication of the weakness of Egypt's internal front, and many questions were addressed to me on this score during my stay in New York.

The fixing of October as a deadline for the termination of direct talks with Israel had likewise caused concern in the US, as that was also the date on which the mandate of the United Nations Emergency Force in Sinai would expire.

I left New York for Paris, where I spent two days, during which I met with the French Foreign Minister, Louis de Guiringeau. He questioned me about developments in our talks with Israel. France was not very sanguine regarding the outcome of these talks and had throughout maintained a position of reserve and caution, and had refrained from showing any support for President Sadat's initiative lest its good relations with the other Arab states be affected. The thrust of our discussions, however, centred on African problems in the Horn of Africa, Zaire and Chad, which were causing serious concern in France.

I arrived back in Cairo on the evening of 10 June, and on 11 June the American Ambassador, Herman Eilts, visited President Sadat and handed him a paper containing some American observations which, in the US view, ought to be incorporated into the Egyptian project.

On 12 June, I left Cairo for Alexandria to meet President Sadat at the Maamoura rest-house. He welcomed me warmly, and I submitted to him the results of my trip, observing that the American side had registered its approval of the Egyptian project and considered it reasonable and logical. The US, I pointed out, were of opinion that the project should contain further details on security, to which the President replied that he had sent me the American proposals handed to him by Eilts the previous day.

I also conveyed to the President the concern and dissatisfaction I perceived in the United States and France with regard to the legislation and other measures he had set forth in the referendum. I pointed out that it could be construed as a renunciation of democracy on his part and a weakness on his internal front, adding that Israel was inciting the US information media to criticize those actions.

President Sadat replied: "Poor things, they are incapable of understanding the state of affairs here, or the fact that the measures I have taken signify increased democracy in Egypt!"

I was just about to leave when the President turned to me and said: "By the way, I received a phone call from President Carter; he proposes a tripartite meeting between the Foreign Ministers of Egypt, Israel and the US. He seemed very keen on it, and I gave him my approval, on condition the meeting takes place anywhere but in Egypt or Israel, as I promised President Numeiry.

This habit of his of placing me before the *fait accompli* without prior consultation irritated me.

"Everything you have said," I replied, "has so far shown that you have no intention of again engaging in direct negotiations with Israel unless it changes its position. And less than two weeks ago I reached an agreement with the Saudis to drop negotiations with Israel unless it modified its stand. With this understanding, they are now making the appropriate contacts to bring about an Arab reconciliation and arrange for the convening of an Arab summit at the proper time. Apart from all this, the US government put certain questions to Israel regarding the future of the West Bank and Gaza Strip over a month ago, to which Israel has so far not replied.

Camp David

"How [I went on] can we approve, in principle, of a meeting with Israel when we do not know its position and are unable to assess whether or not its response is favourable? In fact, I have been informed by Secretary of State Vance that he was not at all optimistic that the Israeli reaction would be positive. Frankly speaking, I am not at all happy at Carter's inconsistent position.

"I met Vance ten days ago and he made no reference at all to any such meeting, saying merely that after he had received the Israeli reply he would be paying a visit to the area to reach an understanding on the next step." The conversation continued:

Sadat: "President Carter was most insistent that I agree to his proposal, and you know how much importance I attach to an United States role, and how eager I am for the United States to assume the role of a full partner in the negotiations. So I don't want to upset President Carter."

Myself: "Well, I can understand that: what I *don't* understand is why the Americans seem so unwilling to play out the scenario agreed at Camp David. Wherever we have tried to improve our relations with Arab countries, they have raised some obstacle or other, whereas we need the support of the Arab states, particularly Jordan. Otherwise, we will be left alone to tackle problems we have not been empowered to deal with."

Sadat: "King Hussein has not yet taken a stand – he probably expects the West Bank to be returned to him on a silver platter. Anyway, I told President Carter that my agreeing to a tripartite foreign ministers' meeting was a concession and a special favour to him on my part. I made it plain to him that this was to be the only and final such meeting. He has agreed, and proposes it be held in London."

When I got back to Cairo, I set up a working group to look into the American proposal for amendments to be introduced to the Egyptian project regarding the West Bank and the Gaza Strip. The group set to work and came up with a new project which included certain of the American proposals, in a modified form to suit our own position. I approved of the project, and so did President Sadat.

On 13 June, in a statement before the US House of Representatives' Foreign Relations Political Committee, the Assistant-Secretary of State for the Middle East, Harold Saunders, said: "The American position now can be summarized in the need to know Israel's position on the West Bank and Gaza and the necessity for an Israeli announcement that it intends to withdraw from those territories, formerly under British mandate, which do not fall within Israel's 1967 borders."

Saunders added that the withdrawal aspect would have to be decided as a basic issue while security and sovereignty issues were being discussed. If Israel did not make such an announcement, countries such as Jordan would not be able to join in the talks. He went on to inform the House Foreign Relations Committee that, in Washington's view, the future of the West Bank depended on the existence of links between that territory and Jordan, therefore the creation of a Palestinian state was a realistic solution.

On 15 June, I received the US Ambassador, Herman Eilts, and handed him our amended project entitled: "Proposals on withdrawal from the West Bank and Gaza Strip and Security Arrangements". I made it plain to the American Ambassador that we did not want our project made known to the Israelis until they had replied to the questionnaire submitted to them by the US, and I asked him to fix a date, in agreement with us, when the American side would inform the Israelis of the project. Eilts assured me that this would be done. The Americans, he went on, hoped the Israelis would reach a decision on those questions at a meeting of their cabinet within the new few days. Begin, he added, was attempting to compromise in view of the great differences within the cabinet in this respect.

I referred to President Carter's suggestion to President Sadat for a meeting of foreign ministers of the three states, pointing out to him that this did not conform to the scenario agreed upon with the US. I told him his country had to pressure Israel into modifying its stand as a condition for the holding of such a meeting. The Ambassador replied that there was some truth in this, but the American President's position would be strengthened if a new round of negotiations was held. In this way, if Israel maintained a negative attitude, he would be able to convince the Congress and US opinion that he (Carter) had been obliged to put forward American proposals in view of the inflexible Israeli position. My response to this was that while I regretted Begin's attitude, it had to be admitted that he alone never wavered from any line he had committed himself to, whereas Presidents Carter and Sadat proceeded in uneven fashion, that is, one step forward and another step back, and this had encouraged Begin to maintain his inflexibility.

On 17 June I submitted to President Sadat a memorandum on the American proposal to hold a meeting in London. It included the following points:

1. It is evident from reports emanating from Israel that the Israeli Cabinet is in a dilemma. It is divided within itself as to the replies to the questions put to Israel by the United States. Under such circumstances, our acceptance of the American proposal would afford the Israeli government the opportunity to avoid giving a reply

Camp David

until it had been apprised of the outcome of the Foreign Ministers' meeting.

Mindful of the need not to give Israel such an opportunity, I have notified the American Ambassador – in accordance with your instructions – not to convey our project to the Israeli side before it has replied positively to the questions put to it.

This position is also in accordance with the American position as publicly voiced by Saunders and Atherton, indicating that a positive reply on the part of Israel is necessary before direct negotiations can be resumed.

2 On the other hand, you have made statements to the effect that we would be ready for another round of talks were some new development to occur to change the Israeli position. You have also informed President Numeiry of this.

3 More than a month has passed, and no reply has come from the Israelis. There is thus no need for Egypt to show any marked enthusiasm for the American proposal of a tripartite meeting. This being so, may I observe the following:

(a) Were we to accept the proposed meeting as a concession to President Carter, it should be accompanied by a pledge on his part that the American project for the West Bank and the Gaza Strip would be as close as possible to our proposals and ideas.

(b) We may inform the US government of our acceptance in principle of its project, and simultaneously inform it that the meeting could not be held unless the Israeli replies indicated that some improvement had taken place in the Israeli position.

(c) On the timing of the meeting: if Vance cannot be present in London save at the proposed time,[1] a meeting could be held later in Washington or in any other place suited to Vance when the Israeli replies had been received. The meeting could also be postponed to a date after the conclusion of Vance's tour of the area and in the light of anything it might have achieved to modify the Israeli position.

(d) Dayan's[2] request for a tripartite meeting is part of the internal struggle between him and Begin on the one hand, and between him and Weizman on the other. At best, there is no guarantee that any agreement with Dayan will be approved by the Israeli cabinet, especially since there is always the possibility that Begin's government will be replaced, whether for health – or for political reasons.[3]

4 Egypt, as well as the United States, is seeking to induce more countries to join in the negotiations, and acceptance of the tripartite meeting without some positive move by Israel does not serve our purpose.

Such being the case, we propose the following reply:
(a) Acceptance in principle to hold the meeting.
(b) A positive Israeli reply has to be received prior to holding the meeting.
(c) The meeting need not be held in London if Mr Vance's schedule does not allow him to absent himself save on this proposed date. The meeting could be held in Washington whenever it suits him.
(d) A meeting could be held if positive developments appeared in the Israeli position following Mr Vance's visit to the area.

On 18 June, Israel sent in the replies to the American queries addressed to it more than two months before, as follows:

After five years have passed, allowing for the establishment of an administrative local government in "Judea", "Samaria" and the Gaza Strip, the Israeli government agrees to discuss the nature of future relations with any party that proposes to do so. Any agreement requires negotiations between the parties themselves, with inhabitants of the territories, elected according to the system applied by the existing local government, participating in these negotiations.

I feel that this reply – if it may be described as such – speaks for itself!

Footnotes

1 The American Ambassador had informed us that it would be convenient for Vance that the meeting take place on 9 July.
2 Dayan proposed through the American Embassy that he come to Cairo for a meeting with the President, but we excused ourselves.
3 There were reports of serious differences between Begin and some of his ministers on the one hand, and between Igal Yadin and his supporters on the other hand.

Chapter Twenty Four

Israel Rejects the Egyptian Project Before it is Presented

Israel's reply was so negative that there was no way of denying it, this was felt even by part of its staunchest friends in the US. The official State Department spokesman, Hodding Carter, expressed the American government's regret that the Israeli government had not responded to the American queries. The reply it had given was, he said, no reply.

However, the Israeli reply did contain, in its intricate and ambiguous formulation, a simple, clear signal, namely that Israel had no intention of withdrawal from the West Bank and the Gaza Strip after the transitional period, which was only a breathing-spell in which to entrench its occupation of the territories as a prelude to their final annexation and absorption. Israel would only condescend to offer the wretched Palestinians a local administrative government on those territories under the authority of Israel.

Personally, I considered that Israel's reply had finalized the situation and had definitively closed the door to any resumption of negotiations between Israel and ourselves. It was incumbent upon the United States to fulfil its responsibilities, namely, to present proposals on the basis of its repeated intention to indicate in them that the withdrawal provision contained in Security Council Resolution 242 would be applicable to all occupied territories. This had been stressed anew by Mr Saunders in an official statement to the House Foreign Relations Committee a few days earlier.

It was quite clear to me now that President Carter's telephone call to President Sadat, calling for a tripartite foreign ministers meeting, had been motivated by the previous knowledge that the Israeli reply would be negative. Neither can I exclude the possibility of some sort of co-ordination between the United States and Israel to ensure the continuation of direct negotiations between Egypt and Israel, to consolidate Egypt's isolation from the Arab world and the conclusion of a separate peace with Israel.

The Israeli reply was followed by a period of confusion in which a series of Egyptian and American statements were made, numerous meetings with the American ambassador were held, and exchanges of messages between Sadat

Israel Rejects the Egyptian Project Before it is Presented

and Carter took place. For my part, I announced that the Israeli reply reflected Israel's determination to enforce its project for local administration as submitted in Ismailia, and which had been rejected at the time as it was now. The project completely disregarded the principle of withdrawal, and in view of this, I said, we deemed it futile to resume negotiations with Israel.

President Sadat also proclaimed before the Central Committee of the Arab Socialist Union that the Israeli reply had not been positive or specific but that we were still prepared to discuss safeguards and arrangements, although we would not negotiate one inch of Arab territory.

The US Ambassador, Herman Eilts, acted swiftly in an attempt at securing the agreement reached between Carter and Sadat on the tripartite foreign ministers. My stand was that the agreement was overtaken by events and of no further consequence in view of the negative Israeli reply.

Elits nevertheless succeeded in persuading President Sadat that such a meeting would be useful to help President Carter implement the plan agreed to in the Camp David scenario. President Carter would have found it no easy task to put forward American proposals to resolve the conflict unless he could produce evidence which would satisfy US opinion – and particularly Jewish and Zionist groups and Israel's friends in Congress – that direct negotiations between Egypt and Israel had brought about no result. Carter stressed that the best and only method of achieving this was the holding of a tripartite meeting.

The plan agreed to by Egypt and the US at Camp David was highly secret and could not be disclosed as the reason for the holding of a tripartite meeting. On the other hand it would have been difficult for Egypt – with an eye to the Arab states and Palestinian people – to agree to take part in such a meeting after Israel had replied negatively.

The American side were also at a loss regarding the Egyptian proposals which, it had been agreed, would not be revealed until Israel had replied to the US questionnaire. After talks with the American side, we decided that Egypt's justification for meeting with Israel and the United States would be based on the project it was currently preparing. Egypt would present its project as a new element in the negotiations in the hope that the parties would reach an acceptable formulation. American statements were issued to pave the way for the submission of the Egyptian project. On 24 June an American proposal was announced calling for a meeting between Vance, Dayan and myself to be held on 9 July.

The Israeli cabinet met on 25 June and an Israeli government spokesman stated after the session that Israel considered the Egyptian proposal a precondition for peace, and Israel was determined that there would be no preconditions.

The Egyptian Foreign Ministry, in a comment on the Israeli rejection of the Egyptian project, declared that:

Camp David

> This decision once again raises the question as to Israel's true intentions. It is, indeed, strange that Israel – which has taken over a month to reply to the US queries, even though the so-called reply is merely a restatement of previous positions and is noteworthy for its inflexibility and refusal to go along with the sincere peace efforts – should now proceed to reject a project about which it knew nothing and which is still incomplete.
>
> It now seems as if Israel, by adopting such a position, which betrays its nervousness and irritation at the world-wide response to the idea, whose broad lines were revealed to the press by President Sadat, is attempting to close the door to peace efforts. This attitude is likewise reflected in Israel's response to queries by the American government, which was seeking a suitable basis for progress in the achievement of a just and comprehensive peace which President Sadat has already embarked upon and which Israel has sought to impede from the very beginning...

Israel's rejection of the Egyptian project confused the American government, since it removed the pretext for the tripartite meeting. On 26 June President Carter announced that Israel's replies to the US queries had been disappointing, and he regretted Israel's rejection of the Egyptian project before it had even been finally drafted. Carter added that the time was ripe for a tripartite foreign ministers meeting, and that Egypt and Israel could have new ideas to put forward. Such a meeting could take place after the final drafting of the Egyptian proposals had been made and conveyed to Israel via Washington.

Israel at once withdrew its rejection of the Egyptian project, and an official statement was issued on 27 June by the Israeli cabinet declaring that since Egypt had not submitted a peace plan to Israel, the latter could not have rejected such a plan. The way was thus once again cleared for the holding of a tripartite meeting on the basis of the Egyptian project.

Begin then issued a statement calling for the resumption of negotiations with Egypt, and I replied with one to the effect that:

> The Prime Minister of Israel appears to forget that current peace efforts are the fruit of President Sadat's peace intiative, whose purpose was to dispèl doubt and work sincerely for a comprehensive and just settlement of the Middle East problem on bases acceptable to the international community, namely full withdrawal, recognition of the legitimate rights of the Palestinian people and safeguarding the security of all parties.
>
> If such sincere efforts have met with difficulties that have led to the stalling of negotiations, this is mainly due to the positions adopted by Begin. These indicate that he has not abandoned his out-dated

Israel Rejects the Egyptian Project Before it is Presented

concepts, which cannot provide a suitable groundwork for the establishment of a lasting and stable peace. It is indeed strange that Begin should call upon Egypt to come up with a peace project, while at the same time assembling his cabinet to announce his rejection of the Egyptian peace project, even before it appeared in its final form. . . This attitude of Begin's is an indication that Begin, despite his claims, is constantly striving to block all avenues likely to lead to the peace aspired to by the states of the area.

During this time, an emergency session of the Arab League Council – which was not attended by the rejectionist states – was held at ministerial level to discuss the complaint of the Yemen Arab Republic against the People's Democratic Republic of Yemen for the latter's part in the assassination of the former's President Ahmed El Ghasmy. He had been killed as a result of an explosive charge contained in a message conveyed to him by a Yemeni envoy from Democratic Yemen.

In the evening, when the meetings were over, I set out to meet the Saudi Foreign Minister in a luxury flat overlooking the Nile owned by his uncle, Sheikh Kamal Adham. We talked until a late hour, and with us was the Bahreini Foreign Minister, a personal friend of Prince Faisal. I had no alternative but to acquaint him with the fact that I had been obliged to go against what we had agreed upon in Jeddah, namely to cease all direct contacts with Israel in view of Sadat's agreeing to attend the tripartite meeting proposed by Carter. I explained to him the reasons that had led to the meeting, emphasizing that this would be the last. Prince Faisal showed understanding and expressed the hope that this would indeed be the last of such meetings.

Around this time, the United States announced that the US Vice-President, Walter Mondale, would be carrying a message from President Carter to both Menahim Begin and Sadat aimed at activating peace efforts in the Middle East.

On 1 July President Carter said in a statement that he did not think the Egyptian peace proposals would be totally acceptable to Israel, and he added that the US role was to consider the possibility of achieving a compromise by examining the points of agreement and difference between the two countries. Carter went on to say that if a compromise was not reached at the proposed tripartite ministerial meeting in London, there would be no alternative but to go back to the United Nations and the Geneva Conference.[1]

Following Carter's announcement, I issued one of my own in which I said that President Carter's statements were not at all encouraging, and that we did not understand what the Americans implied when they spoke of the need to find a comprehensive formula for the West Bank and Gaza Strip, adding that our demands were just and had been endorsed by the international community. Some principles, I said, were not subject to bargaining.

On 3 July Mondale arrived in Alexandria from Israel and was helicoptered from Gianaclis airport to the President's Maamoura rest-house. President Sadat and I had previously agreed that he accept to hold the tripartite conference with the proviso that, should the talks fail, the US would align its position with ours and not seek to establish a compromise formula as recently proposed by President Carter. Yet no sooner had Sadat learned from Mondale that Begin was prepared to send his foreign minister to London to take part in the tripartite meeting, than he agreed, without further ado, to attend. When I reproached Sadat for his attitude, he replied that he considered it best, since Begin had agreed to it unconditionally, not to link our decision to attend with any conditions, lest we appear intransigent.

After the talks, President Sadat and Vice-President Mondale held a press conference in the rest-house garden, at which Mondale announced that President Sadat had agreed to accept Carter's invitation to participate in the tripartite conference with the proviso that, should the talks fail, the US that Moshe Dayan should attend the meeting, and that 17 July had been fixed as a date for the meeting.

Sadat, in turn, said he had agreed to send his foreign minister to London, adding that Egypt had presented its peace project to Vice-President Mondale for transmission to Carter, who would then pass it on to Israel. Sadat declined to disclose any detail on the Egyptian project, saying it would be revealed fully after Israel had received it. Egypt, the President went on, was doing its utmost to achieve peace. Egypt was prepared to go to Geneva, but to do so would imply failure or court disaster unless there were sound prior arrangements.

On the tripartite meeting in London Sadat said, and I quote: "I have made some proposals concerning this meeting to Mr Mondale, and I have suggested alternative venues for it, such as El Arish, the capital of Sinai. I have, however, agreed that it be held in London."

I should like to draw the reader's attention to this paragraph, in view of its subsequent repercussions. After the news conference, William Quandt, a member of the US National Security Council and a member of the Mondale delegation, came up to me and asked: "Did President Sadat mean that a tripartite meeting would be held in London, to be followed by another in El Arish?"

My immediate reply was: "He meant one meeting only. He spoke of El Arish as an alternative venue to London. If you want my opinion, the situation calls for no meetings at all." This answer amused Quandt.

I had been told by President Sadat to hold myself ready to leave for Vienna with him at the beginning of July at the invitation of Austrian Chancellor Bruno Kreisky. He had indicated at the time the possibility that Kreisky would also extend an invitation to Shimon Perez, the leader of the

Israel Rejects the Egyptian Project Before it is Presented

Israeli Labour Party, with a possible meeting between himself and Perez. The daily *Al Ahram* newspaper had referred to this Kreisky invitation the day Mondale arrived in Cairo. The press seized the opportunity offered by the press conference to question Sadat on the proposed visit: he was asked if he was going to meet Shimon Perez. Sadat, however, refused to answer to this.

Following the press conference, Sadat informed me that, on second thoughts, he deemed it best that I should not, after all, accompany him to Vienna. He would, he told me, be meeting with Shimon Perez and former German Chancellor Willy Brandt in Vienna in their capacity as party leaders. He would be meeting as the leader of the Arab Socialist Union, consequently it would be purely a meeting of parties. He considered that it would be embarrassing for me to attend party meetings. I replied that I saw his point and could see no reason to go, especially since I already had more than enough to do preparing for the London meeting.

On 4 July, the United States delivered to Israel the Egyptian project on the West Bank and Gaza Strip. On 5 July, Egypt published the full text of the project.[2] This was warmly received by the Europeans and won the support of Jordan.

Footnotes

1   *Al Ahram*, 3 July 1978.
2   See Appendix 1 for the text of the amended Egyptian project (according, to the American proposals).

Chapter Twenty Five

Believe it or Not!

At 6.30 a.m. on 7 July I was awakened by the ringing of my telephone. Vice-President Mubarak was at the other end of the line. He asked banteringly: "Are you still asleep, Mohamed Bey?" I replied in the affirmative, pointing out that I had stayed up late. Mubarak then asked me: "Are you ready for the trip to Austria?" I replied: "I am not leaving: I was told so by the President a few days ago." The Vice-President answered: "But you are leaving: I was talking to him yesterday, and he told me to let you know you were leaving so you could get ready. The President will be taking off from Gianaclis airport at 11 a.m. this morning. I shall be travelling with you to Alexandria to see him off. Please meet me at Almaza [the military airfield near Heliopolis] and we will leave together."

Accordingly, I roused first Ahmed Maher and then Amr Hamdy (who had my passport). I told them I was leaving and they were to pick me up at 9 a.m. on our way to the airport. My wife quickly packed a suitcase while I contacted my secretary at the Ministry and asked her to cancel all my appointments for the coming week.

We arrived at Gianaclis at 10.30 a.m. followed by the President and his wife fifteen minutes later. They had travelled from Alexandria by helicopter. When the departure ceremonies were over, the plane took off at 11 a.m. for Vienna.

The President was fasting as was his custom every Thursday. Ahmed Maher and I sat beside one another on the plane, reviewing papers until 12.30 a.m. when I proceeded to the President's lounge and sat with him and his wife. Our talk was general until the conversation came round to the tripartite ministerial meeting scheduled for London in ten days time. The President began by saying: "I do not expect it to achieve any positive results, but it will assist President Carter in coming forward with American proposals and will be an opportunity to reveal the falsity of Israel's claims to peace."

He added: "I really wanted the meeting to be held in the city of El Arish and not in London. In the first place, El Arish is our territory and the capital of Sinai and such a location would have great significance, and in the second it is close to Cairo and Israel. If a matter requiring consultation were to arise, you could easily fly back to me in Cairo within half an hour and return. And if other Arab parties, such as Syria and Jordan, wished to join the talks, the distance would not be far from Damascus and Amman."

I replied that I, for my part, would not agree to go to El Arish. "Why?" Sadat wanted to know. "For two reasons [I answered]: Firstly, you promised President Gaafar El Numeiry when you met him last May, that if the need arose for direct negotiations between Egypt and Israel, you would hold them outside Egypt and Israel that is, in a third country such as Romania, out of consideration for the Arab states who called on us to declare that direct negotiations were no way to help the Arab solidarity committee discharge its functions under President Numeiry."

At this the President smiled and said: "I did not say outside Egypt and Israel, but outside Cairo and Jerusalem."

My response was quick in coming: "No, Rais, I recall perfectly that you said: 'Outside Egypt and Israel', and, anyway, this was what President Numeiry understood and conveyed to all the Arabs."

The President remained quiet for a moment, then asked: "What is your second reason for not wanting to go to El Arish?"

I replied: "I'll be hanged if I'll go to El Arish and negotiate on my own territory with the Israelis under their flag and guarded by their occupying forces."

The President looked at me for a moment without saying anything. Then he stood up and announced he would go to sleep for a while to rest from his fasting before we arrived in Vienna.

I remained alone with Mrs Jihan El Sadat, who asked me to have lunch with her. Mrs Sadat had regarded me with esteem ever since her visit to Germany in 1974 which had left a favourable impression on the German people and officials. While we were having lunch, she said: "For Heaven's sake, Mohamed Bey, don't leave the President alone during his talks with Shimon Perez in Vienna." I told her I was really embarrassed, and recounted all that had occurred with regard to the cancellation of my departure for Vienna in view of the unofficial nature of the President's visit, followed by my being notified that morning to prepare to accompany him. Mrs Sadat again pleaded with me not to leave him alone with them – the Israelis, she said, were very sly, in contrast with Sadat, who was frank and outspoken. They would, she continued, seek deliberately to play on those qualities of his. I said: "Well, why don't you ask him?" She replied: "He gets angry when I discuss his work with him. However, he likes you and will not object to your presence if you ask to be there." I told her I would do what I could.

After lunch, I thanked her and took my leave. Back in my seat, what she had said rang in my ears, and I wondered why she had said what she had. Mrs Sadat was intelligent and observant. She, too, was very close to him, and pride makes it difficult for some people to reveal their feelings. However, she was aware that my relationship with her husband went back more than thirty years, and she knew she could trust me. Why was she worried? She must have noticed something in Sadat. Perhaps he no longer handled matters with the same consideration and perception. Perhaps she realized that he was over-conceited and had thrown caution to the winds. Perhaps she had noticed that he had become unduly optimistic, perhaps, perhaps, perhaps! . . . Yet something had driven her to say what she had said to me. An idea suddenly occurred to me: could it have been Mrs Jihan El Sadat who was behind his change of mind regarding my departure for Vienna?

Our plane touched down at Vienna airport, where the Austrian President and Chancellor Bruno Kreisky were on hand to greet us. We were lodged in the Imperial Hotel with its memories of the great days of the Austro-Hungarian Empire, and the tales and tragedies of the Hapsburgs who ruled for centuries until the end of World War I.

President Sadat invited me to dine with him in his suite (it was Iftar time for him). I turned up at 7 p.m., when we discussed various matters before proceeding to the dining-room. We then resumed our conversation. Midway through dinner, the President's secretary entered to inform him that Mr Hassan El Tohamy was present. Sadat asked that he join us. Tohamy came in and embraced the President, who introduced me, and we shook hands. He was a fine figure of a man, with a powerful frame, average height and blue eyes. His strength and vitality were reflected in his bearded face, and his eyes held a strange glitter.

Although this was our first meeting, I had heard queer stories about him. Having led a tumultuous, carefree life in his youth, he had suddenly turned to religion and Sufism. He had been one of the officers who had carried out the 23 July Revolution in 1952, later serving in military intelligence, and subsequently became Egyptian Ambassador to Austria – a post he held for many years during the sixties. He later became Secretary-General of the Islamic Conference, and subsequently established a reputation for communicating with genii, the prophets and the dead.

President Sadat told me that he had been keen to introduce Hassan El Tohamy to me. Tohamy, he confided to me, had been a member in the military wing of the clandestine organization of which Sadat was the leader and I a member of its civilian wing!

Tohamy himself told me he had been eager to meet me. He said that, in the time I spent in prison, he had learned a great deal about me. Perhaps I was not aware, he continued, that he had prepared a plan to enable us to escape from prison if we were sentenced by the court for the political assassinations of 1946. Tohamy went on to recount stories of his heroic deeds, and these included the most unbelievable escapades. He spun his tales so confidently and with such self-assurance that one was almost

Believe it or Not!

inclined to believe them. His conversation, though exaggerated, was amusing, in the style of the *Arabian Nights*.

I understood that he had arrived some time previously to prepare for Sadat's visit and arrange for the meeting between President Sadat and Shimon Perez. In this task he had been helped by a Jewish-Austrian businessman by the name of Karl Kahan, who was a friend of Chancellor Bruno Kreisky.

After dinner we returned to our rooms.

On 5 July, I had submitted to the President, before his departure for Vienna, a comprehensive memorandum on the positions of the Israeli Labour Party and its leader, Perez, with regard to a settlement of the Middle East crisis and the future of the West Bank. The memo pointed out that the main differences in the views of Begin and Perez concerned the West Bank and the degree to which Resolution 242 was applicable to it. It also centred on the feasibility of creating a federal state of Jordan and the West Bank, with an Israeli military presence in the latter.

This is not the place to discuss the position of the Labour Party on a settlement, but my memorandum drew the President's attention to some of the following points:

> ... Your meeting with Perez, Mr President, will take place immediately before the tripartite foreign ministers meeting in London. With this in mind, the following points have been drawn up for your consideration:
>
> (a) Any flexibility that might be shown by Egypt could be made public by Perez or leaked by him to the Israeli goverment. This would cause the latter to adopt a more intransigent attitude in London, since it would be aware that the declared Egyptian positions at the meeting were not its final ones. In this respect, news reports indicate that Perez, in response to Dayan's attack on him for meeting with you, particularly before the tripartite meeting, has pledged to inform the Israeli government of the outcome of his meeting with you.
>
> (b) Perez may also leak information on the flexibility of the Egyptian position to show he was capable of doing so and exploit the fact in his struggle to assume power. This is not inherently bad, since it could contribute to weaken Begin's position, but it could also make it appear that Egypt was adopting a dual approach, and thus encourage the American government to exert increased pressure on us to achieve more flexibility than we are prepared to show.

On 8 July, President Sadat met with Shimon Perez. The meeting was

Camp David

attended by Kreisky and Willy Brandt, the former German Chancellor, who had succeeded Kreisky as Chairman of the Socialist International. The four held a press conference afterwards, and what they had to say may be summed up in the need to reach a just and comprehensive settlement. They announced that there had been a serious exchange of the various viewpoints. Willy Brandt said he was pleased that the Socialist International had managed to arrange a meeting between President Sadat and Shimon Perez, the Leader of the Israeli Labour Party, acting on the principle that international disputes should be settled through peaceful dialogue.

After the press conference, Sadat affirmed to me that the get-together had been useful and that Perez, unlike Begin, was open-minded and was prepared to make concessions. He indicated that they had agreed to find a formula that would both meet Israel's security requirements and ensure the rights of the Palestinian people.

In the evening Chancellor Kreisky and his wife gave a lavish dinner banquet attended by Sadat and his wife, ex-German Chancellor Willy Brandt, the speaker of the Austrian Parliament, the Foreign Minister and their wives and myself. Various subjects were discussed. Then Kreisky observed that the time had come for King Hussein to join in the peace negotiations to settle the Palestinian question, especially since the Egyptian project involved restoring the West Bank to the Jordanian administration. He had no sooner said this than Sadat affirmed that King Hussein was pursuing an opportunist policy. King Hussein, Sadat claimed, wished to risk nothing and was waiting for the West Bank to be handed to him as a gift. He described King Hussein as a person who took the wrong decisions at the right time, for he had joined President Nasser in the 1967 War only to lose the West bank, and had refused to join with Egypt in the 1973 War, and so did not share the Arabs' victory. King Tallal, Hussein's father, the President averred, had died insane, and he had been given to understand that signs of schizophrenia were beginning to appear in King Hussein.

I was very upset by what the President had said, I felt everyone else was uncomfortable too. Both Kreisky and Brandt praised King Hussein's policy, and expressed admiration for his courage and intelligence. They showed understanding for the difficult circumstances in which Jordan found itself.

Our visit to Vienna had ended and we were to spend a few days in the lake region of Salzkammergut, near Salzburg, for a little bit of relaxation. Hassan El Tohamy had joined us on the plane to Salzburg, and our conversation there centred on his feelings of distrust for Foreign Minister Dayan. Without warning, Hassan El Tohamy abruptly declared that he believed Dayan was the false Messiah predicted by the Old Testament, adding that he had told Dayan this in Morocco. Here he was interrupted by President Sadat, who told him: "We do not wish to raise this subject now".

Tohamy fell silent. Until then, I was unaware that a meeting between

Believe it or Not!

Hassan El Tohamy and Dayan in Morocco had preceded the Sadat initiative.

We travelled by car from Salzburg Airport through one of the world's most beautiful regions, covered with mountain valleys and lakes, arriving eventually at the Fortress of Foeschel, now converted into a hotel, where the President had stayed three years ago when he had met with American President Ford. I was given a small, picturesque bungalow on the edge of the lake, and in the evening Ahmed Maher picked me up for dinner at the restaurant. We were looking over the menu when Hassan El Tohamy came in and spotted us. He came over and asked whether he might join us for dinner, and we welcomed him. A few minutes later he was again on his hobby-horse, recounting his adventures and spinning his tales. Conversation turned to the Jewish religion, and he informed us that he had made a close study of it, having read both the Old Testament and the Talmud. He had also had access to several documents and manuscripts, among which was a secret document nobody knew about except for a few select Jews. According to this document, the Jews were to live as a Diaspora for over two thousand years, after which they would return to Jerusalem to be slaughtered. We did not understand this, and asked him to explain. Tohamy intimated that, exasperated by the Jews, God had ordered them out of Jerusalem to live in exile dispersed around the world. They had complained to God, repented and asked for forgiveness. As proof of such forgiveness, they pleaded to be allowed to return to Jerusalem, the promised land, to be slaughtered in expurgation of their sins. They would thereby have been forgiven their sedition, abated God's wrath and gained His pardon.

Tohamy confided us that, following his perusal of this document, he had engaged in further study and research before meeting some Jewish rabbis in London. According to him, they were first amazed and then terrified when he told them what he knew concerning the document. In vain they attempted to learn how he had gained access to this vital secret, but were finally convinced of his sincerity, believing that his coming to them was a sign from the Almighty. They begged him to return to them in six months time, and when he did so, he was informed that they had discussed the matter and agreed that his information was correct. They asked for five years' grace to put their affairs in order before being put to the sword. Here, Tohamy looked at his watch, and, seeing it was half an hour to midnight, got up and left. Ahmed Maher and myself followed him out of the room with our eyes and then burst out laughing together.

Whether the reader believes it or not, this story was the obscure basis for some proposals concerning Jerusalem made by President Sadat two months later at the tripartite summit in Camp David! I shall be going into this more fully when the time comes.

On 10 July the President sent for me to accompany him on a tour of the lake. As I was setting out, I encountered Tohamy who, after shaking hands with me, said he had decided to make me a gift of the entire collection of his secret file! It contained, he confided, secret information of great importance. He was doing this, he added, because he appreciated my patriotism. He had (Tohamy went on) refused to hand it to any of the foreign ministers who had preceded me! He began to talk about the forthcoming foreign ministers meeting in London, impressing upon me the fact that he knew Moshe Dayan well. If Dayan happened to be difficult during the talks all I had to do (he said) was to tighten my right fist while fixing him with my gaze, then open it and spread my fingers before his face, at the same time crying out: "Tohamy." This, Tohamy averred, would make him return to his senses immediately, and I would be able to communicate with him!

A member of the secretariat now approached me suddenly to inform me that President Sadat was about to begin his tour of the lake. I took my leave of Tohamy and started off.

We took a small motor-boat operated by electric batteries. I sat in the rear with the President, with the driver and guard in front. The surface of the water, as we cruised along, reflected the mountains, the greenery of the trees and the azure sky. The weather was invigorating and sunny and the calm all-embracing save for the waves thrown up by our bow as we cut through the water. We reached the far shore of the lake in half an hour and went to a beautiful lakeside café set in a flower-garden. Many people gathered around us to shake the President's hand and ask him to sign autographs and photographs of the spot. It was obvious that they greatly admired the President and hoped he would bring peace. The President took time off to sign autographs, and he was still engaged in doing so when we were joined by Ahmed Maher and Amr Hamdy, my personal guard. We remained upwards of an hour in the café, drinking *Apfel saft*, the romantic atmosphere surrounding us inclining our conversation to the beauty of nature and the pleasures of life far removed from politics and problems. We then took the boat to return to the hotel.

Back in the bungalow, our press counsellor in Bonn, Hamdi Azzam, who had come to Austria to cover the President's visit, phoned to tell me that a press statement had been issued by Willy Brandt and Bruno Kreisky in the name of the Socialist International.

The statement, he added, had been made in German, and as soon as he had translated it, he would send me a copy. Both Ahmed Maher and myself got down to studying the statement. In it, Brandt and Kreisky gave it as their considered opinion that the principles stated therein truly represented the thinking of the Socialist International on settlement of the Middle East dispute. They intended, in the light of those principles, to arrange for a discussion during the meeting of the Socialist International Bureau in Paris in September.

This was followed by the test of the four principles, consisting of first, the establishment of peace through uninterrupted negotiations; secondly, that peace should be based on the establishment of normal relations; and the setting-up of a system of regional co-operation in the area; and the fourth concerned the settlement of the Palestinian problem according to the Aswan formula. The third principle was set out as follows:

> An important element in the peace settlement is the establishment of secure boundaries in accordance with Security Council Resolutions 242 and 338. Israel would withdraw in each sector to the secure boundaries thus agreed. The exact location of the peace boundaries remains to be determined in the peace negotiations. There should also be provisions for demilitarization and for Israeli security measures in such areas as the needs of security call for.

Whereas we had no serious objections to principles one, two and four, principle three was a cause of great concern to us.

The effects of the morning's excursion soon wore off, for the matter was a serious one, advocating as it did Israel's theory of regional security, which had as its object to expand under the pretext of security. This constituted a flagrant violation of Resolution 242, which openly stipulated the inadmissibility of acquiring territory by war. Even more serious was the fact that the statement had been issued by Brandt and Kreisky after their meeting with Sadat and Perez, which signified that President Sadat had approved of its contents.

Our silence might be interpreted as an acceptance of the principles inherent in the statement, which would encourage Dayan during the London meeting to propose that they be considered as a declaration of intent upon which the settlement would be based. This was particularly so, since Shimon Perez had made a statement to the effect that President Sadat was prepared to withdraw the Egyptian project on the West Bank and Gaza if Israel approved a declaration of intent. This statement might even encourage the United States to formulate its proposals along the same lines. Moreover, the Socialist International represented a considerable international political force, and if its Bureau were to approve these principles at its forthcoming meeting in Paris, they would carry a not inconsiderable weight.

Together with Ahmed Maher, I undertook to prepare a statement immediately to clarify our position with regard to the Kreisky-Brandt statement. This defined our position on the withdrawal and security issues, which would have to be of an international, not an Israeli, nature, and be in the interests of all the parties concerned, not of Israel alone.

As soon as we had concluded our statement, I proceeded to meet the President in his suite at 7 p.m. I found him in his dressing-room, sitting watching television with his wife. He asked me to be seated and I remained a few minutes with them exchanging small talk as I did not wish to broach the subject in front of Mrs Sadat. However, I was in a hurry to show him the statement I had prepared so that it might be published at the appropriate time and appear in the morning newspapers together with the Brandt-Kreisky statement. So I asked the President if he had read the Brandt-Kreisky statement. He replied: "No, I haven't. What was it like?" – "Horrible," I said. At this juncture, Mrs Sadat saw I desired to see him alone, and left the room.

When I had explained to him the third principle of the statement, he replied that he had not agreed to it. I then enquired about the statement by Perez on the President's alleged readiness to withdraw the Egyptian project if Israel would agree to a declaration of intent. Sadat replied that he had not said this exactly, but had shown he was prepared to be flexible if Israel agreed to an acceptable declaration of intent. I told him that Begin had not budged an inch on his autonomy project since he had submitted it to us in Ismailia, and that it was a mistake to offer to withdraw our project before discussing it with Israel at the London meeting. If the Israelis and Americans were not convinced we would adhere to our project, then they would attempt to exploit us.

The President pondered a while, then said: "Issue a statement expressing our views on the statement by the Socialist International," I shot back: "I have it ready to show you before we make it public." I then read out to him our draft, and when I got to the part indicating the possibility that we might agree to minor modifications in the West Bank provided these were carried out on a reciprocal basis for humanitarian and administrative reasons, Sadat broke in: "And add: 'for security reasons'." I indicated to him that this was precisely the point we objected to. He replied that he (Sadat) had agreed with Begin to reach a compromise formula ensuring a balance between Israel's security and the rights of the Palestinian people. I said: "Security may be established in various ways, and we cannot accept that this should be brought about through Israel's annexation of Arab territory."

After some reflection, Sadat advised me, in his words, to "content yourself, then, with the phrase 'slight modifications', without referring to a 'humanitarian or administrative nature'." This I did.

We were eager to have the statement appear in the Cairo morning papers, and Ahmed Maher spent over an hour at the phone, due to faulty connections, but finally succeeded in transmitting it for publication on time.

Chapter Twenty Six

Let's Topple Begin !

Sometime later in the evening, Hassan El Tohamy rang me up and intimated that he wished to see me urgently on an important matter. We met, and Tohamy told me that the internal situation in Israel was in a shambles. For one thing, people were divided for a number of reasons; there were some strongly in favour of peace, and these called for the occupied territory to be restored to its owners. And a split had occurred within the Israeli government with respect to a number of topics, notably on the creation of settlements and on how to reply to the American questionnaire. There was also growing opposition to Begin, whose intransigence had metamorphosed into inflexibility, and this posed a threat to the peace for which President Sadat's initiative had paved the way. Begin's health, too, was failing, and the latent conflict between himself and several other ministers had now come out into the open and was becoming violent. Tohamy confided to me that there had been a rapprochement between Perez and Weizman, adding that what he called his private sources provided him with the most detailed information from within Israel itself. We must, he urged, strike while the iron was hot. We had achieved a major success in organizing the meeting with Shimon Perez, and this had weakened Begin's position while strengthening that of Perez. The next step, he proposed, should be to invite Weizman to meet President Sadat in Foeschel, since this would help to further sap Begin's position, topple his government and lead to the formation of a new government whom it would be easier to communicate with.

    I am inherently opposed to intrigue, as it can prove a two-edged sword. There was, moreover, no need of it so long as the course to be followed was clear and our line well defined. I told Tohamy that his description of the internal situation in Israel was largely correct and would undoubtedly be of great benefit to us, as it constituted a form of opposition to Begin's policy of refusing to conclude a comprehensive peace settlement. However, I added, we had to realize that the wellspring of Israel's internal agitation was Israeli fear that the intransigent policy Begin was following would destroy the opportunity for peace afforded by President Sadat's peace initiative. We could enhance this feeling by sticking to our guns and by affirming our desire and readiness to provide Israel with all necessary safeguards for its security, at the same time assuring it that we sought to live together in peace and establish good neighbourly relations with it. What we had to do, I proceeded, was to address ourselves to Israeli public opinion by sticking to this line. It would be better, I added, to let such inter-actions grow and develop. Thus the change would come from within Israel itself. Were the Israeli people to feel that we were seeking to topple their government, they would, in a natural and spontaneous reaction, rally once more around Begin and his government.

Tohamy, however, remained unconvinced and kept harping on the importance of not letting such an opportunity slip. He finally proposed that we go to the President and submit this idea to him. I replied that I had no wish to force such tactics on the President. I added that the President had come for a few days' relaxation and we should refrain from disturbing him. I needed rest myself.

That evening Hassan El Tohamy failed to turn up at the restaurant as was his custom, and was nowhere to be found!

On 12 July (the following day), a member of the Secretariat informed me that the President wished to see both Tohamy and myself at 10.30 that morning on the hotel terrace.

I was at the appointed spot at 10 o'clock. With me were Hassan Kamel, President's Chef de Cabinet; Ambassador Ahmed Osman, who had just assumed his functions as Egypt's Ambassador to Austria; and Ahmed Maher. We sat by the lake drinking coffee and admiring the splendid view. At precisely 10.30 the President joined us with Hassan El Tohamy. I rose to greet them and then sat at a separate table with them. Sadat let me know that he had called us in order to discuss an important subject, namely the invitation to Foeschel of Weizman to meet the President. He asked us what we thought, and since Tohamy remained silent, I asked: "What lies behind your idea of inviting him over here?" "To put further pressure on Begin by making the situation around him more uncomfortable," came the reply.

I said: "Rais, Weizman is a Minister in Begin's cabinet and a member of the Hirut. He may be more moderate than Begin, even have his differences with him, but that does not mean he will join with us against Begin."

Sadat said, "What objection could there be to his coming here for discussions? He could then convey our views to Begin."

What, I wanted to know, was the hurry, since I myself would be leaving for London in few days' time to attend the tripartite meeting with Dayan and Vance. At this meeting we would submit our project and Dayan would convey our view to his government. I went on: "We have nothing to say to Israel at the moment. All we have to do is submit our project, which will be the concern of the Israeli Foreign Minister, who will be in the British capital. What, then, are we to tell Weizman now?"

Tohamy then spoke up, to the effect that Weizman's meeting with the President where they were now would make Dayan even more circumspect and increase the differences between Weizman and Begin and Weizman and Dayan. I responded that we should adopt a far-sighted policy and exercise patience. We were, I went on, on the threshold of the London meeting so why not base our future action on the outcome. An approach to Weizman (I continued) might be useful after the tripartite meeting, but any attempt to do so now would only paint Weizman out of the picture. There was a short silence, then the President turned to Tohamy saying: "Take the following cable, Hassan." After Tohamy had produced a notebook and pencil, the President dictated a cable to be sent to General Gamassy, the Defence Minister, requesting him to contact Weizman through the Israeli mission in Gianaclis and ask him to come over to meet the President the following day. Gamassy was himself asked to come too. Our meeting then broke up.

Next day, 13 July, I was having breakfast with Ahmed Maher on the hotel terrace when General Gamassy arrived at about 9.30. The President had not yet left his room, and Gamassy sat down with us to drink a cup of coffee. He handed me the Cairo morning papers, and I was immediately struck by the blaring headline in *Al Ahram* announcing: "Gamassy-Weizman meeting depends on outcome of London conference". The report beneath the headline ran:

> Gamassy affirms there will be no new meeting of Egypt-Israel military unless there is a change in the Israeli position during the London conference. Weizman recently asked to meet Gamassy before the London meeting, but the latter refused.

At three in the afternoon Weizman arrived on the terrace of the Foeschel Hotel, accompanied by Karl Kahan. He shook hands with General Gamassy and myself, and I left them sitting with some of my colleagues.

The President was soon informed of Weizman's arrival, and a short time later summoned him to his suite. Weizman left the terrace with General Gamassy, who conducted him to the President and left them alone together.

The meeting lasted for approximately three hours, when Weizman returned to the terrace where General Gamassy and Kahan were awaiting him. A few minutes later Kahan approached me and said he would be honoured if I would accept his invitation to have dinner with him. General Gamassy and Weizman, he added, had already agreed to come. I excused myself, saying I was busy, but they insisted, so I agreed to spend some time in their company before dinner.

That evening, I took Maher and proceeded to the restaurant where the dinner was to be held. The view there was breathtaking, with the twinkling of the lights from the mountain villages. Fifteen minutes later I returned to my hotel in the company of Maher, where I was informed that the President had left a message for me to join him in his room immediately upon my return.

I directed my steps to the President's chamber with a heavy heart, but he received me warmly:

"I asked for you to tell you of the meeting I had with Weizman, which I believe was a fruitful and successful one, although you objected to it at the time. I made it clear to Weizman that Begin's actions would result in the loss of the peace opportunity, since his behaviour had shown that he was totally ignorant of politics: if he had had any political sense whatsoever, he would have matched my initiative. However, he failed to seize its implications and showed inflexibility, thus setting the world against him. He could, for instance, have pulled back his forces from Sinai to the El Arish-Ras Mohamed line. The ball would then have been in our court, and it would have been our turn to take a similar step in reply. His intransigence and covetousness, however, have blinded him. I told Weizman that I could not engage eternally in futile negotiations, and that if no radical transformation occurred in the Israeli position before October [the date when the mandate for the presence of the UN forces was due to expire], the situation would be very serious indeed. And I suggested that Weizman should try to convince Begin of the need to make some progress before that date, such as returning the city of El Arish to Egypt and flying the Egyptian flag. Then it would be possible to negotiate with the Israelis, and allow the Syrians and Jordanians to go there should they decide to join the talks. [1]

"He could also restore to us Mount Sinai, where I intend to build a religious compound for the Jewish, Muslim and Christian religions to stand as a symbol for the unity of religions as well as for love and peace." [2]

The President added that he had invited Weizman to come to Cairo after the London meeting. When he had finished speaking, I said nothing, so in a moment or two he asked me: "What's the matter with you, Mohamed – is anything bothering you?" Although I was boiling with anger and about to explode, I replied "No." "You seem tired," he rejoined. "Try to get some rest – you have a lot of work to do before going to London."

I took my leave of him with feelings of resentment and disgust, with Sadat, Begin and Tohamy and with Sadat's working style. What was Sadat playing at, I wondered? Had he found no better way to pass the afternoon in this beautiful place, to which he had come to relax, than to call up Weizman? How could we call for withdrawal from Sinai, the Golan, the West Bank and

Let's Topple Begin!

Gaza and in the same breath summon the Israeli Defence Minister and plead with him to intervene with Begin to get him to condescend to give us back El Arish, which would then become an island in the ocean of Israeli-occupied territory that belonged to us? How could he possibly bring himself to ask for Weizman's mediation: was it so that he would build a pyramid for himself on top of Mount Sinai when it was restored? To say nothing of the fact that it would then be our turn to make concessions to Begin if he responded to our pleas.

The Sadat-Weizman meeting (that had been inspired by Tohamy) had further complicated the course of events, which I shall be dealing with in due course.

I went back to my room, where Ahmed Maher was waiting for me. Before I briefed him on my meeting with the President, we looked over some press reports, among which was one broadcast by the American CBS station to the effect that both Egypt and Israel had agreed to carry on peace negotiations at ministerial level at the conclusion of the London meeting. The prospective meetings (the report continued) were to take place in El Arish, on a date to be agreed upon in London. Another news item carried a report that Israel had accepted Egypt's proposal to resume negotiations after the London conference. Yet another report revealed that Dayan had expressed Israel's readiness to attend the El Arish meetings and that the agenda of the London meetings could be expected to include:

1 The recent Egyptian peace proposals.
2 The Israeli peace plan.
3 The establishment of a framework for the continuation of negotiations between Egypt and Israel.

Clearly, the United States – whether on its own or in connivance with Israel – had concocted this report (a fabrication from beginning to end) which was diametrically opposed to the Egyptian position. The US had deliberately leaked it in an attempt to place us in an embarrassing situation and so force us into accepting a *fait accompli*, namely acceptance of another round of negotiations with Israel even before the London meeting had taken place. I suddenly recalled to mind the question put to me by William Quandt following the Sadat-Mondale press conference in Alexandria. I cursed the moment Sadat had pronounced the fateful words "El Arish" as an alternative to "London".

The purpose of the US in doing all it could to encourage and sustain direct negotiations between Egypt and Israel was to postpone the moment of truth, when it would be obliged to face Israel with its proposals in accordance with the pledge given by President Carter during the Camp David meeting in February 1978.

The United States had procrastinated and had done everything it possibly

Camp David

could to avoid calling upon Israel to abide by 'international law' and withdraw from territory it occupied thanks to American weaponry, and as a result of which its greed and desire for expansion had been given free rein.

The United States was well aware that a third, or even a fourth meeting between the Israelis and Egyptians would make no progress, since Israel refused to loosen its hold on our territory or remove its stranglehold from the Palestinian people. Nothing showed this more clearly than Israel's refusal to reply to the queries addressed to it by the United States itself on the future of the West Bank and Gaza – a precondition (assuming the replies were positive) for any resumption of negotiations.

The United States was pursuing this line with complete disregard for the damaging effect such continual meetings would have on Egypt, and the humiliation and indignity it would bring on the Arabs in the eyes of the international community.

The fact that Israel was in such a hurry to agree to subsequent meetings could be well understood, for this was God-sent opportunity to split the Arab ranks and increase Egypt's isolation by dragging us into negotiations while proclaiming in advance that it (Israel) would neither withdraw from occupied Arab territory nor recognize the rights of the Palestinian people, which it had uprooted from their homeland and dispersed throughout the world.

I made it plain to Maher that I was not much concerned with the manoeuvres of the US and Israel, since each was acting to suit his purpose and serve his interests, and we had to be prepared for such situations. Responsibility for resisting and defeating such manoeuvres lay with ourselves. I told Maher I would not take part in any meeting following that of London if no radical transformation had occurred to change the Israeli position and justify the holding of a subsequent meeting.

What I was mainly concerned with, however, were the improvised and impulsive actions of President Sadat which he undertook without prior notice, thus deviating from the political and tactical line we were pursuing, and which would likely have an adverse effect on our position and require additional and strenuous efforts on our part to correct. I asked Maher if it were possible that Sadat was oblivious of their machinations. Menahim Begin never acted in a given situation until he had thoroughly studied it with his cabinet. I admitted to Maher that I was completely at sea and was experiencing great difficulty in working with Sadat. Then I recounted to Maher the story of Weizman's visit to Foeschel, and the manner in which Sadat had consulted me over it. I had (I went on) told him that in all honesty I was against the visit, and this for reasons which I considered both sound and logical. I would have been prepared to let it pass if he had had strong reasons for wanting to meet Weizman which he did not wish to reveal to me. When, however, he informed me of what had occurred and of the senseless

Let's Topple Begin!

conversation I realized (I told Maher) that it was pure whim that had impelled him to invite Weizman over without due preparation.

Maher attempted to soothe my ruffled feathers by affirming that the President's responsibilities were both heavy and tedious, and he sometimes acted like this out of concern at seeing time pass with no tangible results to show for his initiative. Sadat, Maher continued, believed that such actions would activate matters, and he advised me to remain by Sadat's side, since my presence was of the utmost importance and Sadat listened to me without losing his temper. This was not the case with others who chose not to reveal what they really thought for fear of angering him. Moreover Maher concluded by assuring me that this was my main responsibility as Foreign Minister.

We went on to evaluate Sadat's visit to Austria, and decided it was negative, in view of the fact that the President, in his meeting with Shimon Perez, had approved Israel's theory for regional security. This theory was based on achieving a balance between Israel's security and the aspirations of the Palestinian people. Both Kreisky and Brandt had issued their statement on these grounds, as I have mentioned earlier. In Sadat's meeting with Weizman the discussion had side-stepped our project for the West Bank and Gaza Strip to focus on side issues, such as the restoration of El Arish and Mount Sinai which, far from achieving progress, would only set us back. These secondary issues, moreover, constituted a deviation from our declared and immutable policy lines and added nothing of value to the discussions.

The following day, 14 July, we boarded the plane for home.

On 15 July, I received a visit from Herman Eilts, the American Ambassador, and we discussed arrangements for the tripartite foreign ministers conference which was originally scheduled to be held in the Churchill Hotel, but which the British government was now, for security reasons, transferring to Leeds Castle in Kent.

In the course of our conversation, Eilts asked me casually what our reaction would be if events obliged us to postpone the search for a solution of the Palestinian question to a later stage and instead concentrate upon a partial settlement between Israel and Egypt on Sinai. I told him that we should reject this out of hand, since to do so would destroy the foundations upon which President Sadat's initiative had been grounded, namely the achievement of a comprehensive settlement to the Arab-Israeli conflict, and would have serious consequences. Whereupon he asked: "What if President Sadat were to consider it best to attain this goal in stages?" To this I replied: "My course would then be clear: I would hand in my resignation." Eilts was immediately shocked into saying: 'Good God, I hope you will never come to that."

The effects of our Austrian trip had still not worn off and I was soon to have good reason for feeling depressed. I had spent the afternoon at home with Ahmed Maher looking over some papers for the tripartite meeting when Hosny Mubarak phoned me at 11 o'clock the same evening to give me President Sadat's directives on the Leeds meeting. I told him there were several points in connection with the meeting I wished to clear up with the President prior to my departure on 17 July. He replied that the President was presently engaged, but would be in constant touch with me during the conference. This incensed me and I shot back that I could not work that way. My relationship with Mr Mubarak was based on mutual respect and frankness, for he was a man of unimpeachable honesty and integrity, and as straight as a die.

An hour later Mr Mubarak was on the line again to say the President would meet with us the following morning at eleven at his Maamoura rest-house.

After I had just completed my review of the approach to be adopted at the Leeds meeting Sadat turned to me and said: "I have observed a change in you lately; could you have discussed our plans with some member or other of the opposition and have been influenced by them?"

I replied tartly, "I am not in the habit of discussing our plans with anyone. I put my plans into practice after I have discussed them thoroughly with my Foreign Ministry experts in the utmost secrecy."

Sadat went on, "I would like to ask your opinion on a particular person, namely Nabil El Araby."

Nabil El Araby, our current Ambassador in New Delhi, was then Director of the Legal Department at the Foreign Ministry and was related to Mohamed Hassanein Heikal, the former editor-in-chief of *Al Ahram*, who was opposed to the President Sadat initiative.

I answered, "Nabil El Araby is a competent diplomat, and is dedicated and dependable. I am confident he would not pass secret information about his work to anyone." Then I lost my temper and really let fly: "You are well aware that I did not seek to become Foreign Minister, and I only agreed to assume the post because of our old association and out of a sense of national duty to assist you in serving our cause. I am not afraid of you and I am after neither the position nor the glory. However, I do feel duty-bound to give you some outspoken and heartfelt advice. Decisions, of course, are yours alone to make, and any time you wish me to leave the ministry I shall at once do so, whether you choose to dismiss me or whether I am given the option of tendering my resignation."

President Sadat was moved, and confided me that he had selected me for what I was, adding that he had complete faith in my sincere intentions and my integrity. He continued, "I do not want any assistant of mine to take my words at their face value without due discussion. There was no reason for you to flare up. I asked you a simple question, and I accept your answer. The matter is closed."

The President then shook hands with me and wished me every success at

Let's Topple Begin!

the London meeting. I left Maamoura for Cairo in the company of Mr Mubarak, for we were to leave the next day for London.

Footnotes:

1. Here I recalled the conversation I had with the President on the plane about El Arish.
2. See *The Battle for Peace*, Weizman, p.313.

Chapter Twenty Seven

Inside the Ramparts of Leeds Castle

On the afternoon of 17 July, the Egyptian delegation to the tripartite meeting boarded the plane for London. The delegation consisted of myself and Ambassadors Ussama El Baz, Nabil El Araby, Abdel Raouf Al Ridi and Ahmed Maher El Sayid, as well as First Secretary Ahmed Abou El Gheit from my office, a very promising young man. The atmosphere was gay and festive, for the group rejoiced in its team spirit and was conscious of its national and Arab responsibility. We were, moreover, carrying with us a well-balanced, solid project that would be hard to argue against.

We landed at Heathrow, and were met by a British Foreign Office representative and Samih Anwar, the Egyptian Ambassador in London. A quick look around showed the extent of the security measures taken by the British authorities to ensure the safety of the three delegations. The place was crowded with armoured vehicles, tanks and troops.

We then proceeded to one of the airport holding areas, where I told the journalists assembled there:

> This meeting, as you know, has been arranged on the initiative of the United States, in pursuance of its efforts to achieve a just and lasting peace in the Middle East. We have come here with open hearts and minds, and are determined to explore all avenues to attain the peace to which all the peoples of the region aspire. We hope the Israeli government is imbued with the same spirit, and if it is, we shall undoubtedly achieve the progress so ardently desired.
>
> Peace is possible, and so are good-neighbourly relations and security for all parties, but only if a given party does not attempt to use these legitimate aspirations to conceal goals and ambitions that are inconsistent with "international" law and the spirit in which we have come here . . . Expansionism does not build confidence. Annexation never leads to true or permanent security. Infringing the rights and sovereignty of others inevitably leads to violence. These are elementary truths recognized by the entire world, and these should be our beacon and guiding principles during this meeting.

Inside the Ramparts of Leeds Castle

We helicoptered to Leeds Castle, sixty miles inside the Kentish border, overflying the splendid panorama of the English countryside. My arrival at the castle was mingled with regret at not having visited this place as a tourist. The castle gleamed like a diamond in a calm and tranquil sea. The water around it reflected its walls and towers while black and white swans cruised majestically. Surrounding the castle were vast stretches of hills and valleys covered with a rich carpet of green sprinkled with centuries old oak trees. The castle was built at the time of William the Conqueror, and had witnessed the centuries of British history. King Henry VIII lived there for a while with his second wife, Anne Boleyn.

We entered the castle and its Keeper greeted us and took us to our rooms, which were in a separate wing. Other wings had been set aside for the American and Israeli delegations. When I entered my room, I felt as though I was in another world. The room was a vast one, with a very high ceiling, and facing the door was a spacious, elevated, three-bayed Oriel window overlooking a breath-taking panorama. In the middle of the room stood a four-poster bed. The walls were covered with portraits of persons who had lived and died here hundreds of years before I was born. There were also paintings of hunting-scenes. I could not but feel a very profound sense of history replete with its splendours and tragedies.

The three delegations assembled in the Festival Hall for drinks to break the ice before dinner. I went over and stood with Vance. Moshe Dayan, whom I had not seen since the Political Committee meetings in Jerusalem the previous January, joined us. A bronze statue of an Egyptian cat dating from the Pharaonic period engaged Dayan's attention and became the focus of his conversation, since he had a passion for archaeology.

Later I had a word with Herman Eilts, who informed me that Weizman had given an account of the meetings between himself and President Sadat in Salzburg to Samuel Lewis, the United States' Ambassador in Tel-Aviv. What Weizman told Lewis was much the same as what Sadat had told him (Eilts) that Weizman had requested the President to desist from his attempts to create divisions within the ranks of the Israeli government. Weizman had returned from Salzburg in very high spirits, but these had soon sunk to zero following the Israeli cabinet meeting. Weizman had told Lewis that if he received another invitation from Sadat to visit Egypt, he very much doubted whether he would be allowed to accept it. He had been exposed to a violent attack on the part of Ariel Sharon, in which Begin had played the part of a spectator. Eilts likewise informed me that Dayan had conferred with Weizman prior to coming to Leeds Castle. He (Eilts) also hinted at the possibility that Israel might consider what Sadat had told Weizman in Salzburg, as new Egyptian proposals. I at once denied that we had any fresh proposals, adding that we had nothing else to discuss but the project previously submitted to Israel via the United States. And I asked him to convey this to Vance.

Camp David

We then went in to dinner and members of the three delegations sat intermingled around a long table bearing delicious dishes denying the notoriety of English cuisine. Gay Vance radiated an atmosphere of cheerfulness by her charming conversation.

At eleven o'clock that evening, Vance visited me in the company of Eilts. Ahmed Maher was also present. Vance informed me that he wished to come to an understanding with me before the meeting, and that he had seen Dayan before coming to us. He indicated that he had observed many points of similarity in both the Israeli and Egyptian projects for the West Bank and Gaza. For example, each stipulated a five-year transitional period and a kind of autonomy. Both projects also included security arrangements during and even after the five-year transitional period, provided that Jordan assume a role if it so desired. And both projects aimed at establishing a true peace and normal relations.

Vance added that the real difference consisted in the period following the five years for the withdrawal and the Palestinian self-determination. He believed the Aswan formula was the solution, and was of the opinion that he found more common ground between the two projects than he had previously imagined possible. It would therefore, he added, be appropriate to explore those common grounds and identify the points of disagreement and subject them to a thorough and open discussion.

I replied that we appreciated his role but that the method he proposed would lead to nothing as the two projects were completely different as to their basic philosophic and ultimate goals. Egypt's philosophy was based on Security Council Resolution 242 whereas the Israeli project reflected its disregard for that Resolution, alleging that it did not apply to the West Bank and Gaza. Consequently (I continued) any points of similarity were superficial as both the initial and final points were in total contrast.

I then went on to point out that if we admitted there *were* points of similarity, Dayan would spread the word that we had accepted things which in fact we had not, with the aim of impairing our Arab image. Any convergence of views on sub-issues was of no value unless these formed part of the framework of agreement on fundamental issues.

Vance said he understood our point perfectly and assured us he would deal only with fundamentals. The United States, he declared, were committed to what had been agreed at Camp David, but a serious and direct discussion in which the points of similarity and difference would be underlined was needed to make it possible for the United States, as a concerned and friendly party to both countries, to put forward proposals that would be acceptable internally, internationally and also be accepted by Israel. Only in this way, he averred, would the US position acquire greater support.

To this I replied that we wished to co-operate with and assist the United States to undertake that role agreed upon, and we would not object if Vance felt the need to point to the similarities and differences, but that we, for our part, would always emphasize the points of difference were, in fact, the fundamental points which alone were capable of either reaching settlement or of leading to an impasse, depending on Israel's position.

Vance asked me how the meeting should conclude, and suggested that we announce that the meeting had been useful and that a subsequent meeting would be held on an agreed date and venue.

I told him I could not agree the use of the words "useful meeting" in advance. As regards a subsequent meeting with the Israelis, I had no instructions to that effect. This, I added, would depend on the Israeli position and on whether the outcome of the matter could be considered.

Vance declared that he did not want to tie us to anything and would not insist on a joint declaration. What he had in mind, he assured us, was to issue a statement to the effect that the meeting had been an occasion for serious discussion; that he had surveyed the points of similarity and difference; and that he would be leaving for the area at the beginning of August to prepare for a new meeting, with Atherton preceding him there for that purpose.

To this I agreed, objecting only to the words "new meeting". I suggested he use only the term "for a visit to the region". As far as I was concerned, I told him, I would comment on the points of similarity and difference, as I had earlier explained to him.

Vance enquired as to what proposals Egypt could submit as security arrangements. I indicated the six points [1] already put forward by President Sadat and noted that new arrangements could be added when other parties joined the talks. The reason why Israel (I explained) had to be committed to withdraw in principle was to enable enlarged negotiations including Jordan and the Palestinians to take place in which each would express views on security provided this did not constitute an infringement of territory or sovereignty.

Here Vance informed me that the United States was now less keen to get Jordan to join in the talks, adding that President Sadat had informed Weizman in Salzburg that he (Sadat) was prepared to represent the West Bank alone to the exclusion of Jordan.

My response to this was that it was impossible for Egypt alone to assume this responsibility in the absence of Jordan, and that the President must have been trying to find a solution to Jordan's refusal to join the talks despite the existence of acceptable conditions. However, I added, Jordan would inevitably join in the talks if Israel pledged to withdraw.

Vance observed that it was very possible that Dayan would raise the subject of what had transpired between Sadat and Weizman in Salzburg, to which I replied that I was there to discuss the Egyptian project which we had handed to them and which they in turn had passed on to Israel. Israeli hints as to the alleged existence of another Egyptian project based on what had taken place between Weizman and Sadat at Salzburg were devoid of any foundation, and the encounter referred to had been held within another framework about which I knew nothing and on which I refused accordingly to base myself.

Vance, however, persisted, and suggested that if Dayan referred to what had transpired between Sadat and Weizman, I could confirm it provided it was accompanied by an Israeli withdrawal. This I again categorically refused to do, making it plain that I would in no way go beyond discussion of the Egyptian project and was prepared to further clarify security arrangements on the frontiers with Egypt alone. I told him that when other parties, such as the Jordanians, joined, then additional ideas could be considered.

Vance wanted to know what difference Jordan's participation in the talks could have on security arrangements to which I replied that there were basic points that could not be discussed in the absence of Jordan, such as the relationship between Jordan and the Palestinian state and the minor alterations in the West Bank demarcation lines. I added that I found it unacceptable that Dayan should be allowed to side step the basic issues and draw us into a maze of details and procedural matters. The main question to which he must provide an answer, I stressed, was whether he agreed to the principle of withdrawal. He also had to inform us of what they really wanted, as this would determine the course of the discussions and decide whether there was any chance of progress.

The first priority, I pointed out, was to draw the other Arab parties into the negotiations and this would never take place so long as we succumbed to Israeli manoeuvres. It could be done, however, if the United States were to adopt positions in conformity with its declared principles, while taking into account the size and nature of its relations with Israel. To give Israel the opportunity of wriggling out of its present dilemma, I went on, would be to expose the region to many internal as well as external dangers.

At the end of our meeting, Vance asked me if I thought it best that the next meeting include the ministers of defence and foreign affairs to both sides. I replied that we should not consider another meeting when we did not know the outcome of this one.

I cabled President Sadat, who was preparing to leave for Khartoum to attend the Organization of African Unity's summit meeting. In it I informed him of my encounter with Vance, and the next day I received a cable from the President, which ran:

1   I approve of the line you are pursuing and do not deviate from it. You must show flexibility over the Egyptian position in London and attempt to win Vance to our side.
2   In any discussion with Dayan, adhere to the information in your possession and if he alludes to any new topic on the pretext that Weizman had discussed it with the President, indicate that you are not authorized to take a decision on it and know nothing about it.
3   Do not commit yourself to fixing the date or place for any future

conference, as it is obvious that Dayan wishes to hold a conference in El Arish. If the Israelis come forward with new ideas, the situation will be different.

The following morning at 9 o'clock the first meeting was held between the Egyptian, American and Israeli delegations. After Vance had spoken for a few minutes and expressed the hope that progress would be made in the direction of a peaceful solution, he gave the floor to Moshe Dayan. Dayan explained the Israeli autonomy project, specifying that it was no more than a proposal subject to discussion and modification. They had no desire to intervene in the lives of "Arab Palestinians" (as he called them). Rather, said he, they sought to live side-by-side with them. He added that the project included the termination of the Israeli military administration with the object of ending Israel's control over Palestinian Arabs and to give them the opportunity to handle their affairs themselves. The project also provided for the possibility of reviewing the situation after the five years had elapsed. Dayan turned to Barak, the Israeli General Prosecutor, and asked him to give a detailed explanation of the project.

Barak embarked upon his task by attempting to make his project more palatable, but failed, as the Egyptian proverb has it, "to make sherbet out of stale fish". Despite the glitter he tried to endow the project with, it remained clear, that it was intended to allow Israel enough time to entrench itself in the West Bank and Gaza by creating a new status quo in the territory and establish Israeli settlements and so alter the demographic composition of the area and, in brief, to set the scene for the annexation of those territories to Israel. Barak's explanation ended by saying that the Israeli project deferred a solution to the regional problem but found one for the Arab-Jewish Palestinian problem out of humane consideration.

When he had completed his submission of the project, I declared that I did not approve of the Israeli project previously rejected in Ismailia, as it was inconsistent with Security Council Resolution 242, which stipulated the inadmissibility of acquiring territories by war and thus the withdrawal of Israel from the occupied territories. And I added that the project disregarded the legitimate rights of the Palestinian people and transformed them into second-class citizens in their own houses and territory under Israeli occupation. I then called upon Ussama El Baz to present the Egyptian project. This he did in a masterly, forceful and touching way, bringing out its plausibility and logic and its commitment to the United Nations resolutions on the settlement of the Arab-Israeli conflict in all its aspects. He denied the Israelis any loophole through which they could attack the project, and when he had concluded, Dayan asked if Egypt was prepared to sign a peace agreement on Sinai, the West Bank and Gaza – or even on Gaza alone – should Jordan refrain from joining the negotiations for any reason?

El Baz replied that this was a hypothetical question that was out of context since agreement on the principle of withdrawal would constitute an irresistible inducement to Jordan to join in the negotiations. Dayan seized the opportunity to ask whether the Egyptian six points on security arrangements included freedom of navigation in the straits of Tiran, and whether Egypt considered the Israeli project on Sinai an acceptable basis for negotiations? El Baz replied that these subjects lay outside the context of the issue then under discussion, namely the West Bank and Gaza.

Dayan wanted information on the envisaged schedule of events in the Egyptian project, to which El Baz replied:

> *First*: Agreement on the project.
> *Second*: Negotiations between Egypt, Jordan and Israel to decide on the commencement of the transitional period and arrangements for transferring authority in the West Bank to Jordan and Gaza to Egypt.
> *Third*: Election of the Palestinian self-governing that would appoint Palestinian representatives to the quadripartite negotiations comprising Egypt, Jordan, Palestinian representatives and Israel. These negotiations would determine the details of the transitional period and establish a time schedule for it.

At this point Dayan broke in to say that they had categorically rejected all the United Nations resolutions on refugees as well as the creation of the Palestinian state.

Vance pointed out at this juncture that there was a difference between an independent Palestinian state and one that was joined to Jordan, and he wanted to know Dayan's motives for rejecting a federal solution. Dayan replied that they had not considered such a possibility.

The first meeting lasted two hours, and, truth to tell, it was totally dominated by Ussama El Baz. The Israeli side was singularly unable to either embarrass him or prevent him from answering their questions clearly and firmly. He was, indisputably, the star of the meeting, and we had good cause to be proud of him. He also won the admiration of the Americans, while the Israelis were subdued.

In the chapter in his book dealing with the Leeds Castle meeting, Dayan gives the following description of Ussama El Baz:

> The principal Egyptian spokesman was El Baz, an incisive, knowledgeable, Harvard-educated jurist. Slight of nature, thin and sallow-complexioned, he tried to avoid the social side of such gatherings as much as possible. At dinner he would sit silent, and only peck at his food. But at the conference table he came to life. His strength lay in the sharpness of his tongue, his expert familiarity with every subject under discussion, the clarity of his formulation, and his cutting replies in arguments, which at times verged on the offensive. I

could not tell whether or not he was genuinely committed to securing a peace agreement.

We resumed our meetings after lunch at 3 p.m. and El Baz continued to expound the project's time schedule and the six points on security. Dayan then observed that the presence of United Nations forces in demilitarized zones was of no value. He added that they did not trust the United Nations. He stressed that security arrangments had to include an Israeli presence in the West Bank and Gaza even after the transitional period. He also emphasized that the West Bank and Gaza had to be completely demilitarized except for Israeli weaponry.

Vance noted that they wished to avoid the presence of Palestinian forces in the areas which had limited demilitarization. However, they would consider establishing a Palestinian police force there. Furthermore, he wished to know how terrorism could be prevented during the transitional period. Dayan replied that this could be resolved by settling the Palestinians in the Arab countries in which they found themselves at the time. Vance asked why they (the Israelis) did not accept a federal union between the Palestinian state and Jordan. Dayan told him that they did not object to the West Bank as a homeland for Arab Palestinians, but the Jews would have to share equal rights with them there. He added that Israel distinguished between the people and the territory. It was seeking to resolve the problem of the people by establishing administrative autonomy, though it could not consider Israelis residing in West Bank territory as foreigners.

I made it plain that we categorically rejected the idea of any distinction between people and territory. Israel was attempting to treat the Palestinians – who were the true owners of the land – as inferior creatures, I noted, although they had the same rights as other people, to self-determination.

Dayan wanted to know if this meant that the Palestinians should have the right to an independent state? Certainly, I replied, stressing that this was a matter of principle which may not be contested, but that as we were desirous of satisfying their security demands, we had expressed our views on the possibility of setting up a Palestinian state linked to Jordan. We were prepared, I said, to work toward that end. I thereupon asked Dayan another direct question: did they intend to implement Security Council Resolution 242 on the West Bank and Gaza? Dayan replied that Resolution 242 did not call for withdrawal from all occupied territory. Israel interpreted the Resolution as the removal of its military administration from the West Bank and Gaza. Israel, he continued, was prepared to discuss any idea that offered a compromise for the West Bank along the lines of the Allon project.

I told him that this was totally unacceptable and asked him whether their purpose was to ensure their security or to expand or both?

Dayan replied that a return to the 1967 borders was not acceptable to them, as this did not ensure their security. Neither did they trust the presence of any United Nations forces and so could not risk withdrawal for the time being as any change in Jordan could pose a threat to some of their populated areas, which were no more than eighteen kilometres wide in some places. Israel, he went on, wanted a portion of territory for its security. Any security framework should include the presence of Israeli forces in the West Bank, otherwise, Israel would not consider itself secure, he concluded.

My rejoinder to this was that he seemed to be living in the past, when war was the basis of our relations. Egypt, I added, was now offering an integrated and genuine peace philosophy and this could not be implemented by the usurpation of other peoples' rights. Israel had to understand this new situation and react to President Sadat's initiative, for past experience had shown that expansion was not, and would never be conducive to peace.

A brooding tension settled over the meeting, and Vance suggested that it adjourn.

In the evening Vance came to my room, accompanied by Eilts. Ahmed Maher was with me. Vance intimated that he still considered it necessary to hold a subsequent meeting, to be attended by the foreign and defence ministers of Egypt and Israel, to discuss details of security arrangements, as this point had been raised by Israel, as a pretext for not withdrawing. Vance added that he wished to announce, during the closing session the following day, that the parties agreed to such a meeting. I made it clear to Vance that I had specific instructions from President Sadat not to commit myself to any further meetings unless a transformation in the Israeli position had occurred. Only a few hours before, I told him, Moshe Dayan had proclaimed to all and sundry, including the American delegation, that Israel would not withdraw from the West Bank and Gaza and that it accepted no other substitute for territory as its security.

Vance argued that they needed another meeting to declare their position. I replied that Egypt and the United States had first to agree on the American proposals: once this was done and it became clear to us that the Americans were in need of another conference prior to declaring the position agreed upon, they could rest assured that President Sadat would give this matter due consideration when I had supplied him with the facts of the case. I concluded that I personally, believed that the Leeds meeting sufficed for the United States to state their positions.

Their position, Vance persisted, would be very close to Egypt's. I asked him what their position would be if Israel rejected the American project out of hand as soon as it had been submitted. Vance looked at me meaningfully and confided to me that he would impart to me something of a highly confidential nature provided I let no one else know apart from President Sadat and his Vice-President. When I had promised to do so, he informed me that after presenting the proposals, President Carter intended to sidetrack the Congress so as not to clash with Israel's supporters, and address the American people directly on the US position on the issue and the reasoning

Early associations: fellow conspirators on trial for the assassination of Amin Osman Pasha, 1946; Anwar El Sadat (left), Mohamed Ibrahim Kamel (left behind Sadat), Hussein Tewfick (center).

The meeting of the Egyptian and Israeli delegations at Ismailia, December 25th, 1977.

At Ismailia: left to right, Ahmed Maher, then senior official of the Egyptian Foreign Office, Alfred Atherton, then American Assistant Secretary of State for the Middle East, Herman Eilts, the U.S. Ambassador to Egypt and M.I. Kamel.

The Dome of the Rock, Jerusalem.

The meeting of the Egyptian National Security Council in Cairo, January 1978. Its members included Vice-President Mubarak, Premier Salem, Mr Sayed Marei, Dr Mustapha Khalil, Lieutenant General El Gamassy, Mr Nabawy Ismail, Mr Kamal Hassan Aly, Hassan El Tohamy and M.I. Kamel, then Foreign Minister.

The inaugural session of the Political Committee on January 16th, 1978, in Jerusalem: the Egyptian, Israeli and American delegations.

Mohamed Kamel commenting on Menahim Begin's speech in Jerusalem, January 17th, 1978; left to right, Mrs Moshe Dayan, Mohamed Kamel, Menahim Begin, Cyrus Vance and far right, Moshe Dayan.

The meeting of the Egyptian and American delegations in the Barrage rest-house after the Jerusalem talks ended, January 1978.

The Wailing Wall, Jerusalem.

Mohamed Ibrahim Kamel talking to Kurt Waldheim, Secretary General of the United Nations on the eve of his address to the Tenth Special Session of the General Assembly devoted to disarmament on May 31st.

At Leeds Castle, Kent, England, July 18th, 1978: Cyrus Vance, Mohamed Kamel and Moshe Dayan. (Press Association Photograph)

Premier Menahim Begin, President Jimmy Carter and President Sadat in President Carter's bungalow, "Aspen", at Camp David in the run-up to the signing of the Camp David Accords, September 17th, 1978.

behind it. Later, he went on, they would try to win Congress support and the support of the Jewish groups. He hoped this would induce Israel to submit to the American proposals, but if it did not, they (the Americans) intended to ask the Security Council to adopt an additional resolution based on their proposals.

At this point, Ambassador Eilts told me that Vice-President Mondale objected to this scenario, but the US administration was determined to go through with it. I replied that I had the same confidence in him (Vance) as had President Sadat in him and in President Carter, and I added that I approved of the scenario but it was important that they agreed with us on the proposals before submitting them.

The following morning Vance again came to visit me before the meeting, to inform me that he had had a lengthy talk with Dayan that very morning in the light of our encounter the day before, and had made it clear to him that it was necessary that Israel tackle the question of sovereignty and the future of the West Bank and Gaza after the five-year transitional period. He told him that Egypt could not accept a situation which perpetuated the Israeli occupation, and Dayan had said he was aware of this and now believed that the Israeli replies to the American queries ought to have been more positive. Vance added that he had made it plain to Dayan that they had to distinguish between annexation of territory and the feasibility of deploying Israeli forces under the sovereignty of another state in accordance with a prior agreement. He had specified that the presence of Israeli forces in the West Bank after the expiry of the five-year transitional period could be considered if an agreement to this effect was reached within the enlarged negotiations. Dayan asked Vance to raise these subjects with Begin when he visited the region.

Vance asked me if he could announce to the press following the closing session that he would be visiting the region to discuss the possibility of holding another meeting, and I replied that I had no objection.

On the morning of the following day, 19 July, the three delegations held their final meeting. Dayan started the ball rolling by putting a question with regard to the slight alteration in the West Bank that we had proposed, and sought to ascertain their extent and nature. I replied that in principle Israel should announce its commitment to withdraw before any discussion of border alterations. The demarcation lines on the West Bank could be examined at the expanded meetings entrusted with the task of discussing security arrangements. Egypt's position, I went on, was that alterations should be in the interests of both sides and be carried out for administrative or humane reasons in the most restricted manner. However, I added, the decision was ultimately not ours to make, and the agreement of Jordan and the representatives of the Palestinian people was necessary. Dayan then asked about our position on Jerusalem. I emphasized that the withdrawal also applied to Arab Jerusalem, though we did not want to set up any

Camp David

barriers or obstacles between the two parts of the city.

Dayan thereupon asked if we would be prepared to conclude an agreement on freedom of access to the Holy Places, pointing out that this was not intended as a substitute proposal for what we had put forward, to which I replied that it was only natural that the agreement contain a provision on freedom of movement and access to the Holy Places, but that what we were insisting on was the restoration of Eastern Jerusalem to the Arabs. Dayan observed that the Israelis had stated that everything was subject to negotiation, including Jerusalem, and the decision to annex it to Israel did not alter that fact. He personally believed, he confided, that the Jerusalem issue presented no difficulty so long as everybody agreed that it contained Holy Places for all religions; that there was a need for free movement and access to the Holy Places: and that it should not be divided. A formula for Jerusalem satisfactory to all parties could be found, he added.

Vance then proceeded to read out his draft statement to the press, to be made public after the conference had approved it. Dayan said he would announce that he had heard nothing from the Egyptian side to indicate any changes in the Egyptian position, and added that he would also say that the meetings had been useful in clarifying the positions of each party, and that details had been discussed.

I, for my part, declared that I would announce that Egypt was totally prepared for peace, security arrangements and good-neighbourly relations, provided Arab territory or sovereignty were not infringed upon. I asked Dayan to convey this to his government and call upon the latter to adopt a more positive stand in order to achieve peace.

The meetings in Leeds Castle thus drew to an end.

The results of the Leeds Castle meetings can be summarized as follows:

1. We succeeded in refuting the Israeli project completely while at the same time focusing attention on the Egyptian project which soon became the centre of discussion. The Israelis were unable to find any loopholes and were constantly obliged to adopt a defensive position.
2. After Dayan had attempted to elude and evade the issue, he finally found himself obliged – under Egyptian pressure, and with the Americans looking on – to divulge Israel's real intentions as reflected in their continued occupation, their desire to expand and their refusal to recognize the national rights of the Palestinian people. The American side witnessed this at first hand.
3. We refused to commit ourselves to a subsequent meeting, despite American pressure, choosing instead to await the outcome of the Israeli cabinet meeting after it had considered the Dayan report and after both Atherton and Vance had visited the region.
4. The American side sat listening to the debate for most of the time,

and addressed few questions to Dayan, these being usually in a form implying criticism of the Israeli position.
5 Vance confided to me what President Carter intended to do if Israel rejected the American proposals.

This position had its significance and indicated American preparedness to firmly confront Israel should the latter turn down their proposals. However, one aspect giving cause for concern with regard to the American position lay in the point made by Vance to Dayan on the need to distinguish between the annexation of territory and the right to maintain Israeli forces on territory not subject to Israel sovereignty. This showed that the United States approved the permanent stationing of Israeli forces on West Bank territory after the Israeli withdrawal. I told Vance it was for the Palestinians to decide on this.
6 Dayan made no attempt to raise the question of what had transpired between Sadat and Shimon Perez in Vienna or what had taken place between Sadat and Weizman at Foeschel. That this was so, was due to my categorical refusal to discuss this question with Vance when he alluded to the possibility that Dayan might raise the matter during the meetings.
7 At one point Dayan tried to switch the discussion to Sinai, but we refused to acquiesce, pointing out to him instead that the subject under discussion was confined to withdrawal from the West Bank and Gaza Strip, and to security arrangements.

Footnote

1 Statement of the Six Points:
   a Establishment of demilitarized zones.
   b Establishment of early warning stations on both sides of the border, manned by a third party.
   c Establishment of zones of restricted armaments.
   d Stationing of UN forces along the borders and at Sharm El Sheikh.
   e Considering the Straits of Tiran an international waterway.
   f Establishment of a joint Egyptian-Israeli military committee.

Chapter Twenty Eight

Not One Grain of Sand For Nothing

When I returned to Egypt after the Leeds Castle Conference, press reports of a follow-up tripartite meeting at ministerial level started to leak in the United States. The venues suggested for that meeting were as varied as the news reports themselves: one would have it that El Arish had been selected, another that the meeting was to take place at the American early-warning station at Um Khasheiba in Sinai – while a third hinted that the meeting was to take place at sea abroad one of the United States battleships of the Sixth Fleet!

The quick succession of these reports was a source of irritation to me since they seemed to have received a certain amount of official blessing; and all the more so because I had made it clear to the Americans more than once, when the subject had been discussed prior to, and during, the Leeds Castle Conference in talks with Cyrus Vance, that we would never agree to another meeting with Israel unless the latter showed a definite change of attitude. How could they expect that we would agree to such a meeting after Moshe Dayan had reiterated the previous Israeli positions at the Leeds Castle meeting, particularly that there was no alternative to a territorial compromise in the West Bank?

In a well-orchestrated campaign in tune with these press reports, a barrage of statements emanating from the Israelis ran along the same lines. Prime Minister Menahim Begin declared, on 23 July, that both Dayan and Ezer Weizman would be meeting with the Egyptian foreign and defence ministers on 3 August, at the early-warning station in Sinai. According to Begin, Vance had already approved this meeting!

What irked me most was that those reports and statements made no reference to any consultations having been conducted with Egypt. How could a meeting be decided together with its date, and venue, without consulting Egypt and despite Egypt's rejection of the very idea of a meeting unless there was a basic change of heart on the part of the Israelis, which was not in any way evident at that time?

I came to the conclusion that this campaign was designed to embarrass us by presenting Egypt as obstinate and unyielding. It seemed to me that the

United States was reneging on the promises to us, for it certainly did not square with the United States' pledge at Camp David the preceding February to try to effect a change in the Israeli position sufficiently to make possible a resumption of negotiations with some promise of progress.

I was convinced that the Leeds Castle Conference represented the end of one stage of negotiations. It had become clear that the Egyptian and Israeli positions were irreconcilable. The Egyptian position required total Israeli withdrawal from the West Bank and Gaza after the necessary security measures for all parties concerned had been agreed to. Israel, on the other hand, rejected the idea of complete withdrawal. It appeared to me we had no alternative but to suspend negotiations with Israel to be resumed only in the presence of the parties concerned, i.e. the representatives of the Palestinian people, who alone could accept or reject any territorial concessions. The Egyptian project had, for practical reasons, called for the participation of Jordan not as the sovereign power ruling the West Bank, but to supervise the administration which would be the responsibility of the representatives of the Palestinian people during the transitional period. In short, Jordan would be acting in the same capacity as Egypt with regard to Gaza during this period. This would enable the Palestinian people to exercise their right to self-determination within a purely Arab context. If efforts to bring Jordan into the negotiations failed, we should refuse to negotiate the Palestinian issue any further with Israel. There would then remain two choices open to Egypt. The first would be to resume negotiations with Israel for a partial solution or a separate agreement concerning Sinai – an alternative Sadat had persistently rejected from the start. The second was to turn to the Arabs, work to re-establish Arab solidarity, and put into effect the strategy agreed upon at the Rabat Summit conference in 1974, whether by peaceful or other means, if Israel still insisted on holding on to the occupied territories.

I presented the case to President Sadat on my return from Leeds Castle and explained to him why, in my view, the Leeds Castle meeting should be the last at this stage, notwithstanding persistent United States efforts. I reminded him of the fact that he had agreed to the tripartite foreign ministers meetings at Leeds Castle despite Israel's unsatisfactory answers to the United States questionnaire, as a personal concession to President Carter. I furthermore pointed out that he had personally assured me that he had only agreed to one meeting. To allow ourselves to be led into accepting another one, with no apparent change of attitude on the part of Israelis, would induce both the United States and Israel to believe that they could prevail on us to make concessions instead of the other way around. To do so would likewise re-arouse suspicions and further gnaw at our prestige in the Arab world.

Finally, to agree unconditionally to another meeting would restrict our options and render even more remote the possibility of creating a unified

Camp David

Arab front either in the context of the Geneva Conference by way of a preliminary conference as suggested by Waldheim, or, failing this, by referring the case back to the Security Council.

I proposed to the President that we should take certain steps, *viz*.:

1. To begin urgently to explore with King Hussein his willingness to participate in the negotiations. This would, if successful, create a new situation that would make it possible to agree to a resumption of negotiations with Israel if the need arose.
2. To give Saudi Arabia the signal to contact the other Arab countries concerned and work to iron out our differences and prepare for either a full-scale or restricted Arab summit, whichever the case might be, as agreed with the Saudis the previous May.
3. To demand that the United States honour its pledges, given at Camp David the previous February, and ensure that the United States project is brought more into line with the Egyptian position and to accord with the official American interpretation of Resolution 242 as applying to all fronts – and to reflect the United States positions concerning other disputed issues such as the settlements and the return of the refugees.

Sadat agreed with me not to hold another meeting with Israel, and consented to my leaving for Jordan for discussions with King Hussein. I was left, however, with the impression that he was agreeing to this with some reluctance, either because he wished to avoid a clash with the United States, which was pressing hard for the resumption of negotiations, or because he was loath to turn once more to the Arabs after some of them had broken with him, attacking him vehemently in the process; or even because of a natural reluctance to admit the failure of his initiative.

I assured him that his initiative could never be termed a failure, since it had succeeded in unmasking Israel's intransigence, and that when we had smoothed out our differences with the Arabs, we would be the stronger with what the initiative had already achieved, namely the support of the United States and world public opinion.

Be that as it may, unexpected events of major importance put an end to Sadat's hesitation and impelled him into taking a decisive stand against any further meetings with Israel, even if this meant incurring United States displeasure.

A violent crisis erupted as a result of the talks he had with Weizman at Foeschel on the restitution of El Arish and Mount Sinai to Egypt.

No sooner was the Leeds Castle Conference over than the media in Israel began to bandy reports on the subject. They announced that Sadat had asked Weizman to return El Arish and Mount Sinai as a goodwill gesture in answer to Sadat's visit to Jerusalem in November 1977.

Not One Grain of Sand For Nothing

Then Israel Radio announced that the Israeli cabinet would be discussing the "proposal" Sadat had made to Begin via Weizman, and that several ministers were in favour of the Egyptian proposal.

Next, political personalities in Israel began to present Sadat's casual talk with Weizman as a "new Egyptian proposal", and the head of the Parliamentary Coalition Group, the Likud, issued a statement to the effect that while Israel might respond favourably to Sadat's demands, this could not take place before the resumption of negotiations between the two countries. Moreover, the spokesman for the Liberal Party declared that President Sadat was, in fact, asking Israel to make a concession without offering anything in return, while the National Religious Party demanded that Sadat offer some quid pro quo, such as, for example, giving up his demand for the dismantlement of settlements from the north of Sinai. The military spokesman declared that they could not proffer an opinion before they had studied the conditions for the proposed agreement on El Arish and had ascertained what would happen to the airfields and the Israeli camps close to El Arish, as well as to the road connecting El Arish to the rest of Egypt.

This was soon followed by a statement made by Begin at a press conference on 23 July to the effect that the Israeli cabinet had, by an overwhelming majority, decided to reject Sadat's request that they give up El Arish and Mount Sinai, since "no one person or country has the right to get something for nothing", adding that the Israeli government had entrusted him with a message for Sadat explaining that such "concessions" could only be granted on a reciprocal basis.

Again, in a televised interview by the CBS, Begin affirmed that his proposals regarding self-government for what he termed "Judea and Samaria" represented a major concession on the part of Israel. He then went on to say that he had refused Egypt's proposal for handing back El Arish and Mount Sinai to Egyptian administration, accusing Egypt of rejecting a territorial compromise on the West Bank and Gaza during the Leeds conference, averring that the Egyptian Foreign Minister had thrice said "no" in reply to Dayan's question as to whether Egypt was prepared to discuss these territorial concessions.

On the following day, 24 July, the Israeli Premier, speaking in the Knesset, proclaimed: "Israel will not give away a grain of sand as a present, but is ready to negotiate on the principle of reciprocal concessions." And he added: "If President Sadat is prepared to sign a peace treaty, we are ready to work for a settlement with patience, persistence and the necessary forcefulness . . . if no peace treaty is signed, we shall work to establish a relation of peaceful co-existence with our neighbours similar to those obtaining in Europe between the states of Western Europe and those of Eastern Europe following World War II. If, however, Sadat agrees to negotiate directly with us once more, we shall offer him a certain proposal in return for the restitution of El Arish and Mount Sinai."

Israeli observers speculated that this "certain proposal" was an Israeli demand for Egyptian recognition of the Israeli settlements and military facilities in Sinai.

Those Israeli statements angered Sadat very much for he saw Begin and his government playing havoc with his initiative. In exchange for the comprehensive settlement Sadat was offering the Israelis were using the initiative to barter and haggle over the territories. For each grain of sand Begin was exacting a price. All was for sale, up for barter at usurious rates of interest, in instalments – harsh-term instalments, by the piece, by the metre, by the foot and by the inch! And he had had all the time in the world, and may the best man would win!

Sadat's reaction began with a violent explosion: Field-Marshal Gamassy, the Defence Minister, had been handed a message from Begin to Sadat via the Israeli military mission in Gianaclis. This was the message that Begin, following the meeting of the Israeli cabinet, declared he would send to Sadat, but whose content he had already divulged to all the news agencies, to the effect that there would be no one-sided concessions, that Egypt would not have El Arish without giving something in return, and that he would be expecting an answer from Sadat, and that if the Egyptian President agreed to negotiate on the principle of reciprocity, then he, Begin, would be pleased to meet him in order to resume negotiations.

But Field-Marshal Gamassy refused to acknowledge the message on instructions from President Sadat, on the grounds that it dealt with a political issue, which did not come within his purview as a military man.

Begin tried once again to deliver the message, this time through the American Embassy, and at a meeting with Herman Eilts, at which the latter presented me with the message. I, in my turn, refused to accept it on the grounds of form, since the Prime Minister of Israel had revealed its content to the news agencies prior to sending it to President Sadat. This, I informed him, went against all the conventions of diplomatic usage and was unprecedented. Furthermore (I pointed out) we rejected it in substance and could not accept Begin's presentation of the subject of El Arish and Mount Sinai as "a new Egyptian proposal", and we dismissed out of hand Begin's claim that we should offer territorial and strategic concessions in return for our territories or parts of them – territories seized by force of arms!

President Sadat asked me to draft a message from him to President Carter which would detail the developments since the Leeds Castle meeting, and point out that Israel no longer made any secret of its intentions; its insistence on territorial concessions in connection with the occupied Arab territories, made any resumption of meetings with Israel – which the United States had been working for – meaningless.

It had been decided that I should leave for Jordan on the morning of 26 July to meet with King Hussein. However, Sadat convened a meeting of the National Security Council early the same day, and I had to postpone my trip to Amman until after the meeting. The Council gathered at Sadat's resthouse at Maamoura in Alexandria. At the start of the meeting, Sadat asked me to make an oral report to the Council of the negotiations at Leeds Castle. He followed on explaining the El Arish and Mount Sinai incident, vehemently attacking Begin's attitude. He declared he would not cede an inch of the occupied Arab territories, emphasizing that he had not embarked on his initiative and visited Jerusalem to allow things to come to such a pass. He had, he informed us, decided that there should be no further negotiations with Israel, as they would lead nowhere – indeed, they might make things even worse by impelling both sides to take up unyielding positions. He thereupon announced that he had decided to expel the Israeli military mission in Gianaclis, since its presence no longer served any useful purpose.

At this point, Dr Mustapha Khalil, the Leader of the Socialist Union Party and later Prime Minister, attempted to intervene, expressing his fear that the expulsion of the military mission was a very sensitive matter, and might complicate the situation. Sadat, however, shook his head and, addressing El Gamassy, demanded that the necessary steps be taken for the Israeli mission to leave Egypt within forty-eight hours. I felt Dr Khalil's hand on my shoulder – he was sitting on my left, and as I turned to him he whispered: "Please, Mohamed, talk to the President, persuade him to revoke his decision, or at least postpone it for the time being!" "Why?" I wanted to know. "Because the military mission is under Weizman's authority and its expulsion would be a personal slap to him. He is the only member of the Israeli government we can consider a friend, and if we lose him, we lose all means of contact with the Israelis." "Are you asking me to plead with the President to reconsider his decision to expel the Israeli military mission? I, who, ever since becoming Foreign Minister, have tried to get rid of the mission? To hell with Weizman and the military mission, which is nothing but an official centre of espionage! If ever the need should arise for a renewal of contacts with Israel, then let it be done through the American Embassies in Tel-Aviv and Cairo!"

The President then requested me to read out to the Council the message I had prepared to be sent to President Carter, which I hereunder quote in full so that the reader may judge for himself Sadat's attitude at this stage, which no doubt constituted a turning-point, with the Leeds Castle meeting behind us and before further developments led to the agreement on the tripartite summit meeting which was later held between Presidents Carter, Sadat and Menahim Begin at the beginning of September 1978:

My dear friend President Carter,
   In the light of the latest developments in the Middle East, I wish to exchange my views with you, as has become the regular practice between us, in order to assess the situation and consider what steps can and should be taken to bring us nearer to our common aim: a just,

lasting and comprehensive peace in the area.

I think that we have now reached important and crucial crossroads, and that it would be useful at this juncture, to ponder over what has happened since my visit to Jerusalem.

The objective of my peace initiative, as I stated in my speech before the Knesset of 20 November 1977, was, and still is, to achieve peace. In that speech, I said: "I have come to you to build a new life and to establish peace . . . In the history of nations and peoples, there come moments when it becomes imperative for those endowed with wisdom and clear vision, to overcome the past with all its complications and residues, to move towards new horizons. We must all rise above every form of fanaticism, above self deception and above theories of superiority." I added: "The Arab world is not seeking a durable and just peace from a position of weakness or instability. Rather, it possesses all the potentialities of power and stability. Hence, its position stems from a genuine will to achieve peace, from a civilized awareness that in order to avert a definite catastrophe [for all] we have no other alternative but to establish a durable and just peace, a peace that cannot be shaken by storms, or tampered through doubts, or shaken by ill intentions."

In that same speech, I stated that peace is possible provided that the Arab territories occupied in 1967 be restored, and the legitimate rights of the Palestinian people be recognized. This has been my constant attitude which I repeated over and over again: yes to peace, to security, to normal and good neighbourly relations, but land and sovereignty we cannot and will not concede. All my actions have proceeded from my, and my people's, deep and sincere dedication to peace.

Unfortunately, this spirit has not been reciprocated. From the very first moment, it became clear that Prime Minister Begin was unable to overcome his dangerous illusions, and was not ready to face realities and engage sincerely in the peace process. Throughout all the meetings which followed my visit to Jerusalem (at the Cairo Preparatory Meeting in Ismailia, in the Political and Military Committees), the attitude of Mr Begin's government has been to cling to obsolete conceptions. However, since peace is a cherished goal, we have, at each and every time, overcome our growing doubts as to the real intentions of the Israeli government in the hope that they would come to understand that peace is worth giving up ambitions of annexation and expansion. This is, Mr President, the only obligation we ask of them, and this is what they refuse to commit themselves to. And yet, when you thought that another round of direct negotiations was necessary in order to allow the United States to position themselves and prepare for playing the active role on which we agreed at Camp David, I agreed to a meeting of the three foreign ministers in London, despite my doubts and reservations. I thought it was also a good opportunity to explain directly to the Israelis our plan which deals with the core and crux of the conflict: the Palestinian problem.

This plan, as you know, is based on a true interpretation of Resolution 242, and of the obligations of all the parties as spelled out in that Resolution. It was a translation into the fact of the equation: withdrawal plus security equals peace, good neighbourly relations. This was so clearly obvious that the Foreign Minister of Israel could not, in the presence of Secretary Vance, say that he rejected our plan. But, on the other hand, he clearly stated, also in the presence of Mr Vance, that Israel does not want to restore the land, that it wants to continue military occupation, to annex Arab territories, that it wants to deny the national rights of the Palestinian people, and refugees to abide by United Nations Resolutions pertaining to the Palestinian Refugees.

Dear Mr President, if the aim of the Leeds Castle meeting was to clarify the positions of the parties in order for the United States to be able to assume the responsibilitites they have agreed to shoulder, as a full partner, then I believe that this has been achieved. It would not, in my judgment, be useful to hold a new meeting while the Israeli position remains as it is. The parties would only repeat their positions, perhaps hardening them in the process, and we would be faced with an even more complicated situation. This is why I feel that, unless Israel shows its sincere readiness for adopting attitudes and policies which can help the peace process, a new meeting cannot be justified. All the more so, as Israeli declarations and attitudes have since shown that they have decided to continue on this dangerous course. They try to mix the issues, and divert us to side issues. I even sometimes feel that Mr Begin wants to treat the peace process as a commercial transaction and solve it by barter. This is a distortion of the spirit of my initiative, and will lead us nowhere. We ask for no concessions, the land is ours and we cannot concede it. Peace will not be built on "barter basis" . . . It can only be durable if it is just, and if it creates conditions for good neighbourly relations, otherwise any agreement would bear the seeds of further strife and conflict. Unfortunately, Israeli statements show that they have not yet come to this logical conclusion; and they adopt attitudes similar to those which made it necessary to withdraw the Egyptian delegation from Jerusalem, in order to deprive Mr Begin of the opportunity to completely destroy the peace process.

Mr President, Secretary Vance will be coming soon to the area. I will be discussing all these issues with him. But I wanted to acquaint you, in advance, with my present thinking in all frankness and sincerity. I think the peace process can be saved, provided that the Israeli government can be made to understand that it will not be allowed to continue to exploit the process as a veil for its illegal aims and ambitions. Otherwise, we will all be faced with a situation fraught with great dangers.

It is peace that you and I, Mr President, are seeking and working for. We are working for the future. If Mr Begin agrees to look with us in the same direction we will be very near our goal. If, on the contrary, he chooses to remain prisoner of old ambitions, conceptions and misconceptions, he will bear, before the world and his people, the terrible responsibility of letting a unique chance fade away.

Yours truly

26.7.1978.   Mohamed Anwar El Sadat

President Sadat approved the letter as it stood and ordered that it be despatched to President Carter. Mr Sayed Marei commented on what he described as "your excellent English", but I told him the letter was given final expression by Ambassador Ahmed Maher El Sayid, not myself. At this, Mr Marei looked askance at me, remarking, "In all my born days, I've never met a politician who refused well-deserved praise!" My reply was that I was no politician, simply a man trying to serve his country!

I hurried with Ahmed Maher El Sayid to Alexandria to take the plane from Nouzha, where President Sadat's private Mystère was waiting to fly us to Amman.

We took off at three-thirty.

Chapter Twenty Nine

A Meeting With King Hussein

The lowering sun was setting as we touched down at Amman Airport after a three-hour flight, the journey taking longer than usual as we flew by a roundabout route in order to avoid flying over Israel and occupied Sinai.

We were met by the Jordanian Information Minister, (deputizing for the Foreign Minister) and the Interior Minister. The reception committee accompanied us to a reception-hall at the airport, where a number of reporters representing the mass media were waiting for us. As I answered their questions, King Hussein contacted the airport, enquired about our aircraft, and left a message to say he was expecting us at the Royal Palace after we had rested from our flight.

The Deputy Foreign Minister told me the King had been worried about the delay in the arrival of the Egyptian delegation and had hoped we would get there before dark because of the troubled conditions in the area: he had been checking with the airport frequently to assure himself of our safe arrival. When I heard this, I decided to go straight to the Palace from the airport so as not to keep him waiting.

I have always felt a great deal of admiration and respect for King Hussein who is, in my opinion, a unique personality among the kings and heads of the Arab world. He came to the throne in the troubled times which followed the assassination of his grandfather, King Abdullah, as he was leaving the Al Akhsa mosque in 1951, in full view of his grandson Hussein, who was still a child. Hussein has courage, intelligence and savoir-faire. Nor is he lacking in eloquence, and all these qualitites have served him in good stead in the many crises and personal and public experiences through which he has passed and which he has invariably confronted squarely and unflinchingly. He is a tough man as well as a wise one, and is without doubt an experienced politician.

He received us cheerfully and unassumingly as we entered his private wing. He invited me to be seated, and, having done so, I automatically reached for my packet of cigarettes, took one out, placed it between my lips, and was on the point of lighting it when I came to my senses! I at once removed my cigarette and apologized to the King, explaining that I am incapable of talking without smoking! I then asked his permission to do so and, with an amused smile, he graciously gave his consent.

I next apologized for my dishevelled appearance, explaining that I had come straight away to meet him just as I was, without even washing my face or changing – though I had bought a new suit especially for the occasion – so as not to keep him waiting! The King laughed and said: "Consider yourself at home." He asked after President Sadat and, after conveying Sadat's best wishes, I renewed to him Sadat's invitation to visit Cairo. The King replied that he had already received an invitation from Vice-President Mubarak, and he hoped to be able to take advantage of it as soon as possible.

The King observed that they had been following my every move and statement since becoming Foreign Minister, and had formed a very good opinion of me – an opinion that was shared by their Ambassador in Bonn, Ibrahim Ezzeldin, who was a colleague during my ambassadorial years in the Federal Republic of Germany. The conversation continued for a further half-hour and dealt with general subjects, and then the King took me out onto the terrace, where Mr Abdel Hamid Sharraf – the King's Chef de Cabinet and later Premier – the Minister of Information, the Egyptian Ambassador in Amman, Ezzaf Abdel-Latif, and Ahmed Maher El Sayid were, and the talks began.

I gave a detailed explanation of the Egyptian project on the West Bank and Gaza Strip, and followed this with a detailed account of what had passed at the Leeds Castle Conference. I asked King Hussein to lend all the assistance he possibly could and contribute to ensure the success of the forthcoming stage, in particular by influencing the United States to make a greater commitment to the principles governing the Egyptian project.

The King replied that they had already studied the Egyptian project and had publicly announced their support for it. The King went on to detail Jordan's position, which may be summarized in the following:

1 They were keen to have a peace based on Israel's withdrawal from the occupied territories, the restitution of Jerusalem, and the recognition of the legitimate rights of the Palestinian people. The moment they felt the possibility of this, Jordan would unfailingly assume its responsibilities.
2 It would be difficult for Jordan to participate in the administration of the West Bank while Israeli troops were still there, for such troops would be, in effect, the ruling power.
3 Although there were, undoubtedly, many impediments to peace, including Israeli arrogance, the most serious was the weakness and fragmentation of the Arab position.
4 The King observed that he had made it clear to the American Envoy, Alfred Atherton, that, as far as the Arabs were concerned, there existed no scope for manoeuvre: their demands were for territory and sovereignty, and these were not – and would never be

– negotiable. The King added that Atherton had informed him that the US was considering the possibility of presenting some ideas of its own.

5 The King said he fully appreciated the importance of Egypt's peace efforts, adding that despite his not having been consulted and the fact that Sadat's initiative took him by surprise while he was preparing for a Geneva Conference, he had been quick to declare his support for the move and had toured the Gulf States to urge them to take a positive stand vis-à-vis the initiative, although by so doing he had impaired his relationship with Syria.

6 King Hussein intimated that his fixed target was to enhance Arab solidarity so as to avoid negative implications of the existing divisions in the Arab World which are impeding the peace efforts.

7 He also remarked that, during his visit to Syria the week before, he had observed a marked change of attitude and a readiness to move in the direction of the Geneva Conference, although President Assad remained guarded in referring to President Sadat. Assad, he reported, expressed surprise that Egypt singled out Begin for attack, although the attitude of the Israeli Labour Party was no less extreme, as past experience had shown, the only difference being that they were less open and at the same time more intelligent than Begin.

8 The King owned that it was not easy to understand Saudi Arabia's position, since one and all left that country with the impression that the Saudis agreed with them! He gave an example of this: Vice-President Mubarak had informed him, in the course of his visit, that the Saudis were prepared to back Jordan in carrying out its responsibilities with regard to the West Bank; yet when he himself (King Hussein) visited the Saudi Kingdom, they had informed him that their position on this point remained unchanged.

King Hussein had been deeply hurt when he was informed that President Sadat had accused him of changing position with regard to his role in the West Bank. The Saudis, in fact, never ceased to impress on him their support for the establishment of an independent Palestinian state even going so far as to apply pressure on him to that effect. This would ensure the security of Saudi Arabia and prevent undesirable influences infiltrating across the borders.

9 The King stressed the fact that he was committed to the resolutions of the Rabat Summit meeting on the Palestinian people's right to self-determination, and he observed that Crown Prince Fahd of Saudi Arabia was attempting to start a dialogue between Jordan and the PLO – a subject that was likewise discussed with President

Camp David

   Assad. He said there had been some direct contacts between him and the Palestinians for the same purpose, but that nothing had so far materialized.
10 The King pointed to the explosive situation in Lebanon and the need to keep a close watch on it because of the latent dangers that Syria and Jordan might be drawn into it.
11 The King devoted much of what he had to say to the subject of Jerusalem and changes being brought about there by the Israelis. He pointed out that the importance of Arab Jerusalem called for moral, political and material support. He was working, he said, to that end, his visit to Iran being a step in that direction.
12 On the international situation and the danger posed by Communist encirclement of the area, the King believed in the necessity of a more unified Arab front to stem the communist tide, and he was also of the opinion that such unity alone could guarantee an effective resistance to Israeli expansionism.

When the King had finished his exposé, I thanked him, assuring him that we fully appreciated Jordan's difficult position, and its vital role in any settlement of the Arab-Israeli conflict. Egypt, I informed him, relied on him to make the appropriate moves in this direction and counted on Jordanian participation in the forthcoming critical stage. I told him we were in total agreement on the need to restore Arab unity as a mainstay of our strategy. As for the danger of a Communist encirclement, I pointed out to him that this factor could be used to pressurize the United States more effectively, so that it, in turn, would put pressure on Israel for the achievement of a comprehensive settlement.

It was now almost midnight, and I requested permission to leave. The King, however, rose, saying: "I want to show you something before you go." I followed him to the edge of the terrace overlooking the valley, and he pointed to a spot ablaze with light amid the surrounding darkness, "That," he told me, "is Jerusalem." There followed a moment of pregnant silence, and I felt a tremor pass through my whole frame, while my heart beat wildly with the conflicting emotions of sadness, bitterness, yearning, hope and grim determination.

We left when the King bade me farewell and requested me to convey his greetings and best wishes to President Sadat, and to thank him for having sent his Foreign Minister for consultation, stressing the need for continuous contact and co-ordination. This, the King told me, constituted the ideal working method, ensuring that no party would be taken unawares by any unexpected move on the part of the other.

The following morning, 27 July, I paid a visit to the Jordanian Premier, Mr Modar Badran, to whom I reported what had taken place between Sadat and Perez in Vienna, and between Sadat and Weizman in Salzburg. I likewise

A Meeting With King Hussein

gave him a detailed account of the conference at Leeds Castle. I indicated to him how necessary it was for Jordan to consider taking a more active part, especially in view of Vance's visit to the area and in the light of certain indications that the United States might be ready to present its own ideas for a solution. I stressed the fact that Israel was pressing for Jordan's exclusion from the peace efforts.

Mr Badran thereupon explained his position as follows:

1 Events had shown the soundness of Jordan's stated position at the Rabat Conference, namely that Jordan itself should be the party calling for the restitution of the West Bank.
2 The Israeli Labour Party was no less extremist than the Likud Coalition. It was the leadership of that Party that had, throughout the ten years of occupation since 1967, planted the settlements and sown the seeds of expansion. The only difference was that Begin had said openly and shamelessly that expansion was his true aim, whilst Labour had been more subtle about it.
3 Israel had already made plans to bring down the Jordanian regime and establish a Palestinian regime that would owe allegiance to Israel. By so doing, Israel hoped to solve the Palestinian problem once and for all by giving the Palestinians control over Jordanian territory, and he, Badran, was convinced that Israel was grooming Palestinian personnel to replace them at the appropriate time, as they did for the West Bank prior to the 1967 War.
4 King Hussein had assured President Assad, in the course of his last visit to Damascus, that Egypt was not after a separate peace, and that King Hussein had detected some flexibility in the Syrian stand and a desire to go back to the Geneva Conference.
5 The Jordanian military position admitted only limited possibilities and, militarily-speaking, Jordan was in an awkward position, so the Jordanians' desire for peace was genuine. However, their freedom of action was restricted by the complexity of Arab and Palestinian politics towards Jordan.
6 Brezinski, had lately asked them to take a more active part in the peace efforts, and the Jordanians had answered saying that, although they were not laying down pre-conditions, it was necessary to agree on certain principles for their participation. These were: the assurance of an Israeli withdrawal from the West Bank, and the Palestinians' right to self-determination in their own land. The Jordanians had stated their readiness to offer security guarantees, but not at the expense of any territory.
7 Atherton had brought with him nothing new on his last visit to Amman, and such was also Saud El Faisal's impression when he met with him in Saudi Arabia.

Camp David

8 Begin was aiming at putting into effect the Allon Plan, for what the Israelis were now proposing with regard to autonomy had earlier been proposed by the Israeli Labour Party in 1974, under the heading "Civil Administration". Jordan had at the time cautioned citizens and civil servants in the West Bank against falling for this Plan, and had been instrumental in its failure.

Badran went on to state that Israel was now concentrating on inviting over the largest possible number of immigrants to swallow up yet more territory. Badran told me he could not imagine Israel withdrawing under any pressure that did not emanate from the Arabs themselves.

I told Badran we were not in the least concerned about Begin and whether or not he remained in power, nor did we think there was much to choose between Begin and the Israeli Labour Party, but that if he were to run into trouble or his government were to be threatened, that would be a factor likely to affect the Israeli position. Be that as it may (I went on) our main concern for the present was to pressure the United States into aligning itself with the Arab position. There could be no doubt that if we could bring about a greater understanding of the Arab viewpoint in both United States governing circles and public opinion, this would greatly facilitate any moves by the United States administration along such lines. President Sadat's initiative had already accomplished much in this direction, but Arab endorsement would be of great assistance. Such support was, I believed, already taking shape and would soon produce results; Arab efforts in that direction are needed and could be useful. It was my belief, for instance that Jordan had both a responsibility and a duty to be more active and more forceful in its dealings with Vance. It would certainly be useful if Jordan were to take a more positive attitude in support of Egypt's effort for a comprehensive settlement.

I drew several conclusions from my talks first with King Hussein then later with Premier Modar Badran, which may be summarized as follows:

Firstly: the Jordanian Premier had numerous reservations concerning Sadat's initiative, and, furthermore, did not believe it was possible for the initiative to achieve any positive results. He was therefore of the opinion that they (the Jordanians) ought to proceed with caution and not get Jordan involved, as it was a rather weak gamble. He was attuned to the Syrian position, and was for turning anew to Geneva.
Secondly: and most importantly I realized that the Jordanians knew the West Bank better than anyone else, and despite over a decade of Israeli occupation were aware of all the developments in the territory. This was not only due to the fact of having controlled the West Bank from the time King Abdullah annexed it in 1948 until its occupation by Israel in 1967, but also to intermarriage and security considerations,

A Meeting With King Hussein

and the presence of Israeli forces on the West Bank made that knowledge more imperative. Badran – during our conversation lasting for several hours – left me with the definite impression that he had a very thorough and detailed knowledge of the West Bank. He knew every hill and valley, field and garden, village and hamlet. He knew the people, the families, their women and who was married to whom, what land and what houses they owned, and how they earned their living. He knew who had dealings with the Israelis and who had not, who was for the PLO and who merely went along with it. Furthermore, he was informed of every step taken – or even about to be taken– by Israel in the West Bank and could take the measure, without a poll, of public opinion there, how it changed and what influenced it, with great accuracy. As a result of all this, I became increasingly convinced that no one could decide the fate of the West Bank and so solve the Palestinian problem in the absence of Jordan: it had to take part in any settlement, even if temporary, until we had succeeded in regaining the territories, and so make it possible for the Palestinian people to determine their future either by joining Jordan or having their own independent state, or forming a confederation with Jordan.

Thirdly: King Hussein still resented the fact that no one at the Rabat Summit in 1974 heeded his plea that he be authorized to claim the restoration of the West Bank as Jordanian territory – as Sinai is to Egypt and the Golan heights are to Syria. The heads of state likewise rejected his proposal to be entitled in conjunction with the PLO to make the claim, so as to make the PLO the sole representative of the West Bank – which would result in Jordan losing all claim to it. Had they agreed to do so, the whole situation would have radically changed, and Israel would have had no pretext for refusing to discuss the West Bank, since, as matters now stand, and because Israel does not recognize the PLO, there is no representative with whom to discuss the West Bank.

As I have already stated, Jordan's claim to sovereignty over the West Bank – though it went unrecognized by the Arab states at the time of the annexation – is no less valid than Israel's claim to sovereignty over the Palestinian territories it has occupied over the years, over and above the territories allocated by the United Nations General Assembly resolution on partition.

Yet, despite the bitterness felt by King Hussein, I had no doubts of his readiness and resolve to carry out his responsibilities and participate in the negotiations for the restitution of the West Bank. Nonetheless, the situation was far from simple, for he was entangled in complex and sensitive issues – on the one hand, doubts and mistrust on the part of the PLO, and on the other the doubts and mistrust of some of the Arab countries which, at Rabat, had relieved him of that responsibility. I could understand why he should hesitate to involve himself in this matter without receiving an unequivocal mandate from the Palestinians and the Arab nation. Failing this, he needed, at the very least, an equally unequivocal United States commitment that the negotiations would be conducted on the principle of an Israeli withdrawal from the West Bank. His involvement in the negotiations without both or at least one of these alternatives would constitute an adventure into the unknown. And nobody can claim King Hussein is lacking in good sense!

After my meeting with the Jordanian Premier, I headed for the house of El Sharif Abdel Hamid Sharraf, who had invited me to lunch for further counsel and discussions.

The late Abdel Hamid Sharraf was an intelligent, well-informed young man, looked upon very favourably by King Hussein who appreciated and trusted him. The Jordanian Premier, Deputy Foreign Minister and Interior Minister were present at that luncheon, while I had with me the Egyptian Ambassador in Amman and Ahmed Maher El Sayid.

The informal gathering was characterized by complete frankness, coupled with trust and an honest desire for understanding and co-operation. I started the ball rolling by saying that there were certain indications that the United States were preparing to present its ideas for resolving the Arab-Israeli conflict, and that it was therefore absolutely essential that we should stand together to influence the American position so that what they had to offer would be as near as possible to the Arab position.

I pointed out that Israel was attempting to undermine the Egyptian project on the return of Gaza to Egyptian administration and of the West Bank to Jordan on the grounds that Jordan was not prepared to take part in the negotiations. Dayan nearly convinced Vance of this at Leeds Castle, but I countered it at the time, assuring Vance that there was nothing to prevent Jordan from joining the negotiations provided that they would be conducted on the basis of the implementation of United Nations Resolution 242 calling for an Israeli withdrawal from the occupied territories.

Therefore (I explained to Badran) I thought it desirable that Jordan should make clear its position at this critical stage, so as to give the lie to the Israelis and make it possible for the United States to come up with ideas that would coincide with the Arab position.

A lengthy discussion ensued, in which Badran indicated that Jordan could not take a leap in the dark, but that they were ready to move once they were convinced that the principle of withdrawal was undisputed. I responded by throwing out a suggestion: why should not Jordan declare that its participation in any negotiations was conditional upon the United States committing itself to the necessity of an Israeli withdrawal from the West Bank; failing that Jordan would then be free not to negotiate? Thus, Jordan, as I saw it, would not be coerced into doing anything, while officially demonstrating its

A Meeting With King Hussein

readiness to participate in the negotiations on the basis of the Egyptian project.

Badran attempted to argue the usefulness of such a declaration, especially since Jordan's position was well known to the Americans and the Israelis, to say nothing of the Steadfastness Front, who were all aware that Jordan was prepared to take part in the negotiations if it could be assured beforehand that they would lead to an Israeli withdrawal.

Abdel Hamid Sharraf broke in to intimate that the thrust of what I was suggesting had already been expressed in various statements by King Hussein after Sadat had acted on his initiative, whereupon I again pointed out that such a declaration from Jordan would have considerable impact at that particular time, as it would come on the heels of the Egyptian project, which was built around Jordan's participation. From what I could sense from the United States attitude at Leeds Castle, I could see no harm in such a declaration – especially if it were made before Vance arrived in the area.

Sharraf seemed to have come round to the idea, and ended by saying he was sure King Hussein and his government could find a formula containing my suggestions. He said he would bring the subject up with the King. The important thing, he went on, was to keep up the pressure on the United States of America, and he assured me that Jordan was prepared to contact the Arab countries, notably Saudi Arabia and the Gulf states – and even Syria – to this end. He also advised that Egypt should concentrate its efforts on inducing Saudi Arabia to bring pressure to bear on the United States both before and during Vance's visit.

With lunch over, we bade the Jordanians goodbye and left Sharraf's house for the airport on our way back to Cairo. I felt the visit to Jordan had been constructive and had added one more brick to the edifice of renewed Arab friendship and co-operation. Arriving at Cairo airport, I went straight home and had a hot bath, after which I sat down to watch Sadat's televised speech at Alexandria University. The occasion was the 26 July celebrations marking King Faruk's departure in his private yacht *El Mahrussa* for Italy after his abdication in favour of his son, Crown Prince Fuad.[1]

On TV, Sadat made a violent attack on Israeli Premier Begin, describing him as a thief who never returned all he had stolen, but always kept back something, like the cattle-thieves of Egypt in time past, who, when forced to make restitution, were in the habit of first snatching a third or a half of their plunder! Said Sadat: "'We won't allow him [Begin] to turn the Temple of Peace we have built into a market-place as happened in the Lord's Temple in the time of Christ. At the same time, however, I repeat to the Jewish people in Israel, Europe, and the world at large, that Israel has a right to peace and a right to good-neighbourly relations, but has no right to infringe on our sovereignty or steal our territory."

Camp David

Footnote

1   King Faruk remained in Italy until his death in 1965. President Sadat respected his death wish that he be buried in Egypt. He now lies in the family vault in the Al-Rifai Mosque at the foot of the Citadel. He was buried without any ceremony.

Chapter Thirty

The Last Stand

When it was agreed at the Leeds Castle Conference that Alfred Atherton should visit Egypt, Hodding Carter, spokesman for the State Department, gave out statements setting the tone for the visit. On 25 July, he announced that the United States would be having talks with both Israel and Egypt in the coming month, and that Vance was hopeful that this meeting would take place. He added that it had not yet been decided where they would be held, but suggested that Sinai was one of the venues being considered. The impression the United States was trying to give was that a meeting would be held soon since both Egypt and Israel had assured them that they were keen on reaching a settlement of the Middle East conflict as early as possible.

On 26 July, the spokesman declared that the United States appreciated Israel's efforts during and after the Leeds Castle Conference to work out solutions for the main problems that had obstructed the negotiations, and hoped that those efforts would lead to positive results that would enable the negotiations to start again.

It is only true to say that I was both perplexed and a bit frustrated that the United States was once again making noises about a future meeting without justification, save perhaps an agreement between the United States and Israel to force that meeting on us irrespective of the results. I was keenly aware that the second statement of the United States spokesman had gone beyond all bounds and was intended as a direct provocation to us. What were these so-called efforts on the part of Israel purportedly at Leeds Castle that the United States considered so encouraging? We were there, and so were the Americans, yet neither party saw or heard of any efforts likely to yield positive results and ease the situation – unless, that is, the Americans considered the Israeli Foreign Minister's insistence, towards the end of that conference, on the need to partition the occupied territory, as a positive effort?

It was in this frame of mind that I received Mr Atherton on the afternoon of 28 July following his visit to Saudi Arabia, Jordan and Israel. The meeting was attended on the United States side by Messrs Herman Eilts and Atherton, and on the Egyptian side, in addition to myself, by Mr Ahmed

Camp David

Maher El Sayid, and the discussion lasted nearly three hours.

Atherton began by alluding to the success achieved by the Egyptian delegation at Leeds Castle – a success he described as instrumental in clarifying the problems to a much greater degree even though it had not led to any change of attitude by either party, so that the basic differences between Egypt and Israel remained. For this reason (he continued) it was necessary to continue negotiations to crystallize the positions and enable the United States to fulfil its commitments undertaken at Camp David as regards the active role to be played, by the United States. President Carter's views on this, he declared, were unchanged. These were that Egypt should commit itself to one more bout of direct negotiations, at which the Egyptian foreign affairs and defence ministers would meet with their Israeli counterparts, with the participation of the American Secretary of State, to enable the United States to put forward its proposals since, were the United States to present these in a vacuum, the result would be inevitable failure. Atherton added that he was carrying a message to President Sadat on this point.

Turning to his visits to Saudi Arabia and Jordan, Atherton said these were intended to acquaint the leadership of those countries with the American evaluation of the Leeds Castle talks and why the United States considered them constructive, and inform them of how the United States would proceed in the future. He had, he added, attempted to win their support for the American efforts, and their endorsement of a new round of direct negotiations. He had, he affirmed, assured them that this was not an Israeli demand but an American proposal basically for domestic purposes. However, he had to confess that he had failed to convince them since they were not in favour of another round of negotiations unless something positive were achieved. Both Prince Saud El Faisal and King Hussein had their doubts, and King Hussein explained that while he would not participate in the negotiations, nor would he put any obstacles in their way until he saw the results. Prince Saud El Faisal had said much the same thing – if the United States was determined on another round of negotiations, he would not oppose it.

After Atherton had spoken, I told him that I would as usual, speak frankly as that was in the interests of the mutual trust existing between us. I reminded him that Secretary of State Vance had already asked us to agree to a second meeting. This was at Leeds Castle, before the negotiations had got under way, and I had then replied that we could hardly agree to a second meeting until we had completed the first and provided the Israelis had shown more flexibility. I had also informed him that I had instructions from the President not to commit Egypt to another meeting unless the Israelis showed a change of heart, as to do otherwise would be to waste time and energy and allow Israel to minimize the American role.

However, I had told Vance that when he visited the area after the Leeds Castle Conference, he might at the time propose another meeting – to be the

The Last Stand

last – if Israel showed readiness to enter into negotiations based on the principles laid down in United Nations resolutions.

Dayan had, in fact, made very clear the Israeli position at Leeds Castle:

1. Continued occupation of the West Bank and Gaza.
2. Territorial security, i.e. forcibly annexing territories.
3. Refusal to abide by United Nations resolutions on refugees.
4. Refusal to allow any form of self-determination to the Palestinian people.
5. Claiming sovereignty over the occupied territories.
6. Retention of settlements under the guise of the right of the Jews not to be considered as aliens in the West Bank.

Vance had nevertheless requested me to acquiesce into expressing his hope that a further meeting would be convened. It was his right, but we had reservations which we expressed in private and in public for I stated that we did not object to further meetings on condition that Israel react positively to our peace efforts and added Peace: Yes. Security: Yes. Good-Neighbourly Relations: Yes. However, on territory and sovereignty there can be no compromise. So far we could detect no change in the Israeli position.

This had been made clear in Sadat's message to President Carter on 24 July. The message had been both clear and frank and was based on the faith Sadat had in Carter and in his determination not to give Begin the chance to completely wreck the peace process.

And here I told Atherton that, "I take strong exception to the American attitude, for despite our very definite stand on further meetings and despite the fact that the United States government was well aware of our motivations, American officials have been repeating over and over again that a meeting will take place, just as if our views did not matter. Furthermore, the Israelis are announcing its date and venue on the basis, so they claim, of information derived from you! It seemed to me that what is intended is to embarrass the Egyptians and drag them into a futile exercise which would be detrimental to Egypt's position Arab-wise and internationally.

"Again, and despite the rigidity and obstinacy of the Israeli attitude, the official United States spokesman, Hodding Carter, gave out statements two days ago in which he blatantly observed that the United States appreciated the Israeli efforts at Leeds Castle and later, what were these efforts?

"In fact Israel's attitude is intransigence incarnate! Land and occupation is all that interests them! What does it all mean? Can't you understand, or do you think we don't? What did Dayan say at Leeds? Didn't he say – and you heard him – he was prepared to discuss any Arab proposal for a territorial compromise? In other words, that we should allow him to retain our territories so that he may bargain over the part he should like to keep? Hasn't he announced his readiness to discuss the sovereignty of the West

Camp David

Bank and Gaza after five years? He knows – and you know – that this is completely unacceptable! There can be no sovereignty for Israel, neither has Israel any right to claim such sovereignty. Are these, then, the 'efforts' likely to end the stalemate? And while I'm about it – I was quite surprised about what Eilts said that Dayan had not presented the Allon Plan at Leeds Castle. Are we supposed to offer them thanks for this? Whether or not he presented it is irrelevant, since the Allon Plan does not go beyond the gist of what Dayan has put forward.

"Even more maddening is the fact that Eilts looks upon this as a positive sign since otherwise 'the United States would have had to take it into consideration'! How are we to take this? Does it imply that if Israel were to propose the occupation of Egypt, then America would have to take this into consideration, adopt a middle course and offer Israel a third or a half of Egypt? How can we go on trusting the impartiality of any ideas the United States may eventually submit? The US has taken up clear positions and has made firm and unambiguous statements on withdrawal. This, as we understand, is the formula laid down in Resolution 242, and this is the way the United States has interpreted it ever since it was adopted.

"That is what the United States should take into consideration when presenting its proposals, not the Israeli attitudes and proposals, which square with no known logic, justice or law!

"Then there is that question of points of differences and agreement. We made it perfectly clear at Leeds Castle that this method was both meaningless and unproductive. All it did was to ease the pressure on Israel and was unacceptable to us.

"The main issue is: 'Will Israel withdraw or not?' We are aware that the Saudis have laid stress on this point, as have the Jordanians, who have shown their readiness to join in the negotiations if these result in withdrawal. This seems to me a very logical attitude, for one should know where a road leads before starting out on a journey!

"Friendly Arab states are never tired of repeating that, whether we are dealing with Begin or anyone else in Israel, no results can be adopted for unless the United States take a firm stand. This means that if your proposals represent ambiguous, middle-of-the-road solutions which do not tackle the main problem – withdrawal – then all efforts will be in vain and will lead nowhere. They will only contribute to further complicate matters for both Egypt and the United States, perpetuate the conflict and waste a unique opportunity for peace, to say nothing of the fact that the resulting Arab frustration would provide a golden opportunity for the Soviet Union to reactivate its role in the area! The experience of Dulles and the High Dam in 1956 is still fresh in people's minds. We don't understand why we need another meeting . . . positions were made quite clear at Leeds Castle, and so was the deadlock. Now is the time for the United States to submit its proposals after first discussing them with us: if, however, the idea is just for a meeting for the sake of a meeting then, this would only embarrass us, for we have repeatedly announced that we have no intention of attending a meeting unless the Israelis furnish proof of more positive thinking. This position should hardly come as a surprise since it has been made clear to you in private talks, and it really seems as if your purpose now is to show that Egypt can be led by the nose, and this is something we cannot accept, whether from you or anyone else.

"Furthermore, as you are perfectly well aware, Israel wants to bar everyone, including you, from the whole process, and if we were to agree to a meeting under such circumstances, we would be giving the Israelis the opportunity to influence American public opinion, for Israel would then be able to say: 'Direct negotiations are continuing, so why should the United States submit ideas or proposals? You should let us solve our own problems with the Egyptians!' If this were to happen, the United States would not be in a position to fulfil its pledges made at Camp David last February.

"We do not ask you to be biased in our favour – merely that you hold to the principles you believe in and which you reaffirmed following Sadat's visit in a White House communiqué issued on 8 February 1978. President Sadat has faith in both the United States and Carter, and we hope you will not abuse this faith or impair Sadat's position after he risked a great deal through his confidence in you!

"If you really want a meeting, then kindly inform us of any change you may have observed in Israel's attitude constituting any sort of improvement, to make such a meeting realistic.

"You heard from Saudi Arabia and Jordan exactly what we heard, namely that it was pointless to continue with direct negotiations, and we ourselves, despite our concern for peace and Sadat's initiative, are beginning to feel that this may well be the case.

"Do you, following your visit to Israel yesterday, have anything to convince those countries and ourselves that a further meeting might be useful and fruitful and might even help us a little way along the path to peace? If you have, then we are ready and willing – if not, then I must make it clear that we are not prepared to waste time or bear the indignity of being at Begin's beck and call, that is final."

Atherton was on the defensive throughout the entire interview and could not provide a single satisfactory answer! He attempted vainly to shake my determination not to accept any further meetings. To tell the truth, both he and Eilts felt we were on solid ground.

And so the interview ended.

President Sadat agreed to receive Mr Atherton at 11.30 of the morning of 30 July: he was to meet him at the rest-house in Maamoura. I spent an hour with the President before the meeting briefing him on what took place between Atherton and myself. I told him the Americans should understand that when we said something, we meant it and stuck to it. I informed him that

Camp David

I, personally, would never agree, under any circumstances, to take part in a further meeting with the Israelis unless there was some justification for doing so through a change of attitude on their part. Sadat approved, and confided to me that he could not understand the American attitude, especially after the long and clear message he had sent to Carter on 26 July.

Atherton began by conveying President Carter's greetings and best wishes to President Sadat, and he intimated that he was the bearer of a message which had been given to him the day before. In his turn, Sadat thanked Carter and requested Atherton to pass on to Carter his own best wishes to himself and his family, and to inform him that, despite everything, he (Sadat) remained optimistic.

Atherton read out the main points in Carter's message. He (Carter) was grateful to Sadat for the frankness with which he had dealt with the situation in his message of the twenty-sixth, and expressed the hope that their dialogue and exchange of ideas would continue. Carter said he understood and appreciated Sadat's concern at the delay in moving towards a peaceful settlement which (he went on) called for tireless efforts on both their parts to foil the attempts being made in some quarters to wreck the peace initiative. Although the Leeds Castle talks had been constructive, they had not solved any of the principal problems still pending between Egypt and Irsael. For this reason (the message continued) and in order to keep to the line laid down between Egypt and the United States at Camp David, it was necessary that Egypt show a willingness to keep the negotiations going by agreeing on another round of talks, to be attended by the foreign and defence ministers of Egypt and Israel, and in the presence of the United States Foreign Secretary. When this had been agreed, Vance would visit the area with a special message from President Carter.

Sadat expressed his high esteem for President Carter, and told Atherton that I had acquainted him with what had taken place two days before. Sadat said that, before discussing the matter, he would like Atherton to give him some details regarding the latter's visit to Israel, the more especially since the visit had coincided with Sadat's announcement of his refusal to receive the message Begin had addressed to him, because the Israeli Premier had made its contents public before sending it. Atherton's visit had also occurred while the Egyptian President was delivering a speech at Alexandria University on 27 July. Sadat signified that he was anxious to know the results of Atherton's trip to Saudi Arabia and Jordan as well. Atherton accordingly made the following points:

> *First:* There were signs that several members of the Israeli cabinet and Knesset felt unhappy and embarrassed by the manner Sadat published his discussions with Weizman at Salzburg, and also with the manner in which Begin had handled the matter.

The Last Stand

Second: Begin's position in the Knesset was unchanged, and he still enjoyed majority support. There were no indications of an imminent change.

Third: He had met with Begin, Ygal Yadin, Dayan and Weizman and had discussed with them America's evaluation of the Leeds talks. During these discussions, he (Atherton) had thrown out suggestions that they should modify their attitude in view of what might occur following the five-year transitional period. The fact that Begin had listened without saying anything was, in Atherton's view, significant, since Begin had always been quick to answer in the past. His silence on this occasion could be taken to mean that he (Begin) did not reject the proposal out of hand, in fact, some of those around him felt he was in a more flexible frame of mind, as he had told them that "it was possible to re-phrase the Israeli answers to the American questionnaire". Dayan had already, after Leeds Castle, hinted at the possibility of modifying the Israeli response. Begin, moreover, had finally agreed on the possibility of discussing the question of sovereignty over the West Bank and Gaza following the five-year transitional period.

Atherton added, that although this did not constitute an acceptable answer to the American questionnaire and was otherwise unsatisfactory, yet, compared with Begin's previous attitude, it might be looked upon as some sort of progress, and as opening the door to further possibilities. There were those in Israel who interpreted this to mean that, for the first time, the Israeli government did not exclude the possible recognition of Arab sovereignty. Several newspapers had reflected similar ideas, and neither the government nor cabinet members with whom he talked had denied them. That, added Atherton, might be some kind of opening.

Fourth: With regard to the personal attack on Begin, he felt this was being resented, and might have an adverse effect and that was also his opinion. Atherton said he would return to Israel to await Vance and that he had left them several questions to which he expected answers.

Fifth: As regards his visits to Saudi Arabia and Jordan, Atherton repeated what he had already told me which I had already conveyed to Sadat. Before concluding, he said, he wished to explain that the United States laid great importance on this second meeting they were proposing. The United States was unswerving in its intentions, and was acting throughout on the lines of the Camp David scenario. The question was how the United States purposes could best be achieved. It was necessary that President Carter gain the support of United States public opinion and so influence opinion within Israel. For the fact was that although Saudi Arabia, Jordan and we in Egypt were aware that matters had reached a dead end, the public in the United States was as yet unaware of this.

My reply to all this was that we had been talking about it for the last two days, while the main differences between us were twofold. The first was the way in which the United States had handled the question with complete disregard for our circumstances and our point of view. The second was that basic US ideas would not give us what we wanted but, instead, coincided with what Begin would like to achieve, namely to restrict commitment to negotiations during the five transitional years, whereas we were emphasizing that our starting-point was a commitment by Israel to withdraw, given all the necessary security measures. I assured Atherton that if they were thinking in terms of a compromise between the Israeli and Egyptian proposals, then we would not get anywhere, since we had submitted our proposals at Leeds Castle for the West Bank and Gaza but they were determined to divide the territory. Although we rejected this, we were prepared to receive their suggestions through the United States, provided that these were serious and worthy of consideration, unlike Begin's offer (mentioned by Atherton) to discuss the sovereignty issue when five years had elapsed.

Our proposal was that, if the United States wished to resume direct negotiations in the absence of an Israeli commitment to withdraw, then they should submit a project – after discussing it with us – stating the declared US position on withdrawal and other issues. To put it in another way – we could not resume direct negotiations without a commitment by Israel that the framework for such talks would be withdrawal or, if that were not possible, the American proposal should contain an explicit commitment that the essence of the negotiations lay in the implementation of the withdrawal in return for security measures for all parties. Without such a commitment, from either Israel or the United States, any resumption of negotiations on our part would be like sowing in the wind.

There was, I added, another matter, namely, that the Egyptian proposals were based on the assumption that Jordan would participate in the administration of the West Bank during the five-year transitional period, and it was a well-known fact that Jordan's condition for taking part in the negotiations was a clear understanding that such negotiations would end the occupation. Without Jordan, the negotiations between Egypt and Israel would be limited to Gaza, without the West Bank, and this was unacceptable for it would fritter away the Palestinian cause and thus undermine it. The Israeli intention to exclude Jordan had now become clear, and this invalidated the Egyptian proposals.

Atherton replied that: "I may not have explained our position clearly yesterday. We do ask of Israel a commitment to negotiate: there may be some ambiguity as regards the withdrawal, but we do insist on it."

To this I retorted: "We are not renegotiating Resolution 242 – that has already been done in the Security Council. The negotiations should be confined to its implementation."

It was then Sadat's turn to speak: "After hearing President Carter's message and Mr Atherton's evaluation of the situation, I have this to say. You may recall that before the meeting of Leeds Castle I had announced that I could not deal with the Israelis unless something new appeared in their attitude. But when Mr Carter asked me for one more bout of negotiations, I agreed, and because of our personal friendship I accepted that the meeting be held in Leeds Castle instead of El Arish, which I favoured as the venue for the meeting.

"After my visit to Jerusalem, I believed we had gone beyond the stage of doubts and complexes: however, it became clear that the Israelis were constantly raising obstacles. This was obvious at every stage – in Jerusalem, at Ismailia and at the meetings of the political and military committees. And though I knew their aim was expansion and the acquisition of additional territory and establishing new borders for Israel, my goal has ever been to push forward the peace process and to make it easier for them to accept peace. Yet they swept this aside and let greed dominate their every action.

"Then came the Leeds Castle Conference, and what I had always expected materialized for they showed themselves for what they really are and revealed their goal to be possession of land.

"In my talk with President Carter, prior to the initiative, in April 1977, we discussed three topics: Territory, the nature of peace, and the Palestinian problem. There was no essential difference between us, save as regards the nature of peace, for I believed (after thirty years of hostilities) that it would not be easy to establish normal peaceful relationships at one go. Carter had talked with the Israelis before our meeting, and they had informed him that all they aspired to was recognition of their country; direct negotiations with them; the normalization of international relationships and the establishment of co-operation and peaceful co-existence. They had told Carter at the time that no Arab could possibly agree to their demands.

"In November, however, we left all that behind, and acquiesced to their presence in the area, our readiness for direct negotiations, recognition of their state and all the security they could wish. We likewise proclaimed our preparedness to establish normal relations, open our borders and co-operate on the principle of co-existence. This remains my attitude. We offered them something they never imagined possible in their wildest dreams, but they were defeated by their very nature and their propensity to take all while demanding still more. This truth was revealed for all to see at the Leeds Castle Conference, when we submitted our proposals and the six-point security plan and, in addition, declared that we did not even object to the United States having a defence pact with them.

"The Israeli answer was that their security lay in dividing the territories – which is something we have no power to do. Begin's attitude was extremely arrogant, not to say impertinent, when he proclaimed that not a grain of sand would be given away without something in return. The same goes for Dayan, who said they could not give us Christmas presents for nothing. That is why I ordered the Israeli military mission back to Israel.

"Now President Carter, in this most recent message of his, is asking for further talks with Israel, to be attended by Vance and the foreign and defence ministers of both countries. I regretfully have to state that my attitude at present is that no further talks will be held at any level unless they declare that territory forms no part of any compromise. In return, we would be prepared to go to the ends of the world to give them the security arrangements they need. We must not waste years in discussions and talk about meeting them halfway, possible compromises, and so forth. Land and sovereignty must remain outside the bargaining framework: we are not in the jungle where people seize other people's property, although they in Israel, led by Begin, are trying to transform Israel into a great power in the area at the expense of our territory, while obtaining security and peace at the same time!"

Sadat fell silent for a while, then said in a strong – almost an emotional – voice: "Egypt and the United States enjoy close ties of friendship which we cherish and wish to strengthen, through increased co-operation. Yet at this very moment, the Pentagon transmits to Israel twice daily information concerning our defences by American satellite! We, for our part, have no one to provide us with pictures of Israel, although we definitely wish to feel secure!

"Personally, I am very surprised by the United States attitude. How can you allow such exploitation by Israel? You give them everything, yet Begin defies you in the most insolent way and you can do nothing! As for providing Israel with aerial maps, which threatens our security, I should be very loth to spoil the image our peoples have of America, so I am requesting officially, and confidentially, that the United States should inform us of all it has provided and is providing Israel with concerning our defences. This could be useful in case they should insolently proclaim that they refuse to be pressured by the United States.

"You can ask Kissinger what Israel asked you for four days after the start of the October War, and what you have offered in the form of the most sophisticated equipment both then and afterwards.

"Please inform my friend President Carter that I will not embarrass him – all I ask is that you preserve your country's image in the eyes of the Arabs,

The Last Stand

for Israeli arrogance and insolence spring from their possession of American-made weaponry, with which you so generously supply them, to say nothing of the co-operation with the Pentagon! My people will most certainly be aware that there are Americans fighting in the ranks of the Israeli armed forces! So far everything you have done has gone to help bring about Israeli occupation of Arab territory. I could proclaim this far and wide, but I won't because of my friendship for Carter and my gratitude to the American people! My advice, however, is that you try and repair the American image, and you will find in me a true and reliable friend. As a matter of fact, King Khaled recently sent me a message requesting me to break off all contacts with Israel now that such contacts have proved utterly useless. I feel it is now up to the United States to clarify its position, which so far it has not done. We are ready to listen to anything new, but I repeat that our readiness for direct negotiations, for all the necessary security arrangements, for normalization of relations and open borders, does not include the giving up of a single inch of territory, and Israel must remove all its settlements on the West Bank. This has, ever since 1967, been your position too, and even Goldberg the Zionist was in favour of an Israeli withdrawal with minor modifications. I do not insist that withdrawal should take place before negotiations are begun – they can state their acceptance of the principle with an American guarantee. Israel's aim is to exclude the United States from the negotiating table in one way or another so they may have us to themselves.

"I would have been prepared to countenance this, had they wished to live like any other country of the Middle East, but since they do not, I shall always insist on your presence during negotiations, because we want you to bear witness to their behaviour. Indeed, they actually requested me to agree to a twosome, but I refused, and when Weizman informed me that the whole world would give me credit for my peace efforts, I told him I would leave that credit to President Carter.

"I wish to convey all this to Carter as well as to Vance in order that he may bear it in mind during his next visit to the area, and please make it clear to Carter that I have no desire to embarrass him in any way. Kindly also touch on the fact that I sent him a letter informing him of my meetings in Austria and ensuing developments.

"You must know that we do not want to be forced to reject any American project, for this we will do if it is designed to curry favour with the Israelis by seeking a compromise. Although I realize that this might cause Carter some embarrassment, I would like you to explain to him that I would have had no other alternative. What is important is that he should not come up with something that would harm his image in this area, for he is still my friend, and all we are asking is that you should be firm with Israel and ascertain whether or not they are prepared to abandon their claims for territory and sovereignty and sit down with the Arabs to negotiate peace."

Camp David

There followed a lengthy exchange between Sadat and Mr Atherton which, for convenience sake, I shall set down as follows:

Atherton: "Mr President I shall certainly convey to President Carter everything you have just said: he reciprocates your feelings for him, and the whole world is aware of the great affection and respect America has for you. I agree that negotiations may be protracted over many years, and that if we are not a party to them they would drag on for even longer. The United States, however, will not allow this to happen, for our presence will prevent this: although it is difficult for us to place much faith in the future if there should be no way to resume negotiations. We still stand by our commitments at Camp David, but I cannot see how we are to play our part unless negotiations are continued."

Sadat: "That is understandable, and we are, of course, prepared to negotiate and be patient and flexible, but it is Israel which is obstructing. The situation is clear for all to see: they occupy our territories and wish to retain part of them, so don't place me in a position in which the Israeli Premier is enabled to formally announce that his principle is never to give anything away for nothing! Or had I, perhaps, been mistaken all along, and what they have really been doing is giving me parts of their own territory? The fact is, of course, that they are nothing but marauders! Since, however, we are not living in a jungle, the decisive moment for us came when, at Leeds Castle and in the course of discussions in the Knesset, they made known their government's decision not to give back anything for nothing. At that time, when I met Weizman, I did not claim El Arish, since I might just as well have claimed the whole of Sinai. I merely discussed the future with him and suggested that any future meeting be held in El Arish and Beersheba.

"The Israelis should be made to understand that I am not a weakling and that they will never succeed in forcing any territorial concessions from me. I told Weizman that the way to win the trust of the Egyptian people was never to touch their land, and they would then never have anything to worry about on this score. This is my second initiative, following the first of November 1977. It means I am ready to negotiate anything save territory and sovereignty, but will never tolerate any attempt to plant a great power in the area that would impose its will on us. The Egyptian people might understand the fact that the United States guarantee Israel's security, but only provided you make it clear to Israel that it must not use the weapons you have supplied to it to expand and lay claim to other people's territory. Should you fail to do this, my people will lay the blame on you, and it won't be through any fault of mine."

The Last Stand

Atherton: "You will see, Mr President, that our positions will be clear for all to see, and we are really sorry, for we thought we were drawing closer to the crucial points at issue."
Sadat: "The fact is, you were never close, and you will never get closer as long as territory is the Israeli objective. New approaches must first emerge."
Atherton: "I didn't mean we were close to bringing about an agreement between Israel and yourselves, only that we were close to achieving what we agreed upon at Camp David in February 1978. In order to carry through that agreement we must have negotiations as a framework."
Sadat: "That's true for nothing can be achieved without sitting around a negotiating table: the Soviets asked me to sit down with Golda Meir in Tashkent in 1972, but I refused because I was the defeated party: now, however, you are asking me to sit down with the Israelis after Begin has informed me in a tone of finality that he is not prepared to give land away for nothing! This I cannot accept, and that's all there is to it!"
Ambassador Eilts: "Can we not say that you suggest a normalization of relations in return for restitution of the territories?"
Sadat: "I've offered more than that."
Ambassador Eilts: "What I am now proposing is this: may we look into what Your Excellency has offered – which in itself is more than they ever dreamed of – and maybe consider it as part of a package deal, and couldn't this be done through a second meeting?"
Sadat: "You've heard what I had to say and I trust you will relay it to President Carter. I am leaving the whole affair in the hands of President Carter, the Congress and the American people."
Atherton: "We know President Carter feels that he has an obligation towards you, and believes that in order to achieve anything, he needs another meeting, as we have explained to you. We have a problem and only another round of negotiations will serve. We hope no announcement will be given out to the press, so as to keep all the options open."
Sadat: "I've explained where I stand both to you and to my people in my 27 July speech."
Atherton: "As regards the new approach you are calling for, would it be sufficient for the United States to announce that it feels progress is being made?"
Mohamed Ibrahim Kamel: "Of course it wouldn't! But if, in your invitation to negotiate, you were to make a commitment to the effect that the meeting would be based on the implementation of withdrawal, as explicitly laid down in Resolution 242. . ."
Sadat: "No . . . No . . . No . . .! We have now reached the point of no

return – either Peace or No Peace . . . And I beg you to make it clear to Carter that Israel is not ready for peace and Begin will not be a peacemaker. The Israelis feel they are entitled to take decisions, but so do we, and I call on the whole world to bear witness as to who is in the right and who in the wrong! When they have shown themselves up for what they are, then the whole world will pass its judgment on this thoroughly spoilt child of yours. The day will come when the world will realize that the Israelis have destroyed that last hope of peace. As for us, we are certain we will emerge victorious and regain our territory in spite of everything!"

Ambassador Eilts: "I am aware of what you are asking us to get from Israel, but how can we incorporate this in an American proposal?"

Sadat: "If you want to know what I think, and if you are asking me how you should go about doing it, I suggest that you refrain from going into details and simply submit a paper setting forth the principle of inadmissibility of acquiring territory by force; the paper should also set down what you have already stated, namely that settlements are illegal. Once this has been done, the parties can get together to discuss other matters, security included. Nobody can object to either the resolutions of the UN or the inadmissibility of acquisition of territory by force.

"The whole world knows that Israel cannot survive without your help, and Goldman told me he had contacted Erlich, the Israeli Finance Minister, and Shimon Perez, and they were all looking to America to rid them of "that man Begin". The United States should assume its responsibilities!"

Atherton: "Mr President, how are we to submit our proposals in the absence of negotiations?"

Mohamed Ibrahim Kamel: "We had negotiations at Leeds Castle, at which they clearly stated – in your presence – their resolve to divide up the territory. The United States could use the outcome of that conference to present it proposals without dragging us into a new negotiating farce."

Ambassador Eilts: "Mr President, when we suggested the Leeds Castle meeting, we did not expect anything positive to come out of it. The scenario was that each side would explain its position. Atherton and Vance would visit the area and, finally, another meeting would be held.[1] We would then put forward our proposals.

"We have worked on this basis, and we must not appear to be bringing pressure to bear on any of the parties, the important issue being that we are in dire need of another round of negotiations before we can submit our proposals. Mohamed Kamel says there is no need for a further meeting before this can be done, yet our position is that, without this meeting, the impression will gain ground that we are

The Last Stand

trying to impose a definite line of thought on one side and that therefore there must be another get-together.

"Mr President, may I put a question to you? If the United States were to issue a general statement setting forth the main outlines, would you then agree to a further meeting?"

Sadat: "I advise you to take your time and not to do anything that would harm your image in the area. It is not our wish that the United States should present a definite proposal, since that would satisfy nobody. My view is that we should avoid going into details and that your communiqué should deal with nothing but the principles on which we all agree.

"So all I am asking is that, at a time convenient to the United States, it should issue a communiqué with some such wording as follows: *In accordance with the international code of morality*, and in pursuance of the spirit of and principles of the United Nations Charter and Security Council Resolution 242, any solution to the conflict between the two sides demands an end to the territorial occupation and their joint co-operation for peace and security. The United States will join in the negotiations.

"President Carter is at liberty to add any security measures he may deem appropriate to satisfy the needs of both parties. He may also refer to normalization, recognition, open borders and co-operation between neighbouring nations. He may likewise give all the necessary guarantees, while at the same time expressing America's desire to participate in such guarantees."

Ambassador Eilts: "This is different from what we agreed to."

Sadat: "Of course it is: certain unfortunate developments have occurred, beginning with Leeds Castle, and these were compounded by Begin's letter – a letter which denotes his arrogance and insolence!"

Ambassador Eilts: "It is obvious that the letter caused you great displeasure!"

Sadat: "Not really: it merely exposed him for what he truly is, for I would have wished it otherwise. It signified that we were at a crossroads: we could either continue on the road to peace – within a definite framework – or we could allow Israel to win on points, for it is a sad fact that, while they have no case, if we do not face them firmly they will win hands down and we shall have irretrievably lost our chance for peace."

So ended the meeting. I accompanied Mr Atherton and Ambassador Eilts to the door where a number of newsmen were gathered, and then made my way back to Sadat. Kissing his forehead, I said: "Bravo, Rais!"

He smiled as he replied: "What did you expect, Mohamed?"

Camp David

Footnote

1 President Sadat never hinted at a second meeting to follow that held in Leeds Castle when I returned from the latter conference, saying only that he had agreed to the Leeds meeting solely as a gesture to President Carter, and that it would be the last.

Chapter Thirty One

The Leap To The Summit – Why?

Mr Atherton left Egypt for Washington with President Sadat's final decision not to attend a meeting of foreign and defence ministers as proposed by the United States, and to participate in direct negotiations only if these ruled out any discussion on territory or sovereignty.

This attitude was a disppointment to the American government, for it put paid to the continuation of the direct negotiations and forced it to seek another way out. This it found by deciding to bypass the proposed meeting at ministerial level and, instead, leap to the level of a tripartite summit, to be attended by President Sadat, Premier Begin and President Carter.

It was decided that the Secretary of State should travel to the Middle East carrying with him Carter's invitation to such a conference, to both Begin and Sadat, and that his mission should include a visit to both Saudi Arabia and Jordan in an attempt to allay their apprehensions and induce them to support the idea of the conference. Since all this was held to represent a great risk to President Carter's political career, the purpose of Vance's trip was kept a closely guarded secret.

Before giving the background to this decision, I would like to cite two incidents that occurred at the time, the first being the visit of Crown Prince Fahd of Saudi Arabia to Alexandria after Atherton had left. Meeting with Sadat, he blessed his refusal to resume negotiations and expressed the readiness of his country to carry out its role of regrouping the Arabs as a first step towards an Arab summit.

The second incident was a statement to the United States Senate attributed to the US Secretary of State carried by some of the news media to the effect that Sadat's refusal to resume negotiations is considered "an obstacle to peace". I immediately sent for the American Ambassador and demanded an explanation. The Ambassador denied all knowledge of the statement, and the following morning presented me with the text in which Vance had expressed his belief in the need for negotiations between the parties concerned so that the Americans could submit their ideas should the negotiation run into difficulties.

To go back to the reasons for the American decision to pass over a ministerial meeting in favour of a tripartite summit at Camp David, I am here basing myself on the minutes of the meeting of Mr Harold Saunders, the Assistant Secretary of State for Middle East Affairs, with the accredited reporters to the State Department, on 3 August 1978, to explain the reasons for Vance's visit to the area.

The minutes, covering forty-nine pages,[1] were kept reasonably secret, in the sense that those present pledged not to reveal in their comments or reports concerning Vance's anticipated visit to the Middle East, even by insinuation, their sources of information.

Saunders began the interview by explaining that the course taken by the State Department, and which it intended to follow up, was the continuation of direct negotiations to which President Sadat had put an end at his last meeting with Atherton on Sunday 30 July. It was for this reason that Vance was being despatched to the area on a fact-finding mission to ascertain the best way of resuming them.

Saunders declared that the Leeds Castle talks had been useful in that they had helped in bringing to the negotiating table many matters of deep import, regarding which the United States needed to be able to help the two parties formulate a compromise. With regard to the highly complicated problems of the West Bank and Gaza Strip, some ideas had emerged that would help to crystallize the thinking of the two sides; so much so, indeed, that it became apparent that even hitherto intractable problems might, in the final analysis, be solved – problems such as security, bringing Jordan into the negotiations, etc.

The American plan was that the projected meeting could be expanded into a second meeting of foreign and defence ministers the following week so that matters could be considered in greater detail, and also to enable the parties concerned to further clarify the attitudes they intended to adopt with regard to territorial questions. President Sadat, however, had suddenly decided he could not proceed with the talks until the land question had been settled. In his (Saunders') opinion Sadat's action was based on two reasons: in the first place he lost patience with and faith in the negotiations, believing that the Israelis, for their part, were using them to stall and gain time, whilst the Americans were employing them to avoid having to take a decision to pressurize Israel into declaring its commitment to withdraw from most of the territories in the West Bank and Gaza Strip. Saunders averred that loss of patience was a characteristic of Sadat's – he went to Jerusalem last Fall, said Saunders, when he lost patience with the way the Americans were handling the preliminary arrangements for a Geneva conference which he felt would lead to nothing; and he was now, true to form, holding out against entering into any negotiations unless the land sovereignty issue was excluded from them.

The second reason which led to his decision was that his friends in the Arab world informed him that his position there was eroding and had almost

The Leap To The Summit – Why?

reached zero-point. There was no doubt (said Saunders) that the Saudis were truly worried that one of the main moderate Arab leaders should have forfeited his credibility in the Arab world, and felt that something should be done to bring him back into the Arab fold. They had opened doors for him to return to the Arabs without losing face, and he would naturally be thinking of this once he felt that his initiative would achieve nothing.

Saunders added: "If Sadat becomes solidly entrenched in his position that there will be no more negotiations until the territorial issue is resolved, that becomes a respectable position for him in the Arab world, but it's not an easy one for us to deal with in keeping the negotiations going." Saunders went on to say that the continuation of negotiations was vital, both as regards major American interests and those of their friends in the areas, and they felt that time was fast running out. He revealed that the purpose of Vance's visit to both Jerusalem and Alexandria was to hold detailed talks with each party in order to ascertain how each wished to resume the negotiations. This, Saunders told them, would give him an opportunity to evaluate the situation and obtain a better idea of how matters stood.

Saunders concluded by observing that it was difficult to anticipate what the next move would be until Vance had returned to Washington and submitted his report to President Carter.

A question-and-answer session followed, and Saunders was asked whether Vance's visit would have the result of putting pressure on Israel as Sadat believed, but Saunders vehemently denied this, adding that United States policy was not conducted along those lines, and consequently Vance would not be "playing into anybody's hands, particularly Sadat's hands". The United States plan, he explained, was to keep the negotiations going by hook or by crook, with both parties being asked to think in terms of a compromise on the main issues.

To a question on whether the United States intended to submit an American plan, he replied that the United States had previously submitted plans such as the Rogers Plan and the Brookings Report. Such proposals, however, could not be imposed on either party, contrary to what some people believed, for they remained no more than United States-inspired suggestions – made in the United States in a vacuum – and neither of the conflicting parties had been consulted. Thus (said Saunders) United States policy was to leave it to the parties to negotiate, with the Americans standing by to offer suggestions on how to bridge any gaps that might open up between the two sides. Such, Saunders went on, was the technique employed by Kissinger in his shuttle diplomacy to overcome the disengagement stalemate in 1974–75. He would listen to each side, put his finger on the points agreed by both, and then offer suggestions to resolve any particularly intractable issue. In the files on those disengagement talks, said Saunders, were to be found documents entitled "An American Proposal", the reason being that one of the disputing parties had asked for a United States

Camp David

suggestion since they were, as they put it, unable to propose anything that touched on their sovereignty and restricted their right to deploy their forces in their own territory; but that, however, if the suggestion came from the Americans, then they would accept it.

For this reason, no United States proposals would ever be made but as a result of what came out of the negotiations. The United States would neither submit a comprehensive project, as Sadat would like them to do, nor would they come down in favour of Israel or Egypt, but, instead, would seek compromises. When Saunders was asked whether Israel was prepared to modify its position on withdrawal from the West Bank in accordance with the United States interpretation of Resolution 242, he answered that it had not, but had insisted that the issue regarding the soverignty of the West Bank should be shelved. Israel, he told them, was adopting a wait-and-see attitude with regard to what might happen in the West Bank and Gaza Strip, preferring to put off territorial questions to a later date. Israel, he went on, did not wish to commit itself to anything, beforehand, and felt that the negotiations would be more realistic if they "could be worked out in the context of a real situation on the ground which has evolved over a five-year period". The Egyptian attitude, on the other hand, was that the territorial issue should be decided on there and then, leaving the negotiations to deal with the details. The United States government, for its part, considered the Israeli attitude – not because it is Israeli necessarily – more in line with the American way of handling things. It would, in the United States' view, be difficult to go along with the Egyptian attitude that they should first settle the territorial issue and then go on to discuss details. The United States, said Saunders, saw the possibility for compromise between both positions and that was where the United States expected to be effective.

The question was put to Saunders: "Assuming that United States mediation at a non-crucial point was successful, what if the gap between the two parties was such as to threaten the negotiations with total failure – would the United States then submit a proposal to bridge the gap which might appear to Israel as an imposed settlement and to Egypt as United States participation as a full partner?"

Saunders replied that we should distinguish between two types of differences, namely those for which there are solutions through compromise, with or without United States assistance – and other, basic differences, one of which was the major issue of whether or not Israel would honour its commitment to withdraw from the West Bank. Saunders averred that, to be frank, he failed to see how the United States could submit a proposal settling this point.

Yet he continued: "But I think even there, there are ways of dealing with it, where a United States suggestion could be useful in the sense that there are different ways of making that decision. One extreme is to insist that the Israelis agree today that at a certain point in the future, they will totally

The Leap To The Summit – Why?

vacate the West Bank.

"Now I don't think anything the United States could do or say would produce that decision. But the other end of the spectrum is to simply say: 'Well, we came to negotiate a solution on the West Bank, so let's just get the negotiations started, and let's not have any guidelines to the negotiators about where it will come out.' Well, somewhere in between there . . . that is where we are trying to find our way, in this middle ground."

Asked to explain what he meant by "that it is important that matters should be kept going", he said that it was some kind of "a fuzzy formulation" which would imply that the peace-seeking impetus be maintained, and what he was really getting at was that negotiations should be resumed with the main focus on what had been dealt with so far. He could not be definite as to how this might come about, whether this should be by a shuttle process or a conference and whether it should be direct or indirect negotiations, until Vance had returned and submitted his report to the President.

When told that Vance's efforts to ascertain the "bottom line" required by each party had so far been in vain, Saunders replied that the "bottom line" could never be known until the time came when a decision had to be taken.

One last question was put to Saunders, whose answer was implicit in its very phrasing, and which faithfully reflected the American situation, which I here quote in full:

> "You started out by saying that we were pretty close to running out of time. And I have just been trying to put together in my head all what you are saying, how it fits together. And it seems to me an argument could be made that you really are trying to prevent this thing from total collapse.
>
> "There is no programme. You are afraid to present a programme. The Israelis are frozen. The Arabs are moving away from negotiations. And the only programme you really have is to keep talking in order to prevent a public admission that the thing has failed, the Sadat initiative and all that was involved in it."

In the hope of throwing more light on the American way of thinking, it has been judged useful to give some of Saunders' answers to additional questions put to him: thus, when asked why he did not exert pressure to bring about a separate Israeli-Egyptian settlement, rather than waste their effort in trying to achieve a settlement embracing the moderate Palestinians and Jordan, he replied that the problem was that Sadat had been adamant the preceding Sunday (during his meeting with Atherton) in his refusal to negotiate until the territorial issue had been resolved in such a way that it would not be subject to negotiation, and it had consequently become virtually impossible to reopen the negotiations without coming to grips with the West Bank and Gaza.

Said Saunders: "It's common knowledge that the Israelis are looking for a separate settlement, and we have not sought to impose our views in this matter, while President Sadat keeps repeating he is unable to proceed alone in seeking a solution to the Egyptian-Israeli dispute without some other move on the other fronts. He's said he's prepared to be flexible with regard to such a move on the other fronts, but must not appear as the man who abandoned the Palestinian cause and betrayed the other Arabs. It is for this reason he has so repeatedly and insistently called for a declaration of principles."

When asked what would happen if the United States failed to resume negotiations between Egypt and Israel, Saunders remarked: "The only sensible policy for the United States in the Middle East is, namely, the pursuit of peace which permits us to maintain our relationships on all fronts in the Middle East... If you've lost the centre piece of your strategy in the Middle East you've suffered a major loss, which doesn't lead tomorrow to war or to any immediate consequence, except you don't have a policy any more that makes sense.

"...Part of what we are trying to do in the Middle East is to build and strengthen a coalition of moderate Arab states and leaders – Saudi Arabia, Egypt, bring Syria into that, Jordan, of course, Morocco, Tunisia, Kuwait. That strategy has a lot of reasons: it has peace-making reasons, it has oil-related reasons, it has contain-the-Soviet-Union reasons, and so on. It's the overall approach to what we want in this part of the world . . .

"I think the consequences on the ground would be moves toward Arab summits and so on, which would rigidify the Arab position . . . An Arab summit which would lock the Arabs up and put an end to the Sadat initiative and to anything perhaps except sort of starting over with Geneva, and all of that. If the progress toward peace stalls, you are back to square one trying to get to Geneva and all of that business where we were a year ago. . .

"So if you just let the no-peace-no-war situation go on, not to say that Sadat will be toppled immediately, but you risk movements in that direction both in Syria and Egypt and a very different kind of Middle East, different for Israel and different for us, so it is for this reason that we want to keep the momentum towards peace going, because that keeps the moderate leaders engaged. It promotes a relationship with the key countries that we need and it permits us to have the close relationship with Israel which you are going to have; at the same time we can have a close relationship with the Middle East."

In answer to a question as to whether Sadat was ready to go back to the Arab fold, Saunders replied: "Just technically, the point at which that happens is when they arrange and agree on an Arab summit. And I am hopeful the Secretary can give him enough to work with, to suggest enough that we might work with together, so that that decision won't be made."

When I was through reading the minutes of the Saunders interview, a copy of which came into my hands two weeks later, a fortnight before the Camp

The Leap To The Summit – Why?

David Summit, my apprehensions concerning the United States attitude grew, and my faith in their motives was shaken. Saunders' answers to the numerous questions with regard to the American proposal left no doubt in my mind that the American stand – whichever way you looked at it – was to keep negotiations going until a compromise was reached, which itself depended on concessions from both sides, not, however, in connection with security measures or the normalization of relationships – areas where compromise was possible – but on the very substance of the issue, land and sovereignty, which Sadat had asserted were not negotiable.

The United States had, to all intents and purposes, set aside Resolution 242, upon whose implementation any settlement should be based, which had been agreed internationally and to which both Egypt and Israel had subscribed. The United States seemed oblivious of all their publicly declared statements on withdrawal from the West Bank and Gaza with minor modifications, and of the White House communiqué following Sadat's visit on 8 February 1978. Even more disquieting was that they had turned a blind eye to Carter's pledge to President Sadat and the scenario the two presidents had agreed upon in the course of the aforesaid visit.[2]

All that had gone with the wind and the American position shifted towards driving the parties – especially Egypt – into resuming negotiations until they came up with a compromise involving the territory issue, and this despite Israel's stated intention to annex the Arab occupied territories, which Dayan declared publicly at Leeds Castle. Thus the resumption of negotiations had become, for the United States, an end in itself, not only in the hope that Egypt might, at last, concede some of the territory on the West Bank which did not belong to it, but to prevent the alternative – a halt to the negotiations coupled with Egypt's return to the Arab ranks, followed by an Arab summit and a return to the Geneva Conference, where the Soviet Union would co-chair the meeting, which was precisely what both Israel and the United States did not want.

The final purpose of the United States was to isolate Egypt from the Arab world, so that an ostracized Egypt might fall an easy prey and submit to a separate settlement, thereby increasing Arab dissension.

To get around the difficulty created by Sadat's conditions for a resumption of negotiations and to prevent Egypt from returning to the Arab fold and to shut the door on the reconvening of the Geneva Conference (which would spell the failure of the United States to achieve results at the tripartite talks), the United States came up with the idea of a summit at Camp David, luring Sadat with the bait that the United States had decided to assume the role of "Full Partner".

Footnotes

1 Department of State: background briefing, Thursday 3 August 1978.
2 *Vide*, p. 91 above.

Chapter Thirty Two

You And I Will Make History

The month of Ramadan had begun by the time Vance visited the area, arriving in Jerusalem on 5 August 1978, where he had private talks with Begin and his aides lasting two days. A Voice of America broadcast announced that it was being conjectured in Middle East circles that the United States was seeking to arrange a tripartite summit meeting with President Carter. The Voice of America broadcast added that Begin had announced that he was ready to study the proposal if it were put to him: according to Begin, Vance had not asked Israel, during his visit there, to modify its attitude to the Middle East problem in any way. The Egyptian President, Begin was reported to have said, had to agree to a tripartite meeting without preconditions.

Apart from that broadcast, both the Americans and the Israelis were silent on the purpose of the visit by Vance, who declared he would only be prepared to give any details after he had completed his talks with Sadat.

Before moving on to discuss Vance's visit to Alexandria, it would be in order at this point to refer to the fact that Israel had taken advantage of Vance's visit to launch a large-scale campaign in the media, assisted by the Israeli lobby in the United States, in an effort to regain the ground they had lost following Sadat's initiative putting the blame on Egypt for obstructing negotiations. The campaign also aimed to sow the seeds of discord between Egypt and the United States. It was carried along the following lines:

1. To present Egypt's position, as expressed by Sadat at his meeting with Atherton on 30 July, as adopting a new, hard-line stance, further claiming that Egypt had not given the negotiations a chance in fact. After his meeting with Vance, Begin actually described the Egyptian position as obstinate and inflexible, rendering further discussion on the Middle East impossible!
2. To imply that the change in the Egyptian position was the result of Saudi pressure, and to suggest that Egypt had to choose either to continue working for peace, or return to Arab solidarity.
3. To demonstrate that Israel had spared no effort to achieve peace.

The campaign even claimed that all the ideas that had been put forward were Israel's, including the proposal for a partial settlement with Egypt on Sinai, and that it was now up to Egypt to present its suggestions! The campaign claimed that even a provisional agreement between Israel and Egypt would be a positive step and might provide the opportunity for a comprehensive settlement. Begin declared he was still as good as his word in his offer to bestow limited autonomy (under Israeli military supervision) on the Palestinian Arabs in the West Bank and Gaza Strip. Moreover [he said] he was prepared to discuss the question of sovereignty of "Judea and Samaria" and Gaza five years after peace had been established and his autonomy plan implemented.

4 To exploit the disagreement between the United States and Egypt on the procedure for the settlement so as to cover up the fact that American positions on substance were closer to Egypt than to Israel.
5 To portray Sadat as using the United States to pressurize Israel, accusing him of deliberately, and consistently, creating an atmosphere of crisis and tension to finally get the Americans to put forward a United States peace proposal that would be as close as possible to the Egyptian position.
6 To resort to threats, for in one of Begin's declarations he hinted at the possibility of Israel waging a preventive war. This was aimed at increasing tension in the area which would not fail to leave its impact on Egypt and the United States!

On 7 August, United States Secretary of State Cyrus Vance arrived in Alexandria from Jerusalem accompanied by several aides, among them Atherton, Saunders and Quandt, checking in at the Palestine Hotel[1] which has been built in the grounds of King Faruk's palace at Montazah.

Vance was to meet Sadat at his rest-house in Maamoura at 8.30 that evening, but at four o'clock the American group, headed by Vance, met with the Egyptian team led by myself. Vance was not very talkative, so I seized the opportunity to elaborate on the Egyptian position since the Leeds Castle meeting, and to refute Israel's accusations. I then set out our views on what we expected from the United States.

I began by making it clear that we intended to proceed with our peace effort, which we have sustained since Sadat's speech in the Knesset in November 1977. We would also abide by our pledges with regard to security, peace and good-neighbourly relations, even beyond those which were contained in Resolution 242. I likewise expressed our readiness to pursue direct negotiations with Israel provided they were carried out on the basis of clear and accepted principles, thus offering a genuine opportunity for peace.

I brought out the fact that, as far as we were concerned, Arab solidarity was no alternative to the peace initiative, and that Egypt's position was to strive for Arab unity, while at the same time preserving its freedom to seek the most appropriate method to achieve the comprehensive peace settlement with Israel agreed to by the Arabs at the Rabat Summit Conference in 1974.

I concluded by stressing the importance of the time factor, pointing out the dangers besetting the area as a result of the faltering peace efforts which were attributable to the stubborn and unyielding Israeli attitude. I emphasized the need for the United States to step up its efforts and to deny Begin the opportunity of disrupting the relationship between the United States and the Arab world, and so tarnish the image of the United States in the eyes of the Arab nation.

Vance said nothing about President Carter's message to President Sadat, nor did he mention anything of his recent talks in Israel.

At 8.30 that evening, Vance and the American delegation arrived at the rest-house in Maamoura. Sadat was seated at a table set in the garden where the meeting was to take place. Present were Vice-President Mubarak, Prime Minster Mamdouh Salem, Defence Minister Gamassy, Dr Boutros Ghali, Ambassador Ghorbal and myself. After exchanging greetings, the Americans and the Egyptians sat down together and refreshments were handed round. TV cameramen and news photographers took pictures, and minutes later Sadat led Vance away out of earshot, their meeting lasting well past midnight. When they returned, Vance shook hands with Sadat and all present and took his leave. I rode with him in his car back to the Palestine Hotel, and on the way there he informed me – his face beaming with pleasure and his voice gushing with enthusiasm – that Sadat had accepted Carter's invitation to a tripartite summit meeting, which he suggested should be held in Camp David on 5 September. He revealed to me that Begin had already accepted the meeting when he visited him in Jerusalem, and Vance assured me that everything would be all right. The conference, he said, must be successful, or it would mean the end of Carter's political career, and for this reason the American President intended to throw his whole weight to bring about the peace we desired, with the United States taking an active and positive part in the talks.

I walked with Vance to the lift and was about to ride up with him on my way to my room when a sudden thought struck me. I bade him goodnight there and then, left the hotel, got into my car and requested the driver to take me back to the Maamoura rest-house! I must admit that the news of the impending tripartite summit came as a complete surprise to me, as I was in no way expecting it. I was under the impression that the purpose of Vance's visit was to persuade Sadat to resume negotiations at ministerial level, as before, with the added inducement of American promises to guarantee progress in the talks along lines satisfactory to us.

In truth, I had very good reasons to rule out the probability of such an invitation from Carter at a time when Israeli and Egytian positions were diametrically opposed, which would make an intervention on the part of Carter at this particular time a very hazardous adventure and an even riskier gamble.

It was almost one o'clock in the morning when I arrived at the rest-house, and I was afraid the President might have retired. Furthermore, it must be said that there was no urgent necessity for a meeting at this hour; I could easily have put it off until the summit meeting. At the door I ran into Mr Hassan Kamel, the Chef de Cabinet of the President's office, on his way out, and in answer to my enquiry he informed me that the President was having his "Sohour" (the pre-dawn meal of Ramadan) in the garden and together we went to where Sadat was sitting at a sumptuous table covered with the choice dishes characteristic of Ramadan. Looking up, he saw me and promptly invited me to be seated, but said nothing and, instead, set to eat with gusto. After a moment of silence, I let him know that Vance had told me about the impending summit in Camp David and the fact that he had agreed to attend. "Yes . . . yes, that's what I've been working upon from the very beginning: my idea is that America should act as a full partner, and Vance informed me that he had been asked to convey Carter's assurance that was precisely what he intended to do. Remember, Carter has put his career on the line, and I feel sure we'll succeed. Whether the conference succeeds or fails depends on us, and it's about time the United States pressurized Israel and cut Begin down to size! Haven't I always told you that I was full of optimism and my initiative could never fail." "God willing, we shall succeed!" I replied – and suddenly found I had no more to say.

Silence reigned for a while, while I helped myself to a bunch of grapes and began to eat them abstractedly, one at a time. "Do you remember when we were in prison?" asked Sadat. "You'll have a place in history with me, Mohamed!" I answered automatically: "In Sha'allah," with a sense of awe: Camp David seemed to me a journey to a mysterious, unknown world, I simply could not take in the idea of a tripartite summit, much less fathom its pros and cons! Suddenly I blurted out: "I need a vacation!" The President looked at me in surprise, and shot back: "What do you mean? We have a great deal of work to do!" I replied that it was precisely because I was aware of this that I felt I needed three or four days' rest. "Why don't you go to the beach at Sidi Abdel Rahman?" the President suggested. "That's an excellent idea!" I agreed.

The President finished his meal and sent for Mr Hassan Kamel to inform him that the official Egyptian delegation to Camp David would consist of Hassan El Tohamy, Mohamed Ibrahim Kamel, Boutros Ghali, Ussama El Baz and himself, and instructed him to advise them to be ready to leave, whereupon I shook hands with the President and departed.

The following morning, 8 August, I had a meeting with Mr Vance at which we discussed the deteriorating situation in Lebanon. Vance, who seemed

Camp David

somewhat worried about it, asked what I thought of the Syrian presence there, and I replied that, to be frank, I was in complete disagreement on that score with Sadat, who was calling for "all hands off" and a Syrian withdrawal from Lebanon. For my part, I felt he was taking this stand out of his personal feelings for President Assad. However, in my view (I told Vance) the Syrian presence at the present time appeared to be the most effective factor in securing at least a measure of stability to prevent a slide towards the worse since Syria would be the first to feel the effects. I added that if the Syrian forces were to pull out of Lebanon, the situation would certainly get out of hand, and that country would be fragmented into small states and warring factions. And that (I went on) was precisely Israel's aim, in the pursuance of its territorial ambitions in Lebanon, for although Israel claimed to have withdrawn its troops from Southern Lebanon, it had not, in reality, done so, but had established a fifth column in the persons of the dissenter Major Saad Haddad and his militia, which it was storing with arms and supplies on the pretext of protecting the Lebanese Christians – an old formula that the former imperialist nations made use of to justify their colonialism in the nineteenth century. The operation was designed to give Haddad and his ilk a free hand in the south and so keep the road for an eventual Israeli invasion of Lebanon open. Haddad was fomenting trouble and helping to spread chaos by attacking the United Nations peace-keeping forces and preventing them from performing their duties, in addition to keeping the Lebanese army from entering Southern Lebanon. By so doing, he was attempting to undermine and bring down the legitimate government in Lebanon, thus allowing Israel to fish in troubled waters and achieve its goal of expansion in Lebanon.

Vance gave me to understand that he concurred in my analysis of the situation.

At noon, a White House press release expressed Carter's satisfaction at the acceptance by both Sadat and Begin of his invitation to come to Camp David on 5 September for a meeting designed to seek a framework for peace in the Middle East. Carter added that each of the three heads would be assisted by a restricted number of top aides and that no time limit had been set for the duration of the meeting.

The same evening, after breaking his fast, Sadat, in the company of Vance, gave a press conference at the Maamoura rest-house. Most of the questions dealt with the matter of the United States becoming a full partner in the talks to be held in Camp David. Sadat expressed his satisfaction at this development, adding that America's responsibilities as a superpower made this incumbent upon her. Answering a question as to why he had accepted a resumption of direct negotiations with Begin, he replied that he was not going to Camp David to meet Begin but in answer to Carter's invitation to go there.

Vance, for his part, stated that the United States was ready to play the role of full partner because peace in the Middle East was not only the concern of the United States, but of the whole world as well. On full partnership, Vance acknowledged that their efforts would evolve within the framework of Resolution 242.

The following morning (9 August) Vance flew back to Washington while Quandt headed for Israel to inform the government there of what had transpired during Vance's talks with Sadat. Atherton went on to Saudi Arabia and Jordan to brief them on the latest developments and try to gain their support for the tripartite summit in Camp David. As for myself, I took my family and my car and went down to the beach at Sidi Abdel Rahman!

Sidi Abdel Rahman is situated on one of the bays of the Mediterranean about 120 miles west of Alexandria, only a little way from El Alamein. The shore there is quiet and untroubled, with its fresh crisp sea breeze, white sands and calm, turquoise waters. There is nothing there but a small hotel and a few beach-houses in a setting of palms and fig-trees, and this was the first holiday I had had since I was appointed Foreign Minister. It was also the first time I had been able to really get together with my family, especially my two sons Ahmed and Aly, whom I hardly ever saw – and even when I did, I was usually exhausted and tense, so I decided to devote these few days to them. It was likewise an opportunity to really relax and shut out all that was happening beyond that beautiful, isolated beach!

And I did just that, making no attempt to read the newspapers or even to listen to the news on the radio! I spent the time strolling along the waterline, swimming, lying on the sand, and occasionally lending a hand with an indoor game or two. However, I found I could not stop myself from thinking about the impending Camp David Conference, which would sometimes force itself on my consciousness.

What bothered me was the American attitude, which I could not understand. What made President Carter gamble his career and risk his position as United States President, now it had become apparent that the Egyptian and Israeli attitudes were diametrically opposed? Why had Vance made his proposal to the Israeli Premier first? Was it only coincidence? For logic demanded that the proposal should have first been put to President Sadat, as he represented the party that was opposed to any ministerial meeting as long as the Israeli attitude remained unchanged. The Israelis on the other hand were the party waiting with baited breath to resume the meetings in co-operation with the United States. Had Vance approached the Egyptians first, they would have had the opportunity to refuse it unless it were to be underpinned by definite American guarantees of a positive change in Israeli attitudes. Offering the proposal, however, to Sadat after it had already been accepted by Begin, meant that Sadat was being presented with a *fait accompli*, which he would either be obliged to accept or face the charge of back-tracking on his peace efforts.

I wondered what had really taken place during those long hours of talks

Camp David

Vance had alone with Begin in Jerusalem, and later with Sadat in private session in the garden at Maamoura. Did either of them offer concessions? What Sadat had told me after his meeting with Vance was that President Carter had agreed to act as a full partner, throwing his full weight into the role; while Begin had declared, following his meeting with Vance in Jerusalem: "The United States has not asked Israel to change its attitude as regards the Middle East problem."[2] And if concessions *had* been made during the private talks Vance had had first with Begin and then with Sadat, what could these be? One can hardly imagine Begin informing the United States Secretary of State that he had changed his mind about Israeli expansion and the annexation of the West Bank and Gaza – his lifelong dream – he, who declared right after his appointment as Prime Minister that "Judea and Samaria" were Israeli liberated territory, a claim which had been repeated emphatically two weeks ago by Dayan at the Leeds Castle meeting though in a different form, when he had stated that there was no alternative to territorial compromise!

On the other hand, was it imaginable that Sadat could have told Vance that he had changed his mind with regard to the principle that territory and sovereignty were not negotiable? And if so, did he have the right to concede territory not belonging to him, together with the rights of a whole nation – he, who had travelled to Jerusalem to solve that very problem?

It is my belief that neither Begin nor Sadat promised Vance any such concessions. So what was the United Stated striving for or hoping to achieve by the tripartite summit meeting at Camp David?

I came to the conclusion that the idea of a summit conference was a gamble on another round of negotiations at heads of state level, leading one or both parties to make major concessions, and the way to achieve this was for the American President, with his moral and material resources and personal influence, to put pressure on both Begin and Sadat – brutally if necessary – to force either or both into yielding maximum concessions and finally come up with a compromise. The pressure would take the form of the old "stick and carrot", with the United States alternately threatening and enticing with what lay within its power to grant or withhold, since both parties were vulnerable vis-à-vis the United States; with Carter constantly bearing in mind that failure to reach some sort of solution would cost the United States its standing and the United States President his career.

The conclusion I had reached was not a source of great concern to me, for if the United States were to alter its stand and show partiality to Israel at Camp David, this would still not be the end. Arab potential was considerable, and we had a strong and just case. Our position did not allow for any compromise over our future and the fate of the Arab nation – all we had to do was stand firm, insist on our legitimate rights, reject whatever did not conform to this stand and continue to strive for the realization of a comprehensive peace. Nothing should be allowed to stand in the way, and no power can force us to concede or abandon Arab territory or our sovereignty. As for United States prestige, that was not our responsibility, nor was Jimmy Carter's future our concern!

I recalled what Sadat had said to me while at his Sohour in the garden at Maamoura, to the effect that the success or failure of the Conference rested with us. I had no doubt that he understood, and was fully aware of the implications of his words, and I assumed that what he meant by them was our own success and not that of his friend Jimmy Carter.

What a simpleton I was!

Footnotes

1   The Israeli delegation to the talks on the Egyptian-Israeli Peace Treaty later refused to set foot in the same hotel for the talks, simply because it bore the name of "Palestine". While later, too, Menahim Begin was to insist on the need to hold the talks on autonomy for the Palestinians in Jerusalem, as being the eternal capital of Israel.

2   Israel Radio, 7 August 1978.

Chapter Thirty Three

Fasting While Others Work

I came back from my brief holiday in Sidi Abdel Rahman feeling revitalized and more energetic, and at once got down to the task of preparing for the Camp David Summit, together with my working group, composed of Ussama El Baz, Ahmed Maher El Sayid, Nabil El Araby, Abdel Raouf Al Ridi and a host of Foreign Ministry advisers and specialists. A series of protracted meetings and discussions followed, at which every possibility was explored, and at which every anticipated move and assumption was set down in the form of memos and research papers. The group worked with dedication, interspersed with lighter moments, and the team spirit prevailed at all times. We were fully aware of the importance of the Camp David meetings and the significance of what might come out of them, while realizing that, even if the results were inconclusive, no harm would be done to our cause, although we felt it highly improbable – failing a miracle – that the proceedings would culminate in a final, comprehensive settlement to the Arab-Israeli dispute. There were, in fact, two possibilitites, both good: either President Carter would succeed in overcoming Israel's stubborn resolve to hold on to the occupied Arab territories, thus achieving some progress with respect to the implementation of Resolution 242 and induce other Arab parties to join in the negotiations at a later stage – or the Conference would fail to achieve any progress in that direction. In the latter case, we would have lost nothing, provided it was made evident to the United States and the world at large that responsibility for the failure of the Summit lay solely with Israel, which was unlawfully occupying territory it had won by force of arms and which, by refusing to give it up, was rejecting our offer of a comprehensive peace. This in itself would constitute a gain for us and a point of departure for future moves, for Israel found itself baulked by the peace initiative, which was every day attracting new adherents. And, when all was said and done, the future lay before us!

Great interest in the Camp David Conference had been aroused throughout the world and this was reflected in the mass media, which gave prominence to the attitudes and policies of the states concerned, together with an assessment of the probable outcome of the Conference and its future implications. In fact the media had a field day, publishing, commenting, analyzing and conjecturing!

In Israel, Begin held lengthy meetings with his cabinet and the Knesset and with committees, advisers and experts to prepare for the Camp David meetings. Much the same thing was taking place in the United States, with President Carter devoting much of his time preparing for the Conference, spending whole days and nights away from Washington closeted with his aides and counsellors. But where was President Sadat, and what was he doing all this time? Well, he was fasting, and moving from one rest-house to another in Maamoura, Ismailia, Suez or Port Said! Wherever he went, I rang him up to brief him on our work and ask for guidelines on this or that point. He seemed, however, to show no particular interest in these proceedings, generally agreeing to everything I said or contenting himself with some minor, irrelevant observation. He spent most of the day in listless indolence, had his "Iftar" at sundown, and passed most of his evenings organizing his National Democratic Party, (he had announced the establishment of this party in a speech at Alexandria University on 27 July), and receiving well-known national figures and delegations who were quick to join the party for one reason or another. He was engaged in appointing committees, distributing offices, convening symposia and giving lectures, and would hold forth on any subject, whether it was history, politics, economics, the philosophy of life, the relation of party to modern technology, or village morals and values. He would expatiate on episodes in the national struggle, the merits of his initiative, or indeed on any topic that occurred to him! His audience would consist of locals from around the rest-house he happened to be staying at, led by the Governor and the senior officers of the governorate in question, who one and all applauded him effusively and indiscriminately, but had nothing to say!

When preparations had reached the stage where they would have to be approved by Sadat, I asked to see him, along with the working group whose assistance I depended on in making my arrangments for the Conference. Sadat, however, requested that our meeting be postponed for the time being, since he was fasting and to work during Ramadan exhausted him! Undiscouraged, I again put in for a meeting, but was again put off on some pretext or other! This greatly surprised me, for not a week had passed since my appointment as Foreign Minister in which we had not either discussed affairs over the phone or in person, in connection with issues of far less importance than those we were now embarked on. I could not understand his behaviour and his indifference to a matter that might not only determine his and Egypt's future but also that of the entire Middle East region! Was it because he failed to realize the importance of preparing for the Conference? Was he over-confident of success, and did he look upon it as strictly a one-man show? Was he relying on definite commitments by Carter (conveyed through Vance) in the form of reassurances that he (Carter) would be

Camp David

with him all the way? Or did he, perhaps, have something else in mind which he wished to keep to himself until the last moment, as he had when he took the world by surprise and visited Jerusalem?

I began to feel seriously worried, and finally decided to contact him by phone at his Ismailia rest-house. I told him I could not work in such a manner: we were not (I reproached him) going to Camp David to relax or see the sights. It was necessary that we should adopt common attitudes and a joint strategy at the Conference, as otherwise I would not go at all! At which Sadat said he would naturally be meeting me before the Conference – a few days before, in fact (and he named 2 September) – when he would be convening the National Security Council at the Ismailia rest-house!

In the meantime, the United States Ambassador Herman Eilts called on me several times before leaving for Washington to prepare for the Conference and to join the American delegation. He gave me an account of the arrangements that had been made, such as the number decided upon for each delegation: accommodation in Camp David, he said, was limited and would be shared out equally between the delegations. President Carter had decided against allowing the media access to the meetings or enabling it to relay its findings to the outside world, being intent on providing a peaceful atmosphere for the Conference far removed from tension and outside influence. The strangest aspect of the information conveyed to me by Eilts was that Carter had decided that the Conference would be convening for at least a week! I said this sounded very like a prison sentence! Eilts' reply was to the effect that the intention was to provide a chance for a breakthrough and a softening of attitudes, adding with a smile that it was also a kind of precautionary measure to prevent a recurrence of what had occurred in Jerusalem, when President Sadat decided to withdraw the Egyptian delegation to the Political Committee before it had completed its scheduled meetings!

I, for my part, emphasized to Eilts the need for United States proposals to the Conference to incorporate the declared United States stands on withdrawal, settlements and the Aswan formula on the Palestinians, with any United States project being submitted to us for consultation before it was tabled. I received Eilts' assurance that previous commitments would be honoured.

Ambassador Eilts also informed me that, during his visit to Saudi Arabia and Jordan, Mr Atherton had successfully urged the two states to announce their endorsement of the tripartite summit conference, and this had been confirmed to us in reports coming out of Amman and Riyadh. Atherton, Eilts continued, had made it clear to them that the United States attitude at the meeting would be very close to Egypt's.

A few days before the National Security Council was due to meet, I received a visit at my office from the Chief of Army Intelligence, General Kamal Hassan Aly, who was also a member of the Council. He handed me a memorandum on the Intelligence Bureau's evaluation of the situation and its proposals for Camp David. The memo detailed all aspects of the Arab-Israeli dispute and the minimum Egypt should be prepared to accept on all points. I read the memo in his presence and then expressed my appreciation and satisfaction at the fact that its recommendations coincided so completely with the conclusions reached by the Foreign Office.

On 28 August – five days before the meeting of the National Security Council – I despatched a memorandum to President Sadat setting forth the results of our studies with regard to our targets at Camp David and the strategy we proposed for the settlement of those targets. The memo ran as follows:

28 August 1978   *Highly Confidential*

MEMORANDUM
To the President of the Republic
on the
Tripartite Camp David Meeting

I *Introduction*
1. Egypt regards the Camp David meeting as a successful development brought about by the Egyptian stand, which was able:
   a) To prove Egypt's flexibility while at the same time adhering to basic principles governing Arab strategy.
   b) To expose the Israeli intransigence before the United States and the world.
   c) To force the United States to modify its role from that of mediator to that of full partner, and induce President Carter to throw the full weight of his prestige into the balance in seeking a settlement. This factor assumes importance due to the fact that the formally declared American positions were closer to the Egyptian than the Israeli.
   d) To obtain the support of Saudi Arabia and Jordan.
2. In the face of such Egyptian successes, Israel seeks – and will continue to seek, both inside and outside the Conference – to dissuade the United States from assuming the role of full partner with views of its own, and instead to induce it to assume that of a mediator attempting to reconcile the conflicting attitudes of the two parties.
   To this end it will:
   a) Exploit the Zionist lobby in the United States to bring pressure to bear on President Carter to discourage him from tabling any United States proposals.
   b) Assume a deceptive flexibility to create the impression that

Israel is moving forward and imply that continued negotiations will create the necessary momentum which will enable the two parties to reach an agreement without the intervention of the United States. Numerous statements had already been made by United States Senators cautioning the American administration against tabling any United States project while stressing that the Egyptian-Israeli dialogue must be maintained. Furthermore. Israeli statements seek to create the impression of flexibility, since:
- they give exaggerated importance to the mere fact of Israel's agreement to consider the sovereignty issue after the five-year transitional period;
- they purport that Israel is considering a number of alternatives as proof of its good intentions, while making out that Israel's readiness to consider the concept of a territorial compromise (should Egypt suggest this!) constitutes an important concession;
- they are designed to give the impression that Israel would like to make things easier for Egypt by not insisting that a Peace Treaty be signed, and that it would, instead, settle for a partial settlement although this would, in fact, meet all Israel's demands as regards the normalization of relations without fulfilling any of the Arab demands Egypt is fighting to secure.

3 To sum up, while it is conceivable that President Carter's personal intervention may be considered as a form of pressure on the United States government to bring about a just settlement, lest failure deal a direct blow to the standing and prestige of the United States President, Israel seeks to make use of that very intervention as leverage against Egypt by:
   a) insinuating that Egypt's reluctance to offer concessions could affect President Carter's position;
   b) hinting, in an orchestrated campaign, that, if the Camp David meeting were to fail, this would be due to the Egyptian attitude, thus exonerating Israel from all responsibility for the Summit's lack of success.

There can be no doubt that Israeli levers within the American public and the United States administration itself enables Israel to influence the United States decisions in its favour. Egypt, on the other hand, enjoys no such support, so we should show extreme caution with regard to any political stances we may adopt during the meeting and the line we intend to take with the mass media both during and following the meeting.

4 It is noteworthy that the manoeuvres of Israeli statements have had their

their effect on United States attitudes for, as we can see, after agreeing to undertake the role of full partner the United States is showing reluctance to do so and is giving signs that it does not have the intention of tabling a comprehensive American project. Although this could be interpreted as a tactical manoeuvre designed to confront Israeli pressure, it could also denote that the United States is yielding or beginning to yield – for any number of reasons, some of which may be internal, in view of the closeness of the mid-term Congressional elections – to the Israeli lobby. This is a possibility we have to contend with.

II *The Objectives of the Meeting*

1 The basic concept is that the meeting is designed to arrive at a general concensus on the principles of a settlement which shall be applicable to all fronts, deal with all aspects of the problem, and provide for the expansion of the scope of the negotiations so as to include other parties (such as Jordan in a first stage), and securing wider Arab support.
2 However, it now appears that the United States is considering going beyond these "principles" to handling details relating to the West Bank, Gaza and the Palestinian problem.

III *Egypt's Objectives of the Conference*
1 Egypt's target with respect to the declaration of principles is that this should be as clear as possible. It should not include ambiguous provisions allowing for different interpretations, for this would lead us back to the vicious circle Sadat's initiative was intended to break.
2 With respect to the Palestinian problem, Egypt's objective is to come up with a formula according with the project it has itself submitted:[1]
   a) effect withdrawal from the West Bank and Gaza;
   b) ensure the right of the Palestinian people to self-determination.
Within the context of the foregoing two targets, we might be in a position to show some flexibility in the actual application.

IV *A Proposed Egyptian Strategy for the Meeting*
1 The American concept is that the Conference should last for approximately one week, the possible objective being to allow time for a softening of stands. Egypt's best course then would be to initially adopt a relatively hard stand and progressively show flexibility within limits previously agreed, provided that such

flexibility be invariably in response to the American stand. Here it would be useful to consider the philosophy and guidelines of a settlement before discussing specific formulae.

2. It is important that Egypt should, in the course of the meeting, concentrate on refuting Israeli positions and show them to be basically inappropriate for a settlement, and might even lead to a stalemate. The United States would thereby be induced to intervene to avert failure by tabling proposals. Within the context of such refutation, we could concentrate on:

    a) the fact that expansion under pretext of security – to say nothing of its violating international law – will not bring about security because the usurpation of the land will be a constant source of friction. Real security consists in Israel's acceptance by its neighbours, and this will be realized only if they feel Israel does not covet their land or seek to usurp their rights;

    b) that the allegation that the settlements represent an element for peace . . . since they allow Israelis and Arabs to live side by side, is both erroneous and unsound since the settlements, according to Israel doctrine, are separate and form armed Israeli islets in the sea of Arab land. If the Jews really want to live with the Arabs, this implies that they should have – like all foreigners – the right to apply for residence on an individual basis.

3. With an eye to the possibility of the meeting failing to achieve any positive results, it is important that the Egyptian stand should strike a delicate balance between:

    a) holding on to what is basic in our position; and,

    b) presenting our position in a clear and flexible manner so as to win the approval of the United States and the world at large. This would enable us to point to:
    – Israel's clear responsibility for the failure of the Conference.
    – The clear conformity of the American and Egyptian stands vis-à-vis the rigid and thoroughly intransigent Israeli stand.
    – The need for the United States to be persuaded that the continuation of negotiations for their own sake will not yield the desired results.

    Were we to achieve this objective, we could then consider ways and means of rallying a unified Arab stand in a continuation of rather than an alternative to the Egyptian peace initiative.

4   There is no doubt that the failure of that conference under the conditions set forth would be preferable to achieving vague results which would enable Israel to continue to evade the issue, as this would eventually turn the tables against us.

V *The Position on the Elements of a Settlement*
Our position will consist in our insistence on complete withdrawal from the Arab territories occupied in 1967 and the right of the Palestinian people to self-determination. During the negotiations, and in response to United States initiatives, our position could gradually evolve as follows:
1   *Withdrawal*
   a) It is important that the formulae on withdrawal underscore the twin principles of the inadmissibility of acquiring territory by force, and the non-alteration of existing international borders.
   b) As regards the formula entitled "Alterations in the borders of the West Bank which realize both the Palestinians' aspirations and Israel's security", although our interpretation of this formula is clear and unambiguous, it is to be feared that its use would open the door for a multitude of Israeli interpretations inconsistent with our own.[2]
   c) Accordingly, it would be appropriate, in view of our experience of Israeli tactics, to amend the formula as follows:
   – qualify the alterations as minor;
   – to use the term "lines" with regard to the West Bank instead of borders;
   – to stipulate that the alterations should obtain the approval of the Representative of the Palestinian people, who alone can make the final decision thereon;
   – not to tie in "Palestinian aspirations" with "security", while assigning a separate paragraph to "the rights of the Palestinian people" rather than "the Palestinian aspirations".
   d) In the light of the foregoing, to agree to consider, at an advanced stage of the negotiations, minor alterations to the proposed formula would read "withdrawal from the occupied Arab territories since 1967 with the possibility of effecting minor alterations in the lines of the West Bank, to which all parties would agree for administrative and humane considerations and in order to guarantee their mutual security."

Camp David

2   *The Palestinian Issue*
   a) Refuse to consider Begin's project as the basis for a solution.
   b) Insist, during the negotiations, on making the Egyptian project the basis for the talks, and be ready to accept the Aswan Formula's three points, namely: the solution to the Palestinian problem in all its aspects; the legitimate rights of the Palestinian people; and their right to participate in determining their own future (self-determination).

   We should insist that the American side refuse any Israeli amendments to any of these points, since it is a United States formula and must be binding on the American negotiator.

3   *Jerusalem*

   Emphasize that Israeli withdrawal applies to Arab Jerusalem, and affirm Arab sovereignty over it. As a corollary, Egypt could take detailed proposals to ensure the preservation of the unique nature of the city through guarantees allowing freedom of access and worship and non-establishment of barriers in the city.

4   *Security Arrangements*

   To submit detailed Egyptian proposals on security arrangements on all fronts based on the six Egyptian points, guarantees for the maintenance of such arrangements (Egyptian and Jordanian, as well as International guarantees, whether collective or bilateral).

5   *Peaceful Relations*

   To submit an integrated Egyptian approach showing how it envisions peaceful relations without committing Egypt in any peace treaty to any specific measures, which may detract from the internationally accepted norm that relations among states are subject to the principle of sovereignty and freedom of choice.

6   *The Colonies*

   Insist on the Egyptian-American stand on the illegality of settlements and the need to dismantle them, while flexibility could be shown with regard to the timing and method of dismantling such settlements. Agreement should be reached immediately on the suspension of all Israeli activities in this connection.

7   *Refugees*
   a) Insist on the right of the post-1967 displaced persons to repatriation to the West Bank, and their participation in determining the future of the West Bank and the Gaza Strip.
   b) Show readiness to discuss, in the presence of all parties, the methods and stages of implementation of the 1948 United Nations Resolution 194 on refugees.
   c) Not to discuss the issue of "the Jewish refugees from the Arab states" raised by Israel.

VI *Conclusions*
1. It is advisable that the Egyptian position should be firm in the initial stages of the Camp David meetings. The firmness would gradually thaw in response to American initiatives, giving proof of flexibility without prejudicing our basic principles.
     The flexibility could show itself, in the following:
     a) Prolonging the period of withdrawal.
     b) Permitting a limited Israeli military presence in specified areas during the transitional period.
     c) Security arrangements not infringing of the principles of withdrawal and sovereignty.
     d) The scope of peace and peaceful relations.
2. To encourage the United States to reiterate its previously declared positions conforming with our own.
3. Were the meeting to fail, we would be shown as having co-operated and responded to the United States call for flexibility; Israel would not be in a position to lay the blame for the failure at our door. This in itself represents an asset we could build on for the future. We must, however, be careful not to let the United States seek another meeting between ourselves and Israel without it having previously taken a firm attitude towards Israel and a clear position that it could carry through.
4. If, however, the meeting produces a declaration of principles – which may be considered as marking some progress towards the implementation of Resolution 242 – which induces Jordan to join the negotiations and wins the support of Saudi Arabia, it is conceivable that a series of negotiations will follow.

Special efforts will henceforth be needed to co-ordinate efforts as to the stages, framework and the venue of those negotiations (such as the Geneva Conference, etc.).

Respectfully,

Mohamed Ibrahim Kamel
Foreign Minister.

Footnotes:

1. The project was submitted at the Leeds Castle Conference.
2. This was the formula Sadat approved during his meeting with Shimon Perez in Vienna, published in the communiqué of the Socialist International issued by Brandt and Kreisky in June 1978. See p. 196 of this book.

Chapter Thirty Four

Strange Symptoms and Many Question-Marks

At 7.30 p.m. on 30 August, and in the company of Ambassador Ahmed Maher, I arrived at Almaza Military Airfield, followed by the separate arrivals of members of the National Security Council. [1] When we were all together a Soviet-made Antonov aircraft belonging to the air force flew us to Ismailia. On our arrival we drove to "L'île Des Chevaliers", where President Sadat's rest-house was located. Just as the car was about to stop at the entrance to the rest-house, I spotted Ambassador Ussama El Baz standing near the building. I could not understand why he was in Ismailia, since I had met him only the day before at the Ministry, when he had said nothing about it. I waved to him and he waved back, then he seemed to disappear into thin air.

The guard led us to the spacious terrace over-looking the Bitter Lakes, through which the Suez Canal runs. President Sadat was sitting watching one of the popular Ramadan quiz show serials on TV. Sadat stood up to receive us, but when my turn came to shake hands with him, I sensed a coolness on his part which did not exist before. This feeling was accentuated because we had not met for some time. However, I felt little concern, and the President soon left us and went into the rest-house.

We followed the TV show for a while, and we were offered traditional Ramadan sweets, nuts and drinks. Meanwhile, a long table was brought out onto the terrace and chairs were placed around it. The President soon returned, and invited us to be seated at the conference table. A moment of silence ensued, then Sadat suddenly clapped his hands and, when the guard appeared, enquired: "Where are Himmat and Saad Zaghloul? Summon them and prepare a place for them close to the conference table . . . "

The guard hurried inside and a moment later Mrs Himmat Mustapha, the Director of the Television Authority, and Mr Saad Zaghloul Nassar, Press Officer to the Presidency, made their appearance, with pencil and paper. They took their seats round a table set for them close to the President.

I was dumbfounded! Meetings of the National Security Council were a serious business, the subjects discussed and the words exchanged of the greatest importance and the proceedings were highly confidential. No re-

Strange Symptoms and Many Question-Marks

cords were kept of the gathering or the information made available at the meeting; instead, at its conclusions, and if he considered it appropriate, the President would instruct one of two members – the Prime Minister or Foreign Minister – to issue a communiqué on whatever he (Sadat) wished to publish on the meeting. On this occasion, the meeting, which had been called to discuss the Egyptian approach to Camp David, was of a particularly weighty nature, since it had to deal with the strategy and tactics we intended to adopt at the Conference – questions of a highly sensitive nature and of the utmost secrecy. Had a secret record of the meeting been required, one of the Council members could – as we have seen – have been assigned the task.

None of those present paid the slightest attention to what had occurred, but I felt uncomfortable and somewhat resentful, for although I had nothing but cordial feelings for Mrs Himmat Mustapha and Mr Saad Zaghloul, I felt that their presence was a constraint on my freedom of speech. With them attending, I should not be able to disclose matters of importance, which should be confined to the participants. Nor would I be in a position to argue with – let alone oppose – the President, if need be, in their presence. Leaving my chair, I walked up to him, intending to point this out, but when I reached him I hastily checked myself, realizing that to do so might embarrass both of us. It would be difficult for him to ask them to leave the room, since he had summoned them in full view of the Council members. Moreover, if he were to override my objection and insist on their attendance, I would be put in an awkward position.

Sadat stared at me and said: "Is anything the matter, Mohamed?" And I answered: "Ussama El Baz and Ahmed Maher are here; I request that they be allowed to attend the meeting." Sadat replied that he had no objection to this.

Before setting down what Sadat said at the meeting I must warn the reader not to be shocked at the President's contradictions, his truncated and unfinished sentences, and his irritating habit of jumping from one subject to another. To be frank, I record his words with a feeling of shame and sorrow, since I feel it unseemly for the President of the Republic of Egypt to so lower the standard of debate at the National Security Council, in the presence of the most senior officers of the state, though I must admit that he was not at his best that day!

The President began with an introduction, in which he reviewed the Arab-Israeli conflict, the 1967 defeat and finally the 1973 October War, which enabled him to put forward his peace initiative. After giving an account of his visit to Jerusalem in 1977, he went on to detail the monumental achievements of the initiative in winning over both United States and world opinion. He touched on Begin's rigidity and intransigence and the latter's attempts to stifle the initiative by adopting an unyielding and uncompromising stand in the hope of attaining a partial or separate settlement. We had countered his machinations by adopting a firm stance which

Camp David

eventually succeeded in modifying the United States approach and finally induced the Americans to undertake the role of a full partner – just as we intended it should from the outset!

The tripartite summit meeting in Camp David proposed by President Carter (Sadat said) was similar to his own visit to Jerusalem in that it was designed to further remove suspicions and psychological barriers. Our own efforts had yielded positive results the world over, even in Israel, but not with Begin or his retinue. Sadat then added:

> When Vance visited me to convey President Carter's invitation to a summit in Camp David I accepted at once. I intimated to him that I had intended to suggest such a conference to them, but they had anticipated my thoughts. Nonetheless, I addressed two questions to Vance:
>
> First, how do President Carter and yourself stand on a comprehensive settlement[2] and, secondly, how far are you prepared to go towards this end?
>
> To this Vance replied: "We stand on firm grounds, and President Carter is prepared to go all the way. He has reached the point where he is no longer so interested in being re-elected now that he has a chance to solve the Middle East problem and take his place in history as a hero of peace. He has not set a deadline for the Conference, and is leaving his schedule flexible."
>
> That being so, I agreed to attend the meeting. Vance hinted that Begin was making encouraging noises, and I replied that we were opening a new chapter. The Camp David meeting, I added, was even more portentous than my Jerusalem visit. However, I went on, Begin is pooh-poohing the Conference, and will pull every string to have it followed by others. And he will ask Carter to confine himself to the role of honest broker, although I shall insist that his role be that of a full partner.
>
> When he met with his cabinet, Begin did not come up with anything new, and he will insist on the project for self-rule in the West Bank and Gaza submitted in Ismailia and rejected by us. Begin and Dayan form a single camp, and have completely isolated Ezer Weizman, but it is my belief that Begin is fighting a losing battle.
>
> I asked Vance whether he was aware that they would have a confrontation in Camp David and that, if they did not, the Conference would yield nothing.
>
> I told Eilts [the United States Ambassador] before he left for Washington to make it clear to President Carter beforehand that I intend to reject any proposals which in any way prejudice issues of territory and sovereignty.
>
> Here we are faced with a problem, which Begin will exploit to the

full. The 1967 borders dominate the thinking of the Israelis: Tel-Aviv, for instance, is within shelling range of Jerusalem. Begin's preparations for Camp David are based on the assumption that I shall ask for a declaration of principles, and he will seek a separate or partial solution with us, such as withdrawal from Sinai to the Arish Ras Mohamed line. However, I did not go to all the trouble of launching the initiative just to come out with a separate or partial solution.

Begin's attitude will be that the restoration of the 1967 borders applies to Sinai and the Golan but not to the West Bank and Gaza, for the latter constitute a threat to Israeli security. This is true because urban centres in Israel would be within range of gunfire from the West Bank and Gaza.

My view of our strategy is that a declaration of principles is not a problem to be discussed at our level in Camp David. Camp David is the practical application of my peace initiative, and it would be futile to discuss the question of a declaration of principles at the meeting of the three leaders, for to do so would give Begin a free hand! I have, accordingly, decided to discuss a 'framework of peace' rather than a 'declaration of principles'. With this framework, we shall prepare for peace, cutting short Begin's manoeuvres. The preamble to Resolution 242 stipulates the inadmissibility of occupying territory by force. Well, this has to be implemented. As for the discussion of security arrangements in the West Bank, I approve of it, although I did receive two cables, one from [King] Hussein and one from [King] Khaled: I say to them, Why are you foreclosing on us? . . . [He did not answer the question].

Our objective is a framework of peace: it should in fact be more than a mere framework, in the sense that it should clearly and firmly indicate the steps to be taken in solving the problem. With Begin, no word should be obscure, or there will be no end to the matter. What we are after is to win over world opinion. President Carter is on our side. This will end in Begin's downfall! The United States position is geared to finding a framework for peace in the Middle East. The minimum they will accept is agreement to continue negotiations between Egypt and Israel after Camp David, and the maximum is a declaration of principles to govern the peace progress.

In the four power talks, the Rogers' initiative, and the United Nations Resolution, the United States has invariably insisted that the two parties agree on secure and recognized borders. Our project on the framework of peace will include two points: the first concerns the West Bank and Gaza. In Vienna, Kreisky, Brandt, Perez and myself agreed on a formula outlining the borders in such a manner as to meet both the Palestinians' legitimate aspirations and Israel's security. There will have to be concessions on the West Bank, and it is important that we discuss and define such concessions with Begin before he backs out.

The second point concerns self-determination for the Palestinians after a five-year transitional period. Gaza will be restored to Egypt and the West Bank to Jordan. This is approved by everyone. Were King Hussein to refuse (he is preparing to grab the West Bank and turn it into a Jordanian governorate), I shall not hesitate to pursue the negotiations and will pay no heed to their allegations that I am not entitled to speak on behalf of the Palestinians. I have full right to solve Egypt's problem, and I cannot do this without solving the Palestinian problem.

We wish to lay down a pattern, which anyone is free to join or ignore. I shall tell them openly that any decision for war or peace rests with Egypt, which speaks for half of the Arab nation.

With respect to the question of a Palestinian state, our project maintains the stand we adopted three years ago, namely that "the Palestinians have the right to self-determination, with a tie to Jordan". I want to go to the limit. I shall object to the PLO even if it is accepted by Israel!

The framework of peace will be a package deal and we shall ask for guarantees from the United States, the Security Council and its permanent members.

When Sadat had ended his presentation, he asked whether anyone wished to speak, but none of those present expressed a desire to do so, whereupon he turned to me, and in a low voice which appeared to me to contain the hint of a threat, said: "Mohamed, is there anything you wish to say?" Seething with anger, I replied hotly: "Yes, I do: there are quite a few things I wish to say!" At this, Ahmed Maher whispered in my ear: "Cool down, Mohamed Bey!"

I have to confess that Sadat took me by surprise. I had rather expected him to concentrate on the memorandum I had sent him some days earlier on our strategy at Camp David: the memo represented the conclusions arrived at by the Foreign Office as a result of extensive studies and deliberations. Sadat, however, had made no mention of the memorandum, either directly or indirectly. Instead, and just a few days before the Egyptian delegation was due to leave for Camp David, he sprung his surprise on the National Security Council and his Foreign Minister. The project had not even been completed and Sadat's ideas had barely been aired. They had not been adequately discussed. Moreover, they involved matters of a most serious nature.

In taking the floor, I chose to begin with what appeared to me the nub of his exposé, namely his assent to a formula tracing the borders between the West Bank and Gaza on the one hand, and Israel on the other, so as to satisfy both the Palestinian people's aspirations and Israel's security. I said that to approve such a formula would imply a renunciation on our part of an established strategic target and a backing-away from what the President had always maintained – his insistence that territory and sovereignty were not subject to negotiation. At the same time, it implied acceptance of the Israeli security theory we had repeatedly and rightly claimed the October War had forever refuted.

To consent to territorial concessions in the West Bank and Gaza which Israel was now demanding for its security would get us nowhere with Begin, for no sooner had he wrested an admission from us on the need to alter the borders to secure Israel's security, than he would go on to insist that Israeli security requirements embraced all the territories of the West Bank and Gaza. He might even demand that the same principle be applied in Sinai and the Golan, since this would suit his declared expansionist designs. We should thereby have grossly impaired the Palestinian cause without achieving either peace or stability!

Events (I went on) had overtaken the term "Palestinian aspirations" – an old expression used by Britain in the 1917 Balfour Declaration. At that time the Jews had no support for their claim to a national homeland in Palestine except their longings. What did apply to the Palestinians was the term "the legitimate rights of the Palestinian people", which was an absolute right as enunciated by the United Nations General Assembly and endorsed by the international community. There was therefore no need for us to substitute for it such a confusing and unsatisfactory term.

Again, nothing entitled us to negotiate territorial concessions in the West Bank or Gaza; did we (I asked) possess the right to concede territories which did not belong to us, without either the permission of, or a mandate from, their legitimate owners? Were we to attempt to do so, we would only aggravate matters and alienate all Arabs, whether hardline or moderate, and Jordan and the Palestinian people would not be in a position to take part in the negotiations . . .

President Sadat made absolutely no comment on my response contenting himself with giving the floor to any who wished to speak, and although Engineer Sayed Marei and Mustapha Khalil took advantage of the offer, neither of them made the slightest allusion to my comments, behaving as though I had not uttered a word! Instead, they digressed into side-issues, such as enquiring as to the United States position on the future of the settlements in Sinai. Field-Marshal El Gamassy, alone among the speakers, dealt with what I had said, indicating that he concurred with the Foreign Minister that territory and sovereignty were not negotiable, since to bring them into the discussions might prejudice the issue of Sinai itself.

When it came to Tohamy's turn to address the gathering, he burst out: "Brother Mohamed, why do you object to the term 'Palestinian aspirations'? In English the word 'aspirations' has stronger connotations than the word 'rights'." Not quite knowing how to answer him, I merely replied, "Perhaps!" I recalled the memorandum that had been submitted a day or two earlier by Mr Kamal Hassan Aly, who sat facing me, and I attempted to no avail to attract his attention to get him to put in a word for me.

The meeting then broke up and the President, followed by the Council members, trooped to the terrace entrance. They stood around him wishing him a happy Bairam (that feast was due to begin in a few days) and success at Camp David. The President told them of his hope and confidence that the Conference would accomplish its mission and, turning to me, said: "Mohamed, prepare yourself, for we are leaving the day after tomorrow." I answered that I was ready, but that I had a suggestion to make: "The Americans have informed us that the Conference will last at least a week; now, you may find it advisable right at the beginning to take a tougher stand than that provided for in the Egyptian project, since this would give us some elbow-room in dealing with the Americans and cushion the project against pressure designed to secure concessions from the outset."

As though he had been waiting for a word from me to give vent to his suppressed feelings, he burst out laughing dramatically, and with malice in his tone asked loudly: "Do you imagine yourself to be a diplomat, Mr Mohamed?" and, oblivious of the embarrassment of those standing by, he again laughed with amused scorn: "By God, Mohamed, you're no diplomat! What week are you talking about? As soon as I arrive there, I intend to spring my project on them, wreck the Conference and return to Egypt within forty-eight hours!" Controlling myself, I laughed in my turn at the nonsense he was talking and the spectacle he was making of himself before this select group of the country's leaders and prominent figures. Although I was very surprised at his conduct, for he had never before addressed me in such a manner publicly I felt strangely confident, and with a broad smile I could not conceal, replied: "You are naturally free to do what you want, Rais, and, anyway, I have never claimed to be a polished diplomat!"

We returned to Cairo on the Antonov, and although conversation aboard was general, a mixture of serious and not-so-serious, the meeting of the National Security Council was never mentioned. Why dwell on the past? It was over and done with. As for the future – well, the President would take care of everything, and our sole topic of conversation became: how should we all be spending Bairam?

Happy Bairam, all!

I spent the whole night until daybreak reviewing recent events and developments, trying to get to the bottom of Sadat's strange exhibition, see into his mind and discover, through careful scrutiny, his real aims and purposes. By so doing, I hoped to form a general idea in the light of which I could determine where I stood and what I should do.

My initial conclusion was that Sadat had deliberately been avoiding me, and I had a feeling that this had begun after Vance had conveyed to him the invitation to Camp David at his Maamoura rest-house on 7 August. From then on, Sadat had deliberately avoided me until the National Security Council was convened in Ismailia on 30 August just prior to our departure for Camp David on 4 September. It had become clear to me that he was dodging my repeated telephone calls, and that his excuses for not being able to meet me due to "exhaustion through fasting" and his "preoccupations with the establishment of his new Party" was so much subterfuge and camouflage. I realized it was all intended to conceal a secret intention, and I remembered he had acted in a similar way when preparing for the October War.

So why was the President avoiding me? The answer was that he had decided to depart from the position we had adopted and the principles to which we had committed ourselves from the very outset of the initiative. Our attitude up to now had been to stand firm on the issues of territory and sovereignty. Sadat had shown this clearly and decisively during his lengthy meeting with Atherton and Eilts on 10 July. At that meeting, he had announced that we would not resume direct negotiations with Israel unless it was agreed that neither territory nor sovereignty were to be subject to negotiation, and had even termed this attitude his "second initiative" – the first being his visit to Jerusalem.

When, where and how, then, did this change occur? I came to the conclusion that it had come about in the course of the meeting with Vance on 7 August in the gardens of Maamoura. This private interview had lasted a long time – from nine in the evening until after midnight – so that, although Sadat may not have decided on the change at the actual meeting itself, Vance had definitely planted the seed then. I would be naïve to assume that Vance spent the entire time explaining to Sadat that the United States intended to play the role of full partner and unreservedly endorse Egypt's stand on total Israeli withdrawal from all occupied Arab territories, while the remaining members of the two delegations sat yawning fifty yards away.

I based my conclusions on the following premises:

1   The attitude of the United States had, since the very beginning, been aimed at enlarging as far as possible the scope of the negotiating process to enable it – as a third party – to break any deadlock on any subject submitted for discussion. This breakthrough would thereby influence the remaining topics and provide the guiding thread to any eventual solution by keeping up the momentum. This was clearly apparent in the agenda the United States had suggested for the Political Committee which met in Jerusalem in January 1978. It would have been only logical to begin by an agreement on principles which would govern the peaceful settlement. Once that had been accomplished,

negotiations would begin on the implementation of those principles.

Three items figured on the American agenda:
- A declaration of principles governing the negotiations on the realization of a comprehensive peaceful settlement in the Middle East.
- Directives for the negotiations on the West Bank and Gaza.
- The elements of the peace treaties between Israel and its neighbours.

At the meeting between Presidents Carter and Sadat in Camp David in February, the American side urged us not to confine ourselves to a declaration of principles, but to submit a proposal on the West Bank and Gaza, in the hope that they could achieve a breakthrough at some point.

Proceeding along similar lines, Vance, at the Leeds Castle Conference, sought to enlarge points of agreement between the Egyptians and Israeli projects to achieve a breakthrough.

2 Carter called for the summit when he realised the chasm that existed between the Egyptian and Israeli positions, and that the situation had reached an impasse.

Could any person in his right mind imagine a United States president, with the approval of his advisers, embarking so lightly on a course that would result in the destruction of United States prestige and his own political career?

He must have based his initiative on the assumption that a compromise had to be reached. Was he not aware of Begin's stone-wall intransigence, supported as he was by the Zionist lobby and those Congressmen who had the power to either push his policy through Congress or block it? Why should he not try his hand with Sadat? Vance, who was an able lawyer, must have couched his demand for concessions on the West Bank and Gaza in such a way as to suggest to Sadat that any concessions would be minimal! He must have impressed upon Sadat that Carter was in a tizzy, with his position and future threatened, and was looking to Sadat to rescue him. He (Carter) would never forget this service, and would reward him when he was re-elected and able to bring greater pressure to bear on Israel in the interests of a just and honourable solution to the Palestinian problem. The doors of the United States Treasury would be thrown open to Egypt, and United States weaponry would be placed at Egypt's disposal . . . and so on and so forth!

3 Sadat had been careful to point out, in the National Security Council, that the idea of the "framework of peace" was his own. However, in a slip of the tongue he inadvertently blurted out:

Strange Symptoms and Many Question-Marks

"The American stand aims at seeking a framework for peace."

Be that as it may, I had no objection to the idea as such so long as it adhered to our established strategical targets, although it would be true to say that I was against tabling a new project at every meeting. We had submitted a project on a declaration of principles in Jerusalem, and a project on the West Bank and Gaza at Leeds Castle, while Israel did not budge nor had it introduced any improvements on the two projects on Sinai and autonomy submitted by Begin on 25 September 1977.

Now, if Sadat were to decide on a new project, it was absolutely necessary that he instruct the Foreign Office from the outset to study and prepare such a project, and then discuss it with the experts and myself. Once an agreement was reached on a formula, it could be submitted to the National Security Council if Sadat so wished.

It was not permissible that the President should, so to speak, go into hibernation and then wake to spring a new project on us without prior consultation with the competent authorities. This type of behaviour, was unacceptable both in form and substance. Such portentous matters should not be dealt with casually, yet I was prepared, in spite of myself, to overlook all this and deal with it as a natural disaster, for such was Anwar El Sadat, and he was the President! What I could not overlook, however, was his disclosure to the National Security Council that he had accepted the Israeli security theory, for by so doing he had strayed from the targets neither he nor anyone else was entitled to forego. This was made worse because he had, until then, bragged unceasingly about his insistence on those objectives!

I resumed my attempts to unravel what went on in Sadat's mind, and concluded that had I been able to meet with him prior to the National Security Council meeting, we would quite naturally have discussed the memorandum prepared by my Ministry, which had been sent to him earlier. Sadat would then have had to decide whether to approve, amend or reject it.

So why did he, in the event, reject it without discussion? The memorandum adhered to the essentials of our position; the strategy we proposed – if intelligently applied – would have achieved one of two things: we would either gain or still lose nothing, and our position would have been foolproof, irrespective of whether the United States supported or forsook us, whether Begin proved intransigent or indifferent, for either the negotiations would culminate in a declaration of principles, which would be a step forward in the implementation of Resolution 242 (thus enabling Jordan to join the negotiations and obtaining Saudi support along the road to a comprehensive settlement), or the meeting would end inconclusively, in which case Israel would be unable to blame us for the failure in the eyes of the United States. The door would have been left open for the Arabs to rally and continue with the peace initiative rather than seek an alternative to it.

All this was well and good, and would have been fine in other circumstances – if, say, the tripartite meeting had been at ministerial, rather than presidential level. However, another factor had been introduced, and that was President Carter's personal appearance in the arena! This fact should have made Sadat wary and induced him to display the greatest possible caution. With Carter leading the United States delegation to Camp David, the confrontation was no more between Sadat and Begin only but rather involved some sort of confrontation between Sadat and the United States President, although for different reasons. The success or failure of the Conference, in the eyes of the world, added up to success or failure for Carter, and this was so often repeated in the media that it eventually became a slogan! A question which imposed itself was, how Carter could succeed if he were not able to achieve a compromise? This, in turn, implied that Begin and Sadat would each have to make concessions of a kind!

Were it (for the sake of argument) possible for Begin to concede what did not belong to him, might Sadat, in his turn, concede what belonged to others? Relations between the United States and Israel were strong. They were based on historical, spiritual and even strategic ties, cemented by built-in support in the administration, the Congress and United States public opinion. And to crown it all, there was the quasi-sacrosanct American commitment to safeguard Israel's security and interests. By contrast, the American-Egyptian relationship was still in its infancy, and had only come into being after a long estrangement. It was, as yet, fragile and weak, and was mainly of a personal nature, since it was based on a relationship between Sadat and Carter. Israel could easily put up with the anger of the United States President without damaging or in any way affecting its strong ties with the United States. To whom, though, would Sadat be able to turn if he provoked Carter's anger and resentment? He had blown up many bridges with the Arab and non-aligned states, the Soviet Union and others.

The situation was hardly reassuring. What now, I asked myself. Sadat has decided to go to Camp David free from all ties and restrictions, whether in the form of commitment to the views and ideas of his assistants, an established stand, a declared target, a plan of action, or a previously planned strategy! He had even decided to throw his very project, "a framework of peace", on the negotiating table almost at once, when attitudes would be at their most rigid, so that it would be torn apart! He would then be free of the constraints of his own project, and would be able to adopt his attitudes accordingly, with his eyes perpetually fixed on the United States President. Above all, he would have to be careful not to strain Carter's good humour. In order to guarantee himself freedom of action, he would ignore the Foreign Ministry! He would throw its memo, the fruit of so much toil and trouble, into the waste-paper basket and loudly announce, to the distinguished members of his National Security Council, that he had accepted

Strange Symptoms and Many Question-Marks

territorial concessions in the occupied land, and were there any objections? He would thereupon declare, in full view of the most prominent figures of the nation, that his Foreign Minister understood nothing about diplomacy, hoping to silence him and his sharp tongue with a crude warning!

Such were my conclusions to the foregoing events. I could, of course, have been wrong, but the reader will perhaps allow me to wager that it was, in fact, far closer to the truth. My responsibilities as Foreign Minister impelled me to try and read Sadat's mind and analyze his motives, as much as to gain an understanding of Israeli and American thinking. And it must be said that experience and long association with Sadat, combined with a certain perspicacity, enabled me to read Sadat and what went on inside him.

Two points must be tackled before we end this chapter and move on to the Camp David Conference. It is my belief, however, that the events and analysis detailed in this chapter are necessary to a proper understanding of the events that took place in Camp David for without this background the reader would be unable to understand much of what took place there.

The first point raised the question: since Sadat was incapable of formulating himself his project of "a framework of peace", to whom would he have recourse? In fact, Sadat selected Ussama El Baz for the job, and this for several reasons, among them the fact that El Baz was both Under-Secretary of State of the Ministry of Foreign Affairs and Directeur de Cabinet of the Vice-President. So the task was assigned to a presidential aide with strong ties to the Foreign Office. Again, El Baz was a prominent member of the Foreign Ministry working group which drew up the plans for the Camp David Conference. Another factor determining the choice of El Baz was his total grasp of the Arab-Israeli conflict, while he was adept at both political and legal formulation – an extremely delicate and complex task. I had nothing against Ussama El Baz's acceptance of the task he was charged with by President Sadat at the eleventh hour. Nor could exception be taken to his compliance with his instructions to keep the matter under wraps until the appropriate moment. He was primarily a presidential officer and, furthermore, he had received his instructions from the Head of State, who was entitled to entrust any officer of the state with any task he saw fit.

For my part, although resentful and disturbed at the last-minute change and its attendant circumstances, I was relieved that El Baz was in charge of formulating the project. I was confident of his patriotism, intelligence and efficiency, and was convinced he would produce a no-nonsense and coherent project agreeable to our strategic plans. And that is what, in effect, happened. Ussama prepared a fine, integrated project which would have formed the basis for a just and comprehensive settlement had we gradually led up to the project and submitted it at the appropriate moment, and had not Sadat's propensity to rashness and wastefulness impelled him to throw it away for starters during the initial stages of the negotiations, as I have earlier indicated and will later recount.

Camp David

The second point is that I contemplated handing in my resignation, but after I had thought long and hard on my motives for doing this, I realized that the impulse was due to a powerful feeling of frustration and self-pity. Ever since I first assumed the office of Foreign Minister, I had been exerting strenuous and uninterrupted efforts, working more than fifteen hours a day, holding meetings, giving interviews, reading cables and reports, following-up world developments, and deciding on and taking decisions. During the few hous in which I snatched some sleep, I remained subconsciously awake, so that I often roused myself to put an idea down on paper before resuming my troubled slumber. The whole process would be repeated the following day and the day after that, with no break. Despite the exhaustion, tension and in spite of health problems, I never regretted or complained of my situation. I felt that fate had brought me face to face with an extremely dangerous and ticklish situation, and I ignored all the effort, pain and sacrifice involved in confronting it. On the contrary, every effort I made gave me a feeling of psychological relief, which acted as a spur to my determination and energy so long as I felt my efforts were designed to serve the cause for which we were seeking a solution, namely the achievement of a just and comprehensive peace.

Confronting Israeli artifice and manoeuvre, handling and following-up the changing United States stances, and courting the Arab states in order to gain their confidence, were part of my job. That I should, occasionally, find myself obliged to set all this aside and devote my time and efforts at solving a fresh crop of (adventitious) problems and crises as a result of Sadat's fickle whims and abrupt and indiscriminate changes of behaviour without prior notice and consultation, could hardly be borne. It shook my faith in Sadat's leadership and led me to despair of achieving any progress; it also had the effect of undermining my morale and stultifying any desire for serious work. The reader may recall that earlier I gave several instances of this, among them Sadat's sudden decision to withdraw the Egyptian delegation from the Political Committee meeting in Jerusalem and the invitation to Weizman, the Israeli Defence Minister, to visit Cairo, although the Israeli army was invading Lebanon and the Arab foreign ministers were convening in the Egyptian capital at the time! There had also been his invitation to Weizman to meet him at Foeschel, in Salzburg, his raising of the El Arish and Mount Sinai issues, and his meeting with Perez in Vienna, which resulted in the controversial communiqué released by the Socialist International.

The by-product of all this was the appearance of many other secondary problems and side-issues calling for a solution and absorbing time and energy which we might easily have dispensed with. The result was to cloud our field of vision, confuse our thinking and nullify any progress we might have achieved.

And here we were now, at a crucial turning-point, the Camp David Conference, and he had once again, and without warning, sprung his surprise during the National Security Council meeting in Ismailia! Good grief! How could I fail to be exasperated by it all? Nevertheless, I resolutely cast all such bitter thoughts aside, in the knowledge that it would have been inconceivable for me to have forsaken my duty. I *had* to support Sadat, who was about to face a grave test at Camp David, and I fully appreciated the great responsibilities he was shouldering. So I decided to give him my full backing, while at the same time protecting him against himself! I felt I had a two-fold responsibility, for I was the only one who dared confront and question him without fear or awe. This was, perhaps, due to our old association and our having been moulded in the same furnace of experience during the struggle against British colonialism which brought us together in the forties. Our relationship had indeed been forged in the darkness of the prison, and it would never then have occurred to either of us that fate was to bring us together again, he as President of the Republic of Egypt, and I as its Foreign Minister!

Footnotes:

1 The National Security Council consisted of the following: Sadat, Chairman, the Vice-President, the Prime Minister, the Speaker of the People's Assembly, the Leader of the Arab Socialist Union, the defence, foreign affairs and interior ministers, the Chief of Intelligence and Mr Hassan El Tohamy.
2 I recalled the questions President Sadat said he had addressed to President Ceaucescu in Bucharest: "Was Begin a strong man? Did he want peace?", for it was on this basis that he had decided to proceed with his initiative.

Chapter Thirty Five

On the Road to Camp David

At 10 a.m. on Monday 4 September 1978, together with the other members of the Egyptian delegation to the Camp David Conference, I arrived at Abu Sweir Airport. We were there to receive President Sadat, who had travelled to Suez to perform Bairam prayers the day before. Afterwards, we were to go on to Paris, where we would stop over for a night on our way to the United States of America.

Abu Sweir Airport is situated in the Eastern desert, and is a military airport with no facilities for receiving travellers or visitors. For this reason a large tent had been pitched to give some shelter from the sun to those who had come to see the President off. Among the visitors were statesmen and military men as well as a considerable body of persons who announced that they were members of the Democratic National Party established by Sadat.

Before the President's arrival, I was approached by Mr Maher Mohamed Aly, the lawyer, and Mr Mansour Hassan, the future Minister of Culture. Sadat had given each of them an executive role in the organization of his new party. When they asked when I would be joining the party, I promptly replied that I was not going to join it! "But," protested Maher Mohamed Aly, "you're the Minister of Foreign Affairs!" To this I responded: "And so I was, before the establishment of the party." This caused Maher to exclaim: "But you were a member of the old National Party in your youth, so how come that you're not joining the new National Party now, especially since you're a friend of the President?" "You are quite right," I shot back. "However, I'm no longer a member of the old National Party, since I have violated one of its proclaimed principles, namely that there shall be no negotiation before the evacuation. [1] Yet, here I am, as you can see, on my way to Camp David to negotiate before the evacuation!" Maher was dumbfounded, and looked at me in consternation, as if he doubted my mental faculties!

The fact was that after I was appointed Foreign Minister, Mr Mamdouh Salem had hinted, in the presence of Sadat, that it would be a good thing to join the party. (Mamdouh Salem was the Prime Minister and was Chairman of the Misr Party established by the government in compliance with the

On the Road to Camp David

directives of the President, after the multi-party system had been introduced.) I had told him at the time that I considered myself on a national mission which transcended all parties. After this, Mr Fuad Muhieddin, the Secretary-General of the party, periodically sent me an invitation to join the party, complete with the application form. However, I never answered.

It was not long before the President arrived, together with his wife, two of his daughters and his grandson. These preceded him to the plane, while Sadat shook hands with a long line of people, stretching from the door of the tent to the aircraft, who had come to see him off. I proceeded to my seat on board, fastened my seat belt, and began reading the morning papers.

Half an hour after takeoff, I was summoned into the President's presence. When I entered the private lounge where he was sitting with his family, he greeted me warmly and invited me to join them. We discussed various topics, all far removed from politics. He was particularly nice to me, as if he were trying to make me forget what had taken place between us at the last meeting of the National Security Council.

In Paris, President Sadat put up at the Marigny, where he was visited by French President Giscard d'Estaing – a rare courtesy – who extended an invitation to him to dine at the Elysée Palace that evening. For the rest of our delegation, dinner was served at the French Foreign Ministry (the Quai d'Orsay), at the invitation of Mr Jean François Poncet, the Minister for Presidential Affairs, and Mr Olivier Sterne, the Minister of State for Foreign Affairs, in the absence of the French Foreign Minister.

It was clear, from the discussions that took place, that the French side doubted strongly whether the Camp David Conference would yield any positive results, basing their assessment on the knowledge that Menahim Begin would not budge by so much as an inch from his rigid stand, and on the fact that President Carter was in no position to put effective pressure on Israel, with the mid-term elections to Congress so close at hand. The French were also concerned at the fragmentation and divisions in the Arab states since the initiative, and were worried by the deteriorating situation in Iran, where the Shah's position appeared to be collapsing. They likewise feared that the Communists would lend their backing to the spreading Islamic revolution in Iran until the Shah was toppled and they could seize power.

On the afternoon of the following day, 5 September, we left Paris on our way to the United States. The President's family stayed behind in Paris. Aboard the aircraft, I read, for the first time, the project entitled "Framework for Peace". It had been prepared at the last minute, and its full title was: "The Framework for a Comprehensive Peaceful Settlement of the Middle East Problem". [2] This begins with a preamble which sets forth the elements for a peaceful settlement, and is followed by nine Articles:

Article 1 sets forth the parties' determination to reach a
comprehensive settlement by signing peace treaties based on the full

implementation of Resolutions 242 and 334 in all their parts.

Article 2 indicates that the establishment of peace requires the fulfilment of the following:

1. Israel's withdrawal from the territories it had occupied, in accordance with the principle of the inadmissibility of acquiring land through war. Withdrawal from Sinai and the Golan would be to the international borders; and from the West Bank to the lines of the Jordanian-Israeli Armistice Agreement of 1949 . . . Were it to be decided to make some insubstantial amendments, this shall not reflect the weight of conquest. Security measures would be applied in the Bank with a view to responding to the need of the two parties to ensure their security and safeguarding of the rights and aspirations of the Palestinian people. Withdrawal from Gaza would be to the lines of the Egyptian-Israeli Armistice Agreement, of 1949.
2. Dismantling Israeli settlements in the occupied territories in accordance with a timetable.
3. The establishment of security measures which shall comprehend the six points mentioned above in the Egyptian project on the West Bank and Gaza, submitted at Leeds Castle. A new provision had been added, to the effect that "All parties must, by necessity, accede to the Treaty on the Non-Proliferation of Nuclear Weapons, and pledge themselves to abstain from the production or possession of such weapons". It was noteworthy that Egypt had signed the Treaty, whereas Israel had refused – and still refuses – to do so.
4. That the parties pledge themselves to settle any disputes which may arise, by peaceful means. They shall accept the compulsory jurisdiction of the International Court of Justice for any disputes arising from the interpretation of the "Framework for Peace".
5. The abolition of the Israeli military government in the West Bank and Gaza and the transfer of power to the Arab parties in a peaceful and orderly manner. There shall be a transitional period which shall not exceed five years. During this period, Jordan shall have charge of the administration of the West Bank and Egypt of Gaza, in co-operation with the freely elected representatives of the Palestinian people, who shall asssume direct power immediately after the abolition of the Israeli military government. The Palestinian people shall exercise its basic right of self-determination, and Egypt shall recommend that the National Palestinian entity be connected with Jordan.

   The Palestinian people shall have the right to return or receive compensation in accordance with UN resolutions.

6 Israel's withdrawal from Jerusalem to the 1949 Armistice Lines: Arab sovereignty and administration shall be restored in Arab Jerusalem. A joint municipal council for the city shall be established consisting of Palestinians and Israeli members in equal numbers, and shall have charge of public facilities, transport, traffic, postal and telephone services, and tourist activities in the city.

    The parties shall pledge themselves to guarantee freedom of worship in and access to the Holy Places without discrimination.

7 That, in parallel with the implementation of the provisions on withdrawal, the parties shall proceed to establish relations that normally obtain between states in a state of peace. This shall include full recognition, termination of the Arab boycott and free passage through the Suez Canal.

8 That Israel pledge itself to pay full compensation for the acts committed by its military forces against people and civilian installations and for its exploitation of natural resources in the occupied territories.

Article 3: as soon as this framework considered an intergrated whole is signed . . . other parties shall be invited to accede thereto within the context of the Geneva Peace Conference.

Article 4: the representatives of the Palestinian people shall participate in the peace talks which shall take place after this framework is signed.

Article 5: the United States shall participate in the talks, seeking ways and means of implementing agreements and setting the timetable for the fulfilment of the obligations of the parties.

Article 6: the Peace Treaties shall be signed within three months of the signing of this framework.

Articles 7, 8 and 9 call on the Security Council to guarantee the Peace Treaties, the respect for their provisions, as well as the borders between the member states. The Permanent Members of the Security Council are likewise called upon to guarantee the implementation of the framework and the treaties to be duly signed in good faith in accordance therewith.

When I had finished examining the project, I went straight to the President's private lounge. He was alone. I sat down, and he enquired whether I had read the project, and I replied: "Yes, I have, and find it excellently integrated. Every provision and every word is rooted in law, reason and legality, and it can be easily defended or presented with entire conviction and confidence. However, I remain of the opinion that we should not submit the project from the very beginning, so as to assess the attitude of President Carter, ascertain how far he is prepared to move, and expose Begin's position, which I do not think will change. Begin will continue to be unyielding and intransigent."

Sadat's comment was: "Why go around in circles? Since you say the project is well constucted and may be easily defended, I intend, from the very outset, to lay the project before Carter and Begin. In the end, all depends on whether Carter is really ready to undertake the role of full partner he has accepted, and exert pressure on Begin. If he is not ready, why waste time? I'll pack and return to Egypt to prepare the next step."

His words reassured me. I feared prolonged negotiation because, as far as I was concerned as a result of the firmness of the parties' positions, they would only lead us into making concessions, while Begin could afford to persist in his intransigence and obstinacy (being in possession of the occupied territories) – such was not Sadat's case. Sadat was moody and impatient and worried at the stalemate that had befallen his initiative. I said: "I agree with you; however, we need a good exit so that Carter may not hold us responsible for the failure, which we must lay at Begin's door."

Sadat then confided to me that Vance had told him that Carter was prepared to go all the way, even if that meant he would not be re-elected for a second term. Sadat continued: "He is convinced that if he were to succeed in achieving peace, he would, by all accounts, be an international hero."

After a short silence, I opined: "If you're going to submit our project at the outset, you should insist on all its provisions with the utmost determination, and refuse any amendments unless Begin modifies his position. There is nothing there to get Carter's back up. If Begin can insist on every word, comma and full stop in the two projects he submitted in Ismailia, and this despite their unreasonableness, illegality and injustice, then we are surely entitled to stoutly maintain our project and positions, since these are based on international law and United Nations resolutions. Should it be necessary to make some non-basic concessions it would be up to us. We can, for example, make concessions with regard to the compensation we are claiming from Israel by reason of its unlawful exploitation of the mineral wealth of Sinai throughout the years of occupation."

At this the President burst out:

"Never! not a single cent! We should be compensated for each drop of the oil they have stolen from our soil and our territorial waters . . . !"[3]

I said: "The Conference is going to last quite a time and it will be an exhausting battle of nerves."

Sadat's rejoinder was that we should, rather, "keep our cool". "We have nothing to fear [he went on]. We are in full control of the situation." He then told me we should be passing through Morocco on our way back for a day or

On the Road to Camp David

two's rest. I retorted that, in my opinion, we should stop over in Saudi Arabia rather than Morocco. He asked: "Why Saudi Arabia?" I replied: "To communicate to King Khaled and Prince Fahd the results we have obtained. If we succeed in achieving any progress, then we could invite King Hussein to join us there. On the other hand, if we do not succeed, it will be high time for us to consult the Saudis with a view to convening an Arab summit!"

The President turned his face to the window and appeared to be contemplating the sea of cloud over which we were flying. He did not utter a word!

I returned to my seat and eased it back, and was soon in the land of memories and the years of my childhood and youth . . . what a happy, wonderful life it was, so long, long ago. I was awakened by the hostess' voice requesting the passengers to extinguish their cigarettes and to fasten their seat belts; our plane, the voice continued, would in a few minutes be landing at the Andrews Air Force Base.

The aircraft door swung open to reveal Dr Ashraf Ghorbal, our Ambassador in Washington. He was accompanied by Mrs Dobell, the Head of Protocol at the State Department. We followed the President as he descended from the plane and stepped onto a red carpet. A guard of honour, representing the three services, was drawn up for the President's inspection. Walter Mondale, the Vice-President, and Cyrus Vance approached the President and greeted him. The navy band then played, first, the Egyptian Republican Anthem and then the US National Anthem. Mr Mondale made a short speech saying: "On behalf of President Carter and the American people, I sincerely welcome you, once again, to the United States. Our people greatly admire your wisdom, courage, and political astuteness."

Sadat replied in an address in which, after expressing his gratitude for the welcome given him, he went on to say: "We are interested in establishing a just and comprehensive peace in the Middle East, and we always appreciated the United States' contribution to the peace process. We are now at the crossroads and are facing a great challenge. However, we have no alternative but to take up this challenge because we cannot disappoint the world's hopes for peace. We have no time now for manoeuvres or obsolete ideas."

The President then shook hands with the greeting party. These included the ambassadors in Washington of those of Arab states who had not broken off relations with us, the members of our Embassy in Washington, and those of our Permanent Mission in New York. He then greeted a group of Egyptian students who had come to meet him.

We boarded a helicopter with Vance, and in under an hour we landed at the Camp David military camp. By the helipad stood President Carter and his wife, Brezinski, Harold Saunders, Alfred Atherton, Herman Eilts, Samuel Lewis, the United States Ambassador to Israel, and Quandt.

When he had stepped down from the helicopter, Sadat was embraced by Carter. After guests and welcomers had exchanged greetings, President and

Camp David

Mrs Carter accompanied the Egyptian President to the bungalow where he was to stay during the Conference. This bungalow bore the name of "Dogwood". The other members of the Egyptian delegations were then shown to their quarters. Dr Boutros Ghali, Mr Hassan Kamel, Ambassador Ghorbal and myself were ensconced in "Maple" bungalow. This lay about thirty metres from "Dogwood", which, in turn, was located at the same distance from "Aspen", President Carter's quarters. Each of the three dwellings lay at a point of a triangle of almost equal sides.

Our residence consisted of two bedrooms with twin beds and a bathroom attached to each room. The centre of the bungalow was the living-room, simply but comfortably furnished. The centre-piece was a large fireplace, and across from it was a window running the entire length of the wall, overlooking a picturesque stand of birch and pine.

I chose the inner room, sharing it with Dr Boutros Ghali, while Hassan Kamel and Ashraf Ghorbal occupied the remaining one. Half an hour later, Ahmed Maher came to the bungalow, in the company of Ahmed Abou El Gheit, an attaché in my office and a very promising young man. They invited me out for a stroll to explore the Camp. I changed from the suit I was wearing into a shirt, slacks and a pullover and went out with them.

It was already autumn, and silence reigned over the place, save for the sighing of the breeze through the tree branches and the whisper of the gold, green and brown leaves as they floated lazily down in their interweaving patterns of honey, red and russet, forming a symphony of colours. There was an invigorating nip in the air, encouraging brisk and active movement. Squirrels swung through the trees in search of food to store for the lean winter months.

We walked to the edge of the Camp, overlooking a wide valley ending in a chain of medium-sized mountains which, at a distance, could be taken for a wall hiding a mystery. Continuing our stroll through the forest, we came to a group of small buildings, forming the hub of the Camp's activities. One of the buildings housed comfortable sitting-rooms and a well-stocked library. Attached to it was a dining-room seating thirty persons, and a kitchen. In another building across the way was a small movie theatre, a billiard-room, several meeting halls and administrative offices. We went on to discover tennis-courts, a swimming-pool and a field for trap-shooting. Quantities of bicycles were available for anyone wishing to move around the Camp or those in search of exercise. There was also a number of electrically propelled cars, pollution-free and soundless.

We walked back to my bungalow, where Ambassador Eilts soon paid us a visit. He informed us of the imminent arrival of the Israeli delegation, led by Menahim Begin. Then the gates of Camp David would close upon us, and we would be isolated from the world until the Conference ended in one way or another. A press centre had been established for the newspaper, radio and television correspondents in a village close to the Camp. The sole source of information as to what was taking place inside the walls of Camp David would be Jody Powell, the White House spokesman, who would hold a daily press conference in the centre on activities inside the Conference, from which, however, all reference to the talks would be rigorously excluded.

We repaired to the restaurant in the company of Ambassador Eilts, and there we met the other members of the Egyptian delegation. We had an appetizing meal, prepared by a group of young Filipinos, some of whom were students at US universitites. After dinner, I went together with Boutros Ghali, Hassan Kamel and Ashraf Ghorbal, to call on President Sadat at "Dogwood". It was of similar dimensions to ours, but stood higher, with ten wooden steps up to the front door. It was also more elegantly furnished: hard by the living-room was a wooden terrace covered by the branches of a large tree. This was Sadat's preferred spot throughout our stay, and it was here that President Sadat often met me with the Egyptian delegation.

Sadat's morale was high: he informed us that he had paid a courtesy visit to President Carter and was to meet privately with him for a working session at ten the next morning.

I returned to my bungalow, undressed and got into bed. Ghali did the same in the bed close to mine. We did not speak for some time, but then I remarked: "We have arrived safe and sound in Camp David, but I'm wondering how we shall be leaving!" No answer from Ghali – he was sound asleep!

Footnotes

1 The National Party, established by the National leader, Mustapha Pasha Kamel, to liberate the Egyptians from British colonialism, proclaimed that "there shall be no negotiations except after the evacuation", and it pledged to direct the efforts of the Egyptian people to work for the evacuation of the British by all possible means.
2 See Appendix 2.
3 Egypt did not obtain a single cent in compensation!

Chapter Thirty Six

The Roaring of the Lion and The Wisdom of Monkeys

On the morning of the following day, Sadat met Carter privately in "Aspen". The meeting lasted nearly an hour, and upon his return, Ghali and I paid him a visit. He was in high spirits, and informed us that he had conveyed our project, "The Framework of Peace", to Carter, who had listened attentively without comment. Sadat had pointed out to him that the project included security measures with regard to the West Bank and Gaza which went beyond those set forth in the project submitted in Leeds. He (Sadat) hoped Begin would not raise any objections. The US President had told him he would be meeting with the Israeli Premier privately, after which the three could hold a meeting in the afternoon. Carter had likewise indicated that the Camp David Conference was of the utmost importance, adding that its failure might be taken to mean that any resumption of direct negotiations stood little chance of success. This would complicate matters and a unique opportunity to achieve a settlement would have been thrown away. Such a failure, moreover (Carter continued) would affect his present position and his political future. Sadat had answered, saying that were the Conference to fail, he (Carter) would not be the cause, but Begin, if the latter persisted in his obduracy and intransigence.

After this, Sadat suggested that we take a walkabout with him so as to familiarize ourselves with our surroundings. "Can you believe it [he asked us]? Poor naïve Carter tells me he is afraid Hafiz el Assad might die, as he believed that would be a great calamity."

At that time, there were rumours President Assad had developed a throat cancer and was in danger of dying. On the road we encountered Begin, riding in one of the electric cars. He promptly stopped his car, got down and shook hands with the President, saying he hoped he was well. He shook hands wih me, too, with a "How are you, Mr Minister?" He then went on to embrace Boutros Ghali, telling the President as he did so "Peter's my friend. He asked me, during your celebrated visit to El Qods, to call him 'Peter'." Begin thereupon took his leave of us and proceeded to "Aspen". A little later we accompanied Sadat as far as the bungalow and left.

We met the Israeli delegation for the first time in the dining-hall. They were having their meal with Begin and his wife. Begin, unlike Sadat, who had never set foot in the hall, taking his meals alone in his quarters, continued throughout the Conference to do so in the restaurant. The Israelis seemed happy as we greeted them from a distance and sat down at our table. Weizman then left his chair and approached us. After shaking hands with us, he sat with us for a time, expressing his hopes for the success of the Conference.

In the evening, on our way to the restaurant for dinner, we dropped in on the President, and found him watching one of the *Roots* episodes on TV. He informed us that he had read our project to both Carter and Begin and had given the latter a copy. The three of us (he went on) agreed that the Camp David talks were designed to come up with a framework for a peaceful, comprehensive settlement which would allow the other Arab parties to join in the negotiations on that basis. It was likewise agreed that the three men should meet again the following day, by which time Begin would have had the opportunity to examine the project and so put him in a position to express his views and observations on its contents.

When we entered the dining-hall we found the Israelis sitting around the table with no sign of the merry atmosphere which had surrounded them at noon. Their faces were serious and preoccupied. Seeing this, we, for our part, were inordinately cheerful. Their mood may well have been spoiled by the contents of the Egyptian project. Whoever looks into what Moshe Dayan and Ezer Weizman wrote on the meeting held by the Israeli delegation upon Begin's return from the three-man gathering, carrying a copy of the Egyptian project on the framework of peace, can only – if he is fair – be amazed. The Israeli reaction to the Egyptian project was as though it was the height of profanity and blasphemy, designed to leave Israel defenceless. They looked upon it as the culmination of insolence and folly, whereas in truth the Egyptian project represented no more than an honest and objective application of United Nations Resolution 242 accepted by Israel itself. It provided for the restitution of rights to their true owner and the guarantee of peace and security for all states in the area, including Israel, enabling them to live in stability and achieve progress and prosperity.

In my opinion, there is only one explanation for this. The Israeli attitude rests on an erroneous racist belief, which dominates their thinking and governs their behaviour – namely, that they are God's Chosen People. Accordingly, whatever they believe, their rights transcend the rights of others, however legitimate. In saying this, I am not generalizing but simply wish to indicate that is exactly the frame of mind of the ruling Israeli establishment, led by Menahim Begin.

The next day, 7 September, Cyrus Vance asked me to meet him on the terrace adjoining the meeting-hall that afternoon at four. I asked Ahmed Maher to accompany me. Vance arrived, accompanied by Walter Mondale, the United States Vice-President. Vance informed us that he had read our

Camp David

project, "The Framework of Peace", and desired to discuss a few points with us. First, though he wished to make some preliminary observations. The first observation concerned the second paragraph of Article Two stipulating: "the dismantling of Israeli settlements in the occupied territories according to a timetable to be agreed upon during the period indicated in Article Six."[1]

Vance said the position was clear with respect to the Israeli settlements in Sinai. The Israelis agreed with us on the need to dismantle them. As for the settlements in the West Bank and Gaza, their proposed dismantlement would constitute a serious problem, since Israel could never be persuaded to accept that, considering that this would constitute a threat to its security. I was aware, of course, that Israel would never agree to this, but I nevertheless proceeded to tell Vance that those colonies represented an illegal encroachment on the occupied Arab territories. "You, yourself, [I told him], decided this was illegal and constituted an obstacle to peace. How can we aspire to peace when these settlements – the embodiment of aggression – stand on Arab soil without being dismantled? We must achieve a peace free of all problems likely to eventually threaten it, or else we shall have achieved nothing."

During the discussion that followed, I stood by what I had said until Mondale intervened with, "What do you say to a freeze on existing settlements in the West Bank and Gaza?" They finally proposed the following:

1. A five-year freeze on settlements.
2. Transformation of some of the civilian settlements into military camps, were it decided to retain Israeli forces in specified military camps during the transitional period.
3. Negotiate on the future of the settlements during the transitional period, with Jordan and the Palestinians participating in the negotiations.

It ended in my saying that I personally agreed initially to a five-year freeze, provided the freeze included non-enlargement of the existing area of the settlements and, of course, non-establishment of new settlements. Deep inside, I felt well pleased with this solution, particularly as it was being proposed by the American side.

Vance then made the following observations:

1. With regard to Jerusalem, the Egyptian project did not refer to the undivided city.
2. The three-month period set out in Article 3 should be replaced by the more suitable "promptly".
3. He wished to know whether the compulsory jurisdiction of the

International Court of Justice – referred to in paragraph 4 of Article 2 – had any precedents.
4 He expressed the view that it was preferable to delete paragraph 8 of Article 2 on Israel's payment of compensation for the losses it had caused to the population and to civilian installations and its exploitation of natural wealth in the occupied territories, as this would raise problems.
5 He likewise proposed to delete Article 9 because it was covered by Article 8.
6 He proposed that the United States should not in the text be asked to undertake tasks but should only be invited to do so.

I promised Vance I would give him my answer after considering these observations. Both Ambassador Ahmed Maher and myself were satisfied and felt optimistic with regard to the US stand. If such [we thought] were their initial observations on the Egyptian project, then, by all means, "so be it!".

Proceeding on the theory that what was not disapproved was approved, their observations showed that they approved the basic elements of our project with the exception of the issue concerning the dismantling of the settlements in the West Bank and Gaza. Albeit they proposed a practical solution which would eliminate the danger of any spreading of the cancerous colonial settlements to the rest of the West Bank and Gaza Strip.

After the President had returned from his second meeting with President Carter and Begin, Tohamy, Hassan Kamel, Boutros Ghali, Ashraf Ghorbal, Ussama El Baza and myself visited Sadat's quarters. We sat with him on the wooden terrace, where he confided to us that he had had a stormy discussion with Begin on the Israeli settlements in Sinai. Begin had announced that he would not, under any circumstances, relinquish those settlements. This was not simply a personal wish or a fancy to hang on to the settlements as a souvenir, but rather because they formed a security belt protecting Israel against attack. Neither the Israeli government nor the opposition could ever agree to the dismantlement of such settlements. Israel's security was sacred and vital to all! And Begin indicated that it should be possible to devise an appropriate formula for the retention of the settlements which would satisfy President Sadat and convince him that the maintenance of such settlements did not, in any way, conflict with Egyptian sovereignty over Sinai, which would be restored in toto to Egypt. The settlements could, for example, be placed under the control of the UN.

All this, however, was rejected out of hand by Sadat, who said our land was sacred and that neither the Egyptian people nor himself could accept the maintenance of a single Israeli settlement, settler or soldier on our territory. He said he would sign an agreement only if all such setttlements were dismantled. As to the West Bank and Gaza, Sadat informed us that he had refuted all Begin's arguments, such as the one which maintained that approval of what was set forth in the Egyptian project would result in the establishment of a terrorist Palestinian state which would constitute a danger to his country. Further, Begin had claimed, it would conflict with what President Carter and Sadat himself had told the Israelis of their non-endorsement of the establishment of an independent Palestinian state.

Sadat went on to say that he had answered that all this was true, but that what the framework of peace suggested was the establishment of a Palestinian state linked to Jordan, not an independent state. Such a state, furthermore, could be demilitarized. Sadat told us that Begin had rejected everything in our project concerning the West Bank and Gaza, and that he (Sadat) had replied that there would be no agreement without a solution to the Palestinian question.

Sadat declared before Carter and Begin that he would sign no agreement on Sinai before reaching an agreement on the West Bank and Gaza Strip. Sadat revealed to us that, after Begin's departure, Carter had requested that an American-Egyptian bilateral meeting be held at Presidential level, with no more that three assistants on each side. It was agreed that this meeting would be held following the show to be given by the US Marines in the evening.

Accordingly, Sadat asked Tohamy, Ghali and myself to attend the meeting with him. As we were taking our leave, Sadat told us proudly: "I wish you could have heard President Carter say to me after the tripartite meeting: 'You roared like a lion when you told Begin in front of me that neither yourself nor he, nor even King Hussein, can claim sovereignty over the West Bank and Gaza, and that the Palestinian people were alone entitiled to do so.' " Sadat was pleased at Carter comparing him to that noble beast, and repeated the story several times on subsequent occasions as proof of his fierce defence of the Palestinian people's rights!

After sunset the members of the delegations attended a performance given by US Marines in one of the open Camp David courtyards. A small wooden amphitheatre had been prepared for the occasion. The heads of delegations sat in the first row, with Sadat on Carter's right and the Israeli Premier on his left. In the same row sat the Camp David military, while members of the delegations occupied the rows behind. The media – press, radio and television – had been invited to attend the show, and had been permitted for the first time to penetrate the electrified walls of Camp David. They were not, however, allowed any contact with the delegations, and seating accommodation had been arranged for them on the other side of the courtyard.

The Marines began their show, and their performance was extremely efficient, clever and precise. I was scarcely watching the show, however, my thoughts being absorbed by the bilateral meeting we were about to hold with

The Roaring of the Lion and The Wisdom of Monkeys

the American side led by President Carter. I was curious to find out what his plans were. So much depended on this.

After the show, the representatives of the mass media left the Camp and the members of the delegations made their way to the *al fresco* party being held in their honour. This was designed to melt the ice between Egyptian and Israeli delegations and make them more familiar with one another. There was a barbecue with drinks, salads and sweets while the Marine band played.

The party was strained, however, and there was little mirth. Maier Rosen, a member of the Israeli delegation (he was later appointed Ambassador in Paris), tried to convince me that Israel's retention of settlements in Sinai did not in any way prejudice Egyptian sovereignty, and he and I discussed the subject for some time. When, however, he persisted in his attempts, I asked him whether he really thought I was as naïve as all that!

At around 11 p.m., Ambassador Eilts asked me to leave the party, together with Tohamy and Ghali, to attend the American-Egyptian meeting. The two sides met in one of the small conference-rooms in the building opposite the one housing the dining-hall. The two presidents sat side by side at a round table covered with green baize, illuminated by a powerful light. To the left of Carter sat US Vice-President Walter Mondale, Cyrus Vance and Brezinski. To Sadat's right were seated Hassan El Tohamy, myself and Boutros Ghali.

President Carter began with a speech thanking President Sadat and the Israeli Premier once more for their spontaneous acceptance of the invitation to the tripartite meeting in Camp David, adding that this was a good opportunity to break the stalemate in the negotiations and achieve progress towards peace. He next paid tribute to Sadat for his Jerusalem initiative, commending his courage, wisdom, political acumen, foresight and persistence in the search for peace. Carter then went on, in the same voice and tone, to praise Begin as a courageous leader, a shrewd politician and a man of peace quick to respond to President Sadat's historic initiative!

I glanced at Sadat and immediately noticed that he was annoyed and resented Carter's praise of the Israeli Premier and of his placing him on the same footing as himself. He thereupon said: "It was I who made the peace initative. Had Begin really desired peace, we would have had it for some time now. And there would have been no cause for our presence here now."

He then lit his pipe, exhaled the smoke from his nostrils and stared with expressionless eyes before him.

I suddenly heard Tohamy cry: "Your Excellency!" and when Carter turned to him he continued: "I met Foreign Minister Moshe Dayan twice in Morocco prior to the initiative. At the second meeting, he told me that Prime Minister Begin had agreed to withdraw from the West Bank, Gaza, the Golan and Sinai and that they were ready to accept our conditions for peace. This was in the presence of King Hassan II. However, when I accompanied President Sadat to Jerusalem in November last, a senior member of Begin's inner circle asked me: 'Why have you come to Jerusalem? We are satisfied with the present situation and our occupation of the land we have liberated. Peace at present is not in our interest!' "

The faces of those present were a study! Carter said, somewhat coldly: "It is always possible to say that a person of the inner circle said this or that. However, it would be wrong to rely too much on such utterances. Anyone could attribute any words or any story to me, claiming he is of my inner circle – he could actually belong to it – but his words would not necessarily be true or their sense might have been distorted. It is generally held that President Sadat is flexible, while his close assistants are hard-liners; and that Prime Minister Begin is a hard-liner while his close assistants are flexible! This may or may not be true, but if it is true, then it constitutes a useful and desirable balance. Let us now return to the subject of our meeting."

Glancing at a paper in front of him, Carter proceeded: "I should like to speak first about Sinai and then about the West Bank and Gaza. The main problem in Sinai is that of the Israeli settlements and airports established there. There is clear disagreement between the Egyptian and Israeli positions on the subject. The Israeli Prime Minister believes he has made great concessions on Sinai, as indicated in the project presented at Ismailia. In his view, such concessions exceed by far the concessions previously offered by Israeli Labour Party. As to Charm-el-Sheikh, he feels that UN forces should be deployed there and should not be withdrawn except with the approval of both the Egyptian and Israeli sides together with that of the Security Council."

Vice-President Walter Mondale then enquired what the situation would be if the problem of the Sinai settlements were to be resolved, and would it then be possible to solve other prolems.

Secretary of State Vance replied that there existed no legal or legitimate basis for the Sinai settlements, and Israeli security requirements did not call for them. He added that Dayan and Weizman were more inclined to a resolution of the settlements issue than Begin. As for the problem of the Israeli airfields in Sinai, this was a military problem, which might be considered by the military. Vance indicated that the situation in Sinai and Golan was very different from that in the West Bank and Gaza. There was an Egyptian government with sovereign rights to Sinai, and a Syrian government which could impose its authority in the Golan. The situation was different in the West Bank and Gaza where there was no clear authority or sovereignty.

Brezinski opined that Sinai should be restored to Egypt in its entirety. He proposed that some of the Israeli settlements in Sinai be transformed into training centres for the US army (we learned later that the proposal was made at Foreign Minister Dayan's suggestion).

President Sadat then spoke briefly. He made it clear that there were two

The Roaring of the Lion and The Wisdom of Monkeys

things that were not negotiable under any cicumstances, namely the land and sovereignty. With regard to the situation in Sinai, it was his belief that Israel was reluctant to give up the settlements established there for fear of creating a precedent which might be invoked for the dismantlement of Israel settlements in the Golan, the West Bank and Gaza. As for Brezinski's proposal to transform the settlements into training centres for the US army, he could not accept it, since it would be harmful to both American and Egyptian interests.

Carter once again took the floor to say that, in view of the crucial differences between Egypt and Israel on the West Bank and Gaza, he would submit an American project for a settlement based on the idea of self-rule. The basic issues on sovereignty over the West Bank and Gaza would be deferred for discussion at the end of the transitional period, adding that Begin's was a good project for a transitional period.

On the settlements issue, and despite their being illegal, there was a fundamental difference between the settlements in Sinai and other settlements in the West Bank and Gaza. Israel sincerely believed it needed these settlements for security purposes. Their existence greatly restrained terrorist and extremist activities to which Israel was exposed. Carter went on to say that, were it not possible for Jordan to be involved during the transitional period, he hoped Egypt would accept a presence in the West Bank and Gaza. The United States President added that this project would not go into details, but would be confined to drawing the broad lines for a settlement, since nobody had the right to speak for the Palestinians. A partial or incomplete solution, although it might not be acceptable to all three parties, was preferable to a possible breakdown or suspension of the peace process and a return to the dangers of military confrontation.

On the subject of withdrawal and determination of borders, an understanding could be reached based on the formulae agreed between President Sadat and Shimon Perez in Vienna. These were based on a tie-in of Palestinian aspirations and Israeli security considerations.

Carter concluded his presentation by declaring that, practically speaking, were Egypt, the US and Israel to approve a project based on those premises, there would be nothing to prevent its successful implementation, in view of the authority enjoyed by the three parties. This might induce objections from some of the other Arab states; however, they could not but follow suit eventually.

Vance then again took the floor. He said he wished to put forward some conciliatory ideas. These were that the (Israeli) autonomy project be accepted as a basis for a settlement. Egypt, Israel, Jordan and the Palestinians would be involved during the transitional period. The United States would try to reach an understanding with Israel on the final status of the West Bank and Gaza after the transitional period.

The American side had put its case. My eyes, together with those of all the participants, now focussed on President Sadat to hear his answer to all that Vance and Carter had said, which was very serious and required an immediate reaction. Sadat, however, stared straight in front of him as though he were not there, looking at nothing! He neither moved not uttered a single word – nor did he roar "like a lion". I hurriedly collected my own thoughts so as to be able to speak. Overwhelmed with bitterness at what Carter had said and at what Sadat had left unsaid, I heard the US President say: "And now I should like to hear Minister Kamel!"

I began speaking, directing my words to President Carter. I outlined the background to the Israeli-Arab dispute, following this up with recent developments in the Middle East. I emphasized the role of President Sadat in expelling the Russian experts from Egypt and in reducing Soviet influence in the area. I then spoke of the 1973 October War, which laid the groundwork for a peaceful settlement between the Arabs and Israel and the resumption of diplomatic relations between the US and Egypt. President Carter (I went on) had assumed the office of President after clearly affirming, during his election campaign, that human rights would constitute one of the cornerstones of his policy and preoccupations.

This affirmation was subsequently confirmed by his statements "on the right of Palestinian people to a national homeland". He was the first American President to make such a declaration and to give priority to the quest for a solution to the Middle East problem, whose persistence threatened the political and economic security of the world. This had encouraged President Sadat to take the initiative of visiting Jerusalem. I added that we fully appreciated the importance of US participation in the talks, and its unvarying declarations on adherence to principles and values. I indicated that our positions had been positive and constructive right from the start, and that we had offered Israel all possible security assurances, guarantees for peace, and good-neighbourly relations in the presence and with the assistance of the US representatives. Despite all this, however, Israel had been unresponsive and obdurate and was insisting on the impossible. We could not – and were not entitled to – give up the occupied territories. Even were we, for the sake of argument, to agree to it, this would still not bring about peace and security. We had responded to President Carter's invitation to participate in the Camp David Conference, despite the fact that we remain convinced of Israel's bad faith, because we believed in him as a man of principle who would unflinchingly perform his part by doing all he could to convince Israel that the way to peace was to be found in restoring lands and rights to their rightful owners.

I went on to say that I was not going to speak of Sinai, but rather of solving the Palestinian problem, which was at the heart of the conflict and the key to that just and comprehensive peace we so desired: "I have listened attentively [I told Carter] to your ideas with regard to the American project you intend to submit, but must honestly confess myself shocked at the direction you seem to be taking, which, in my opinion, errs from the road to an overall solution!"

And I went on to declare that my understanding was that they wanted to take the autonomy project submitted by Begin in Ismailia as the basis for a settlement, although it had been rejected out of hand by both Egypt and the Arabs. Moreover, some of Carter's ideas were simply a repetition of Israel's unfounded claims. Among them was deferring consideration of sovereignty over the West Bank and Gaza on the grounds of its alleged ambiguity, whereas there was not the least doubt as to the Palestinian people's right to sovereignty over those territories. The Palestinian people had lived there uninterruptedly for thousands of years until the United Nations General Assembly resolution on partition divided Palestine into an Arab and Jewish state. The legal consequences of that solution were to establish the sovereignty of Israel over the territory allocated to the Jewish state, while at the same time ensuring and affirming the Palestinian people's sovereign rights over the territory allotted to the Arab state, including the West Bank and Gaza. I failed to understand (I continued) why he did not take the Egyptian project as a basis for a settlement. The said project was totally objective and represented an unbiased implementation of Resolution 242 governing the comprehensive settlement.

I made it clear that I refused to accept the Israeli project as a basis for a settlement. At the same time, however, we were not insisting that the Egyptian project should be the basis for such a settlement. What we were truly hoping for was that the American project would reflect declared United States positions on a solution to the dispute. These were: withdrawal from the occupied Arab territories, while allowing for possible slight and relatively unimportant modifications with regard to the West Bank alone, but only on condition that agreement was reached thereon; illegality of settlements; right of Palestinian refugees to return to their homes and compensation; non-recognition of the annexation of Arab Jerusalem by Israel; and, finally, the Aswan formula, formulated by President Carter himself, on a solution to the Palestinian problem.

I told them that I completely disagreed with President Carter's view that, were Egypt, Israel and the US to agree to even a partial or incomplete solution, the other Arab states would be obliged to accept and go along with it. Such a view, in my opinion, was based on an unsound assessment, the fact being that a solution of this sort would result in the isolation of Egypt and further divisions among the Arabs, and would lead to instability in the area which, in turn, would result in a more acute polarization within it, thus opening the way to the restoration of Soviet influence there. Were, however, the USA to use its influence and assist in the achievement of a just solution to the Palestinian issue on the basis of the legitimate rights of the Palestinian people, all the Arab states without exception, both moderate and radical, would feel grateful to the US. Peace would prevail in the area, which would be beneficial to both Israel and the Arabs and would be reflected in improved world security and economy.

When I had done, President Carter remarked: "Thank you, Mr Minister. We shall take what you have said into consideration. I repeat, however, that, were Egypt, Israel and the United States on the same side, then no power outside or inside the area would dare oppose them."

Appalled, I shot a glance at President Sadat, in the hope that he would save the situation by commenting on the dangerous idea Carter had just advanced. Not a bit of it, however: he was still lost in his own world, drawing on his pipe! Perhaps he thought it wisest to follow the example of the three Chinese monkeys – "see no evil, hear no evil, speak no evil"!

The meeting came to an end and I had a feeling that a lot was going on in the dark between Sadat and Carter, and that I should prepare myself for surprises which would probably be unpleasant!

Footnotes

1   Article Six stipulates that "peace treaties shall be established within three months of the signing by the concerned parties of this framework" – thereby proclaiming the beginning of the peace process and the point of departure for "the dynamism of peace and co-existence".

Chapter Thirty Seven

Kissinger's Curse Again

It was after midnight when I retired with Boutros Ghali to our bedroom at the conclusion of the meeting. We donned our pyjamas, but sleep eluded us both, so I sat on my bed while Boutros did likewise on the bed facing mine. I began to speak – or rather to think aloud. I was deeply concerned (I told Boutros) at what had taken place in the last twenty-four hours. Sadat had presented our project (The Framework of Peace) to Carter and Begin and – although I had advised against it – had discussed it with them at the start of the Conference. However, he was perfectly entitled to do so, for I had no way of imposing my views on him. "The account he gave us yesterday [I went on], left us with the impression that he had succeeded, in the presence of the United States President, in making a good case for the Egyptian project."

However, I knew from experience that I could not rely entirely on Sadat's accounts, as he often failed to mention certain points, either because he had forgotten them or because he deemed them of little importance, or again, because they were not to his liking. It might be that he did this when he was unable to refute an argument or – what was even more serious – because he had been lured into making concessions to Carter or Begin, or both. Now it was apparent from what President Carter had said at the meeting that he (Carter) had ruled out the Egyptian project as a basis for negotiation. Even though he had not said so explicitly, he implied it when he had decided to submit an American project to bridge the gap between the Egyptian and Israeli positions. Carter was presenting us with ideas that would later be embodied in a United States project! All these ideas were strongly influenced by Israeli thinking, particularly the deferral of the consideration of main issues such as sovereignty over the West Bank and Gaza to a later stage. The ideas intimated a distinction between the status of the settlements in Sinai and those in the other occupied territories. They played down Jordan's role in the negotiations concerning the West Bank while highlighting Egypt's role. They glossed over certain issues on the grounds that there was no one to speak on behalf of the Palestinians. Withdrawal and delineation of borders were to be effected according to the Sadat-Perez Vienna

Camp David

formula. Had Carter been unable to find a single principle or idea in the Egyptian project he could accept?

And there was Vance, openly, stating that Begin's autonomy project – submitted in Ismailia – would be the basis for a settlement! What Carter and Vance were saying suggested that America would indeed undertake the role of "full partner", but this would be as a full partner of Israel against Egypt! What they were saying implied that the United States would not be submitting its own ideas as had already been agreed.

Be that as it may, the real mystery and disaster was Sadat's attitude. Although the plot was unfolding, he was never roused to anger and never demurred. He neither rejected, refuted, discussed nor explained!

What price now his promises and the threats he hurled at me within sight and hearing of the members of the National Security Council? He pledged to present his project at the start of the Conference, threatening that if it was not accepted as a basis for negotiation he intended to leave the conference and return to Egypt within twenty-four hours! He had reiterated this promise to me during the talk I had with him aboard the plane just a few hours before we reached Camp David! I said to Boutros: "And now look where we are! Here we have the United States President, without equivocation or ambiguity, coming up with the idea of concluding a strategic American-Egyptian-Israeli alliance, while Sadat does not utter a single word! What can be the matter with him?"

Boutros sympathized and said he shared my feelings. He was, he said, surprised at Sadat's attitude during the meeting: "Maybe he was only absent-minded and tired, and did not really understand what Carter was saying. It had been a long, exhausting day. It could be that Carter's aim was to test us by throwing out ideas as trial balloons, just to elicit our views and observations which he would take into account." I had answered Carter well (Boutros assured me) and was well founded in my arguments. Carter had no choice but to take what I said into consideration.

"Maybe so," I replied, "but what value can my words have in the light of the President's silence? Isn't silence a sign of approval, and didn't you notice Carter's sly remark to Tohamy, to the effect that rumours had it that President Sadat was moderate while his assistants were hard-liners? He means us, of course. And do you imagine that Carter would pay more attention to my words than to what Sadat might say or not say? Carter would say that the President's position took precedence over his minister's – and can you blame him?"

Boutros replied: "Anyway, today's meeting was merely preparatory. They are still preparing their project; nothing they may have said necessarily represents their final ideas. We shan't know the conclusions they have reached until they finalize their project and submit it to us – then we shall see. So stop worrying until then and let's get some sleep – it's almost dawn!"

"You're right – good night!" And I put out the light.

Boutros Ghali and I were on very good terms. We saw eye-to-eye on many matters and often reached similar conclusions. The main difference between us, though, was the manner in which each viewed his functions, duties, and working relationships with President Sadat. Boutros believed in blind obedience to the President and felt bound to carry out his decisions, and present them in a favourable light. Boutros believed that the President had an overall view of matters and could see things which might have escaped us; his decisions would be taken accordingly. If we were to give an opinion or propose an idea to the President – if he happened to be in a good mood, that is! – matters should not, in Boutros' opinion, go beyond suggestion.

I, on the other hand, was of quite a different view, believing that our duties and functions extended beyond advice and consultation to making him aware of shortcomings, flaws, or dangers in his decisions. We were his ministers and advisers, not employees in a private enterprise he owned, and we were not now dealing with his private affairs but with a complex issue pertaining to the fate of a nation. No individual, whatever his capacity or intelligence, could undertake that task single-handedly. This, however, did not mean that we should impose our views on him for he was, after all, the President and had the final say. We were to acquaint him with both sides of the picture.

This is not intended to single out Boutros, nor to blame him for his attitude. In this, he is no different from the majority of ministers. I am making this point because of the reflection of this attitude on our work in Camp David. The official Egyptian delegation consisted, apart from the President, of Hassan El Tohamy, Hassan Kamel, myself, Boutros Ghali and Ussama El Baz. To begin with Tohamy, besides not being specialized in the type of work we were engaged in, had odd ideas, which neither I nor anyone else could readily understand. Hassan Kamel, by reason of the many years spent dealing with questions of protocol and later in administrative work when he was appointed Chef de Cabinet of the President, was out of touch with the intricate issues of the Arab-Israeli conflict.

That left myself, Boutros and Ussama, whose responsibilities were, consequently, so much the greater. I must acknowledge the fact that Ussama El Baz had his own flexible manner of supporting my ideas before the President. And although he had his limits, he would often skilfully redress matters when Sadat entrusted him with the task of formulating his ideas. As for the excellent team of advisers and experts from the Foreign Ministry, which served as an operations-room for the delegation, it had contact with us only. It had no direct contact with the President, save in special circumstances.

The members of the official delegation normally met with the team of advisers before meeting with the President. We usually, after the discussion, reached the same conclusions so that, when we met later with the President, and he held a contrary view to ours, matters ended by my appearing as the only opposer of his ideas, since most of the members would either show their support for his views or keep silent. This in itself did not trouble me. What did was that, had they expressed their views, the President might have been better advised.

I recall, at the conclusion of one of the meetings with the President, Boutros advising me – perhaps for my own good – in the following terms: "Please, Mohamed, don't argue with the President in the delegation's presence!"

To which I replied: "How can I not? It is my duty and yours and that of the other members to argue with the President and to express our views. He included us in the delegation for this very purpose. Otherwise, why are we then here?"

"It is best to say what you want to say when you're alone with him. I've noticed he becomes angry when you speak to him in front of us."

"I don't believe he can get angry at hearing views expressed which, while useful, do not bind him. I invariably address him with the respect due to him as President but if, notwithstanding, he loses his temper, then that's his privilege!"

On the morning of the following day, I was breakfasting with Ahmed Maher when Brezinski, Carter's National Security Adviser, came in and joined us. He broached the subject of the freeze on settlements on which we had agreed with Mondale and Vance. He told us that he was in complete agreement with regard to the non-establishment of new settlements in the West Bank and Gaza. However, there was a problem with a freeze on the horizontal expansion of existing settlements. What, for example, would be the position if a family living in one of the existing settlements had one or more children? Would it then not be entitled to add a room to its house to accommodate the new members of the family?

I replied that what was meant was non-establishment of new buildings or installations to receive new settlers. Brezinski then turned to the situation in the Middle East, averring that the area was about to witness upheavals. He referred to Afghanistan where a Communist government had seized power after toppling the monarchy, and to the deteriorating internal situation in Iran, which posed a real threat to the Shah's position. He also referred to the situation in the Horn of Africa. The US, he said, was concerned over these developments and sought to contain these situations, while preparing itself to confront them should it fail to do so. The US was thus very much interested in easing the Arab-Israeli conflict by securing some sort of settlement.

My response to this was that we had come to Camp David for that purpose, and that it would be possible if the US put sufficient pressure on Israel to induce it to give up its policies in the occupied territories. Brezinski rejoined that there were limits to what they could do, and it would be difficult to bring about a settlement at one stroke. We should, he advised, proceed gradually, step by step, over a period of time which would culminate in a comprehensive settlement, and he went on to explain his theory of "The Dynamics of Situations". As I could understand it, situations are not entirely static, but enjoy an inherent dynamism and momentum forcing them to develop. Each situation paves the way for a new situation. He likened that to a snowball falling from the top of a mountain. Similarly, ending Israeli military rule in the West Bank and Gaza and ensuring the Palestinians' exercise of self-rule there, and putting a freeze on the settlements, which would result in the suspension of the Israeli settlements, would all constitute a point of departure for successive developments. These would finally lead to the Palestinians exercising their full legitimate rights, including the right to determine their future.

I made it plain to Brezinski that I was not against his theory as such. We had no objection to a transitional period which would eventually lead to the exercise by the Palestinian people of their right to self-determination and their sovereignty over their territories. There was one basic requirement, however, and this was that Israel should not, during the transitional period, be in a position that allowed it to impede the attainment of such objective. This condition was not met in Begin's autonomy project for the West Bank and Gaza. The United States, I told Brezinski, had shown an inclination, at the last meeting, to opt for that project as a basis for a settlement. Israel's intentions to proceed with the annexation of the West Bank and Gaza were an open secret. Begin's successive statements on their being liberated Israel territories, followed – since the occupation – by the implementation of a settlement scheme designed to engulf the territories piecemeal, were alone sufficient proof! There was not the slightest doubt as to the Israeli intention to annex those territories. Israel was using security as a cover up, any remaining doubts should have been completely dispelled by Begin's announcement that his country was just one party among others (i.e. the Palestinians and Jordan) entitled to claim sovereignty over the West Bank and Gaza. Begin (I told Brezinski) could not now claim sovereignty, as this would be unacceptable. How, then, could he sustain his claim to sovereignty? An illegal occupation of territories could not give him such a title – sovereignty was the right of the Palestinian people whose land this was. Begin therefore had to defer the settlement of the issue of sovereignty over the West Bank and Gaza until the end of the five-year transitional period. Begin by that time would have been able to create a factual situation in the territories to enable him to exercise *de facto* sovereignty without the need to proclaim it. All would be over. Any subsequent claim by the Palestinian people and/or Jordan to sovereignty would be hopeless and useless.

In the afternoon a meeting was held between the Egyptian and United States delegations at foreign minister level. Vance began by saying that they had invited us to the meeting in order to discuss a few ideas which they had not, as yet, formulated. They wished to ascertain our views before incorporating them into the American project they intended to submit to us in the following day or two (Saturday or Sunday). Vance added that the general framework of their project would be based on the Egyptian project – "The Framework of Peace". He believed, he said, that President Sadat would find it acceptable.

Together with my Egyptian colleagues, I felt a wave of optimism in the wake of the overwhelming pessimism induced by President Carter's words at our previous meeting. I replied that such remarks were encouraging and accorded with the closeness of the Egyptian and American positions on a settlement. Carter's words the day before (I went on) had aroused our fears. We had been left with the impression that he wished to take the Israeli autonomy project as a basis for a settlement. Vance, however, assured us that this was a false impression, and that all Carter had said was that he saw the merits of the idea of self-rule (as outlined in the Israeli project) during the transitional period. This did not mean, he added, that they were going to incorporate the Israeli project in their proposals.

My response was that the project we had submitted at Leeds Castle also contained the concept of self-rule during the transitional period. Vance admitted that the United States position differed from both the Egyptian and Israeli positions on that point. Whereas the Egyptian project confined the role of the supervision of the authority in charge of self-rule to the Arab parties (Egypt and Jordan), during the transitional period, the Israeli project confined that role to Israel. By contrast, the American view was that the controlling authority, during the transitional period, would be shared by Egypt, Israel and Jordan. And Vance added that the American ideas were designed to reach a solution clearly favouring Arab interests.

Dr Boutros Ghali specified that our aim was to ensure such conditions as would guard against placing Egypt in an embarrassing position. Thus, maximum guarantees for the Palestinians should be provided for to avoid any comparison between what was applied in Sinai and what obtained in the West Bank. Egypt must be in a position to defend the United States ideas.

In the following pages I shall be recording the broad lines of the US ideas on a comprehensive settlement. These ideas were submitted by Vance during this meeting which was attended, on the American side, by Vance, Brezinski, Atherton and William Quandt, and on the Egyptian side by Boutros Ghali, Ashràf Ghorbal, Ussama El Baz, Ahmed Maher, Nabil El Araby and Abdel Raouf Al Ridi. Before doing so, however, I wish first to indicate that these American ideas did not entirely agree with the Egyptian position on many points, but they constituted, nonetheless, a sound foundation to build on and develop. I am certain that the spirit of the American team – composed of United States State Department officers – reflected a sincere desire to achieve a just and comprehensive settlement, while taking into consideration the reasonableness and justice of the Egyptian position

Kissinger's Curse Again

since it was based on universally recognized principles and the unanimous resolutions governing the settlement of the Arab-Israeli conflict, at the same time safeguarding any vital United States interests in the Middle East without prejudice to Israeli security.

These ideas, however, never saw the light of day since they eventually clashed with Israeli expansionism and proved a threat to the political futures of Carter and Mondale, as I shall shortly show.

The American ideas put forward at the said meeting consisted of the following:

1. That the preamble to the Egyptian project be retained.
2. That Egypt, Jordan and Israel reach an agreement on the transitional period, allowing the Palestinians to exercise self-rule during that period.
3. That the United States purpose in holding the Conference was to come up with a general framework which would form the basis for negotiations during the next stage.
4. That the Peace Agreement should be concluded on the basis of Resolution 242.
5. That they (i.e. the US) were still considering the manner in which the transitional period would end, though it was clear that the Palestinian people would themselves decide on their future at the conclusion of that period. Furthermore, the Palestinians would themselves be signatories of the peace treaty at the expiry of that period.
6. That the American ideas did not tackle the subject of sovereignty over the West Bank and Gaza, the American position being that the issue of sovereignty would be considered at the end of the transitional period, in view of the conflicting claims. The sovereignty issue would be settled through the conclusion of peace agreements which would determine the relations between the parties at the conclusion of the five-year period.
7. That the Aswan Formula would deal with the solution to the entire Palestinian question.
8. That, with respect to the right of the Palestinian people to self-determination, this could be based on a number of alternatives such as the establishment of a federal or confederal regime with Jordan.
9. That sovereignty over the West Bank and Gaza would not be absolute. Certain measures applied there, such as security measures, and these would undoubtedly affect sovereignty.
10. That the American objective at present was to effect basic changes in the situation which could affect the general environment in the Middle East in the short term, which would not fail to have an

impact on the outcome of the transitional period.
11. That the United States envisaged the following steps in the near future within the framework of its proposals:
   a) An agreement on a total Israeli withdrawal from Sinai.
   b) The establishment of a Palestinian authority in the West Bank and Gaza.
   c) A freeze on Israeli settlements in the West Bank and Gaza.
   d) The return of individuals and reuniting families.
12. That the United States proposals were intended to create conditions likely to strengthen the Arab position, while circumscribing and halting the Israeli presence in Arab territories, leading progressively to its reduction. The United States would not, for the time being, force Israel to give up its claims to sovereignty. However, the conditions obtaining at the conclusion of the transitional period would lead to voiding such claims of any content.
13. That, with respect to the settlements, these must be dismantled in Sinai within a given period of time and in accordance with a timetable. As for the settlements in the West Bank and Gaza, these must be frozen. When Jordan and the Palestinians joined the negotiations, their future would be one of the subjects of negotiations.
14. That the United States ideas would include proposals on the Palestinian refugees based on the principle of compensation and return and the establishment of a body entrusted with implementation, with the participation of all parties concerned.
15. That United States ideas would include Jerusalem, e.g. the right of access to the Holy Places and the non-redivision of the city. The American side was fully conscious of the sensitivity of the Jerusalem issue. Its proposals, however, would not deal with details, but would leave such details to negotiation, it being noted that the United States had well-defined and clear positions with regard to the city and did not recognize its unilateral annexation by Israel.

Such were, in general, the United States ideas submitted at the meeting, which lasted for more than three hours. I need only add that the Egyptian side explained its position firmly, effectively and skilfully when the ideas came up for discussion, dealing with the inherent contradictions, shortcomings and negative aspects of the proposals and the loopholes which could enable Israel, during the transitional period, to thwart the objective of the comprehensive settlement. Ussama El Baz, Al Ridi and El Araby participated actively in these discussions. As a result the American side undertook to review their proposals in the light of our objections.

Kissinger's Curse Again

After dinner, I went across to President Sadat's bungalow. As I sat with him, I gave him an account of what had taken place at our meeting with Vance and the American delegation. I had nothing but praise for the efforts of Ussama, Araby and Ridi, and Sadat expressed his satisfaction at what he heard. It was clear that he was eagerly anticipating that the finalized American project would, on most points, go along with the Egyptian project. Tohamy, Ghorbal, and Hassan Kamel came in shortly afterwards, and though we chatted until midnight, the Middle East was hardly ever touched upon. There was a very simple reason for this – there was nothing we could do but wait for the American project to be submitted. Only then should we be able to determine our next step.

Next day I again proceeded to the President's bungalow, where I found him wearing his track-suit getting ready for his daily constitutional. He requested me to accompany him. He walked with quick, energetic steps calling for great physical fitness. Sadat walked regularly every day, and often he told me that, however busy he might be, he did at least four kilometers a day.

After nearly half an hour of earnest walking, he confided to me that Camp David reminded him of his days in the detention camp. I told him I had the same feeling, adding: "What makes things even gloomier is the fact that our intramural colleagues are, of all people, Begin and Dayan, with whom we have to deal!"

He rejoined: "We are dealing with the lowest and meanest of enemies. The Jews even tormented their Prophet Moses, and exasperated their God!" And after a while he went on: "I pity poor Carter in his dealings with Begin, with his stilted mentality." Whereupon I asked whether he (Sadat) believed that Carter would put real pressure on him? His rejoinder was: "Of course he will, otherwise the Conference will flounder, and that would affect Carter's position. I have made it clear to him that I have offered everything in order to bring about a peace which the Israelis could never have imagined in their wildest dreams, and I told him there was nothing left for me to concede."

We resumed our walk, this time in silence. On our way back we ran into Weizman on a bicycle. He promptly stopped and hailed us, Weizman asked Sadat if he could see him that day, to which Sadat replied: "Of course: it's always a pleasure to talk to you!" Weizman had visited Sadat two days earlier, but Sadat had not disclosed to me what had transpired between them.

To tell the truth, I was not happy about Weizman's private meetings with Sadat. I feared the mischief and danger inseparable from such meetings, and have mentioned instances of the problems and complications resulting from them, as when they met in Egypt in March as the Israeli army was invading Lebanon and the Arab ministers were gathering in Cairo. Then there were the complications resulting from their get-together in Austria at the beginning of July.

Camp David

Sadat described his relationship with Weizman as one of friendship, and I do, in fact, believe that Sadat actually felt genuine affection for Weizman. This may have been due to several factors: there was Weizman's open and cheerful personality, at odds with the usual Israeli closed, cautious nature. Then there was the genuine zeal he professed in the search for peace. He was convinced, too, that Israel had to pay a price for that peace, though I am unaware how far he would have been prepared to go in that respect. However, he certainly appeared more flexible than the obdurate Begin, who wanted peace and the occupied Arab territories as well. And it was a well-known fact that Weizman's relations with Dayan were none of the best, and this for personal reasons going back to the days when Dayan was married to Weizman's wife's sister and his subsequent ill-treatment of her. Sadat for his part, had a particularly strong aversion to Dayan, for reasons best known to himself. It may have been that Dayan was living proof of the 1967 defeat. Sadat avoided meeting or talking to him, and whenever anyone mentioned his name, he would call him a liar and a braggart. Perhaps Sadat believed that his enemy's enemy was his friend, as the saying goes!

In addition to all this, Sadat believed he could use Weizman both to convey a particular message to Begin and to sound out Israeli thinking. He kept him in reserve, so to speak, against crises with Menahim Begin. I must add that Sadat nursed the hope that Begin would be brought down as a result of his hard-line policy, or would die or retire for health reasons. He hoped Weizman would succeed him as Israeli Premier or at least occupy an influential post. If this happened, Sadat's relationship with Israel would become much easier and possibilities for agreement closer.

On the other hand, I cannot claim to know anything of what Weizman felt for Sadat: all that concerned me in this matter was my apprehension at the Israeli foe's direct access to the President's thoughts. There was a potential danger in the fact that the Israeli War Minister could meet the Egyptian President alone in his own house on an intimate, friendly and affectionate footing.

As we ate lunch in the restaurant, I asked Ambassador Eilts for news of the project. He replied that it had been prepared, and would be submitted to President Carter. I said I hoped they would abide by their promise to consult with us before submitting it to the Israeli side, and Eilts told me they would give us a copy that afternoon. He added that he thought the project a reasonable one which would be acceptable to us. However, he gave me no definite information as to its contents but told me that it had been decided that the three delegations would go to visit the site of the battle that took place to the west of the city of Gettysburg in 1863, during the American Civil War.

That evening at dinner, I told Ambassador Eilts that we had not received the project. He replied that they were perhaps introducing some minor

Kissinger's Curse Again

amendments, but that it would surely reach us the following day after the visit to Gettysburg.

The members of the Egyptian delegation met each evening in my bungalow. We usually talked of the American attitude. Some were optimistic, others pessimistic, but, as I indicated earlier, there was nothing we could do until the Americans had submitted their project. The members usually brought with them some items of petty news which then became the object of smalltalk, such as who met who, who went to the cinema, whose face reflected assurance and confidence, and who appeared concerned and gloomy, who had been in and out of Begin's bungalow, and so on.

Time dragged slowly and wearily on until Tohamy, his mysterious rounds completed, joined us in the bungalow. He was the only member of the delegation who had his own private bungalow. He and Begin were the only persons who insisted on wearing a formal suit and tie throughout the Conference. He could hardly cross the threshold of the bungalow before all the weariness, gloom and anxiety disappeared like magic, to be replaced by joy, liveliness and jest. And we were all ears!

He began with the latest news. He would say, for instance, that Dayan had agreed an hour earlier to restore Jerusalem to the Arabs. He would go on to talk about mysticism and the interpretation of dreams, before turning to stories and narratives. He held forth on how he had solved the problems of the Muslims in the Philippines, and how he had been able to delay the revolution in Malaysia for three years. He regaled us with accounts of how he had treated himself against the deadly poison which had been slipped into his food during one of his visits to an Arab state. He had gone to his room, doubled up with pain, and had then bolted his door. For three days he touched neither food nor water, treating himself with the poison antidote he always carried with him!

Sometimes he would expatiate on the merits of ambergris which, he informed us, was extracted from the kidneys of the whale, and of the wonderful properties of Royal Jelly. Then he would stop abruptly, and speak of Jerusalem. Addressing me, he would say: "Jerusalem has been put in trust with you, brother Mohamed; beware of renouncing it!" Or he would turn to Boutros Ghali – the only Christian among us – and invite him to embrace Islam, the true religion! The members of the delegation would then place bets on whether he would succeed or fail! Somebody might even ask loudly whether anyone would wager the contrary – that Tohamy would embrace Christianity!

All this merriment and laughter masked the concern we all felt, and relieved the prevailing tension.

News of Tohamy's miracles travelled well beyond the circle of the Egyptian delegation, for one day, as we entered the dining-hall for lunch, we found Tohamy standing by one of the Israeli tables. He was surrounded by several Israelis, who were engaged in an animated discussion with him. We discovered a little later that Tohamy had assured them that he could stop his heart beating for as long as he wanted! They had a lengthy conversation before he joined us for lunch. And at dinner that evening, the members of the Israeli delegation invited Tohamy to resume the discussion! They even brought Begin's private physician along with them to discuss the matter scientifically with him!

I can recall a particularly humorous episode: Ghali had once told us of the threatening letters he had received after he had accompanied President Sadat on his visit to Jerusalem. He had added in French: "They are accusing me of being the third generation of traitors in the Ghali family!" I had laughed and said: "How can that be? I know of only two – your grandfather[1] and yourself, so who can the third be?" Boutros had thereupon answered: "They say that my uncle, Nagib Pasha Ghali, was involved with the British during the First World War."

On the morning of Sunday, 10 September, the gates of Camp David swung open to give passage to a motorcade preceded by security cars followed by a limousine carrying President Carter, Sadat and Premier Begin. Behind the limousine came a bus with the other members of the three delegations – save for those who stayed behind – and this was succeeded by another bearing a group of journalists, photographers and news agency correspondents.

The motorcade proceeded to the town of Gettysburg, lying not far from Camp David. It was the first time we had left Camp David (or the "detention camp", as we called it!) since we had entered it on 5 September, and our feeling was one of freedom and elation. The only fly in the ointment was the knowledge that we should have to be back in the detention camp in a few hours, with its atmosphere of tension and anxiety.

On the way to Gettysburg, we noticed that the members of the American and Israeli delegations, with the exception of Dayan and Weizman, had stayed behind and this fact gave rise to much suspicion and speculation. However, we soon arrived at the battlefield and emerged from our cars. The members of the delegations and the mass media crowded round Carter, Sadat and Begin. Despite the presence of specialists, who had been brought over for that very purpose, President Carter had decided to take on the job of guide and narrator. The battle (he informed us) had lasted for three days in July 1863. It had been between the Federal government forces, led by General Mead, whose army consisted of eighty-two thousand infantry, backed by cavalry and artillery, and the Confederate forces, numbering seventy-five thousand infantry, also with cavalry and artillery backing, led by General Lee.

The battle (Carter continued) had had its ups and downs, but had culminated eventually in the victory of the Federal forces. The North lost twenty-five thousand men, dead, wounded or missing while the South lost thirty thousand. The battle was a turning-point in the Civil War, and gave a decisive advantage to the North. For three hours, we moved over the battlefield, listening to Carter's explanations on the details and the outcome of the battle. He recounted the story with incredible accuracy, and appeared to have learnt it all off by heart – so much so, in fact, that a member of our delegation observed laughingly: "Carter should feel no concern for his future. If the Camp David Conference fails, he can always make a living as a tourist guide in Gettysburg!"

When we returned I had lunch and went to my bungalow, as I wished to sleep for a while and relax after our hectic trip.

I was awakened by a call from Ambassador Eilts, who informed me that he had something important he wished to talk over with me. I told him I'd be waiting for him. He arrived five minutes later, and appeared somewhat downcast. "I'm sorry, Mohamed, but something unexpected has happened: Begin has produced a written pledge to the Israeli government, signed by Kissinger in 1975. This commits the United States to abstain from presenting any project on the settlement of the Arab-Israeli conflict without prior consultation with Israel. Consequently, we shall be unable to give you a copy of the project we have prepared."

This piece of news effectively banished all thought of sleep!

Footnotes

1   Boutros Pasha Ghali, the Prime Minister of Egypt, was assassinated by El Wardany in 1909 for agreeing to extend the Suez Canal concession until 1969.

Chapter Thirty Eight

Between The Israeli Hammer and The American Anvil

It will, perhaps, be useful to set the scene for a better understanding of the developments with which this chapter will be dealing by an introduction to the events which led up to them. The fact that the US should have yielded to Israel's request to implement Kissinger's 1975 pledge on US consultation with Israel before submission of proposals for a settlement of the Arab-Israeli conflict, dealt a heavy blow to the Egyptian negotiating position in Camp David. It was also the point at which Israel's fortunes began to show an upturn, made possible by the following:

1. Sadat's precipitate and rash presentation of his project "The Framework for Peace" at the very first working session of the Conference. This was a tactical error which ran counter to the strategy suggested to him by the Foreign Ministry[1] and my advice to him at the meeting of the National Security Council.
2. The United States failure to honour its pledge to show us its proposals prior to their submission, and to play the role as a full partner, with the parties concerned, to which it had committed itself.

It was almost certain that the American project, which was prepared after discussions with the Egyptian and Israeli delegations, would turn out to be a compromise between the Egyptian project ruled out after its rejection by the Israelis and Israeli ideas (based on Menahim Begin's projects for Sinai and for self-rule in the West Bank and Gaza, submitted in Ismailia and rejected out of hand by Egypt).

It had been originally agreed, then, that the project was to be submitted to both the Egyptian and Israeli sides simultaneously, as a proposed basis to any settlement between them. The US had, however, accepted to show it to Israel only, not for informational purposes, but for prior consultation, which promptly developed into an obligation to acquire Israel's prior approval to the American proposals. Israel's rejection of such proposals, on consultation, constituted a kind of veto, and this, in turn, led the US to submit yet other ideas, and so it went. This meant that consultations between the US and Israel, even under the best of circumstances, would only result in a compromise between the original American project and the Israeli ideas advanced during the consultations. Thus, the project, instead of being, as originally intended, a compromise between the Egyptian and Israeli positions, would become a compromise project spawned from the US and Israeli ideas. This, in turn, meant that the project would eventually be cut down to a compromise of a compromise project favouring Israel.

Perhaps I can put it more clearly by resorting to arithmetic, assuming that:

The Egyptian project	=	100% Egyptian ideas
The American project	=	50% Egyptian ideas
	+	50% Israeli ideas
The American project after consultation with Israel	=	25% Egyptian ideas
	+	75% Israeli Ideas.

Now we should bear in mind that the Egyptian "Framework for Peace" project was not intended as the basis for a negotiating position subject to bargaining. Had we had bargaining in mind, the project would have been based, for instance, on the partition resolution. In that case Israel would have been required to return all the territories it had annexed by force from the territory allocated to the Palestinian state by the terms of the said resolution from 1949 to 1967.

Rather, the project depended on the strict implementation of Resolution 242, which contained the basic elements for a settlement of the conflict. These were: withdrawal from the Arab territories occupied in 1967 in return for ending the state of war; and the establishment of peaceful relations between Israel and the neighbouring Arab states.

This illustrates the magnitude of the gap separating the Egyptian project from the project which, though in name "American" was in fact, after consultation, "Israeli". And this was to be presented to Egypt (and also formally to Israel, for the sake of appearances). Were we to oppose or reject the project, we would be accused of rejecting the proposals submitted by the US in the exercise of its role as a full partner, to which we had agreed from the outset. The inevitable clash would then be between Egypt and the US rather than between Israel and the US. Our strategy – which Sadat had unfortunately not followed – in the event the Conference were to fail, would have ensured that the blame for this would have been attributed to Israel, and there would have been close agreement between the American and Egyptian stands in confronting the obdurate Israeli position, which would then stand revealed as it really was, despite all Israeli attempts at misrepresentation and deceit.

Matters could even have been straightened out had Sadat been prepared

Camp David

to follow the line he had laid down at the National Security Council in Ismailia, despite its shortcomings, to the effect that in the event of his framework for peace being rejected, he would withdraw from the Conference and return to Cairo to prepare the next step. However, he set this strategy aside from the very first day of the Conference, and proved himself unable – or else lacked the courage – to take such a decision, thus falling into the trap of projects and formulae, which led to an erosion of his position and its final collapse.

To go back to Kissinger's aforementioned pledge of not submitting any proposals for a settlement without prior consultation with Israel, the singularity of this pledge can be explained only by Kissinger's collusion with Israel and his misuse of his position as US Secretary of State. The USA could have abided by this pledge so long as Egypt pursued its traditional policy. President Sadat's peace initiative and its subsequent development into tripartite negotiations among Egypt, Israel and the US with the latter's assumption of the role of full partner should have terminated the pledge made by Kissinger to Israel, which is nothing less than an insult to the status of a great state. The point in question was not a quarrel on the street, in which two children take sides against a third, but a very serious issue designed to solve a very serious problem on which depended the fate of the Middle East. It made all the difference between peace and war, chaos and stability and had an impact on the interest of the world at large and the interests of the US and its allies.

After this introduction, we may now fairly proceed with events and developments. The US was expected to put its project to us, as it had previously pledged to do, as I had been informed by Ambassador Eilts, and as Secretary of State Vance had reaffirmed. However, this was forestalled at the last moment by Israeli blackmail, and as a result we did not even get to see the American original project as it stood prior to consultation with Israel. Nevertheless, it must certainly have been along the following broad lines:

1. What the US Vice-President and Secretary of State Vance had affirmed to me at our meeting on Thursday 7 September,[2] regarding the US position on settlements, namely:
   a) Complete removal of Israeli settlements in Sinai; and
   b) a five-year moratorium on Israeli settlements in the West Bank and Gaza Strip. The future of the settlements (removal or maintance) would thereupon be negotiated among Jordan, the Palestinian and Israel.
2. What Vance had affirmed at the meeting between the Egyptian and US delegations on Friday 8 September[3] with regard to the American project they were to submit to us on Saturday or Sunday which would be generally based on the Egyptian project would

include the following points:
a) Approval of the Preamble in the Egyptian project.
b) That the peace agreement should be concluded on the basis of Resolution 242.
c) That the Palestinian people would itself decide its stand at the end of the transitional period, and would itself sign the treaty at the end of the period.
d) That the Aswan formula would deal with the solution to the Palestinian question in all its aspects.
e) That the right of the Palestinian people to self-determination would be based on several options.
f) That the American ideas would inlcude proposals on the Palestinian refugees based on compensation and repatriation.

Those were the bases and broad lines which the US project undoubtedly contained. In addition to these, it would also have included some ideas advanced by Vance during the meeting, such as the period preceding the setting up of the tripartite authority (consisting of Egypt, Israel and Jordan) which would supervise self-rule and the measures to be taken during the transitional period; the deferment of the sovereignty issue which would be decided at the end of the transitional period; and what he (Vance) had said with regard to Jerusalem.

At 4 p.m. on Sunday 10 September (the day of the visit to Gettysburg) there was a meeting of the American and Israeli sides. The former was led by President Carter, the other members being Walter Mondale, Vance and Brezinski, while the Israeli side was headed by Begin and included Dayan, Weizman and Barak, the Israeli Attorney-General. The purpose of the meeting was to hold consultations on the American project before it was submitted to Egypt, and it went on until three in the morning. Since this was a bilateral meeting, the Egyptian delegation had no way of knowing what transpired, but through the accounts given by Foreign Minister Dayan and Defence Minister Weizman, who were present.

Let us, then, begin by considering how consultation takes place between the world's most powerful nation and its spoilt, covetous and recalcitrant ally, before trying to assess the results.

In his book, *Breakthrough*,[4] Dayan writes:

> The Americans said there were four major issues which they did not see eye to eye with us. They wanted us to freeze settlements in the territories for five years, namely to establish no new settlements and not to add new members to existing villages. They wanted a categorical decision from us on the manner in which the sovereignty in Judea, Samaria and Gaza would be determined after five years. They wanted to know the source of authority in the territories, namely

whether it would be possible to abolish the autonomy and who would have the authority to do so. (In the American view, Israel should have no authority.) And fourthly, an appropriate formula was required to ensure the implementation of the injunction in Resolution 242 concerning Israel's withdrawal from territories conquered in the 1967 War. Neither these issues nor the respective positions of the various sides were new. The one over which the greatest differences existed was settlements, on which our position was final. I told them we would accept no limitations on this matter.

Then he goes on to say:

The lawyers in our delegation, Barak, Rosenne, and Rubinstein, sat with the Americans to discuss the "source of authority" in the West Bank and Gaza, and all tried to come up with a formula on the withdrawal of Israeli forces that would not be interpreted as requiring their total departure from the territories."

And again:

There was a growing conviction as the discussions continued that, if we were to reach a framework agreement, the only way out of the difficulty posed by the differences of opinion on these major issues was to ignore them – either by leaving them unmentioned in the agreement, or by devising vague formula which each side could interpret in his own way.

Dealing with the practical issues was our main purpose at Camp David. But there was also a problem of certain definitions and expressions which we, and Begin in particular, wanted excluded from the agreement. One, for example, was what was known as the Aswan Formula, which spoke of the "constitutional rights" of the Palestinians and their "right to determine their future"; another was the obligation to fulfil UN Resolution 242 "in all its parts", namely, including its Preamble, which held inadmissable the acquisition of territory by war. We were concerned that when it came to giving flesh to these formulae, we would be told that Israel was obliged to evacuate the whole of the West Bank and Gaza, and that the Palestinians had the right to establish their independent state".

Before summing up, the Israeli position was as follows:

On Sinai, we stressed that our readiness to withdraw to the international boundary was to be read in the context of the peace proposal we had submitted, namely, that the Israeli settlements and airfields in north-eastern and south-eastern Sinai would remain within our control.

As for the West Bank and Gaza, we emphasized that we were not to be obliged to withdraw from these territories. Here we saw the source of danger in the reference in the Preamble to Resolution 242 on the inadmissibility of the acquisition of territory by war. We therefore resolved that this part of the Preamble was not to be included in the peace treaty.

On the subject of the Palestinians, we were determined to avoid a formula which might be interpreted as our agreeing to their right to self-determination and statehood. We proposed that the future of the Palestinian Arabs dwelling in the West Bank and Gaza would be determined at talks to be conducted between them, Egypt, Jordan and Israel.

I cannot conceive of anything clearer than these words of Dayan, so I beg the reader's indulgence if I refrain from any comments on it.

To round off our picture of Israeli "consultations", let us glance at what Weizman tells us in his account. Weizman writes[5]:

The American proposal was seventeen pages of high explosive. In an attempt to manipulate the discussion, the Americans circumvented controversial issues like the fate of the Sinai settlements and airfields; at the same time they added a whole series of worrisome conditions relating to Judea, Samaria and the Gaza Strip.

Within three years, according to this document, talks would commence on the final status of Judea, Samaria and the Gaza Strip – including the question of borders and of Palestinian participation; there would be a self-governing authority – and not a council; the self-governing body would not draw its authority from the Israeli military government; Jordan would enjoy a special status; further settlements would not be established, and the existing ones would be frozen; and a plebiscite would be held to determine the final status of the West Bank and the Gaza Strip.

"Gentlemen," Begin said, "the Americans have simply copied the Egyptian plan." His expression was grim, I was worried over his quiet tone, he was swallowing his anger and I feared the valves of his heart might burst...

Describing the discussions – or consultations, he (Weizman) has this to say:

It was Menahim Begin's night. Seated at the head of the Israeli delegation, he faced Carter and the others: his voice raised to eliminate any doubts or misunderstandings, he rejected or amended considerable portions of the American proposal.

In the course of the discussion, Carter said he intended to bring up the issue of the national rights of the Palestinians, including their right of self-determination.

"Out of the question," Begin replied. He was afraid that such discussion might open up the possibility in the distant future of a Palestinian state.

When the American President proposed a freeze on new settlements, the Israelis rejected it immediately.

Then Carter went on to suggest that Israeli units remain in the West Bank over and beyond the five-year period. At long last, the Israeli delegation found one point on which it could agree with Carter.

But Carter also declared that Sadat would not make concessions with regard to Israeli settlements and airfields in the Sinai and therefore Israel should evacuate them. "We do not dismantle settlements," Begin said with great emphasis. "We do not plough them up or demolish them. . ."

to which he adds:

When we reached the clause about the "Non-acquisition of territory by force" Begin's reaction was extremely fierce. "There is no such situation in our case. The territories we occupy were conquered in a defensive war. You should know Mr President" – Begin pointed at Carter – "that in all the wars we were the victims of Arab aggression." Begin vigorously objected to a sentence in the Preamble that stressed that "occupation of territory by force is unacceptable" it sounded innocent enough, but Begin smelled a trap, foreseeing that it might be used later to dislodge Israel from the Golan Heights. "We will not accept that," the Prime Minister told Carter. "Mr Prime Minister," Carter replied, "that is not only the view of Sadat, it is also the American view – and you will have to accept it." By now it was around three o'clock in the morning. Carter compressed his lips, no longer capable of concealing his fury. He crumpled up the papers lying on the table before him and flung down his pencil, his blue eyes alight with rage. "You will have to accept it." He seemed to be repeating the words to himself.

"Mr President," Begin said tensely. "No threats, please."

Once again I repeat: Israeli intentions, as revealed in Weizman's account, are clear and straightforward, with no attempt at evasion, and speak for themselves. I should like, however, to draw the reader's attention to the fact that the Israeli Premier's words to the American President – "No threats, please" – were neither a plea nor an entreaty to Carter, but a threat and a hint to him that, of the two, it was Begin and not he (Carter) who had the power to threaten.

To threaten with what? Many things. First: in the short term, with the failure of the Camp David Conference, which would be a defeat for President Carter who had convened the Conference. Then, in the medium term, there were the mid-term United States Congressional elections, the Panama Treaty, Carter's energy project, etc. . . Finally, in the long term, there were the 1980 Presidential elections, and Carter's chances for re-election rested in Begin's hands. The Israeli Premier had only to ring the alarm. The Zionist lobby, with its influence in Congress, the administration and the mass media was always ready. Begin was already setting the stage. Weizman, in his book, writes:

> In retaliation against Sadat's proposals, the Israeli delegation spent the night drawing up an impromptu document aimed as a double edged sword against Carter and Sadat. It would be made plain to the other two leaders that publication would automatically entail publication of the Israeli proposals – whereupon the international reaction would get completely out of hand. Begin, like other members of our delegation, attached great importance to winning over public opinion to our side should the conference end in failure. There was talks of preparations for mass rallies and media appearances in Washington if the summit broke up.

When we received the US project[6] the following day, Monday 11 September, it was very different from what we had anticipated. It did not include or reflect the established and declared US positions on the settlement of the Arab-Israeli conflict, and it left out most of the points put forward by Vance at the American-Egyptian meeting the preceding Friday.

The whole project, was clearly marked with the Israeli "consultations". A quick glance at the project showed that the Aswan formula on the solution of the Palestinian question had been thwarted. The reference to the right of self-determination was shrouded in vagueness. The project stipulated neither Israeli withdrawal from Sinai nor from the West Bank. It made not the slightest reference to withdrawal from Arab Jerusalem, nor did it refer in any way to the settlements in either Sinai, the West Bank or Gaza Strip. The project assigned Israel a major role and far-reaching powers in the West Bank and Gaza during the transitional period, while giving a minor role to Egypt and Jordan. The project, in fact, seemed restricted to providing protection for Israel, and did not deal effectively with the issue of the uprooted refugees and displaced persons. In addition, it made security arrangements for Israel alone, to the exclusion of all the other parties. To cap it all, the project contained a strange and troubling provision: it stipulated that were Jordan not to participate in the negotiations, Egypt, Israel and the inhabitants of the West Bank and Gaza would proceed to estabish the autonomy authority and supervise its administration.

In sum, the project was, heart and soul, an Israeli one, while ostensibly of American manufacture.

After lunch, we met with the American delegation at their request. They wished to discuss their project with us without further delay. We told them that a first reading of the project revealed numerous shortcomings, and we needed to study it carefully and in depth so as to be in a position to discuss it and submit alternative proposals. They said we could meet again after dinner, but we insisted on postponing the meeting to the following day, informing them that they had to allow us sufficient time, as they had with Israel.

At the conclusion of the meeting, I asked Vance what was meant by the provision dealing with the case of the non-participation of Jordan in the negotiations: He replied that it meant that Egypt would replace Jordan in the role the latter would have undertaken in the West Bank. I rejoined that if Jordan abstained from participation, so would Egypt. To this Vance replied: "Ask President Sadat: it was he who suggested it and decided it." Controlling my temper, I said: "This article is humiliating to King Hussein, and constitutes a provocation designed to ensure his refusal to participate in the negotiations, which has been Israel's aim from the very beginning. Egypt had no mandate and was not competent to undertake such a role!"

Going over to the President's bungalow, I found him sitting on the terrace with Hassan El Tohamy. Sadat questioned me on what had happened at the meeting. I told him that the United States project was quite unacceptable, and we had asked that discussion of it be deferred to the following day to give us time to prepare counter proposals. In any case, I continued, it was full of loopholes and could not be accepted as it stood, yet it was important to ascertain American intentions by discussing the project with them. I then referred to the provision in the United States project on Egypt's taking over Jordan's responsibilities in the West Bank should Jordan refuse to take part in the negotiations. Sadat observed: "That is correct: I cannot have the initiative depend upon the humour of King Hussein, who wants to be given the West Bank on a salver at no cost to himself."

I replied, "King Hussein's position is that he will not hesitate to enter the negotiations if Israel announces its agreement to implement the withdrawal from the West Bank, or if the United States formally pledges itself to this. This is a natural and logical stand and coincides with our own. What, then, is the sense in our continuing with the talks if we do not know precisely where they will lead? Jordan's role during the transitional period is crucial, and this is stipulated in our own project. Who other than Jordan would have the authority to supervise the administration in the West Bank, in view of the fact that Israel refuses to assign any role to the PLO?"

This drew a firm reply from Sadat to the effect that were King Hussein to refuse, he (Sadat) would undertake the role. I said that that was hardly a practical proposition: to begin with, on what grounds would we be basing ourselves in assuming this role? Then again, what did we know of the West Bank? To say nothing of the fact that our relations with the PLO were strained and our intervention in the West Bank might very well lead to a clash with the organization. Where would we be then?

Sadat answered haughtily: "I shall send Egyptian troops to the West Bank. I am aware that we shall lose some men, but they will kill ten men of the organization for every Egyptian who is killed."

Here Hassan El Tohamy broke in. He told us he knew the West Bank like the palm of his hand. We had, he went on, a large group of officers who were thoroughly familiar with the West Bank from the time of the Joint Arab Command. Turning to Sadat, I tried to fight down my rising anger: "What are you saying? This is sheer madness – our enemy is Israel, not the Palestinian people, whose problems your initiative was designed to solve! Have things come to such a pass that we are now fighting the Palestinians within sight and hearing of Israel? What can you hope to gain from it? Do you want us to get entangled in the West Bank as we were entangled in Yemen, or as Syria has become entangled in Lebanon?"

Sadat said very quietly: "Do not get excited, Mohamed. You don't know King Hussein. Let me tell you something you don't know. In 1973, after I had completed the war plan and was preparing for the war, I sent to King Hussein asking him to allow twenty or thirty Egyptian officers of the commando forces to travel to Jordan. I proposed that they should be joined by a number of Jordanian officers, if he so wished, whose task would be to infiltrate into Israel across the West Bank, so that, once the war began, they could blow up and destroy vital installations inside Israel itself. King Hussein, however, lacked the courage to accept the proposal."

I replied: "Well, after his experience in 1967, you can hardly blame him!"

Silence prevailed for a moment, then Hassan El Tohamy said suddenly: "Important developments are afoot. Reliable information has reached me from my own private sources to the effect that King Hussein intends to abdicate his throne in favour of his brother, Prince Hassan, in a week's time, and that Prince Hassan intends to announce, immediately upon his accession to the throne, that he is going to join the negotiations. The problem will thus be solved!"

Turning to Hassan El Tohamy, I said: "This time your private sources are mistaken. Our information indicates that Prince Hassan – unlike King Hussein – is strongly opposed to Jordan's becoming in any way involved over the West Bank for fear of the consequences."

And once more addressing President Sadat, I said: "I hope you will not impose any role on King Hussein without a prior understanding with him. Assuming we reached an agreement at this Conference – though I have strong doubts as to that – on a role for Jordan, we would make our final decision on it conditional upon King Hussein's approval. It is my belief that your readiness to supersede Jordan in the West Bank is likely to change the course of events and lead to a disaster from which Israel alone would benefit."

At this the President nodded several times, but made no answer.

I left Sadat in a mood of anxiety and depression. After reviewing recent developments, I concluded that the cause of my anxiety lay in the American project, which was submitted to us after consultation with the Israeli side. I felt that this project was a clear warning of the impending danger, and was proof of American weakness in the face of Israeli pressure. It was both inconceivable and unacceptable that the United States, a superpower, should have recanted on its declared positions and the promises given us by its Secretary of State at the meeting with the Egyptian delegation only three days before, after only one meeting with the Israelis. The American side had submitted to us an insipid and distorted project which we were supposed to consider as a basis for negotiations between the two parties! The best we might hope to achieve after amendments would still fall far short of the minimum we could accept – and even then any amendments we made would be submitted to the Israeli side and would, in turn, be subject to pressures and still other amendments. After all these amendments, it would be returned to us and we would attempt to patch it up again, and the whole process would recommence! In other words, we would be drawn into a vortex of projects and counter projects. At best all we could hope for in the circumstances would be to arrive at a compromise which failed to meet our minimum requirements and from which Israel alone would benefit.

I spoke at length with Ahmed Maher on this point, and he was in complete agreement with me. We concluded that we should have to devise a plan which would allow us to emerge from this whirlpool with the least damage, should the need arise.

I returned to the President, who was preparing to retire for the night. I acquainted him with what was going on my mind, telling him that if we were to stumble into the abyss of projects and formulae based on the United States project, our position would be eroded, and we would eventually find ourselves in an embarrassing position vis-à-vis the American side. Sadat replied that I was right: "Prepare a memorandum for me assessing the situation." And I answered, "You'll have it first thing tomorrow morning!"

I asked Ahmed Maher to draw up the memorandum, whereupon he left, while a group of experts attached to the Egyptian delegation spent the night examining the American project in preparation for the meeting. It had been decided that the Egyptian and American delegations were to meet the following day, Tuesday 12 September, at 3 p.m.

On the morning of the following day, Ahmed Maher handed the memorandum to me and I took it over to President Sadat. Finding he had not yet risen, I left it with his secretary.

The memorandum read as follows:

MEMORANDUM (HIGHLY CONFIDENTIAL)
FOR SUBMISSION TO THE PRESIDENT

I *Introduction*:
1. The Egyptian attendance of the Camp David Conference was and is designed:
   a) To obtain, through US pressure on Israel, an unambiguous and solid framework for peace acceptable to both Egypt and the Arabs; or,
   b) To emerge from the meeting with a unified Egyptian-American position, or one which was as close as possible, with which to face up to the Israeli intransigence.
2. In all cases, Egypt will act in accordance with the following dicta in pursuance of any of the two aforementioned aims:
   a) It will show flexibility.
   b) It will take a firm stand on basic issues.
   c) It will strive to preserve Egyptian-American relations and enhance the mutual confidence between Presidents Carter and Sadat.
3. As a result of the meeting between the two delegations and consideration of the American paper, several facts have emerged which may be summarized in the following:
   a) President Carter is being subjected to both internal pressure (represented by the inclinations of Vice-President Mondale) and Israeli pressure, exploiting these internal pressures.
   b) As a result of such pressures, President Carter has agreed to include in the American paper formulae that are far removed from the declared American positions with respect to the basic elements for a settlement, and are closer to the Israeli positions.
   c) In agreeing to this, Carter is misconstruing Egyptian flexibility. He is under the impression that Egypt is willing to make concessions of substance far exceeding what we are actually prepared to accept.
4. These factors taken together explain why President Carter is faced with a basic conflict, for although he was – and still is – convinced that any agreement reached at Camp David must be endorsed by Saudi Arabia and must encourage Jordan to join the negotiations, the proposals he has presented may, in fact, prove to be counter-productive, and even oblige Saudi Arabia to adopt positions that could be harmful to American interests. And whereas Carter's aim

is to reach an agreement which would make the realization of Soviet targets in the area impossible, the paper he has submitted provides the Soviet Union with the opportunity to rally many forces around it in the Middle East, since it can claim that the US is biased in favour of Israel and that the Egyptian policy of co-operation with the US will either end in failure or force Egypt to make concessions unacceptable to the Arabs.

5 All these facts must be taken into consideration in any Egyptian future moves in the light of Egypt's objectives.

II *The Egyptian Move*

1 During today's meeting between the two foreign ministers, the Egyptian side will attempt to amend the US paper by a flexible yet firm approach to bring it more into line with the basic Egyptian position, the more so since the American side has expressed its readiness to consider any amendments suggested by Egypt in a fair spirit. These Egyptian attempts will be based on:
   a) American goodwill;
   b) The US keen desire that, whatever may come out of Camp David, or whatever the American side may achieve, Egypt's position should be consolidated as a major, influential and moderate power in the area to confront Soviet interference.
   c) The fact that previously declared American stands differ only in detail from the basic, non-negotiable Egyptian position.

2 It follows that any Egyptian moves vis-à-vis the USA will result in any of three possibilities:
   a) The possibility of total success. This may be ruled out since it is inconceivable that the US will identify itself completely with the Egyptian stand.
   b) The possibility of limited success. This will require a patient and in-depth examination of what has so far been achieved and to what extent Egypt would be willing to accept it. Paramount consideration should be given to:
       – safeguarding American–Egyptian relations; and
       – safeguarding Egypt's position in the Arab world.

   The two foregoing objectives should not constitute a restriction on the Egyptian freedom of action in the fulfilment of the national interests of Egypt. This implies that neither the Arab world nor the United States should have the power of veto on any Egyptian move, as long as it is committed to the basic principles.
   c) The possibility of failure: the United States might then insist on concepts and formulae which we cannot accept. Were this possibility to arise we must try to ensure:
       – that any formulae proposed by the United States should not

be such as would be acceptable to Israel, so as not to find ourselves in a situation where Israel accepts an American proposal while Egypt refuses it;
- any rejection on our part should not be in a manner likely to damage Egyptian-American relations and act as a damper on President Carter's efforts to continue the role we believe to be vital for the achievement of a settlement.

3 It follows from the foregoing that, were we to be forced to reject the United States proposals, certain important steps would have to be taken, namely:
a) To come to an understanding with President Carter on the method of announcement of the results of the meeting to the American people and the world.

    Here it is important that the United States President be convinced that his announcement should include the following:
    - the affirmation of the United States declared positions on withdrawal, borders, settlements, security, the Palestinian question, normalization of relations, and guarantees;
    - the affirmation that the United States will continue to play the role of full partner.
b) President Sadat should visit Washington to meet with the Congress and the media to:
    - reaffirm our confidence in the United States and our appreciation of its continuing efforts;
    - reaffirm our interest in the maintenance of Egyptian-American relations;
    - highlight Egyptian flexibility since the President's initiative (publication of the Egyptian project);
    - expose Menahim Begin's obduracy which was responsible for the failure of Camp David.
c) On his way back, the President should visit certain Western European states to keep them informed of the latest developments.
d) The President should also contact moderate Arab leaders (Saudi Arabia, Jordan, Morocco, Sudan) to keep them also informed, emphasizing:
    - that a peaceful settlement is still possible;
    - that the United States intends to pursue its efforts;
    - that those Arab leaders should deal with the United States in such a manner as to strengthen Egypt's hand, in its endeavours for a comprehensive settlement.
e) A restricted Arab summit might then be contemplated with a view of creating a momentum for a larger unified participation in the achievement of peace.

Camp David

>   This attempt will – whether it succeeds or fails – determine future steps.
> 4 It is important that such steps take place before 24 October, the date on which the mandate of the international forces falls due for renewal.
>
>   Respectfully,
>
> 12 September 1978
>
> Mohamed Ibrahim Kamel
> Foreign Minister

The reader will note the calm, flexible style of this memorandum. It was intended to reassure Sadat that the failure of the Camp David Conference did not entail the failure of his initiative, and to further assure him that failure to reach agreement would not lead to a clash between himself and President Carter. Sadat had come to believe that Carter constituted his only hope and his strongest ally. Lastly, the memorandum was meant to induce him – without hurting either his pride or his feelings – to turn gradually once more to the Arabs. He would start by establishing contacts with the moderate Arab leaders. This would be followed by a restricted Arab summit which would, in its turn, pave the way for a unified Arab stand on the comprehensive settlement in accordance with the scenario Prince Saud El Faisal and myself had agreed on in May.

Ahmed Maher and I were on our way to the restaurant for lunch when we met President Carter on his bicycle. He stopped to greet us. While we were talking Tohamy appeared and joined the group. The following exchange then took place between President Carter and myself:

Carter: "It has been a week since the Conference began, and I hope we shall be able to reach an agreement within the next few days which will be acceptable to both parties."
Mohamed Ibrahim Kamel: "I am sorry to say I don't share your optimism, Mr President. The Israeli attitude is as obdurate and unyielding as ever. And the US project submitted to us falls far short of the minimum we can accept."
Carter: "This is only a project which is open to discussion. We shall naturally take into account your observations and proposals, and we would amend the text accordingly. What matters is that we reach an agreement which is acceptable to both parties."
Kamel: "Our problem is that we are not entitled to make any concessions on the occupied Arab territories. We can be very flexible on security arrangements and peace relations. However, it is obvious that this is not what Israel is after. Their only aim is, rather, the annexation of the occupied Arab territories or parts of them. I sincerely hope you will not put pressure on President Sadat at this point. He is not in a position to make such concessions and, were he to

do so, the other Arab states and peoples would not approve of any agreement which provided for any such concessions. His position would completely collapse, and we shall have lost the opportunity to achieve peace, and the problem will remain unsolved."

Carter: "It is impossible, at the present stage, to reach an agreement which would solve all problems at once. I believe we should avoid dealing with any sensitive problems that cannot be easily resolved at present, such as the question of sovereignty over the West Bank and Gaza and the problem of Jerusalem. Such problems should be deferred to a later stage." [The President then added]: "The Soviet Union is roaming around freely in the Horn of Africa and the Middle East because it knows that Egypt has five whole regiments pinned down along the Suez Canal which cannot be moved. Were we to reach a peace agreement between Egypt and Israel, there would be no need for the five regiments to be held up on the Canal. President Sadat would be free to deploy them in whichever manner he chose. This would force the Soviet Union to rethink its strategy and make it more likely to observe more caution."

Kamel: "Pardon me, Mr President, but we are meeting here to find a solution to the Arab-Israeli conflict, not to deal with the policies of the Soviet Union. I repeat to you that a just solution to the Palestinian problem will lead to peace and stability in the Middle East and to a reduction of the Soviet Union's influence in the area. If you want this Conference to succeed, an agreement which provides for Israeli withdrawal from the West Bank, Gaza and Arab Jerusalem must be reached. This will induce the other parties to join in the peace process."

Carter: "It seems to me you fail to realize my aim. I don't think it would be fair to ask President Sadat to bear the whole responsibility for the Arab-Israeli conflict. I wish to spare Sadat such a burden with regard to the West Bank and Jerusalem and get Kings Hussein and Khaled to shoulder it."

Kamel: "There we go again! Neither King Hussein nor King Khaled will agree to join the talks unless these were to be based upon Israel's withdrawal from the West Bank and Jerusalem."

Carter: "They will accept: I have sent to King Hussein to come to Washington next week and I have also sent to Prince Fahd; he will be here towards the end of this month."

Kamel: "Believe me, Mr President, they will not come."

Carter: "They will come."

And so saying, he turned his bicycle around and rode away.

Now I should like at this stage to comment on two concepts implied in President Carter's words. The first pertained to President Sadat's aspirations to become not only America's ally, but also America's policeman in the area. He believed that the way to gain United States support, and assistance, was to adopt a firm and hostile attitude towards the Soviet Union and to assume on its behalf the role of confronting Soviet infiltration in the Middle East and Africa. He would also lend his support to the friendly regimes which revolve in the United States orbit, such as President Mobutu's in Zaire. One can even conceive of the idea that at the back of Sadat's peace initiative there was a desire to ingratiate himself with the United States in view of Israel's special relations with the United States.

The second concept was that President Sadat – and perhaps proceeding from the same premises – was convinced that the Saudi Arabia-United States ties, particularly as regards its security, were organic. Consequently Saudi Arabia (to Sadat's way of thinking) was not in a position to go against US policies. He was also convinced that King Hussein, too far apart from his close ties to the United States, could not but go along with Saudi Arabia, since he was largely dependent on it for solutions to Jordan's financial and economic problems.

Many were the times that President Sadat and I had discussed this, for while I agreed that part of his assumptions were well-founded, yet I believed that he neglected an important factor, namely that Saudi Arabia, however liable to be influenced by the United States, could in turn bring *some* influence to bear on the latter. Saudi Arabia enjoyed vast oil reserves on which the West was dependent. Moreover, Jordan could always say "No" to Saudi Arabia on matters it would find unacceptable. For if Israel, that tiny, isolated state, which was totally dependent – economically, politically and militarily – on the United States, complied only with those United States demands it chose to comply with, would it be strange if Saudi Arabia and Jordan did likewise? These two states were linked organically to the Arab League group, spiritually to the Islamic states, and politically to the non-aligned movement. Would Saudi Arabia (I asked him) acquiesce, for instance, to Israel's annexation of Jerusalem were the United States so to require, and thereby endanger its leadership of the Islamic world? Could King Hussein endorse Israel's annexation of the West Bank and thereby sign his own death warrant if the United States asked him to do so?

These, I am convinced were Sadat's views with regard to Saudi Arabia and Jordan, I also believe that he largely succeeded in convincing Carter that things were so. This explains why neither took seriously the opposition voiced by Saudi Arabia and Jordan to certain unacceptable aspects of the agreement. They believed that they would in the end comply with whatever agreement was reached since the United States would be the initiator.

In my opinion this was the greatest mistake both Sadat and the Americans made when they signed the Camp David accords. They had acted on a miscalculation.

When Carter had departed, I proceeded to President Sadat's bungalow to give him an account of the conversation that had just taken place. He was sitting alone and seemed bored and lonely.

Apparently the discussion that had taken place between us the previous day on Jordan's role in the West Bank in any settlement had had an effect on Sadat. After I had finished my account of my conversation with Carter, he informed me that he had telephoned King Hussein that very morning in London, where he was on a private visit. He had, however, forgotten the time differential between the US and Europe, but he had been assured that King Hussein would contact him first thing in the morning. Just then the phone rang and King Hussein was on the line. After they had exchanged friendly greetings, Sadat informed him that the battle was at its height, and the negotiations were fierce and difficult. He had presented his project on a framework for peace, while the USA had submitted its project to us the day before. We were now considering and discussing it, and Sadat said he was not optimistic about reaching an agreement, because Menahim Begin was proving as stubborn as ever and insisted on his outdated ideas. However, he (Sadat) was going to give the matter the time it required for the sake of President Carter, who had made tremendous efforts to bring the positions of the two parties closer. He informed King Hussein of his intention to visit King Hassan in Morocco on his way back, and asked him whether he could meet him (Hussein) there. King Hussein begged off, saying he would have to return to Jordan the following day, whereupon they agreed to keep in touch.

The meeting of the Egyptian and American delegations, co-chaired by the foreign ministers, to discuss the American project began at 3 p.m. I began with an introduction in which I expressed my appreciation of the efforts that had been exerted by President Carter and Secretary of State Vance in an attempt to reach a settlement to the Arab-Israeli conflict. I told them we had come to Camp David in order to co-operate with them in the achievement of a noble aim, namely the establishment of a just and comprehensive peace. I said we were confident the US would eventually abide by its declared positions on a solution to the conflict.

We had only recently, after long expectation, received the American paper, so before making my general observations, I wished (I went on) to indicate the points upon which the US and ourselves were in full agreement. These were, first of all, the importance we attached to American-Egyptian relations; secondly, the importance we attached to the realization of a just and comprehensive settlement of the Middle East conflict (this meant that any results reached there should encourage the other Arab parties to join the peace efforts); and thirdly, the importance we attached to sparing the area a resurgence of colonialism and foreign intervention. This implied that we should avoid any slide towards the creation of conditions which would, in the end, be harmful to the US and the moderate regimes in the area.

I then read out the statement we had prepared containing our general observations:

Camp David

We have examined the American paper with great attention. We have prepared our detailed observations on the paper, which my colleagues will explain. However, I wish first of all to make some general observations. These are:

1. I regret that the US has decided to present its proposals to Israel first, discuss it with her and amend it in the light of Israel's observations. I mention this because I notice that the American proposal, as submitted, reflects many of Israel's ideas, We had hoped, in order to facilitate the work of the meeting, that the American side would submit its paper to the two parties at one and the same time. The paper could then have been prepared on the known and declared US stands as a basis for discussion.
2. I regret to state that the paper favours the Israeli side in that it demands that the Arab side fulfil clear and well-defined obligations (termination of the state of war, full normalization of relations) while only demanding of Israel that it commit itself to negotiations, giving it the right to veto many subjects.
3. The American proposals make no mention of the UN resolutions, but rather of negotiations based thereon, and this makes for a vicious circle.
4. The proposals do not clearly affirm that there should be complete withdrawal from Sinai, but only affirm Egypt's sovereignty over Sinai. Complete withdrawal should be affirmed.
5. The proposals on the West Bank do not include what Dr Brezinski had indicated with respect to the creation of a "dynamism". Instead, it allows Israel the opportunity to prevent the Palestinian people from exercising their rights, and gives Israel powers and rights which in effect enable it to inhibit any development in the situation after the period of transition.
6. These proposals completely ignore the right of the Palestinian people to self-determination, and give Israel the right to veto any exercise of such right. This constitutes a crucial change in the Aswan formula, by deleting all reference to "the Palestinian people".
7. Moreover, the paper neglects to stipulate that withdrawal shall be to the armistice demarcation lines in the West Bank and Gaza, with minor modifications, and instead leaves the way open for Israeli attempts to swallow up the whole or part of the West Bank.
8. The proposals do not give a clear picture of the situation after the transitional period, and while they assign a role to Israel during the transitional period, the proposals give no role to either Egypt or Jordan apart from participation in the negotiations.
9. The paper makes an issue of Jewish refugees where none exists.
10. With respect to security measures, the paper is designed to make

of the security forces, which Jordanians are requested to join, a force whose sole task would be the protection of Israel.
11 The paper contains no provision on the settlements, notwithstanding what Mr Vance had indicated to me on the need to remove the settlements in Sinai and impose a five-year moratorium on them in the West Bank and Gaza.
12 The proposals grant Israel the right to veto many questions such as:
   a) Differences over interpretation of the agreement.
   b) The return of refugees and displaced persons.
13 The proposals on Jerusalem are vaguely formulated and imply the maintenance of Israeli administration of the city.
14 The proposals deal with Israel's security and show no concern for the security of the Arab states.

There are numerous other observations which my colleagues will be making in the course of discussion before submitting any formal amendments. For the present, I shall confine myself to observing that, unfortunately, nothing in either the form or content of the paper indicates that these are American proposals. To put it succinctly, the American proposals place Egypt in an embarrassing position vis-à-vis the rest of the Arab world. A case in point is the reference to our readiness to assume the responsibility of a settlement on the West Bank were Jordan not to join the negotiations. This would constitute an unwarranted provocation to Jordan and will hardly encourage it to join in the negotiations, especially since the American paper makes so little of its participation.

The proposals will not gain the approval of Saudi Arabia, and we are in agreement on the importance of such approval. They do not allow for Jordan's participation. They fall short of the minimum Egypt would be willing to accept for the realization of a comprehensive and just settlement of the conflict.

We have indicated the Egyptian position in our paper, which may be summed up as follows:

a) There should be a balance in the obligations of the parties.
b) The necessity for total Israeli withdrawal with the exception of some minor alterations in the demarcation lines of the West Bank agreed to by the parties.
c) Respect for sovereignty and territorial integrity.
d) Guaranteeing the security of both parties.
e) Ensuring the participation of the rest of the Arab parties in the peace process.

In the light of all this, I now give the floor to my colleagues so that they may, in turn, present their observations. The amendments we are proposing reflect our desire not to come out with a mere paper, which may do more harm than good, but rather to make a real contribution towards a just, comprehensive and lasting peace.[7]

Discussions then began in earnest. The American side was represented by Vance, Saunders, Atherton and Quandt, the Egyptian side by Ussama El Baz, Abdel Raouf Al Ridi, Director of the Department of Planning at the Foreign Ministry, and Nabil El Araby, Director of the Legal Department at the Foreign Ministry. I scarcely exaggerate when I say that our people dominated the discussion from start to finish with their outstanding ability and skill. The American side – and here I bear witness to the courage and spirit of fair play shown by its members, particularly Cyrus Vance – was on the defensive most of the time. They often seemed embarrassed in the face of the clear and sound arguments of the Egyptian side. Vance, at our request, agreed to delete or amend several points in the American project and promised to look into others. I shall always recall the performance of the Egyptian delegation in this meeting with pride.

The following day, I went to see President Sadat, together with Hassan El Tohamy, and the conversation turned to Jerusalem. It must be said that Tohamy never tired of reiterating the need to rescue Arab Jerusalem from Israel's claws. Naturally, the restitution of Jerusalem was a top priority for all of us. Tohamy, however, spoke emphatically about it wherever he happened to be, and with greater earnestness than any other issue. Suddenly Sadat said: "It could be really great if we could swing this idea of one square mile!" When I enquired what that meant, Tohamy explained that Israel would withdraw from one square mile of Jerusalem and we should hoist an Arab or Islamic flag over that mile. However, neither Tohamy nor President Sadat explained further. The issue of the square mile still remains a mystery to me for the rush of events prevented me from seeking satisfactory explanation. I have asked myself: Why one square mile? Was not the area of Jerusalem greater, and was it conceivable that this very old historical city could be confined, architecturally speaking, to one square mile? And even if it could, what of the outlying suburbs beyond that square mile? I finally concluded that this was just another of Tohamy's bright ideas!

Tohamy went on to say to Sadat: "There is one thing I ask of you, Rais, namely that you fulfil your promise of appointing me Governor-General of Jerusalem.

"I have never in all my life asked you for anything, and I have no other requests to make. This is my life's dream and I pray God you will make it come true before I die!"

Sadat mumbled something I could not catch, and I tried to conceal my bewilderment by remaining silent. I do not know why, but I was reminded at that very moment of the story Tohamy told Ahmed Maher and myself when we were having lunch at Foeschel in Austria, concerning the Jews and their

Between The Israeli Hammer and The American Anvil

God and their return to Jerusalem. I looked at Tohamy and imagined him as the Governor-General, in the one square mile, with the people surrounding him absorbing all of his wisdom and omniscience!

I shuddered, and banished the thought!

That day we received a second American project which had been amended in the light of the discussions of the previous day. It was a great improvement on their first. Carter's original Aswan formula, for instance, had been reintroduced. A new provision had been added concerning the freeze on the establishment of new settlements in the West Bank and Gaza as well as the non-expansion of existing ones during the "negotiations". The provision which dealt with the situation were Jordan not to join the negotiations was also deleted. However, the basic philosophy of the project remained unchanged. It gave Israel a central role in the West Bank and Gaza during the transitional period, granting it practically full control and an exclusive right of veto. The project had remained consistent with the Israeli position on deferring the issue of sovereignty in the West Bank and Gaza until after the transitional period, although the sovereignty of the Palestinian people over those territories could not be subject to debate. I was of the opinion that Israel's insistence on refusing to even discuss the issue of sovereignty at that stage was proof enough of its intention to annex those territories in the future. This was so obvious as to be crystal-clear to even the most naive. Why, then, did the United States seek to impose negotiations on us from this point of departure?

Despite those changes the framework of the American proposals, which were, in fact, based on the Israeli autonomy project, remained unchanged. We seemed to be locked in a vicious circle of amendments and counter-amendments which would soon lead us into the abyss of the unknown. Sadat started to lose patience and his nerves were frayed, while Begin, for his part, remained entrenched in his rigidity and intransigence. As for Carter, he was working frantically against the clock as time wore on, his exasperation increased and he seemed to be losing his equanimity. He could not indefinitely stay away from the White House, neglecting the tasks of the Presidency and his country's foreign and domestic problems. He was fully aware that, were the Camp David Conference to end in failure, it would affect adversely his internal position. According to opinion polls, his popularity was at its lowest since he came to power.

Then three things occurred which had the greatest impact on the course of the negotiations:

1. It was brought to our knowledge that Menahim Begin had insisted from the outset that he would not give us the Israeli settlements and airports in Sinai. The American side was intent on keeping this from us, lest it spell death to the negotiation. This explained why none of the formulae they submitted in their projects dealt with this

question, but were confined to Israel's withdrawal from Sinai and the restoration of full Egyptian sovereignty over Sinai. Apparently Begin had privately assured them that this formula did not conflict with the maintenance of Israeli settlements in Sinai.

2. President Carter and Weizman, the Israeli Defence Minister, succeeded in persuading President Sadat to meet Moshe Dayan – for whom he had a feeling of repulsion and whom he had avoided meeting, as indicated earlier. It is not known whether Carter and Weizman had acted in concert or separately to urge Sadat to agree to such a meeting.

3. President Carter, with the ostensible purpose of buying time, decided to assume the main negotiating role. He asked Sadat and Menahim Begin to co-opt a legal adviser from each delegation who would work with him (i.e. Carter) directly. Sadat chose Ussama El Baz, while the Israeli Premier opted for Aharon Barak to draft formulae. He would then set to work out a compromise formula. This did not mean, in theory, that other members of the delegations no longer took a direct part in the negotiations. However, in practice, that is what matters amounted to in many instances. Carter detained both El Baz and Barak in his bungalow where he discussed the various issues with them, had each prepare his formula and again discussed it with them into the early hours of the morning.

Footnotes

1. The Egyptian Foreign Ministry's Memorandum to President Sadat, dated 28 August 1978, p. 273 and later pages.
2. p. 303 and subsequent pages.
3. p. 317 and subsequent pages.
4. Moshe Dayan, *Breakthrough*, p. 165 and subsequent pages.
5. Weizman, *The Battle for Peace*, p.363 and subsequent pages.
6. The American project covered fourteen pages, as compared with the original seventeen pages as submitted to Israel. The US project is given in Appendix 3.
7. It is noteworthy that all the observations and objections to the US project contained in the statement apply almost entirely and in the most minute detail to the Camp David Accords, which were signed at the end of the Conference.

Chapter Thirty Nine

Faint or Feint?

On the morning of Thursday 14 September, Weizman visited President Sadat and spent some time with him. It would seem that he eventually managed to persuade him to see Moshe Dayan, because Sadat invited the latter to meet him that same afternoon.

Dayan writes in his book *Breakthrough* that President Sadat had some reservations about this encounter, fearing that Dayan would try to get him to agree to peace without giving him anything in return. Anyway, as we have seen, the President, at Weizman's urging, asked him to tea. Dayan adds that President Carter, who had prior knowledge of this meeting, requested him to refrain from discussing points of difference with Sadat. He was afraid that if they did, both parties would dig in, and the tension between them increase. Dayan had promised, according to him, but it was Sadat who turned the conversation to the problems which were holding up progress at the Conference, which was drawing to a close without agreement; and the main reason for this was Israel's adamant insistence on retaining the settlements in Sinai.

A discussion between them on the settlements followed. Dayan claimed they had been driven to establish them by Egypt's rejection of the offer to return all of Sinai in return for peace. The answer had come through the Khartoum Conference, which had been called at the suggestion of Gamal Abdel Nasser. It had rejected negotiation with or recognition of Israel or the establishment of peace with it, maintaining that what had been taken by force should be returned by force.

Dayan adds: "The course of this dialogue was not to Sadat's liking. The smile disappeared, and opposite me sat an angry and troubled man. His Foreign Minister, he said, Muhammad Ibrahim Kamel, was anxious to follow his predecessor Fahmi, and resign. His adviser, Al-Baz, was strongly opposed to a peace treaty with Israel, was venomous in his outbursts among members of his delegation, and strengthened their doubts. If there were no change in the negotiations in his favour, he would have to return to Egypt and admit he had failed. We were obliged, he said, to start a new chapter: withdraw from the entire peninsula of Sinai and hand it over to Egyptian

Camp David

sovereignty. My people, he said, will not agree to any foreign regime on our soil, neither the American forces in the Sinai airfields, nor to your settlements, not even one, not even for a brief period. If you want peace with us, the table must be cleared. We fought so that the Suez Canal should remain in our exclusive control. I am now ready to make peace with you, a full and true peace, and ignore the opposition of the Arab states, but you must take all your people out of Sinai, the troops and civilians, dismantle the military camps and remove the settlements."

Dayan writes that he saw no point in debating the question, or telling Sadat that Egypt was always launching wars against them even though the Israeli leadership offered it peace. It was clear that Sadat insisted on the restitution of Sinai, and if they did not withdraw from Sinai, the Camp David conference would end without a peace agreement. He therefore contented himself with telling Sadat that he would be submitting a report on their meeting to his Prime Minister.

From what Dayan says, it would appear that he intended to abide by his promise to Carter when he met Sadat not to bring up any of the points of difference between them, but according to Dayan it was Sadat who had broached the subject of the settlements in Sinai.

Sadat made no mention to me of his meeting with Dayan, either directly or indirectly. However, he summoned Ussama El Baz after the meeting, and, upon his return, Ussama had told me that he had found Sadat in an angry mood. Sadat had given him the following account of his meeting with Dayan.

Dayan told Sadat he was courageous and forthright, and so he (Dayan) would be blunt with him. It was Sadat's belief that the problem centred around the solution to the Palestinian question, whereas the solution to this was easy when compared with the problem of the Israeli settlements and airfields in Sinai. He must know that neither Begin, Perez nor any other leader could under any circumstances relinquish them. It was not that they wished to expand by retaining them, but it was a security matter, since the settlements formed a safety-belt for Israel, and had been designed and built for that purpose. The Israeli people feared no Arab state except Egypt, which was the only state likely to pose a real threat to Israel. The October War had confirmed this feeling. Hence the Israeli people – and consequently the Knesset – would absolutely refuse to relinquish the Israeli settlements and airfields in Sinai. So he must understand that even if Begin agreed, for the sake of argument, to evacuate the settlements in principle, he would be unable to do so until five or six years after the signing of a peace agreement between Egypt and Israel. Then, and only then, after peace relations had lasted for that time, might it be possible to convince Israeli opinion of Egypt's true intention to maintain a lasting peace, and persuade them it was not simply a manoeuvre.

Sadat had asked him: "And what of the security arrangements I have proposed?" and Dayan replied that these were not by themselves, sufficient to give the Israeli people a feeling of security. "Do you imagine [Sadat had reported] that it is possible for me to conclude any peace treaty with you which did not include the removal of the settlements and airfields and the restitution of Sinai with full sovereignty?" Dayan had informed him that, in that case, "We shall continue to occupy Sinai and pump oil." Whereupon Sadat wanted to know why he had not said so from the beginning, instead of wasting Carter's, Dayan's and his (Sadat's) time.

Dayan had answered: "We did say so from the start, but you chose not to believe us. I wished to explain to you the truth of the situation by presenting it clearly to prevent you building false hopes on what it is impossible for Begin to approve of, at least for the time being."

Finally, Ussama El Baz told me that President Sadat had asked him to prepare an "Assessment of the Situation" in the light of Dayan's conversation with him. Ussama believed he would reach the same conclusion we had in the memorandum we had submitted to Sadat on 12 September. His memorandum, Ussama went on, would recommend reaching an understanding with President Carter on ending the Conference without signing any definite agreements.

I myself have no doubt that Sadat's account of what transpired between himself and Dayan, as communicated to Ussama El Baz, was the truth, rather than the tale Dayan recounts in his book. The subject of the settlements in Sinai did not worry Sadat in the least, since he took it for granted that an agreement would be reached over them – and even if he had had the least doubt, he would have remained confident that President Carter would easily solve this problem, as the latter had assured him he would from the start. So there was no reason why Sadat should invite Dayan to meet him just to talk about the Sinai settlements. It was, rather, the subject of the West Bank and Gaza that he wished to discuss with him. This constituted the real difficulty in reaching an agreement on the framework for a comprehensive peace. This is clear from foregoing account.

There cannot be the slightest doubt that Israel was in possession of a complete analysis of Sadat's personality and psyche. Kissinger had contributed to this record by the information he was able to communicate during his shuttle negotiations in 1974 and 1975. There was also Sadat's statements, interviews and behaviour to work on and data provided by Ezer Weizman through his private meetings and lengthy discussions with him, in addition to many other sources.

The fact is that what Dayan told Sadat was neither strange nor unexpected. It was nothing more than a reflection of the true Israeli intentions to make use of the Sinai card as a bargaining counter to ensure the neutralization of Egypt on the main aspect of the Arab-Israeli conflict thus giving Israel a free hand in the West Bank and Gaza.[1]

The ingenuity of arranging the meeting lay in the following:

1 *The specific choice of Dayan*: if what was said at the meeting had been voiced by Menahim Begin, for instance, it would not have had the same disruptive effect on Sadat. Carter had allied himself with Weizman – Sadat believed both men were true friends who gave him genuine advice – to press Sadat to meet Dayan. They argued that he had not had the chance of talking directly with Dayan in spite of his being the Foreign Minister of Israel. They likewise prompted him to do so because (they assured Sadat) they both believed that Dayan was characterized by flexibility, fertility of thought and a genuine desire to achieve peace with the Arabs. Moreover, Dayan had (they claimed) a special relationship with Begin and could influence him. That he (Sadat) should have acceded to their urgings, his hopes from a breakthrough raised by their claims, only to hear what he had from Dayan, must have been highly disappointing and frustrating to Sadat.
2 *The timing of the meeting*: the Conference had been going on for ten days and any hopes of attaining results had faded. Sadat had become nervous and impatient in face of the unyielding Israeli position. Whenever Carter – the full partner – failed to induce any alteration in the Israeli position, he would hasten to President Sadat and appeal for his help to prevent the failure of the Conference, plead with him to save his (Carter's) political future by showing more flexibility and generosity with regard to this or that point.

It did not escape Sadat that the Conference could not be prolonged for a much longer period, that the prospects of the realization of his hopes were vanishing, and that he would soon have to face the moment of truth.

As I see it, Dayan's conversation with Sadat, although it lasted less than an hour, was the last straw for Sadat and a turning-point in his attitude. From then on he became embroiled in a series of concessions. This ended in his total capitulation, and he finally appended his signature to what Israel, in its wildest dreams, never imagined possible.

That same evening, going to Sadat's bungalow, I found him in his bedroom in his pyjamas. He was lying on a sofa, watching TV. After greeting me familiarly with a welcome, "Hi, Mohamed, take a seat!", he resumed watching the TV programme. When it was over, and after enquiring about some relations of mine involved in the Amin Osman case, he then evoked memories of Gamal Abdel Nasser and other prominent personalities of the revolution, telling me stories about Field-Marshal Abdel Hakim Amer's private life, and how this had placed him sometimes in an embarrassing situation vis-à-vis Nasser, since Amer often spent several days and nights in one or other of the government residences without informing the then President, though he would notify Sadat of his whereabouts so that he

Faint or Feint?

could contact him if need be.

Sometimes important business did come up, and Nasser would finally resort to Sadat to enquire as to his whereabouts. Sadat confided to me that he would then have to invent some plausible pretext or other that Nasser would accept. He (Sadat) would thereupon promptly ring Amer up and ask him to return at once.

I listened to him, occasionally putting in a word or two. I did not wish to refer to what Ussama El Baz had disclosed to me regarding his meeting with Dayan, since Sadat had not originally mentioned the meeting to me.

At this point, Hassan El Tohamy, Hassan Kamel, Boutros Ghali and Ashraf Ghorbal came in and sat down with us. We spoke of things far removed from Camp David, and my thoughts must have been elsewhere, for the next thing I knew, Sadat was shouting at the top of his voice: "What can I do? My Foreign Minister thinks I'm an idiot!" Flabbergasted, I turned towards him, for I had not taken part in the conversation and there was no apparent justification for this sudden outburst of anger. I held my tongue, for I found nothing to say, and he cried again: "Get out, all of you!" He repeated these words twice more, and they all stood up and walked out of the room in silence. I followed them to the door, and when they had all left I went back to Sadat. Then my anger got the better of me and, my eyes fairly shooting sparks, I shouted at him in my turn: "How can you allow yourself, in front of all these people, to accuse me of considering you an idiot? Would I work with you if I thought that you were? . . . and how dare you order me out of the room? Do you think that, just because you appointed me Foreign Minister, you are entitled to act in such manner? I shall quit this office as soon as we get back to Cairo." I turned and had nearly reached the door on my way out, when he called: "Wait, Mohamed." As I remained where I stood, he said: "Come and sit down." I advanced towards him, but remained standing. "What's the matter with you, Mohamed? Don't you know what I'm going through? If you don't bear with me, who will?" Feeling some compunction, I nevertheless retorted: "I feel what you feel, but that was no reason for you to address me in such a manner in front of anybody – I wouldn't take it from my own father!" He replied: "I really am sorry, it's all the fault of this cursed prison we find ourselves in. Why don't you sit down?" I told him I would leave to give him a chance to rest. "For my part it's midnight and I feel like a walk!"

At 9.30 a.m. the next day, I was having coffee with Hassan Kamel, Boutros Ghali and Ashraf Ghorbal when Fawzi Abdel Hafiz, the head of President Sadat's private secretariat, came in to tell us that the President had rung him at 7 a.m. in Washington, where he was staying. Sadat asked him to come to Camp David immediately. When he got there, Sadat had ordered him to arrange for the departure of the Egyptian delegation, and instructed him to provide a helicopter to fly him to Washington that afternoon. Hafiz then asked us to pack.

Camp David

This sudden decision astonished us, and we wondered what could have motivated the decision, particularly since we had been in the President's company only the night before and had remained with him until midnight. Yet he had not mentioned this either directly or indirectly. I was about to go to him to find out what had happened when the phone rang. President Sadat was on the line and requested me to come with Ashraf Ghorbal at once.

When we arrived we found him in his living-room. He was in a state of great agitation, and no sooner had he seen us than he asked: "Where's Vance? Tell Vance to come over, I wish to see him at once."

When I asked what the matter was, he replied: "I've decided to withdraw from the Conference, and have issued instructions accordingly. I'm going to Washington to meet with the Foreign Affairs Committee in Congress. I then intend to hold a press conference and appear on TV to explain exactly what happened, after which I shall return to Cairo."

Then I remembered what Ussama had told me about his having met Dayan the day before. I again asked him: "But what has happened to cause you to take this sudden decision?" "It is quite impossible to reach any understanding with Begin," said the President. "He's simply playing with poor, naïve Carter: he wants us to sign only what he feels like signing, and to leave all the rest up in the air. I've decided not to sign anything in Camp David with President Carter, so that whatever is signed may not be used as a basis for future negotiations and likewise be subject to bargaining."

I did not quite get his meaning. Truth to tell, and more particularly during the last few days, Sadat had come to regard me as the immovable obstacle standing in the way of agreement. Carter now also regarded me as persona non grata, and, of course, in Israeli eyes, I had been that right from the very beginning. Perhaps this was one of the reasons why President Carter was handling the negotiations himself, dealing directly with Sadat rather than through the Egyptian delegation. Sadat never gave me any information on what passed between himself, Carter and Weizman, save such information as he believed I would not disapprove of. However, Ussama El Baz had already told me of the concessions Sadat made and which he, Ussama, sought to rectify in the formulation, and that this led sometimes to violent arguments with President Carter. The latter would tell Ussama that this or that was not what Sadat had approved, and Ussama would answer that he was carrying out his (Sadat's) instructions to the letter. It seemed to me, that Sadat's agitation and his stated intention to leave Camp David were due to the fact that in responding to Carter's honeyed promises on the eventual achievement of a comprehensive settlement he realized he had made too many concessions on the West Bank and Gaza. Then he discovered that this friend and full partner was quite unable to extract anything from Begin in return for his concessions. He had woken up to the painful fact that there was nothing to guarantee that he would be able to reintegrate Sinai minus the settlements and airfields. He would thereby disappoint the Egyptian

Faint or Feint?

people, after having lost the Arabs, and would leave the Conference empty-handed.

"I fully approve," I told Sadat "your not signing any document in Camp David unless it clearly stipulates Israeli withdrawal from the West Bank and Gaza, and the Palestinian people's right to self-determination. And I agree that President Carter has shown great weakness and a total inability to confront Begin. You must, however, meet him and explain your position to him so that Israel may not exploit this to cause us to fall out with the United States and give the impression that we were not giving the negotiations their due as happened when you withdrew the Egyptian delegation from the meeting of the Political Committee in Jerusalem.

"I shall have for you in less than an hour a statement which you could suggest to Carter. It would enable him to show United States public opinion that some progress in the negotiations at Camp David has been achieved. The statement would indicate that the gap between the two sides, however, is still too wide for them to bridge and that he (Carter) would maintain close contacts with both sides."

Sadat listened to what I had to say. When I had finished, Ashraf Ghorbal began to speak. He said that President Sadat's withdrawal from the Conference in this manner, after all the time he had devoted to it, would embarrass President Carter and would be exploited by the Israelis. At this, Sadat exclaimed, "Stop – you've got it quite wrong. Ring Vance and ask him to come at once."

Ashraf rang up Vance and was informed that he was at a meeting with Carter and Dayan, but the message would be relayed to him immediately. Vance appeared a few minutes later. President Sadat began: "It has become clear that the Camp David Conference will not achieve any results: twelve days have already elapsed but no progress has been realized. This is due to Begin's rigidity and obstinacy. I have therefore decided to suspend the negotiations and leave for Washington to explain the situation to Congress and the media and pinpoint the responsibility for the failure of the Conference. I shall then return to Egypt."

Vance said firmly: "Mr President, I do not advise you to do that, because it would greatly disappoint and embarrass President Carter. Furthermore, nothing would be gained by it and only Israel would benefit."

Sadat appeared disturbed and somewhat hesitant.

"As you know [he told Vance] I have made many concessions to facilitate Carter's attempts to reach an agreement. However, Begin has not budged an inch and that is why the Conference has failed. There is a tendency to put our signatures to what has already been agreed, but to do so would oblige me to sign away concessions I would never have agreed to were it not that I wished to help Carter by ensuring that the failure of the Conference would not be attributed to him. I cannot sign anything short of a final, complete agreement, and this appears to be impossible due to Begin's intransigence.

To do otherwise would mean that Begin – or whoever succeeds him as Prime Minister – would consider what I had signed as his acquired right, and he would then attempt to extort further concessions on the remaining issues, in search of a compromise. This I can neither do nor approve. It should be understood that the concessions I have made were for the sake of the United States and President Carter personally, not for the sake of Israel or Menahim Begin. Hence, I refuse to put my name to any document of this sort."

It was with bitterness that I heard him speak of concessions to which he had never referred, either directly or indirectly.

Vance said: "Mr President, you can speak to President Carter on this matter, and I am sure he will do all he can to put your mind at rest. I shall inform him of your desire to meet him." Whereupon Vance left the bungalow, while Ashraf and I proceeded with the President to the outer terrace where we found the other members of our delegation standing around wondering what had caused President Sadat to withdraw from the Conference. We all sat down. Sadat was silent and spoke not at all. I felt I should say something, and my words were, in fact, designed to encourage Sadat in his intention to withdraw from the Conference. Addressing those present, I told them: "The President has decided to terminate the negotiations now that it has become certain that we shall be unable to obtain an agreement acceptable to us. He will be meeting President Carter to agree on how this may best be done without embarrassing the United States' President." Most of the present endorsed the idea of withdrawal.

Fifteen minutes later Vance returned in the company of Harold Brown, the Defence Secretary. They then sat down with us and Vance informed Sadat that Carter would be along to see him in ten minutes' time. Conversation then became general, and current events were eschewed. President Carter soon arrived and we rose to receive him. It was not long, however, before Sadat took him by the hand and led him into the living-room. When the door had closed behind them, Vance and Brown left, while I proceeded with the rest of the delegation to my bungalow where we impatiently awaited the outcome of the meeting. Nearly half an hour later Sadat sent for us. He had recovered his liveliness and appeared pleased and in command of himself. We were all ears as he told us: "President Carter is a great man and extremely intelligent. He solved the problem with the greatest of ease, and I am completely satisfied." When we asked how, Sadat replied: "He told me I could make any agreement we signed dependent on the approval of the constitutional institutions of Egypt and Israel – that is, the People's Assembly in Egypt and the Knesset in Israel. Were either or both of these to reject the agreement, any commitments entered into by the two sides with respect to such agreement would be cancelled and would not be binding on us in any future negotiations."

To this I replied that what mattered was the sort of agreement we were

Faint or Feint?

going to sign. "I shall sign anything proposed by President Carter without reading it," was the rejoinder. There was a moment's silence in the room before I said, trying hard to master my feelings: "Why, Rais, sign without reading? If it pleases us, we sign; otherwise we do not." Sadat reacted by rising to his feet and saying in a threatening tone: "No. I shall sign it without reading it."

And he turned on his heel, left the terrace and entered the bungalow.[2]

The afternoon of that day found me engaged in deep thought, pondering my wretched misfortune in having to deal with an impossible situation, cursing the day Sadat had appointed me Foreign Minister. I no longer understood what was going on in his mind; nor did I understand his strange behaviour and his fickle and totally unexpected moods. I told myself that were such a person the head of a small family, the family would have taken prompt action to revoke his legal competence. Would not such action be more imperative if that person happened to be President of Egypt with the fate of forty million people in his hands? Could he possibly be as naïve as he seemed. Or had he lost his senses? And why does he become so amenable to any request from Carter?

Sadat's masseur appeared just then and informed me that the President wished to see Ussama El Baz and myself immediately in his bungalow. Ussama was in his own quarters, so I sent word to him to join me at the President's bungalow. I walked towards it slowly, wondering what he was going to say to me. When I reached the bungalow, the servant showed me into the living-room. I could hear the President's loud voice as he spoke on the telephone from his bedroom to his wife in Paris. He was telling her that there was a possibility that they would reach an honourable agreement within a day or two. He then asked her to give him his grandson, Sherif, which she promptly did. Sadat kept saying: "Sherif, you bad boy!" laughing uproariously the while. He must have said it twenty times at least before he finally came into the room. Greeting me warmly, he enquired about Ussama El Baz. I told him I had sent for him to come over. Sadat then said: "I have asked you here to tell you that my tough stand this morning with Vance and Carter has yielded excellent results." "Good," I said. "Wait," he continued "I'll fetch the document so that you may see for yourself!"

Out he went, to come back a moment later with a paper in his hand. Then he invited me to sit beside him and read the document. When I began, he cried: "No – speak up so I can hear you!" I promptly complied, but before I was through, Ussama came into the room. President Sadat thereupon welcomed him and requested me to start again from the beginning so that Ussama might hear. And I began to read once more.

The paper consisted of a single handwritten page and was addressed to "President Anwar El Sadat, and Prime Minister Begin". At the foot of the page were Carter's initials (J.C.). The paper specified that enough time had elapsed since the beginning of the negotiations to enable each side to express its ideas, views and stances to the entire satisfaction of President Carter. The latter had therefore decided to close the Conference the following Sunday, 17 September. He invited both sides to submit their final comments on the latest formulation of the United States project, which would be laid before them that afternoon, so that it could be available to him by the following day, Saturday 16 September. President Carter would then submit his project on a framework for peace for signature by President Sadat, Prime Minister Begin and himself (as witness to the agreement). President Carter called upon both sides to refrain from making any statements or comments on the agreement after it had been signed until he had read his communiqué to a joint meeting of both Houses of Congress on Monday 18 September.

When I was through reading, Sadat glanced at me and asked: "Well, what do you think now?" "Think about what?" I replied coldly. "Your only flaw, Mohamed is your Turkish blockheadedness. You don't want to understand"! This elicited from me the remark "that I understood only too well". Then Sadat turned to Ussama and asked him what he thought. Ussama looked at me and then looked quickly away again, suppressing his amusement, but said nothing. At this, Sadat patted my knee and said, "Please, have faith in me, don't you have confidence in me?" I replied that what was important was to ascertain the contents of Carter's project. "As for this paper," I went on, "it deals with matters of procedure and is completely worthless." Sadat snatched the paper out of my hands, shouting: "No, it's a very important document, and in Carter's handwriting, too. I intend to take it with me and lock it away in my private safe until the time is ripe."

I looked at him, wondering whether he really thought me that naïve and stupid, or whether he really believed the document was that important.

I stood up. "Excuse me," I said, and left the room quickly.

The bungalow was packed with members of the delegation. Among them were Ahmed Maher and Mohamed Ibrahim Shakir, Minister Plenipotentiary in our Embassy in Washington (he is also my cousin). Everyone wanted to know why the President had summoned me. I told them it was "nothing important". I then asked Maher and Shakir to step out with me. When they had done so, we walked along aimlessly until we came to a clearing among the trees. There on the ground stretched the trunk of an enormous tree. We sat down on it and I told them I had come to the end of the road and had to take a decision regarding my future attitude to Sadat. I told them that I had reached the end of my tether. The real problem, I added, was to be found neither in the intransigent Israeli attitude nor in America's spineless surrender to Israel. The real problem, I said, was President Sadat himself. He had capitulated unconditionally to President Carter who, in turn, had capitulated unconditionally to Menahim Begin. Any agreement concluded now would prove disastrous to Egypt, the Palestinian people, and the entire Arab nation. I was at a loss (I went on) to explain his objectives, conduct and behaviour. Perhaps he had allied himself too strongly to the United States so

Faint or Feint?

that he found it difficult at this stage to extricate himself.

I concluded that in the circumstances I was incapable of doing anything, and my only course was to resign. I could not share the responsibility for the disaster towards which we were heading. I would therefore write out my resignation that very night, stating the reasons which prompted it, and would send it to the President the following morning.

Both Ahmed Maher and Mohamed Shakir expressed sympathy and understanding for my feelings and position. We then spent some time discussing the resignation when Ahmed Maher came up with an idea. He felt that to write a letter of resignation to Sadat, whose quarters were only a few yards from mine, to say nothing of our long association, would be inappropriate. "Why not," he suggested, "go and see President Sadat yourself tomorrow morning and express your views frankly. That will also give you the opportunity to point out to him the dangers inherent in signing any agreement which falls short of our minimum objectives." There was, continued Maher, some slight chance of my getting through to him and straightening things out. If you fail, you can always announce your resignation.

I thought over what Ahmed Maher had just said, then came to a decision. "Yes, I'll do it."

In the evening I leafed through a copy of the American project, which Carter had submitted at 6 p.m. to both President Sadat and Menahim Begin. It was the fourth, and last, American project, and contained the elements of the settlement for the West Bank and Gaza. It also laid down the bases for a peace agreement between Egypt and Israel, without linking it to – or making it conditional on – the settlement of the Palestinian question. The Egyptian President and the Israeli side were asked to give their final observations on the project so as to allow the American President to discuss them with both sides and reach a common understanding. Carter would then prepare the final draft to the agreements. They would be ready for signing at the time set by him for the closure of the Conference, namely Sunday 17 September.

The project had taken the autonomy project submitted by Begin at Ismailia as a basis. However, some amendments of a purely cosmetic nature had been admitted, by assigning a formal and secondary role to Egypt and Jordan in the administration of the West Bank and Gaza during the transitional period, to make it more palatable. Were Jordan to decide to accede to the agreement – its role would not only be ineffective but positively detrimental, since it would condone Israel's illegal occupation during – and after – the transitional period. Israel all along, would be in effective control.

Nonetheless, Israel continued, right up to the last minute, to propose amendments to the project, as I shall shortly be demonstrating.

Camp David

Footnotes

1. See p. 190 of Weizman's book *The Battle for Peace*.
2. More than two years after the signature of the Camp David Accords, Herman Eilts, the former US Ambassador to Egypt, visited Cairo and I and Ahmed Maher El Sayid had lunch with him, during which we fell to recalling several past events. Eilts asked me whether I really believed Sadat intended to leave Camp David that day (Friday 15 September 1978). I replied: "I would not be telling the truth if I were to tell you that I knew anything about his intentions. Sadat's reasoning is based on gambles and calculations incomprehensible to mere logic. However, it is my personal belief that he actually was going to leave after his conversation with Dayan the day before. Were he unable to remove the settlements and airfields in Sinai, how would he have been able to face the people?" Eilts said: "I had the distinct impression he had agreed with Carter on this manoeuvre to enable the latter to put pressure on Begin to evacuate the settlements in Sinai. This impression of mine became even stronger when Carter showed no concern when he learned of Sadat's intention to leave. He told Vance in front of me that he was quite certain Sadat would not walk out of the Conference." Eilts added that Vance had told him, some time later, that he had advised Carter twice in the first week of the Conference to find some way of ending it in view of Israeli intransigence and the great difference in the stands of the two sides, imagining that such a move would open the way to a resumption of future negotiations under more favourable conditions. But Carter strongly rejected the idea and then it was too late to do anything and events led rapidly to the Camp David pitfall.

Chapter Forty

A Last Attempt Before Resigning

I lay awake all night as I contemplated my meeting with Sadat the following day. What should I tell him? I wondered desperately – and where to begin or end? I argued with myself as to which of us was in the right and which of us was in the wrong.

There passed before my bemused vision the succession of events that had occurred since Israel's appearance on the scene in our neck of the woods, giving rise to the Palestinian question and arousing the suspicions and fears of the adjacent states. My mind travelled back over all the international resolutions and the principles of justice and human rights in the context of which any settlement of the Arab-Israeli dispute should by necessity have had to be attained, and concluded that what had been put to us and was apparently accepted by Sadat – either knowingly and intentionally or out of sheer weakness and resignation in the face of Begin's rigidity and President Carter's urging – was most unlikely to lead to a comprehensive, just and lasting peace and the stability sought in the Middle East. Rather, I thought, the area would be plunged into boiling, senseless turmoil and instability. Egypt's isolation from the other Arab states – of which it was the heart and pillar – and the lifting of the siege of righteousness and justice imposed on Israel at both Arab and international level (with the exception of the United States), designed to induce it to recognize the rights of those whose rights it had usurped, would let loose the hideous and destructive Zionist ogre. American sophisticated weapons were the Ogre's teeth and claws, while its incentives and motivations were those of greed, covetousness and control of the area's destinies and the fate of its peoples, and a monopoly of its treasures and wealth. The ogre would pounce on it, plundering, terrorizing and massacring until it had imposed its hegemony over it. It would then turn to Egypt in its isolation – powerless with its hands tied by what it had signed away and accepted – and impose whatever it chose to impose on that country, and hey presto! Israel, the upstart, alien state of three million emigrants, becomes a world power, under the name of the Empire of Zion. It would then comprehend states with great natural riches, human potential and influential strategic location!

Camp David

How different from all this was what Sadat preached in Jerusalem and his dream of a comprehensive peace throughout the area, bringing prosperity and stability where Israel would live in peace and security with its neighbours under the protection of international law, bound by ties of peace, co-operation and good-neighbourly relations!

The night was passing away hour by hour, but the solace of sleep was denied to me. My mind remained awhirl with misgivings, fears and temptations. Here was I, thousand of miles from my own country, alone and defenceless in a camp surrounded by walls, among people some of whom did not like what I said while still others could not tolerate it and rejected it. True, I had around me a group of intelligent young men who were alert and understood what was going on. These shared my views and feelings, though there was nothing either I or they could do that was not endorsed by our President. I fell prey to atrocious nightmares, in which I beheld pictures and scenes from what I had seen and heard on acts perpetrated by the CIA (the American Central Intelligence Agency) and the Israeli Mossad Organization. What if they were to dispose of me in one way or another, making it look like a casual accident or sudden illness? What was I to do if the Conference ended, the conferees left and I was stranded there without friends, with not even a passport in my possession to indicate who I was?

And what of my family and my children's future? How would Sadat treat me after my recalcitrance and insubordination? My relations with Sadat and the position I had acquired with him – I was barely middle aged – would, if I held my peace and went along with him, open up to me all that ambitious fantasy could visualize in terms of wealth, standing and influence! The office of President of the Republic itself would not be beyond the bounds of possibility!

My thoughts harked back to my father, that haughty judge who took so much pride in his self-respect and whom experience had rendered wise. Consumed by grief, he had died some thirty years before whilst I, his only son, a student in his third year in the Faculty of Law, then barely nineteen, lay in Misr public prison with an uncertain future before him. And I heard again the words he had never tired of repeating to me since the most tender age: "My son, all I aspire to leave to you is a good name, a good education, a rich culture and a university degree . . . My son, the most beautiful thing about living is to go through life in a dignified manner, with your head held high, being subservient to none. . . Never sell or humiliate yourself, my son, for were you to do so you would never be happy, whatever the price. . . My son, you must always be brave and say what you feel, doing only what your conscience and honour approve, and never mind the rest. . ."

And I told myself, "No. I shall never allow anyone to point a finger at my children and say their father was reduced to silence and was too much of a coward to express his opinion, being content to hold his tongue about what he believed to be wrong and a great calamity.

A Last Attempt Before Resigning

"Tomorrow [I told myself] I shall speak quietly, firmly and in all honesty to the President. Maybe he will come to his senses and return to the path of righteousness. Otherwise, well, what will be will be: I have met my obligations, relieved my conscience and obeyed my father's recommendation. . . I put my trust in God, who is unfailing."

On the morning of the following day, 16 September, I was awakened by Ahmed Maher and Ahmed Abou El Gheit, first secretary in my office, who invited me to have breakfast with them. I replied that I didn't feel like having any breakfast, having chain-smoked throughout the night. They thereupon left for the restaurant without me, but Abou El Gheit soon returned with a small tray on which were cheese sandwiches, a cup of tea, an orange and a banana! I was still in bed and thanked him. He, however, stood by me without a word. When I asked him what was wrong, he answered: "Excuse me, Mohamed Bey. You're my boss and my minister, but I feel, young as I am, what is going on inside you. Please don't torture yourself unnecessarily. Everybody knows and appreciates your sincerity and all you have done, and nobody can ever blame you for anything. . .".

"Thank you, Ahmed. Don't worry about me. I know what I have to do. Go and finish your breakfast."

Leaving him standing there, I went into the bathroom to wash my face. . .

At eleven I proceeded to President Sadat's bungalow, where I found him sitting on the terrace with Dr Boutros Ghali and Dr Ashraf Ghorbal. I joined them and we talked about various matters. I was anxious to see them go so I could have a word with the President in private before anything else cropped up, so I went into Sadat's living-room, which opened onto the terrace. Sadat had his back to me and I signalled to Ashraf to take Boutros Ghali and leave. I then returned to my seat and some moments later Ashraf stood up and took his leave with Boutros Ghali. I moved my chair closer to Sadat and said quietly: "I want to have a talk with you, not as a Foreign Minister speaking to the President of the Republic, but as a friend and a younger brother. We were together in prison some thirty years ago, and you know my loyalty to both yourself and the truth. I don't want you to embark on something you might later regret." Sadat replied quietly: "You know that you and I can speak without formality, so tell me what you have to say straight out." The following exchange thereupon took place:

Mohamed Ibrahim Kamel: "I have read the project presented to you yesterday by President Carter on the framework for peace, and have concluded that it is extremely unlikely to result in the comprehensive peace at which you are aiming, whose broad lines you so righteously and clearly defined in your speech to the Knesset when you visited Jerusalem. The American project leads to a separate peace between Egypt and Israel which would be completely independent of what

Camp David

might happen in the West Bank and Gaza. There is no link between the two guaranteeing a convenient solution to the problem of Sinai and that of the Palestinians, which is the basic problem. This means there will be a peace treaty between Egypt and Israel while the West Bank and Gaza remain in the possession and under the domination of Israel. The latter will then proceed to implement its schemes for the final annexation of those territories.

"The American project reflects Begin's philosophy on autonomy with regard to the West Bank and Gaza and meets his demand for the suspension of sovereignty over those territories. It has been deliberately formulated in a vague and confusing manner and is full of gaps, this will make it impossible for us to achieve our aim of Israeli withdrawal from the territories and the exercise by the Palestinian people of its right to self-determination. Israeli negotiations and evasions on this issue could go on for decades, whereas we know for certain that all Israel needs is a few years in order to effectively bring the land under its control. The United States scheme gives Israel the right to veto any step or measure it might consider as an impediment to its clear objective – that of annexation of these territories. And whatever the Egyptian side, the Jordanian side and the Palestinian autonomy authority might agree on would not be implemented, since the project makes this conditional on unanimous agreement, including, by definition, Israel's. With regard to this, two important points should be observed, the first being that we have no mandate from the representatives of the Palestinian people – that is their problem – or from the Arab states whom, one and all, share the responsibility for solving the Palestinian problem, to approve and sign a settlement to this problem. Neither the provisions nor the formulation of the American plan will induce Jordan, under any circumstances, to participate during the transitional period. Neither can it expect to win approval in any other Arab state, let alone the PLO.

"The second point is that the Israeli occupation of the West Bank and Gaza will remain an illegal occupation of other people's soil and will be entirely founded on aggression and brute force and, accordingly, will not confer any rights on Israel, however long such a situation may last. Yet the American project attempts to invest this occupation – at least for the five-year transitional period – with an appearance of legitimacy in the form of token participation by Egypt, Jordan and the Palestinians [the Administrative Council which will exercise self-rule]. True, this would only be a tarnished semblance of legitimacy, since we have no mandate from the people most concerned. However, you know how all-powerful Israeli propaganda is. It will make out that the presence of Israel and its forces is

A Last Attempt Before Resigning

supported by a legal instrument and an agreement signed by Egypt, the most important Arab state, to which Jordan is invited to adhere. It will no longer appear as a mere illegitimate occupation supported solely by force, violence and aggression. The result of all this will be to confuse the issue, dissipate international support at state level and diminish the force of world public opinion which we have striven for so long to build up. In addition, pressure on Israel will be weakened.

"I therefore implore and adjure you to refuse to sign such a ruinous agreement."

President Sadat: "You know nothing of the Arabs. I know them only too well. If they are left to themselves, they will never solve the problems, and Israeli occupation will be perpetuated. Israel will end by engulfing the occupied Arab territories, with the Arabs not lifting a finger to stop them, contenting themselves with bluster and empty slogans, as they have done from the very beginning. They will never agree on anything."

Kamel: "I don't agree with you. What you say is not entirely true. The Arabs closed ranks at your own behest, standing behind you and achieving greater solidarity by uniting militarily, politically and economically in the 1973 October War and later. That this is so is an established fact that cannot be denied. It was Kissinger's arrival in the area and the signing of the second Disengagement Agreement between Egypt and Israel that sowed anew the seeds of dissension and division in the Arab world. Now that American impotence and its abandonment of the search for a just and comprehensive peace is clear, do you not see that you should go back to the Arabs again? Let us labour with them to restore the solidarity which was as strong as adamant... And this time our cause will not involve war but a peaceful solution as laid down by the Rabat Summit Conference decisions. You can return to them with the great asset of international support and a fuller awareness of the justice of the Arab cause, thanks to your initiative. The differences will be dissipated like a summer cloud, and the Arab states will rally around you for peace as they had before in war. This is Egypt's responsibility as the leading Arab state. The Saudis, the Jordanians and ourselves understand one another and we have effectively agreed with them on this strategy. They are now only waiting for a sign from us to begin their good offices. Go back to the Arabs with a renewed initiative, as you did with Israel. You can then return to Israel again as the proponent of a new, comprehensive Arab initiative, on a basis similar to that defined in your previous initiative. This time, though, it will be backed by the full weight of the vast Arab potential. And this time, Israel will be unable to abort it, nor will America again succeed in diverting it from its proper course."

Sadat (after a moment of silence): "The autonomy project will lead to the abolition of the Israeli military government in the West Bank and Gaza and will put an end to the suffering of the Palestinians. President Carter has insisted on adding the adjective 'full' to the words 'autonomy', despite strong opposition by Begin, so the powers of the autonomy authority will be fully comprehensive, save for such things as security. The Palestinians will not be alone. They will have Egypt and Jordan with them during the period of transition. Were the Palestinians to disapprove of the solution to end the transitional period, they would have the right to veto it, because they will vote on this solution. President Carter has told me that the language and formulation of the project may be vague, but this is unimportant. What matters is that he is going to be with us as a full partner in the negotiations on self-rule. President Carter has affirmed to me that when he is re-elected for another term, he will be in a very strong position and will be able to put pressure on Israel. And he will then be in a position to correct any flaws and shortcomings in the language and formulation which he is at present unable to improve in view of Begin's rigidity and his [Carter's] desire to ensure that the Conference does not end in failure and so lead to the termination of the peace process between Egypt and Israel and a resuscitation of conditions which might result in the eruption of a new war. Carter has again assured me that he feels a moral obligation to do something for the Palestinians, and that he will be in a position to do this when he is re-elected."

Kamel: "We are only deceiving ourselves if we say this project will end in the realization of a just solution of the Palestinian cause, for Israel will use it as an instrument and a source of support to liquidate the issue in accordance with its expansionist intentions. This is the unanimous opinion of all the advisers in our delegation. Why do you think Begin is fighting so hard and is scrutinizing every word in the project? He is doing so because once we have signed the project it will become the basis for future negotiations. Then neither Carter nor anyone else will be able to go beyond the context of the provisions and formulations. Then again, how do we know that Carter will be re-elected for another term and thereby fulfil his promises?"

Sadat: "No, no, President Carter has told me that if the Camp David Conference succeeds in reaching agreement on the framework for a comprehensive peace, he will be certain to achieve an easy victory in the forthcoming elections. And I am confident he will carry out his promise to me because he is a man of principle."

Kamel: "The agreements – in accordance with the American project – will not lead to a comprehensive solution but to a separate peace between Egypt and Israel. The West Bank, Gaza and the Golan will remain under the Israeli occupation. This will lead to disastrous results, the most damaging being Egypt's isolation from the Arab world and the freeing of Israel's hands in the area. Why do you not insist on what you have always called for, namely that there should be a link between withdrawal from Sinai and withdrawal from the West Bank and Gaza, so that they may proceed in parallel? Each step in Sinai will be made conditional on an equivalent step in the West Bank and Gaza."

Sadat: "There you are, repeating, like a parrot, just what the Soviet Union is saying with regard to a separate settlement. How can there be a separate agreement, when I am committed in the process of self-rule in the West Bank and Gaza during the five-year transitional period and a solution to the Palestinian question in all its aspects? And what sense is there in keeping Sinai under Israeli domination until a solution is reached to the Palestinian problem so that Israel may cover it with new settlements with every day that passes? Wouldn't that be foolish? You're talking like this because you know nothing of the internal situation in Egypt. Nasser left me a heritage encumbered with worries and problems. Our economic and social conditions are extremely bad and the public utilities are in a state of collapse. Egypt will be unable to deal with the deteriorating situation unless it achieves peace and devotes all its resources to development. Egypt will then be in a stronger position to assist the Palestinians in solving their problems."

Kamel: "This is what your initiative is based on, since it focused on a comprehensive solution. Were the matter confined to the restitution of Sinai and the establishment of peace between Egypt and Israel, to the exclusion of all else, there would have been no call for such diversions and evasions. Menahim Begin would have rushed to Cairo at a signal from you to sign such an agreement and restore Sinai to Egypt, and would have felt greatly relieved. He would then have returned to Israel satisfied, not to say delighted. I do not pretend to know much about Egypt's internal problems: you are the President and you are better informed. If, however, the situation is such as you have described, why do you wish to make it appear that you are seeking a just and lasting solution to the Arab-Israeli dispute? By doing so you are giving Israel a handle which will allow it to seize the West Bank and Gaza and shelve the Palestinian problem under the guise of an honourable and just solution to that self-same problem.

"I am still of the opinion that you should not sign anything. Rather, you should go back to the Arabs and work with them in a united front as I have previously indicated. However, if you consider that our internal conditions are such that we are compelled to reach an immediate interim solution, then announce that openly. You could issue a communiqué to the effect that Egypt had borne the brunt of human, financial and economic sacrifices as a result of its confrontation of Israeli aggression on the Arab states in four wars. It had exhausted all its efforts, energy and power. Say that its economic and social conditions have deteriorated to such a degree that it cannot continue to live in a state of no war-no peace, and that Egypt has therefore decided to conclude an interim agreement with Israel, thereby ending the state of war with Israel. Egypt will, together with the other Arab states and the international community, pursue its peaceful efforts to secure an Israeli withdrawal from all the occupied Arab territories and for the establishment of a just and comprehensive peace in the area. . ."

Sadat (interrupting): "What's the matter? Do you want the Soviet Union, Hafiz El Assad and Gadaffi to gloat over me? Do you want them to say that what they had claimed from the start of my initiative was true? That I was aiming at a separate agreement all along?"

Kamel: "If you sign the agreement on the basis of the American project, it will, to all intents and purposes, be a separate agreement. You won't be able to deceive anybody, and it is better, and more honourable, to say so openly rather than hide behind the self-rule charade as set forth in the project."

Sadat: "I am following a long-range strategy which will end in a comprehensive solution in the Middle East. President Carter will be with us and Saudi Arabia and King Hussein will join us."

Kamel: "If you sign such an agreement, Carter will not be able to do anything, and it will attract neither Saudi Arabia nor Jordan under any circumstances. I beseech you, once more, to reconsider the matter and refrain from signing. Go back to Egypt and let us consult with the Arab states on our next step."

Sadat: "No, I know what I'm doing and will go through with my inititive to the very end."

Kamel: "Very well, then. Please accept my resignation."

Sadat: "I was aware from the beginning that these twists and turns were leading up to that!"

Kamel: "Nothing of the sort! I have tried to convince you of my views. I have failed, so this is the only way out for me. I cannot associate myself with what to me appears wrong and dangerous. And I can deceive neither you nor myself and my conscience. I have to live with it night and day."

Sadat: "If it will be of any relief to you, then I accept it. All I ask of you is that it should be kept strictly between us for the time being and until we are back in Egypt."

Kamel: "I'll keep it to myself – I don't want to embarrass you."

Sadat: "We agree, then. Calm down and relax. Everything will come all right in the end."

A Last Attempt Before Resigning

I left Sadat with a heavy heart, overwhelmed with grief and sorrow. However, I felt considerably calmer and at peace with myself.

Ashraf Ghorbal met me and wanted to know what had transpired between Sadat and myself. I replied that I had had a discussion with him on the danger of the American project, but I could see he was not convinced.

When I went into the bedroom with Boutros Ghali, he said to me: "You are in an unusual state this evening. You seem relaxed and happy. What has happened between you and the President?" To which I replied, smilingly: "That is a secret between us!" But he persisted: "Do tell me!"

I thereupon promised him: "I'll do that the moment we reach Cairo!"

Chapter Forty One

The Signing of the Accords
Sunday 17 September 1978

On the thirteenth day of the Camp David Conference, Sunday 17 September, I was leaving the restaurant after breakfast when I became aware of unusual activity in the Festival Hall adjoining the restaurant. Driven by curiosity I entered the Hall. A great change had taken place there – the comfortable furniture had been removed and at the end of the chamber was a platform on which was a long table with seats for three. On the wall hung three big flags: Egyptian, American and Israeli. In front of the table a group of men were placing chairs in rows.

And it came to me suddenly that this was the day President Carter had fixed for the signing of the Accords. They were getting the Hall ready for the signing ceremony, which could take place at any time that day. I had a sudden feeling of panic, for I felt that I faced a problem I had not previously considered. I had promised Sadat not to make my resignation public; nevertheless, I did not have the least intention of taking part in the ceremony for the signing of the Accords, to which I was totally opposed. But how was the absence of the Egyptian Foreign Minister on such an occasion to be justified? Were we outside this accursed camp, I would have some excuse or other to justify my absence. However, trapped as I was, how was I to do so?

I returned to my bungalow worried and preoccupied. A moment later Ambassador Herman Eilts came in to inform us that the signing ceremony was to take place that afternoon in the Festival Hall. As he was leaving the bungalow, I suddenly called on him to wait for me. As we went out together, I said, "I have a problem!" "What is it?" he wanted to know. "I have resigned," I rejoined. Eilts shot back: "Good God, what happened?" "You can guess what happened because I made it clear several months ago that I would do so unless we reached an acceptable agreement." Eilts replied that this was true and that he understood my position. To this I replied: "The problem is not my resignation, but rather that I have promised Sadat not to announce it at present. And I insist on not attending the signing ceremony. I don't know what to do!" Eilts said: "Let me think it over," and as he was

The Signing of the Accords

leaving, I once again addressed him, saying: "Herman, I hope this will go no further." At this he told me not to worry, and took his departure.

An hour later, Eilts rang me to say he had some better news, and when I asked him what this was, he informed me that it had been decided that the signing ceremony was to take place not at Camp David, but in Washington.

I went out for a walk with Ahmed Maher and related to him in detail the talk I had had with Sadat the day before, and concluded by saying: "I cannot understand that man nor what he wants." Maher admitted that this was a difficult question, but said he thought President Carter had let him down. Sadat had pinned all his hopes on him and had been over-eager to believe his honeyed promises.

Upon our return, I was informed that President Sadat had asked for me. Accordingly, I went to his bungalow and found him on the terrace with Hassan El Tohamy, Hassan Kamel, Boutros Ghali, Ashraf Ghorbal and Ussama El Baz. When I entered he stood up to greet me as warmly as if he had not seen me for a long while. He invited me to sit beside him. It seemed to me that the atmosphere was as gloomy as a funeral, with conversation occurring only at long intervals. The accord was not directly mentioned, nor was its impending signature, and I sensed that everyone present, Sadat included, felt that a great calamity was hanging over them, which would give them very little cause for satisfaction. For my part, I was reduced to silence, and felt terribly depressed. Then someone – I do not now recall who – said that what would provoke the opposition of the Palestinians was the fact that the expression "self-determination" was vaguely and indistinctly formulated – or words to that effect. This caused President Sadat to reply: "It was not possible to do otherwise. President Carter confided to me that this phrase would, in his words, 'cost me my job'."

At this I could no longer hold my tongue, and burst out loudly and agitatedly: "And is this the President of the most powerful state in the world? Is this the saint who claims that the defence of human rights, principles and values is the corner-stone of his policy? Is he willing to sacrifice the fate of a whole people in order just to remain President of the United States for eight years rather than four? If so, he is, indeed, an insignificant and despicable creature."

A dead silence reigned in the room, as they all waited to hear Sadat's answer. I am sure that he took my remarks very much amiss. He felt that they were not directed exclusively at Carter, but at himself as well. In the event, what apparently saved the occasion was the fact that he was intent on keeping my resignation secret until the end of the festivities, for after a while he laughed boisterously and dramatically. Then, in a deep, booming voice, laying his hand on my shoulder: "You are no politician, Mohamed!" "If this is politics," I replied "then it is an honour for me not to be a politician!"

Sadat then got to his feet and everybody left.

Begin was not satisfied with all the concessions he had obtained, and it was doubtful if anything could satisfy Mr Begin. Even in the last hours preceding the signing, he never tired of besieging President Carter, pressing him for one concession after another. And since Carter was so set for the agreement to be signed on that very day, he had no alternative but to seek such concessions from Sadat.

Every hour brought reports of further concessions. Begin insisted on deletion of all reference to "the non-admissibility of acquiring territory by force", telling Carter that "if he had to sign or cut off his two hands he still would not sign it." This resulted in the deletion of the reference to this cardinal principle of Resolution 242. It was only with the greatest difficulty that Ussama El Baz was able to add in the reference to Resolution 242 the phrase "in all its parts" to keep the balance. In return for the word "full" that Carter had added to the phrase "autonomy", Begin insisted on inserting the phrase "administrative council" between brackets before the phrase "the self governing authority" so as to minimize its jurisdiction to administrative questions to the exclusion of the legislative and judicial. The reference to the United Nations resolutions on the problem of the refugees was also deleted. These resolutions stipulate the right of refugees to return and to compensation.

Begin left no paragraph, provision or word which would carry any right or semblance of a right for the Palestinians without trying to void it of any content.

It is not my intention to list all the amendments which were introduced on Israel's insistence at the eleventh hour. However, President Carter's most unforgivable concession to the Israelis was the deletion of the provision on the freeze on settlements in the West Bank and Gaza during the five-year transitional period. This was a fundamental issue on which both the Egyptians and Americans held very strong views. The freeze on settlements during that period was in fact the only guarantee to prevent further deterioration of the situation in the West Bank and Gaza. The provision that no settlements were to be established or the existing ones expanded was all the more necessary since the United States project gave Israel a major role in the supervision of the self-governing authority as well as the right to maintain its occupation forces in the West Bank and Gaza during and after the transitional period with the suspension of the sovereignty issue over the West Bank and Gaza until the end of the transitional period. Colonial settlement was the tool to which Israel would resort for swallowing up the land piecemeal, by changing the demographic composition of the territories.

As to the framework for peace between Egypt and Israel, this was, in its turn, subject to numerous amendments. The worst of all, as far as I was concerned, lay in the fact that it consecrated Egypt's estrangement from the Palestinian cause. It ruled out any idea of a link between Israeli withdrawal from Sinai and the settlement of the Palestinian problem. Equally as bad was that full peace between Egypt and Israel was not made dependent on complete Israeli withdrawal from Sinai itself. A provision was added to the effect that, following the Israeli partial withdrawal to the Arish-Ras Mohamed line, to take place after the signing of the Peace Treaty within a period ranging from three to nine months, normal relations between Egypt and Israel would be established. Such relations comprehend diplomatic, economic and cultural relations, termination of the economic boycott, and so on and so forth. All this would take place while a part of Sinai was still under occupation! The Israeli flag would be flying over the territory, and its army of occupation, arms, depots and airports, would be bustling with activity. Israeli settlers would be building their colonies in Yamit, Rafah and other places and spending their holidays on the beaches of Sharm El Sheikh in gay abandon!

The restitution of Arab Jerusalem was, naturally, a top priority with us. The Egyptian side had submitted several formulae, of which the common denominator was the restitution of Arab Jerusalem in accordance with the principle of the non-admissibility of acquiring land by force. The Egyptian formulae also stipulated the non-division of the city and the guarantee of free access for all persons to the Holy Places without discrimination. However, Israel naturally rejected all such formulae.

As for the American side, its projects on Jerusalem included vague and ambiguous formulae concentrating on free access, freedom of worship and the administration of holy religious places by representatives of the respective religions. None of them, however, referred either to sovereignty over Jerusalem or to its final status. We therefore rejected such formulae in our turn.

Finally, Presidents Carter and Sadat agreed to delete all reference to Jerusalem in the agreement: the Jerusalem issue would be dealt with through letters exchanged between Presidents Sadat and Carter on the one hand, and President Carter and Prime Minister Begin on the other, each defining his position of Jerusalem in the letter. President Sadat wrote a letter indicating that Arab Jerusalem was an integral part of the West Bank and should be subject to Arab sovereignty. President Carter answered by letter acknowledging receipt of Sadat's missive, indicating that he would send a copy to Prime Minister Begin for reference purposes. Carter, in his letter, went on to say that the American position on Jerusalem was that expressed by Ambassador Goldberg in his speech to the UN General Assembly on 14 July 1967, and by Mr Yost in the Security Council on 1 July 1969. (The American position does not recognize the Israeli annexation of Jerusalem.) However, Begin categorically rejected such a clear statement of the American position but went along the aforementioned indirect approach.

Menahim Begin addressed a letter to President Carter indicating that on 28 July 1967, the Israeli Knesset had promulagated a law vesting the Israeli government with legislative and administrative powers over any part of the land of Eretz Israel – Greater Israel, i.e. Palestine – and that, in accordance

Camp David

with this law, the Israeli government had decreed in July 1967 that the city of Jerusalem was the unified, indivisible capital of the State of Israel. President Carter answered saying he would send a copy of the letter to President Sadat and that the American stand on Jerusalem was as previously indicated.

None of the foregoing calls for comment – the letters follow close upon each other like a merry-go-round or a children's see-saw, where the wooden horses never catch up and the see-saw is never at rest! I shall content myself with what Moshe Dayan says in his book:

> Since the American and Egyptian letters were not of an operational character, they did not commit Israel to withdrawing from this territory [Jerusalem].

Consequently, Israel was unconcerned about such letters and did not oppose their exchange.

I had no information as to what went on between Carter, Sadat and Begin during those final hours. Ambassador Nabil El Araby, the Director of the Legal Department, came to see me when he heard of the letters exchanged on Jerusalem. He was greatly disturbed, and requested with insistence that I go immediately to Sadat to inform him that the letters were of no legal or political value and would not solve the question. I could not tell Araby that I had resigned, so I suggested he should go himself and put to the President the legal point of view. I added that he was better qualified to do so than myself. Araby's response to this was that we should go together "when [he added] I shall explain the legal aspect". I replied that I was tired and again requested him to go alone. Half an hour later he was back and appeared agitated. He then told me the following story.

He had been to President Sadat's bungalow and had found Begin there. The purpose of Begin's visit was to congratulate the President on having finally reached a peace agreement. He (Araby) had waited until Begin had left, and had then gone in to the President. Sadat had asked him what he wanted, and Araby had replied that he wished to give him a legal opinion on the letters exchanged on Jerusalem. Sadat then said: "Go ahead and explain." When Araby was through, the President asked him quietly and courteously whether there was anything else he wished to put before him?

When Araby had replied in the negative, Sadat proceeded: "Then listen to what I have to say: I heard you out without interrupting you, so nobody can claim that, as is rumoured of me, that I neither listen nor read! I would like you to know, though, that what you have just been saying has gone into one ear and out of the other! You people in the Foreign Ministry are under the impression that you understand politics. In reality, however, you understand absolutely nothing. Henceforth I shall not pay the least attention to either your words or your memos. I am a man whose actions are governed by a higher strategy which you are incapable of either perceiving or understand-

The Signing of the Accords

ing. I do not need your insignificant and misleading reports. And now your Minister, Mohamed Kamel, insults President Carter in my very presence! Does he not realize that President Carter is my trump card for the establishment of a comprehensive peace?"

The President was silent for a moment, then he said: "Are you not aware that your relative, Mohamed Hassanein Heikal, attacks me in all places and is plotting to topple the regime? I lend not the slightest importance to all his lies and absurdities, which are motivated by pure malice and black rancour. However, I shall not overlook this fact and I shall eventually have his head. Now be so good as to leave and do not come back to waste my time with futile legal argument!"

Nabil El Araby spoke hurriedly as he described what had transpired between himself and the President. His nerves were still on edge, for what he had just heard from the President of the Republic had appalled him.

When he had finished, I had a fit of laughter which lasted for sometime, for the worst misfortune is that which provokes laughter. Nabil looked at me in astonishment, but was soon laughing with me!

At around six in the afternoon Camp David was hit by a sudden thunderstorm and the flood-gates of Heaven opened: the rain pelted down, and the scene was lit fitfully by flashes of lightning. I told my colleagues in the bungalow that even the Heavens did not approve of what was about to take place that day!

I was engaged in packing my suitcase to leave for Washington, when I received a phone call from Ambassador Eilts, who told me to expect shortly a call from Secretary of State Vance, who wished to see me. I thanked him, although I failed to understand why it was necessary for Eilts to advise me that Vance desired to contact me! However, Eilts added: "He knows, Mohamed!" I knew he meant the resignation, and accordingly shot back: "You promised not to tell anybody." Eilts assured me he had told Vance nothing. "Then who did?" I queried in astonishment. His reply was that he could not tell me over the phone! This perplexed me still further, as I could think of no one who could have informed him. Some minutes later, though, Vance rang through to ask me if I would like to drop in for a drink and a talk. "I would with pleasure," I replied, "but the storm is at its height." His response was that it would soon be over and he would be awaiting me.

The storm did, in fact, abate soon afterwards, and I went out, carrying an umbrella to shield me from the slight drizzle that was still falling. Ahmed Maher accompanied me to the door of Vance's bungalow and left me. When I entered, Vance greeted me with a friendly smile and asked me to be seated. A moment later Mondale – who shared the bungalow with Vance – came out of the room carrying a suitcase. Shaking hands with us, he informed us he was returning to Washington immediately to supervise the arrangements for the signing of the Accords in the White House before the delegations arrived.

Camp David

After he had departed, Vance enquired what I should like to drink. Then he stood up, prepared two drinks, came back with them and said: "Let's drink to your health!" And after a little while he went on: "President Sadat told me you had resigned this afternoon, and I am very sorry to hear it. However, I appreciate and understand your position. We are, as you know, a democratic country, and freedom of thought is sacred to us. President Carter was sorry too, for he had great respect for you. Sadat himself has the highest opinion of you, and has spoken to us of your long-standing association with him. Speaking for myself, please permit me to affirm to you that I shall always look back on our mutual relationship with pleasure. You were always honest, sober and straightforward, and I hope we shall continue to be friends".

I thanked Vance and told him I also had high regard for him. He asked me what I particularly objected to in the agreement, and I replied that I was opposed to its whole philosophy. It was no more then a spruced-up version of Begin's autonomy proposal, and I proceeded to tell him that I was greatly disappointed in the United States, to whom we looked up to as the upholder of President Wilson's principles. And I was even more disappointed in President Carter, who had upheld human rights. "You have," I continued "renounced your declared positions on the Arab-Israeli dispute and have abjured recognized international principles. You have drafted your project in accordance with whatever was accepted or rejected by Begin. You have exerted pressure on Sadat alone. Now you have come up with this agreement, which will only aggravate the situation in the Middle East – God knows how complex it is already. This agreement, instead of bringing about peace, will perpetuate chaos, turmoil and instability.

"You will live to regret this agreement, which will weaken Sadat and may even topple him. It will affect your position in the moderate Arab states, who are your friends, while all the Arab peoples will resent you. As for Egypt, it will be isolated in the area. No Arab will accept this agreement, which will remain unimplemented. All that will happen is that it will allow Begin a free hand in the West Bank and Gaza with a view to their annexation. Far from providing a solution to the Arab-Israeli dispute, the agreement will only add fuel to the fire."

To this Vance replied: "President Carter rang up King Hussein today, and has invited him to visit him. The President wanted to speak to Prince Fahd, but the latter's limited command of English would have made it difficult for them to have understood one another. Carter has therefore charged our Ambassador in Jeddah to address to him an invitation to pay him a visit." I replied: "They will not come, and I have already told President Carter so."

Vance countered: "What do you think we can do now to help President Sadat?" I replied: "It's too late for that – you missed the opportunity to do so when you surrendered to Begin's pressures. This agreement will always be a black spot for you and Sadat." Vance acknowledged that the agreement was

The Signing of the Accords

not entirely fair: "However, it's a step forward and President Carter will seek to redress the shortcomings during the autonomy talks. He feels a strong obligation to do something for the Palestinian people and believes he will be in a position to do so once he is re-elected." He then again asked me what they could do to help Egypt, and I replied: "About the only thing you can do is to offer us economic and financial assistance." He replied: "I have already spoken to the Secretary for Agriculture to increase the amount of wheat and corn we have been providing." I replied that it was not a question of flour or corn: "Egypt needs billions of dollars for the construction of public utilities, which are in a state of collapse, to be able to stand on its feet. But will Israel allow you to do this?"

As it was nearing 8.30, I shook hands with Vance and left. The storm had completely abated, and when I reached the bungalow all our luggage had been readied for transportation. I perused a copy of the itinerary. It included the precise time of the departure of each helicopter and the names of the passengers making up the members of the delegations. It had been decided that the three leaders would board the same craft, which would be the last to leave. Arrival time was indicated. Here again there cropped up the problem of my non-attendance at the signing ceremonies. The programme indicated that the helicopters would land inside the gardens of the White House. Once again, I felt trapped. I pinned my hope on Herman Eilts, whose name was on the passenger list of the helicopter I was about to board.

My helicopter was due to take off at precisely 9.15, and its passengers were being invited to assemble at the helipad. Hassan Kamel happened to be walking with me, and I felt it would be appropriate to inform him of my resignation, since it would in any case be common knowledge within the hour. He was thunderstruck, and kept repeating: "This is incredible." I replied that there was nothing else I could do, and when the craft had taken off, I again raised the problem with Eilts. "Are you sure," he asked me, "you do not want to attend the signing ceremony?" "Oh, absolutely," I replied. Eilts then assured me that "he would do what he could".

After our helicopter had touched down on the White House helipad we walked towards the cars which were waiting for us. I was to ride in car number one, with Hassan Kamel, El Tohamy, and Mr Amr Hamdy, the security officer who accompanied me. When I got to the car, however, I stood motionless before it, refusing to go in! I had lost Eilts in the crowd, but then I perceived him walking quickly towards me, and got in. It soon appeared, however, that he was telling the driver of his vehicle that he was not travelling with him.

El Tohamy began chattering away about Jerusalem, but I kept silent. The car soon stopped before the entrance of the East Room, guarded by a group of American soldiers. The chandeliers at the entrance shed their light around as Tohamy and Hassan Kamel got out. The latter called through the opened door: "Come on, Mohamed!", but I replied: "No, I'm not going!"

Camp David

At this Tohamy exclaimed: "Why, what's the matter?" During this exchange, the cars following us were fast approaching, while ours still stood before the entrance. Tohamy ejaculated: "It is inconceivable that the Foreign Minister should not attend the signing ceremony!" I promptly shot back: "I shall not attend, so there is no point in insisting and wasting time."

Hassan Kamel closed the car door. Just then, Herman Eilts left the car, opened the door on my side, shook hands with me and said: "Good luck, Mohamed"! He followed this with instructions to the driver to take the Foreign Minister to the Madison Hotel. The car moved slowly away, but soon stopped again at one of the iron gates. A feeling of anxiety took hold of me again, but then the guard opened the gate with a military salute, and the car moved on into the streets of Washington, passing by Capitol Hill and the Egyptian Obelisk before, finally, drawing up at my hotel. I went up to my suite.

The first thing I did was to take a hot shower, after which I donned my pyjamas and asked Amr Hamdy to order dinner to be sent up to our room. I switched on the TV set, which was just then showing the arrival of the three leaders at the East Hall. They were walking towards the dais on which was placed the table at which the accords were to be signed. Behind the table were the Egyptian and Israeli flags, with the American flag between them. The three leaders stood at the table to resounding applause. The members of the delegations to Camp David, a group of Congressmen and other public figures were invited to attend the ceremony. The television camera panned the guests, stopping for an instant at an empty seat in the first row which I had been expected to occupy. It then moved back to the three leaders.

The ceremony began with a speech by President Carter. He paid tribute to President Sadat and Prime Minister Begin to whom belonged the credit for the success of the Camp David Conference. It was the sincerity of their intentions and their determination to achieve peace which made that possible he said. Carter then spoke of the content of the agreement on the framework for peace in the Middle East and then of the agreement on the framework for peace between Egypt and Israel, which were to be signed that evening.

President Sadat followed President Carter to the rostrum. He expressed his thanks and gratitude to President Carter for the time and the courageous efforts he had devoted to the achievement of peace, saying: "You made a commitment to be a full partner in the peace process. I am happy to say that you have honoured your commitment."

Sadat ended by calling upon Carter to continue his efforts so that the peace process might be completed and thereby strengthen the belief of the Palestinian people in the reality of peace.

He was followed by Begin, who said: "The Camp David conference should be renamed. It was the Jimmy Carter Conference . . . President

The Signing of the Accords

[Carter] worked, as far as my knowledge of history is concerned, I think that he worked harder than our forefathers did in Egypt, building the pyramids."

This was greeted with general laughter and resounding applause. There was absolutely no doubt in my mind – in view of my "Beginian" experience – that this was no casual remark, but was quite deliberate and premeditated.

Begin went on to talk of the course the negotiations had taken at Camp David and of the difficult moments it had faced, taking full advantage of the situation to strike impertinently at Sadat as he told them: "We had some difficult moments, as usually there are some crises in negotiations; as usually, somebody would like to pick up and go home."

Laughter broke out once again, and I felt pity for Sadat.

Begin's speech included a word of thanks to Carter's assistants – especially Cyrus Vance – for their help during the conference. He then went on to thank his own aides, mentioning them by name. He likewise thanked the members of the Egyptian delegation, who had worked assiduously to bring about what they were all celebrating at the moment, particularly Deputy Premier Hassan El Tohamy.

Again the TV camera zoomed in on that empty seat. Thereupon President Carter announced that it was time to sign the Accords. When the signing was over, the three leaders stood up and embraced one another. I saw President Sadat embrace Menahim Begin warmly and enthusiastically. I privately wondered how one could do so to a person whom one had, only a few days before, described as "the meanest and lowest of enemies"!

The instant the ceremonies were over, the telephone rang in my room. Amr Hamdy came forward to tell me it was Reuter's correspondent. I said to tell I was not in. Hamdy had barely put down the receiver, however, when the phone rang again! This time, the speaker was the correspondent of another news agency. And the phone kept on ringing, with Amr continuously busy picking the receiver up and putting it down. I guessed that the absence of the Egyptian Foreign Minister from the signing ceremonies had been noted, and accordingly I rang Reception and asked them not to put any more calls through to my room.

Many members of our Embassy in Washington and our delegation in New York visited me. At 1 a.m. Hassan Kamel, Boutros Ghali, Tohamy, Ashraf Ghorbal, Lieutenant-General Mohamed El Mahy, Chief Adjutant to the President, who had remained in Washington during the Camp David Conference, arrrived. They all expressed their friendly feelings towards me. Ashraf Ghorbal told me that, following the ceremonies to mark the signing of the two Camp David Accords, the President had gone to the Egyptian Embassy, for it had been decided that he should stay there for security reasons. He had met with the editors-in-chief of the Egyptian press, and had pointed out to them what he had achieved at Camp David and had indicated the guidelines they were to follow in the presentation of the Accords to the public. When he was through, the editors-in-chief enquired about my non-attending at the signing ceremonies, for they had heard rumours of my resignation as Foreign Minister. Sadat replied that the rumours were true, but requested them not to publish the news without his permission. He told them my resignation was due to a difference of opinion, and that I was his friend and like a son to him. He thus made it plain to them that he did not want anybody to write ill of me.

I felt relieved when I learned that news of my resignation had leaked out. One problem, however, still gave me cause for concern, namely how I was to return to Egypt without being tied to President Sadat's programme on his way back from the United States. I decided, therefore, to seek him out and broach the subject with him.

At 10.a.m. the following day I proceeded to the Embassy. Sadat was with his friend, Henry Kissinger, and when the latter had left I went into the living-room of the Embassy. Sadat seemed surprised to see me, and asked: "Is anything wrong, Mohamed?" I replied: "Yes, there is: Vance came to see me yesterday, before we left Camp David. He told me you had informed him of my resignation despite the fact that you yourself had asked me to keep it secret. I am aware that you met with the editors-in-chief of the Egyptian press yesterday, and that you confirmed the news of my resignation, asking them not to publish it. And I believe you have an interview with telecaster Barbara Walters in half an hour's time. She will certainly enquire about my resignation. What are you going to tell her?"

After a moment's silence, Sadat replied: "I shall tell her that we live in a democratic country and that you are entitled to express your views and resign without being put away in a detention camp!" I thanked him, and was about to bring up the subject of my return to Egypt alone, when he asked: "What do you intend do now?" "Nothing," I said. "I shall live quiely with my family and the children who were not with me for the past ten years while I was living abroad. They are older now and I want to enjoy being with them before each of them goes his own way." "Choose any Embassy," Sadat replied, but I told him I did not want to be an Ambassador. "I have had my fill of that," I added.

To this Sadat retorded: "And be unemployed, without a job! Pick any Embassy now." I explained: "How can you imagine I could be appointed an Ambassador to implement a policy of which I do not approve? I would not dream of doing so under any circumstances!" Sadat replied angrily: "You don't have to do anything in the Embassy, but relax, and spend your time strolling about like a tourist!" I again replied, "As I said before, the answer is no. I want to live with my children." "Fine," he returned irritably. "Stay with your children until you have had your fill of them. I shall be appointing you Ambassador in the Foreign Ministry anyway. And when you change your mind. I shall make you Ambassador in any Embassy you wish." "Have it your own way," I replied, "But as for me, I'm going to live in Egypt!"

Sadat returned no answer, and left me, quitting the living-room, and I was

The Signing of the Accords

still left without a solution to my one remaining problem: how to leave Washington and return, alone, to Egypt!

I made another attempt the following day, Tuesday 19 September, I told Amr to ascertain the President's appointments schedule. He did so, and was informed that Sadat was due to meet the Congress Foreign Affairs Committees that same morning. This was to be followed by a visit to President Carter in the White House. The President would then return to the Embassy for lunch. Amr then kept in touch with the President's movements through the presidential officers by telephone, passing the information on to me. Thus he told me that the President had left Capitol Hill after his meeting with Congress, and was at that moment on his way to the White House to visit President Carter. I promptly went down to the Embassy and waited for him.

He arrived some twenty minutes later, and when he came in at the Embassy door, I was ready for him. He shook hands with me and walked to the lift, with me at his side. As I followed him into the lift, he asked: "Is there anything wrong, Mohamed? I'm tired and want to go to bed." I said: "I'll not keep you longer than a couple of minutes." The lift stopped at the second floor, and he enquired: "What do you want?" "Your permission to leave for Egypt," I replied. "But didn't we agree that you should accompany me on my way back? We'll be stopping over for two days in Morocco to get some rest, and you'll have a good time." His insistence on my accompanying him was intended to show that our differences were not, after all, of a crucial nature, since I should be in his company, and that our relationship had not suffered. That, I rejoined, "was before anyone knew I had resigned. However, now that my resignation has been published by the press, and now that your interview with Barbara Walters – in which you confirmed the news – has been telecast, in what capacity shall I be travelling with you to Morocco?" He hesitated for a space, then said: "If you want my opinion, I advise you to accompany me." "No," I replied, "I'd rather go back now. My family must be concerned over my resignation." "Have it your own way, since you wish to go back. When will you be leaving?" "I shall try to leave this very day." "Then – Goodbye"!

The time was around 2.30 p.m. I immediately went to Mohamed Shaker's office in the Embassy and asked him to make the necessary arrangements for my departure that day. He said: "It's going to be diffficult, but I'll try anyway."

In the event, he succeeded in booking three seats on a TWA flight to Paris. The aircraft was to take off from New York International Airport at 7 p.m. The other two tickets were for Ahmed Maher and Amr Hamdy.

There remained the matter of reaching the airport in time to board the plane. We finally unearthed another plane that would get to New York twenty minutes before ours was due to take off. It was, however, going to land at La Guardia, and not at JFK, and the distance between the two could not be covered in under thirty minutes. Mohamed Shaker contacted the

Camp David

State Department, and they promised to make special arrangements to enable us to catch the home flight in time.

And, indeed, when we touched down at La Guardia, we found a police car waiting for us at the door of the aircraft. The car was preceded by a police officer on a motorcycle. We were hardly inside the car when it whisked away, with the motorcycle in front sounding an uninterrupted wail on its siren. On we sped, disregarding traffic signals and everything else! I was reminded of scenes in American movies of police pursuit, the sole difference being that we were in the car and the people outside were doing the watching!

The car halted on the tarmac at 7.15 p.m. The engines were already turning over as they awaited us on the instructions of the State Department. We went up into the aircraft, where the hostess showed us to our seats and asked us to fasten our seat belts. A minute later, the plane moved forward and rose into the air.

I let out a sigh of relief, and whispered: "A thousand thanks to God! Father, rest in peace!"

Appendix 1

Proposals Relative to Withdrawal From the West Bank and Gaza and Security Arrangements

1 The establishment of a just and lasting peace in the Middle East necessitates a just solution of the Palestinian question in all its aspects on the basis of the legitimate rights of the Palestinian people and taking into consideration the legitimate security concerns of all the parties.

2 In order to ensure a peaceful and orderly transfer of authority there shall be a transitional period not exceeding five years at the end of which the Palestinian people will be able to determine their own future.

3 Talks shall take place between Egypt, Jordan, Israel and representatives of the Palestinian people with the participation of the UN with a view to agreeing upon:

  a details of the transitional regime.
  b Timetable for the Israeli withdrawal.
  c Mutual security arrangements for all parties concerned during and following the transitional period.
  d Modalities for the implementation of relevant UN resolutions on Palestinian refugees.
  e Other issues considered appropriate by all parties.

4 Israel shall withdraw from the West Bank (including Jerusalem) and the Gaza Strip, occupied since June 1967. The Israeli withdrawal applies to the settlements established in the occupied territories.

5 The Israeli military government in the West Bank and the Gaza Strip shall be abolished at the outset of the transitional period. Supervision over the administration of the West Bank shall become the responsibility of Jordan and supervision over the administration of the Gaza Strip shall

Camp David

become the responsibility of Egypt. Jordan and Egypt shall carry out their responsibility in co-operation with freely elected representatives of the Palestinian people who shall exercise direct authority over the administration of the West Bank and Gaza. The UN shall supervise and facilitate the Israeli withdrawal and the restoration of Arab authority.

6 Egypt and Jordan shall guarantee that the security arrangements to be agreed upon will continue to be respected in the West Bank and Gaza.

Appendix 2

Framework for the Comprehensive Peace Settlement of the Middle East Problem

Following: The historic initiative of President SADAT which rekindled the hopes of all nations for a better future for mankind.

In view of the firm determination of the peoples of the Middle East, together with all peace-loving nations, to put an end to the unhappy past, spare this generation and the generations to come, the scourge of War and open a new chapter in their history ushering in an era of mutual respect and understanding.

Desirous to make the Middle East, the cradle of civilization and the birthplace of all Divine missions, a shining model for coexistence and co-operation among nations.

Determined to revive the great tradition of tolerance and mutual acceptance free from prejudice and discrimination.

Determined to conduct their relations in accordance with the provisions of the Charter of the United Nations and the accepted norms of international law and legitimacy.

Committed to adhere to the letter and spirit of the Universal Declaration of Human Rights.

Desirous to develop between them good-neighbourly relations in accordance with the Declaration of Principles of International Law Concerning Friendly Relations and Co-operation Among States in Accordance with the Charter of the United Nations.

Bearing in mind that the establishment of peace and good neighbourly relations should be founded upon legitimacy, justice, equality and respect for fundamental rights and that good neighbours should demonstrate, in their acts and claims, a strict adherence to the rule of law and a genuine willingness to assume their mutual obligation to refrain from any infringement upon each other's sovereignty or territorial integrity.

Convinced that military occupation and/or the denial of other peoples' rights and legitimate aspirations to live and develop freely are incompatible with the spirit of peace.

Considering the vital interests of all the peoples of the Middle East as well as the universal interest that exists in strengthening World Peace and security.

ARTICLE 1

The Parties express their determination to reach a comprehensive settlement of the Middle East problem through the conclusion of peace treaties on the basis of the full implementation of Security Council Resolutions 242 and 338 in all their parts.

ARTICLE 2

The Parties agree that the establishment of a just and lasting peace among them requires the fulfilment of the following:

First: Withdrawal of Israel from the occupied territories in accordance with the principle of the inadmissibility of the acquisition of territory by War.
In Sinai and the Golan, withdrawal shall take place to the international boundaries between mandated Palestine and Egypt and Syria respectively.
In the West Bank, Israel shall withdraw to the demarcation lines of the 1949 Armistice Agreement between Israel and Jordan with such insubstantial alterations as might be mutually accepted by the Parties concerned. It is to be understood that such alterations should not reflect the weight of conquest.
Security measures shall be introduced in accordance with the provisions below mentioned with a view to meeting the Parties' legitimate concern for security and safeguarding the rights and aspirations of the Palestinian people.
Withdrawal from the Gaza Strip shall take place to the demarcation lines of the 1949 Armistice Agreement between Egypt and Israel.
Israeli withdrawal shall commence immediately after the signing of the peace treaties and shall be completed according to a timetable to be agreed upon within the period referred to in Article 6.

Second: Removal of the Israeli settlements in the occupied territories according to a time-table to be agreed upon within the period referred to in Article 6.

Third: Guaranteeing the security, sovereignty, territorial integrity and inviolability and the political independence of every State through the following measures:

Appendix 2

    a)   The establishment of demilitarized zones astride the borders.
    b)   The establishment of limited armament zones astride the borders.
    c)   The stationing of United Nations forces astride the borders.
    d)   The stationing of early warning systems on the basis of reciprocity.
    e)   Regulating the acquisition of arms by the Parties and the type of their armament and weapons systems.
    f)   The adherence by all the Parties to the Treaty on the Non-Proliferation of nuclear weapons. The Parties undertake not to manufacture or acquire nuclear weapons or other nuclear explosive devices.
    g)   Applying the principle of innocent passage to transit through the Straits of Tiran.
    h)   The establishment of relations of peace and good-neighbourly co-operation among the Parties.

Fourth: An undertaking by all the Parties not to resort to the threat or the use of force to settle disputes. Any disputes shall be settled by peaceful means in accordance with the provisions of Article 33 of the Charter of the United Nations.

    The Parties also undertake to accept the compulsory jurisdiction of the International Court of Justice with respect to all disputes emanating from the application or the interpretation of their contractual arrangements.

Fifth: Upon the signing of the peace treaties, the Israeli military Government in the West Bank and Gaza shall be abolished and authority shall be transferrred to the Arab side in an orderly and peaceful manner.

    There shall be a transitional period not to exceed five years from the date of the signing of the "Framework" during which Jordan shall supervise the administration of the West Bank and Egypt shall supervise the administration of the Gaza Strip.

    Egypt and Jordan shall carry out their responsibility in co-operation with freely elected representatives of the Palestinian people who shall exercise direct authority over the administration of the West Bank and Gaza simultaneously with the abolition of the Israeli military government.

    Six months before the end of the transitional period, the Palestinian people shall exercise their fundamental right to self-determination and shall be enabled to establish their national entity. Egypt and Jordan by virtue of their responsibility in the Gaza Strip and the West Bank, shall recommend that the entity be linked with Jordan as decided by their peoples.

Palestinian refugees and displaced persons shall be enabled to exercise the right to return or receive compensation in accordance with relevant United Nations resolutions.

Sixth: Israel shall withdraw from Jerusalem to the demarcation lines of the Armistice Agreement of 1949 in conformity with the Principle of the inadmissibility of the acquisition of territory by war. Arab sovereignty and administration shall be restored to the Arab sector.

A joint municipal council composed of an equal number of Palestinian and Israeli members shall be entrusted with regulating and supervising the following matters:

a) Public utilities throughout the city.
b) Public transportation and traffic.
c) Postal and telephone services.
d) Tourism.

The Parties undertake to ensure the free exercise of worship, the freedom of access, visit and transit to the holy places without distinction or discrimination.

Seventh: Synchronized with the implementation of the provisions related to withdrawal, the Parties shall proceed to establish among them relationships normal to States at peace with one another. To this end, they undertake to abide by all the provisions of the Charter of the United Nations, Steps taken in this respect include:

a) Full recognition.
b) Abolishing economic boycott.
c) Ensuring the freedom of passage through the Suez Canal in accordance with the Provisions of the Constantinople Convention of 1888 and the Declaration of the Egyptian Government of April 24, 1957.
d) Guaranteeing that under their jurisdiction the citizens of the other Parties shall enjoy the protection of the due process of law.

Eighth: Israel undertakes to pay full and prompt compensation for the damage which resulted from the operations of its armed forces against the civilian population and installations, as well as its exploitation of natural resources in occupied territories.

ARTICLE 3

Upon the signing of this "Framework," which represents a comprehensive and balanced package embodying all the rights and obligations of the Parties, other Parties concerned shall be invited to adhere to it under the Middle East Peace Conference in Geneva.

Appendix 2

ARTICLE 4

The representatives of the Palestinian people shall take part in the peace talks to be held after the signing of the "Framework".

ARTICLE 5

The United States shall participate in the talks on matters related to the modalities of the implementation of the agreements and working out the time-table for the carrying out of the obligations of the Parties.

ARTICLE 6

Peace treaties shall be concluded within three months from the signing of this "Framework" by the Parties concerned, thus signalling the beginning of the peace process and setting in motion the dynamics of peace and co-existence.

ARTICLE 7

The Security Council shall be requested to endorse the Peace Treaties and ensure that their provisions shall not be violated. The Council shall also be requested to guarantee the boundaries between the Parties.

ARTICLE 8

The Permanent members of the Security Council shall be requested to underwrite the Peace Treaties and ensure respect for their provisions. They shall also be requested to conform their policies and actions with the undertakings contained in this Framework.

ARTICLE 9

The United States shall guarantee the implementation of this "Framework" and the peace treaties in full and in good faith.

Appendix 3

A Framework For Peace In The Middle East Agreed At Camp David

Muhammad Anwar al-Sadat, President of the Arab Republic of Egypt, and Menachem Begin, Prime Minister of Israel, met with Jimmy Carter, President of the United States of America, at Camp David from September 5 to , 1978, and have agreed on the following framework for peace in the Middle East. They invite other parties to the Arab-Israeli conflict to adhere to it.

Preamble

The search for peace in the Middle East must be guided by the following:

After four wars during thirty years, despite intensive human efforts, the Middle East, which is the cradle of civilization and the birthplace of three great religions, does not yet enjoy the blessings of peace. The people of the Middle East yearn for peace so that the vast human and natural resources of the region can be turned to the pursuits of peace and so that this area can become a model for coexistence and cooperation among nations.

The historic initiative of President Sadat in visiting Jerusalem and the reception accorded to him by the Parliament, government and people of Israel, and the reciprocal visit of Prime Minister Begin to Ismailia, the peace proposals made by both leaders, as well as the warm reception of these missions by the peoples of both countries, have created an unprecedented opportunity for peace which must not be lost if this generation and future generations are to be spared the tragedies of war.

The provisions of the Charter of the United Nations and the other accepted norms of international law and legitimacy now provide accepted standards for the conduct of relations among all states.

The only agreed basis for a peaceful settlement of the Arab-Israeli conflict is United Nations Security Council Resolution 242, supplemented by Resolution 338. Negotiations based on the principles of

Appendix 3

Resolution 242 are necessary with respect to all fronts of the conflict – the Sinai, the Golan Heights, the West Bank and Gaza, and Lebanon. Resolution 242 in its preamble emphasizes the obligation of Member States in the United Nations to act in accordance with Article 2 of the Charter. Article 2, among other points, calls for the settlement of disputes by peaceful means and for Members to refrain from the threat or use of force. Egypt and Israel in their agreement signed September 4, 1975, agreed: "The Parties hereby undertake not to resort to the threat or use of force or military blockade against each other." They have both also stated that there shall be no more war between them. In a relationship of peace, in the spirit of Article 2, negotiations between Israel and any neighbour prepared to negotiate peace and security with it should be based on all the provisions and principles of Resolution 242, including the inadmissibility of the acquisition of territory by war and the need to work just and lasting peace in which every state in the area can live in security, within secure and recognized borders.

Peace is more than the juridical end of the state of belligerency. It should encompass the full range of normal relations between nations. Progress toward that goal can accelerate movement toward a new era of reconciliation in the Middle East marked by co-operation in promoting economic development, in maintaining stability, and in assuring security.

Security is enhanced by a relationship of peace and by co-operation between nations which enjoy normal relations. In addition, under the terms of peace treaties, the sovereign parties can agree to special security arrangements such as demilitarized zones, limited armaments areas, early warning stations, *special security forces*, liaison, agreed measures for monitoring, and other arrangements that they agree are useful.

Agreement

Taking these factors into account, Egypt and Israel are determined to reach a just, comprehensive, and durable settlement of the Middle East conflict through the conclusion of peace treaties which will be negotiated on the basis of Security Council Resolutions 242 and 338 in all their parts. Their purpose is to achieve peace and good neighbourly relations. They recognize that, for peace to endure, it must involve all those who have been principal parties to the Arab-Israeli conflict; it must provide security; and it must give the peoples who have been most deeply affected by the conflict a sense that they have been dealt with fairly in the peace agreement. They therefore agree that this Framework as appropriate is intended by them to constitute a basis for peace not only between Egypt and Israel, but also between Israel and each of its other neighbours which is prepared to negotiate peace with Israel on this basis. With that objective in mind, they have agreed to proceed as follows:

A. Egypt-Israel.
    1. Egypt and Israel undertake not to resort to the threat or the use of force to settle disputes. Any disputes shall be settled by peaceful means in accordance with the provisions of Article 33 of the Charter of the United Nations. In the event of disputes arising from the application or interpretation of their contractual agreements, the two parties will seek to reach a settlement by direct negotiations.

    2. In order to achieve peace between them, the parties agree to negotiate without interruption with a goal of concluding within three months from the signing of this Framework a peace treaty between them, based on the restoration of full Egyptian sovereignty in the Sinai up to the internationally recognized border between Egypt and mandated Palestine, full peace between Egypt and Israel, security arrangements, and all the elements of a normal, peaceful relationship, while inviting the other parties to the conflict to proceed simultaneously to negotiate and conclude similar peace treaties with a view to achieving a comprehensive peace in the area.

B. West Bank and Gaza.
    1. Egypt and Israel will participate in negotiations on resolution of the Palestinian problem in all its aspects. The solution must recognize the legitimate rights of the Palestinians and enable the Palestinians to participate in the determination of their own future.

    2. To this end, negotiations relating to the West Bank and Gaza should provide for links between these areas and Jordan and should proceed in three stages:

    (a) Egypt and Israel hereby agree that the following should be the main elements of a settlement in the West Bank and Gaza: In order to ensure a peaceful and orderly transfer of authority, there should be transitional arrangements for the West Bank and Gaza for a period not exceeding five years. In order to provide full autonomy to the inhabitants, under these arrangements the Israeli military government and administration will be abolished and withdrawn as soon as a self-governing authority can be freely elected by the inhabitants of these areas to replace the existing military government. This transitional arrangement should derive its authority for self-government from Egypt and Israel, and Jordan, when Jordan joins the negotiations. To negotiate the details of a transitional arrangement, the

Appendix 3

Government of Jordan will be invited to join the negotiations on the basis of this Framework. These new arrangements should give due consideration both to the principle of self-government by the inhabitants of these territories and to the legitimate security concerns of the parties involved.

(b) Egypt, Israel, and Jordan will determine the modalities for establishing the elected self-governing authority in the West Bank and Gaza. The delegations may include Palestinians from the West Bank and Gaza. The parties will negotiate an agreement which will define the powers and responsibilities of the self-governing authority to be exercised in the areas now under the jurisdiction of military government. In the West Bank and Gaza withdrawal of Israeli armed forces will take place and there will be a redeployment of some of them into mutually agreed security locations. It will also include arrangements for assuring internal and external security and public order, including the respective roles of Israeli armed forces and local police.

(c) When the self-governing authority in the West Bank and Gaza is inaugurated, the transitional period of five years will begin. As soon as possible but no later than two years after the beginning of the transitional period, Egypt, Israel, Jordan and the self-governing authority in the West Bank and Gaza will undertake negotiations for the peace treaty which will settle all outstanding issues between the parties after the transitional period, the final status of the West Bank and Gaza after the transitional period and its relationship with its neighbours on the basis of all of the principles of UN Security Council Resolution 242, including the mutual obligations of peace, the necessity for security arrangements for all parties concerned following the transitional period, the withdrawal of Israeli armed forces, a just settlement of the refugee problem, and the establishment of secure and recognized boundaries in accordance with Security Council Resolutions 242 and 338. As determined in the peace negotiations, the exact location of the peace boundaries and nature of security arrangements must meet the just requirements of the Palestinians and Israel's security needs. The peace treaty will define the rights of the citizens of each of the parties to do business, to work, to live, and to carry on other transactions in the respective areas.

3. All necessary measures will be taken and provisions made to assure Israel's security during the transitional period and beyond. To assist in providing such security:

(a) Egypt and Israel propose that Jordanian citizens participate in the police forces of the self-governing authority. The police will maintain continuing liaison on internal security matters with the designated

Camp David

Israeli authorities to ensure that no hostile threats or acts against Israel or its citizens originate from the West Bank or Gaza.

(b) The nature of the Israeli security presence will be agreed in the negotiations described above.

4. During the transitional period, the negotiating parties (Egypt, Israel, Jordan, the self-governing authority) will constitute a continuing committee to decide by unanimous agreement:

(a) issues involving interpretation of the agreement or issues unforeseen during the negotiation of the agreement, which are not within the designated authority of the self-government.

(b) the admission of agreed numbers of persons displaced from the West Bank in 1967 and of Palestinian refugees together with necessary measures in connection with their return to prevent disruption and disorder.

5. Jerusalem, the city of peace, shall not be divided. It is a city holy to Jew, Muslim, and Christian and all peoples must have free access to it and enjoy the free exercise of worship and the right to visit and transit to the holy places without distinction or discrimination. The holy places of each faith will be under the administration of their representatives. For peace to endure, each community in Jerusalem must be able to express freely its cultural and religious values. A representative municipal council shall supervise essential functions in the city. An agreement on relationships in Jerusalem should be reached in the negotiations dealing with the final status of the West Bank and Gaza.

6. Egypt and Israel agree to work with each other and with other interested parties to achieve a just and permanent solution of the problems of the Arab and Jewish refugees.

7. If Jordan is unable to join these negotiations, Egypt, Israel, and the inhabitants of the West Bank and Gaza will proceed to establish and administer the self-governing authority.

C. Settlements.

(Language to be inserted)

D. Associated Principles.

1. Egypt and Israel believe that the principles and provisions described below should apply to peace treaties with all neighbours – Egypt, Jordan, Syria and Lebanon.

2. Signatories shall proceed to establish among themselves relationships normal to states at peace with one another. To this end, they should undertake to abide by all the provisions of the Charter of the United Nations. Steps to be taken in this respect include:
   (a) full recognition: including diplomatic, economic and cultural relations;
   (b) abolishing economic boycotts and barriers to the free movement of goods and people;
   (c) guaranteeing that under their jurisdiction the citizens of the other parties shall enjoy the protection of the due process of law.

3. Signatories should agree to provide for the security and respect the sovereignty, territorial integrity and inviolability and the political independence of each state negotiating peace through measures such as the following:
   (a) the establishment of demilitarized zones;
   (b) the establishment of limited armament zones;
   (c) the stationing of United Nations forces or observer groups as agreed;
   (d) the stationing of early warning systems on the basis of reciprocity;
   (e) regulating the deployment of their armed forces and the types of their armament and weapons systems.

4. Signatories should explore possibilities for regional economic development in the context of both transitional arrangements and final peace treaties, with the objective of contributing to the atmosphere of peace, co-operation and friendship which is their common goal.

5. Claims Commissions may be established for the mutual settlement of all financial claims.

6. The United States shall be invited to participate in the talks on matters related to the modalities of the implementation of the agreements and working out the timetable for the carrying out of the obligations of the parties.

7. The United Nations Security Council shall be requested to endorse the peace treaties and ensure that their provisions shall not be violated. The permanent members of the Security Council shall be requested to underwrite the peace treaties and ensure respect for their provisions. They shall also be requested to conform their policies and actions with the undertakings contained in this Framework.

Camp David

> For the Government of the
> Arab Republic of Egypt:

For the Government
of Israel:

_____

_____

Witnessed by:

_____

Jimmy Carter, President of the
United States of America

Appendix 4

Framework For Peace In The Middle East

Muhammad Anwar El-Sadat, President of the Arab Republic of Egypt, and Menachim Begin, Prime Minister of Israel, met with Jimmy Carter, President of the United States of America, at Camp David from September 5 to September 17, 1978, and have agreed on the following framework for peace in the Middle East. They invite other parties to the Arab Israeli conflict to adhere to it.

Preamble.
The search for peace in the Middle East must be guided by the following:

The agreed basis for a peaceful settlement of the conflict between Israel and its neighbours is United Nations Security Council Resolution 242, in all its parts. Footnote: The texts of Resolution 242 and 338 are annexed to this document.

> After four wars during thirty years, despite intensive human rights, the Middle East, which is the cradle of civilization and the birthplace of three great religions, does not yet enjoy the blessings of peace. The people of the Middle East yearn for peace so that the vast human and natural resources of the region can be turned to the pursuits of peace and so that this area can become a model for co-existence and co-operation among nations.

> The historic initiative of President Sadat in visiting Jerusalem and the reception accorded to him by the Parliament, Government and People of Israel, and the reciprocal visit of Prime Minister Begin to Ismailia, the peace proposals made by both leaders, as well as the warm reception of these missions by the peoples of both countries, have created an unprecedented opportunity for peace which must not be lost if this generation and future generations are to be spared the tragedies of war.

> The provisions of the Charter of the United Nations, and the other

Camp David

accepted norms of international law and legitimacy now provide accepted standards for the conduct of relations among all states.

To achieve a relationship of peace in the spirit of article 2 of the United Nations Charter, future negotiations between Israel and any neighbour prepared to negotiate peace and security with it, are necessary for the purpose of carrying out all the provisions and principles of resolutions 242 and 338.

Peace requires respect for the sovereignty, territorial integrity and political independence of every state in the area and their right to live in peace within secure and recognized boundaries free from threats or acts of force. Progress toward that goal can accelerate movement toward a new era of reconciliation in the Middle East marked by co-operation in promoting economic development, in maintaining stability, and in assuring security.

Security is enhanced by a relationship of peace and by co-operation between nations which enjoy normal relations. In addition, under the terms of peace treaties, the parties can, on the basis of reciprocity, agree to special security arrangements such as demilitarized zones, limited armaments areas, early warning stations, the presence of international forces, liaison, agreed measures for monitoring, and other arrangements that they agree are useful.

Framework.
Taking these factors into account, the parties are determined to reach a just, comprehensive, and durable settlement of the Middle East conflict through the conclusion of peace treaties based on Security Council Resolution 242 and 338 in all their parts. Their purpose is to achieve peace and good neighbourly relations. They recognize that, for peace to endure, it must involve all those who have been most deeply affected by the conflict. They therefore agree that this framework as appropriate is intended by them to constitute a basis for peace not only between Egypt and Israel, but also between Israel and each of its other neighbours which is prepared to negotiate peace with Israel on this basis. With that objective in mind, they have agreed to proceed as follows.

A. *West Bank and Gaza*
   1. Egypt, Israel, Jordan and the representatives of the Palestinian People should participate in negotiations on the resolution of the Palestinian problem in all its aspects. To achieve that objective, negotiations relating to the West Bank and Gaza should proceed in three stages:

   (a) Egypt and Israel agree that, in order to ensure a peaceful and orderly transfer of authority, and taking into account the security

Appendix 4

concerns of all the parties, there should be transitional arrangements for the West Bank and Gaza for a period not exceeding five years. In order to provide full autonomy to the inhabitants, under these arrangements the Israeli military government and its civilian administration will be withdraw as soon as a self-governing authority has been freely elected by the inhabitants of these areas to replace the existing military government. To negotiate the details of a transitional arrangement, the government of Jordan will be invited to join the negotiations on the basis of this framework. These new arrangements should give due consideration both to the principle of self government by the inhabitants of these territories and to the legitimate security concerns of the parties involved.

(b) Egypt, Israel, and Jordan will agree on the modalities for establishing the elected self-governing authority in the West Bank and Gaza. The delegations of Egypt and Jordan may include Palestinians from the West Bank and Gaza or other Palestinians as mutually agreed. The parties will negotiate an agreement which will define the powers and responsibilities and the self-governing authority to be exercised in the West Bank and Gaza. A withdrawal of Israeli armed forces will take place and there will be redeployment of the remaining Israeli forces into specified security locations. The agreement will also include arrangements for assuring internal and external security and public order. A strong local police force will be established, which may include Jordanian citizens. In addition, Israeli and Jordanian forces will participate in joint patrols and in the manning of control posts to assure the security of the borders.

(c) When the self-governing authority (administrative council) in the West Bank and Gaza is established and inaugurated, the transitional period of five years will begin. As soon as possible, but not later than the third year after the beginning of the transitional period, negotiations will take place to determine the final status of the West Bank and Gaza and its relationship with its neighbours, and to conclude a peace treaty between Israel and Jordan by the end of the transitional period. These negotiations will be conducted among Egypt, Israel, Jordan, and the elected representatives of the inhabitants of the West Bank and Gaza. Two separate but related committees will be convened, one committee, consisting of representatives of the four parties which will negotiate and agree on the final status of the West Bank and Gaza, and its relationship with its neighbours, and the second committee, consisting of representatives of Israel and representatives of Jordan to be joined by the elected representatives of the inhabitants of the West Bank and Gaza, to negotiate the peace treaty between Israel and Jordan, taking into account the agreement reached on the final status of the West Bank and Gaza. The negotiations shall be based on all the provisions and principles of UN Security Council Resolution 242. The negotiations will resolve, among other matters, the location of the boundaries and the nature of the security arrangements. The solution from the negotiations must also recognize the legitimate rights of the Palestinian People and their just requirements. In this way, the Palestinians will participate in the determination of their own future through:

1 The negotiations among Egypt, Israel, Jordan and the representatives of the inhabitants to the West Bank and Gaza to agree on the final status of the West Bank and Gaza and other outstanding issues by the end of the transitional period.

2 Submitting their agreement to a vote by the elected representatives of the inhabitants of the West Bank and Gaza.

3 Providing for the elected representatives of the inhabitants of the West Bank and Gaza to decide how they shall govern themselves consistent with the provisions of their agreement.

4 Participating as stated above in the work of the committee negotiating the peace treaty between Israel and Jordan.

2. All necessary measures will be taken and provisions made to assure the security of Israel and its neighbours during the transitional period and beyond. To assist in providing such security, a strong local police force will be constituted by the self-governing authority. It will be composed of inhabitants of the West Bank and Gaza. The police will maintain continuing liaison on internal security matters with the designated Israeli, Jordanian, and Egyptian officers.

3. During the transitional period, representatives of Egypt, Israel, Jordan, and the self-governing authority will constitute a continuing committee to decide by agreement on the modalities of admission to persons displaced from the West Bank and Gaza in 1967, together with necessary measures to prevent disruption and disorder. Other matters of common concern may also be dealt with by this committee.

4. Egypt and Israel will work with each other and with other interested parties to establish agreed procedures for a prompt, just and permanent implementation of the resolution of the refugee problem.

Appendix 4

B. Egypt-Israel
1. Egypt and Israel undertake not to resort to the threat or the use of force to settle disputes. Any disputes shall be settled by peaceful means in accordance with the provisions of article 33 in the Charter of the United Nations.

2. In order to achieve peace between them, the parties agree to negotiate in good faith with a goal of concluding within three months from the signing of this framework a peace treaty between them, while inviting the other parties to the conflict to proceed simultaneously to negotiate and conclude similar peace treaties with a view to achieving a comprehensive peace in the area. The framework for the conclusion of a peace treaty between Egypt and Israel will govern the peace negotiation between them. The parties will agree on the modalities and the timetable for the implementation of their obligations under the treaty.

C. Associated Principles
1. Egypt and Israel state that the principles and provisions described below should apply to peace treaties between Israel and each of its neighbours, Egypt, Jordan, Syria and Lebanon.

2. Signatories shall establish among themselves relationships normal to states at peace with one another. To this end, they should undertake to abide by all the provisions of the Charter of the United Nations. Steps to be taken in this respect include:

(A) Full recognition;
(B) Abolishing economic boycotts;
(C) Guaranteeing that under their jurisdiction the citizens of the other parties shall enjoy the protection of the due process of law.

3. Signatories should explore possibilities for economic development in the context of final peace treaties with the objective of contributing to the atmosphere of peace, co-operation and friendship which is their common goal.

4. Claims commissions may be established for the mutual settlement of all financial claims.

5. The United States shall be invited to participate in the talks on matters related to the modalities of the implementation of the agreement and working out the timetable for the carrying out of the obligations of the parties.

Camp David

6. The United Nations Security Council shall be requested to endorse the peace treaties and ensure that their provisions shall not be violated. The permanent members of the Security Council shall be requested to undertake the peace treaties and ensure respect for the provisions. They shall also be requested to confirm their policies and actions with the undertakings contained in this framework.

For the Government of the Arab Republic of Egypt Mohamed Anwar El-Sadat	For the Government of Israel Menachim Begin

Witnessed by:

Jimmy Carter, President of the United States of America.

Annex

Text of United Nations Security Council Resolution 242 of November 22, 1967.

Adopted unanimously at the 1382nd meeting

The Security Council,

Expressing its continuing concern with the grave situation in the Middle East,

Emphasizing the inadmissibility of the acquisition of territory by war and the need to work for a just and lasting peace in which every state in the area can live in security,

Emphasizing further that states in their acceptance of the Charter of the United Nations have undertaken a commitment to act in accordance with Article 2 of the charter,

1. Affirms that the fulfilment of Charter principles requires the establishment of a just and lasting peace in the Middle East which should include the application of both the following principles:
    (i) Withdrawal of Israeli armed forces from territories occupied in the recent conflict;
    (ii) Termination of all claims or states of belligerency and respect for and acknowledgement of the sovereignty, territorial integrity and political independence of every state in the area and their right to live in peace within secure and recognized boundaries free from threats or acts of force;

Appendix 4

2. Affirms further the necessity
A For guaranteeing freedom of navigation through international waterways in the area;
B For achieving a just settlement of the refugee problem;
C For guaranteeing the territorial inviolability and political independence of every state in the area, through measures including the establishment of demilitarized zones.

3. Requests the Secretary-General to designate a special representative to proceed to the Middle East to establish and maintain contacts with the states concerned in order to promote agreement and assist efforts to achieve a peaceful and accepted settlement in accordance with the provisions and principles of this resolution.

4. Requests the Secretary-General to report to the Security Council on the progress of the efforts of the special representative as soon as possible.

Text of United Nations Security Council Resolution 338.

Adopted by the Security Council at its 1747th meeting on 21/22 October, 1973

The Security Council

1. Calls upon all parties to the present fighting to cease all firing and terminate all military activity immediately, no later than 12 hours after moment of the adoption of this decision, in the positions they now occupy;

2. Calls upon the parties concerned to start immediately after the cease-fire the implementation of Security Council Resolution 242 (1967) in all of its parts;

3. Decides that, immediately and concurrently with the cease-fire, negotiations start between the parties concerned under appropriate auspices aimed at establishing a just and durable peace in the Middle East.

Appendix 5

Framework For the Conclusion of a Peace Treaty between Egypt and Israel

In order to achieve peace between them, Israel and Egypt agree to negotiate in good faith with a goal of concluding within three months of the signing of this framework a peace treaty between them.

It is agreed that:
The site of the negotiations will be under a United Nations flag at a location or locations to be mutually agreed.

All of the principles of U.N. Resolution 242 will apply in this resolution of the dispute between Israel and Egypt.

Unless otherwise mutually agreed, terms of the peace treaty will be implemented between two and three years after the peace treaty is signed.

The following matters are agreed between the Parties:
(a) the full exercise of Egyptian sovereignty up to the internationally recognized border between Egypt and mandated Palestine;
(b) the withdrawal of Israeli armed forces from the Sinai
(c) the use of airfields left by the Israelis near El Arish, Rafah, Ras el Naqb, and Sharm el Sheikh for civilian purposes only, including possible commercial use by all nations;
(d) the right of free passage by ships of Israel through the Gulf of Suez and the Suez Canal on the basis of the Constantinople Convention of 1888 applying to all nations; the Strait of Tiran and the Gulf of Aqaba are international waterways to be open to all nations for unimpeded and nonsuspendable freedom of navigation and overflight;
(e) the construction of a highway between the Sinai and Jordan near Elat with guaranteed free and peaceful passage by Egypt and Jordan; and
(f) the stationing of military forces listed below.

Appendix 5

Stationing of Forces
A. No more than one division (mechanized or infantry) of Egyptian armed forces will be stationed within an area lying approximately 50 kilometers (km) east of the Gulf of Suez and the Suez Canal.
B. Only United Nations forces and civil police equipped with light weapons to perform normal police functions will be stationed within an area lying west of the international border and the Gulf of Aqaba, varying in width from 20 km to 40 km.

C. In the area within 3 km east of the international border there will be Israeli limited military forces not to exceed four infantry battalions and United Nations observers.

D. Border patrol units, not to exceed three battalions, will supplement the civil police in maintaining order in the area not included above.

> The exact demarcation of the above areas will be as decided during the peace negotiations.
>
> Early warning stations may exist to insure compliance with the terms of the agreement.

United Nations forces will be stationed: (a) in part of the area in the Sinai lying within about 20 km of the Mediterranean Sea and adjacent to the international border, and (b) in the Sharm el Sheikh area to ensure freedom of passage through the Strait of Tiran; and these forces will not be removed unless such removal is approved by the Security Council of the United Nations with a unanimous vote of the five permanent members.

After a peace treaty is signed, and after the interim withdrawal is complete, normal relations will be established between Egypt and Israel, including: full recognition, including diplomatic, economic and cultural relations; termination of economic boycotts and barriers to the free movement of goods and people; and mutual protection of citizens by the due process of law.

Interim withdrawal
Between three months and nine months after the signing of the peace treaty, all Israeli forces will withdraw east of a line extending from a point east of El Arish to Ras Muhammed, the exact location of this line to be determined by mutual agreement.

For the Government of the
Arab Republic of Egypt:
Mohamed Anwar El Sadat

For the Government
of Israel:
Menachim Begin

Camp David

Witnessed by:

Jimmy Carter, President
of the United States of America

Selected Bibliography

Bull, Odd, *War and Peace in the Middle East*, Leo Cooper Ltd, London, 1976

Dayan, Moshe, *Breakthrough* A personal account of the Egypt-Israel Peace Negotiations Alfred A. Knopf Inc., New York, 1981

Golan, Matti, *The Secret Conversations of Henry Kissinger*, New York Times Book Co., New York, 1976

Haber, Eitan, Zeef, Schiff, Ehud Yaari, *The Year of the Dove*, Bantam Books Inc., New York, 1979

Heikal, Mohamed Hassanein (Hadiss Al-Mubadarah) published in Arabic by Sharikat Al-Matbouat Lel-Tawzie Wa Al-Nashr, Beirut, 1982

Meir, Golda, *My Life*, Dell Publishing Co. Inc., New York, 1976

Orwell, George, *Animal Farm*, Penguin Books in association with Martin Secker & Warburg, London, 1961.

Quandt, William B., *Decade of Decisions*, University of California Press, 1977

Riad, Mahmoud. "Memoires of Mahmoud Riad: The Search for Peace 1948–1978". Published in Arabic by Al-Mouasasa Al-Arabia Lel-De rassat Wa Al-Nashr, Beirut 1981 (Unauthorised Translation).

Sadat, Anwar, *In Search of Identity*, Collins, London, 1978

Weizman, Ezer, *The Battle for Peace*, Bantam Books Inc., 1981

Index

Abdel-Latif, Ezzat, 230
Abdullah, King, 36, 229, 234
Adham, Kamal, 187
Afghanistan, 316
Africa, 38, 39, 52, 74–5, 102, 106, 153, 175, 179 North, 1
Al Ahram, 123, 189, 201, 206
Alexandria, 1
Algeria, 17, 34, 127, 132, 140, 153
Allies, the, 1, 20
Allon Plan, 215, 234, 242
Aly, Kamal Hassan, 48, 272, 286, 294
Aly, Omar Abu, 2–4
Amer, Abdel Hakim, 352–3
America, 10–13, 15–16, 20, 21, 32, 33, 36–9, 40, 41, 45, 48–50, 54, 56, 65–9, 71, 73–4, 76, 78–87, 89–93, 95–6, 102–3, 107, 111–3, 115–6, 120, 134, 138–9, 140–1, 146–7, 150, 155–64, 166, 168, 171–2, 178–83, 184–8, 203–4, 208–12, 216–9, 220–2, 226, 230–4, 237, 239–46, 248–53, 255–61, 262–9, 283, 287–90, 292, 297, 309–11, 313–4, 317–21, 326–9, 331–4, 336–40, 342–4, 346–8, 355, 361–2, 364–5, 376, 389–90, 395–7, 401–2, 406
Amin, Mustapha, 50, 60–1
Amman, 191, 228, 229, 233
Anglo-Egyptian League, 3–4
Anwar, Samih, 208
Arab League Council, 132, 140, 142, 144, 159, 164, 187, 342
Arab Security Force, the, 136
Arab Socialist Union, 9, 185, 189, 293
Arab Solidarity Committee, 140, 169, 170, 172
Arabs, the, 8–11, 13, 14–18, 22–3, 25–7, 28–32, 34–6, 38–9, 43–4, 52, 54, 56–7, 61, 73, 75–6, 85–6, 93–4, 132–3, 150–1, 165, 169–70, 173–4, 221–2, 230–2, 249, 255–7, 261, 365, 367–8, 373, 376
Araby, Nabil El, 41, 165, 206, 208, 270, 318, 320–1, 346, 374–5
Arafat, Yasser, 8
Asia, 39, 52, 153

Assad, Hafiz El, 22, 42, 113–4, 169, 231–2, 233, 302, 368
Aswan, 42, 46, 64
Aswan Formula, the, 45, 95, 155, 197, 278, 311, 319, 329, 330, 347
Ataturk, 121
Atherton, Alfred Leroy, 65, 74, 81, 85, 91, 95, 105, 128–9, 159–62, 178, 182, 211, 230–1, 233, 239–53, 255, 262–3, 267, 287, 299, 318, 346
Austria, 166, 190–6
Ayouby, Salah El Din El, 54
Azzam, Hamdi, 196

Badran, Modar, 232–7
Baghdad Pact, 54
Bahr, 98
Balfour Declaration, 97, 285
Barak, Aharon, 146–7, 173, 213, 329–30
Bar-lev Line, 10, 118
Barre, Syiad, 102–3
Baz, Ussama El, 21, 41, 159–60, 161, 165, 173, 208, 213–5, 265, 270, 280–1, 291, 305, 315, 318, 320–1, 346, 349–51, 353–4, 357–8, 371–2
Begin Menahim, 7, 12, 14, 16–8, 20, 22–7, 30–2, 34, 40, 43–5, 50–2, 54–5, 58–61, 62–70, 72, 82–3, 85–7, 89, 91, 98, 103, 109, 120, 128–31, 136, 143–4, 146, 148, 155–6, 162–3, 181–3, 186–8, 194, 198, 199–204, 209, 220, 224–8, 233–4, 237, 245, 248, 255, 262–9, 271, 277, 282–3, 288–90, 293, 295, 298, 300, 302–3, 305–8, 311, 313, 317, 322–4, 326, 329, 331–3, 347–8, 350, 352, 355–9, 361, 364, 366–7, 372–4, 378–9, 390, 397, 402, 405
Ben Gurion, 105
Brandt, Willy, 189, 194, 196–8, 283, 297
Breakthrough, 131, 329, 348, 349
Brezinski, Zbgniev, 13, 81, 84, 88, 90–3, 233, 299, 307–9, 316–8, 329
Britain, 1, 20, 54, 107
British Mandate (Palestine), 6–7, 55, 97, 181

408

Index

Brookings Report, 12, 257
Brown, Harold, 356

Cairo, 1, 7, 14, 18, 21, 23–4, 56, 63, 66–8, 70, 101, 107, 130, 132, 136, 140, 144, 145–6, 164, 173–4, 183, 191, 198, 226, 237, 360; University, 1
Callaghan, James, 26, 82, 96, 108
Camp David, 81, 91–2, 95, 109, 111, 128, 149, 155, 158, 163–4, 180, 185, 195, 203, 210, 221–2, 227, 240, 243–4, 246, 250–1, 256, 260–1, 265–8, 270–3, 274, 279, 281–4, 286–8, 294–5, 299–301, 302–3, 314–6, 324–5, 326, 330, 333, 337–8, 340, 347–8, 350, 353–5, 366, 370–1, 375, 378–80, 390, 397
Canada, 107
Carter, Hodding, 184, 239, 241
Carter, Jimmy, 12, 15, 26, 42–3, 46, 50, 61, 64–5, 67–8, 72–3, 79, 81–7, 91, 95, 103–4, 109, 120, 138, 148, 155–6, 158, 161–4, 180–2, 184–8, 190, 203, 216–7, 224–5, 228, 240–1, 243–4, 247–53, 255, 257, 264–9, 270–4, 282–3, 290, 295, 298–9, 301–2, 305–12, 313–4, 319, 321–2, 324–5, 329, 332–3, 337, 339–43, 347–8, 349–52, 354–60, 361, 363, 366, 368, 370–9, 381, 390, 396–7, 402, 406
Ceaucescu, President, 43, 99–100, 108–10, 120, 293
Central Intelligence Agency (CIA), 362
Chad, 150, 179
China, 43
Christians, 52, 202, 266, 394
Cyprus, 106–7, 124–5, 177

Dayan, Moshe, 34, 50–1, 53–4, 56–7, 59, 62, 67–70, 72, 79, 87, 106, 126, 131, 136, 156–7, 164, 182–3, 185, 194–6, 200–1, 203, 209–19, 220, 236, 241–2, 245, 261, 268, 282, 303, 307–8, 321–4, 329, 331, 348, 349–52, 354, 360, 374
Decade of Decisions, 110, 117
De Gaulle, General, 101
Deir Yassin, 7, 12, 63
d'Estaing, Giscard, 101, 104, 108, 120, 295
Dinitz, Simha, 110
Dobell, Mrs, 299
Dulles, Foster, 242

Eastern bloc, 76, 103, 168
Ebeid, Makram, 6
Eden, Anthony, 28
EEC *see* European Economic Community
Egypt, 1, 6–7, 8–13, 14–18, 20, 21–7, 31–3, 35, 41–2, 43–6, 47–8, 50–2, 58–60, 62–4, 66–8, 70, 74–6, 79–87, 89–94, 102, 104, 110, 112–7, 118, 124–8, 132–7, 140–2, 144, 145–8, 150–4, 155, 165–73, 175–9, 184–8, 191, 193–4, 202–5, 210–4, 216–8, 220–5, 229–31, 239–40, 242–4, 246, 248, 258, 260–1, 262–5, 273–8, 283–4, 293, 296, 308–12, 313–4, 318–9, 326–9, 331, 333–5, 337–9, 341, 365–8, 372–4, 380–1, 383–4, 387, 390–4, 396–402, 404–5
Ehrlich, 252
Eilat, 24, 404
Eilts, Herman, 41, 47, 81, 85, 160, 163, 166, 179, 181, 185, 205, 209–10, 216–7, 224, 239, 242, 272, 282, 287, 299–301, 307, 322, 325, 360, 370–1, 375, 377–8
Eisenhower, Dwight, 51, 87
El-Afrangy, Abdallah, 127
El Alamein, 1
El Arish, 24, 47, 60, 93, 188, 190–1, 202–3, 205, 207, 220, 222–5, 250, 292, 373, 404–5
El Arish – Ras Mohamed Line, 202, 283
El Kotla National Party, 6
Entebbe, 107
Erhard, Chancellor, 105
Ethiopia, 101–3
Europe, 10, 38–9, 153, 189, 223 East, 223; West, 153–4, 223
European Economic Community, 15, 75, 97
Ezzat, Hassan, 5
Ezzeldin, Ibrahim, 230

Fahd, Prince, 172–3, 231, 255, 299
Fahmy, Ismail, 14–5, 19, 73, 159, 349
Faisal, King, 11, 13, 42, 141
Faisal, Prince Saud El, 141–4, 169–72, 187, 232, 240
Fakhry, Naguib, 2, 4, 6
Falk, Mohamed, 9
Farouk, King, 1, 237–8
Fawzi, Mohamed, 9
Ford, Gerald, 120, 195
Foreigners' Prison, the, 4, 7

409

Camp David

France, 107, 179
Fuad, Prince, 237

Gadaffi, Colonel, 78, 152, 368
Gamassy, Field Marshall El, 48, 113, 147–8, 173–4, 201, 224–5, 264, 285
Garanna, Zohair, 1
Gaza (Strip), 8, 24–5, 27, 29, 31, 33, 39, 44, 47, 49–50, 51, 57, 59, 65, 79–80, 82, 86, 89–92, 95, 96, 99, 129–30, 137, 139, 147–8, 155–63, 165, 171, 178–83, 184, 187, 189, 197, 203–5, 210, 213–7, 219, 221, 230, 236, 241–2, 246, 256, 258–9, 261, 263, 268, 277–8, 282–5, 288–9, 302, 304–9, 311, 313, 316–20, 326, 328, 330–1, 333–4, 341, 344–5, 347, 351, 354–5, 359, 364, 366–7, 372, 383̲–4, 386–7, 391–4, 398–400
Gedi Pass, 24, 116
General Assembly, U.N. *see* United Nations
Geneva Peace Conference, 11, 15, 30, 35, 42, 109, 114–5, 177, 222, 231, 261, 297, 388
Genscher, Hans Dietrich, 16, 48, 97, 105–6
Germans, the, 1–2, 4, 15, 16, 37, 97
Germany, Democratic Republic of, 97
Germany, Federal Republic of, 37, 97, 105–6, 107, 124, 127, 191
Ghali, Boutros, 18, 21, 41, 70, 81, 126, 147, 264–5, 300–1, 302, 305–7, 313–5, 318, 324, 353, 363, 369, 379
Ghali Boutros Pasha, 325, 371
Ghali, Nagib, 324
Ghasmy, Ahmed El, 187
Gheit, Ahmed Abou El, 208, 300, 363
Ghorbal, Ashraf, 81, 88, 177, 264, 299–301, 305, 318, 321, 353–6, 363, 369, 371, 379
Golan, the, 42, 44, 79, 89, 202, 283, 285, 296, 307, 308–9, 366, 386
Golan Heights, 8, 29, 31, 35, 39, 137, 155, 235, 391
Golan, Matti, 110, 117
Goldberg, Ambassador, 249, 373
Goldman, Nahum, 103, 252
Goma'a, Sharawy, 9
Guiringeau, Louis de, 101, 103, 178
Gulf of Aqaba, 404–5
Gulf of Suez, 13, 167–8, 404–5

Gulf States, 35, 231, 237

Haber, Eitan, 45, 46
Haddad, Saad, 134, 266
Hafiz, Fawzi Abdel, 81, 97–8, 101, 103, 353
Hamdy, Amr, 20, 55, 190, 196, 377–9, 381
Hamid, Abdel, 32
Hassan II, King, 34, 78–9, 133, 307
Hassan, Mansour, 294, 335
Heikal, Mohamed Hassanein, 6, 93, 95, 206, 375
Herzl, Theodor, 32
Herzog, Chaim, 176
Hirut Party, 30, 59, 143, 200
Hitler, Adolf, 63, 121
Holy Places, the, 218, 320
Horn of Africa, 101, 103, 179, 316, 341
Horowitz, Yigal, 146
Hussein, King, 114, 117, 126–7, 129, 147–8, 165–6, 180, 194, 222, 224, 229–37, 240, 283–4, 306, 334–6, 341–3, 368, 376

India, 74
In Search of an Identity, 6, 109, 123
Iran, 41, 166, 176
Iraq, 34, 41, 132
Irgun Zvei Leumi, 7, 54–5
Islam, 29, 39, 118, 192, 295, 342
Ismail, Nabawy, 48
Ismailia, 20–3, 27–8, 32, 41–2, 45, 50, 59–60, 68, 87, 93–4, 124, 130, 185, 198, 287, 293, 390, 397
Israel, 7–8, 10, 12, 14–18, 20, 21–7, 28–40, 42–5, 47–52, 53–60, 64, 71, 73–6, 79–80, 82–7, 89–93, 95, 96–8, 106, 110–7, 118, 125–31, 132–9, 140–4, 144–8, 150, 152, 155–9, 165–74, 175–83, 184–9, 190, 197–8, 199–205, 208–19, 220–8, 233–7, 239–52, 258, 262–9, 270–1, 273–9, 282–3, 285, 287, 297–7, 304–5, 307–12, 314, 317–20, 326–37, 339–42, 344–8, 349–52, 356, 358–60, 361, 364–8, 372–4, 383–4, 386, 388, 390–4, 396–402, 404–5
Iran, 131, 158, 316

Japan, 36
Jerusalem, 8, 14, 16, 23–4, 29–32, 43,

Index

48–50, 53–5, 56, 61, 63, 66, 69–70, 82–4, 89–90, 119, 137, 141, 159, 165, 195, 209, 217–8, 222, 225–6, 230, 232, 269, 278, 281–3, 287, 292, 297, 304, 311, 320, 329, 333, 341–2, 345–6, 355, 363, 373–4, 377, 383, 388, 390, 394, 397
Jews, the, 24, 26–7, 32–3, 52, 55, 60–1, 63, 83, 85, 98–9, 103, 127, 148, 156, 162, 185, 195, 202, 285, 394
Joint Arab Defence Charter, 137
Jordan, 15, 21, 29, 35–6, 39, 47, 52, 78, 87, 89–90, 114, 117, 128, 137, 148, 152, 156–7, 165, 168, 178, 180–1, 189, 191, 193–4, 202, 210–12, 214–6, 222, 230–7, 240, 243, 245–6, 255, 256, 260, 272–3, 275, 279, 284, 289, 296, 304, 306, 309, 313, 317, 319–20, 329, 334–5, 342, 345, 359, 364–6, 383–4, 386–7, 392–3, 398–401, 404
Judea, 24, 130, 148, 329, 331
  see also 'Judea and Samaria'
'Judea and Samaria', 25–7, 31, 47–8, 51, 56, 60, 68, 157, 183, 223, 263, 268
July Revolution, the, 7, 9

Kabous, Sultan, 34
Kahan, Karl, 193, 201
Kamal, Moustafa, 1, 123, 301
Kamel, Hassan, 21–2, 201, 265, 300–1, 305, 315, 321, 353, 371, 377–9
Kamel, Mohamed Ibrahim, 48–9, 84, 143, 190–1, 202, 225, 251–3, 265, 279, 281, 284, 286, 310, 316, 325, 340–1, 349, 352–3, 363, 365–8, 371, 375, 378, 380–1
Kamel, Saad El Din, 2–4, 6
Kennedy, John F., 12
Khaled, King, 143–4, 147, 172, 249, 283, 299
Khalil, Mustapha, 48, 147, 225, 285
Khartoum Conference, the, 349
Kyprianou, President, 177
Kissinger, Henry, 9, 11, 42, 93, 101, 110–5, 117, 119, 248, 257, 325–6, 328, 351, 365, 380
Knesset, the Israeli, 14, 17, 31, 33, 59, 69, 126, 223, 226, 244–5, 250, 263, 271, 350, 356, 363
Kreisky, Bruno, 98, 108, 120, 166, 188–9, 192–4, 196–8, 279, 283
Kuwait, 140–1, 260

Labour Party, Israel, 12, 58, 98, 108, 189, 193–4, 231, 233–4, 308
Larnaka, 107, 124–5, 150
Latin America, 39, 52, 153, 175
Lebanon, 89, 136–9, 146, 168, 177, 232, 266, 321, 335, 391, 394 Southern, 31, 134, 136, 150, 266
Leeds Castle, 205, 209, 214, 218, 220–2, 224–5, 227, 230, 233, 236–7, 239–42, 244, 247, 250, 253–4, 256, 261, 263, 268, 279, 288, 296
Lewis, Samuel, 209, 299
Libya, 17, 34, 78, 105, 127, 132, 140, 151–2, 153
Likud Coalition, Israel, 12, 223, 233
Lilienthal, Alfred, 13

Maher, Ahmed, 20, 55, 64, 68, 79–82, 142, 159–60, 165, 169–70, 177, 190, 195–8, 200–6, 210, 280–1, 282, 300, 303, 305, 316, 318, 336, 340, 358–9, 363, 371, 375, 381
Maher, Aly, 6
Mahy, Mohamed El, 379
Malawi, 176
Marei, Sayed, 48, 73, 81, 88, 89–93, 228, 285
Mariut, King, 94, 166
Masry, Aziz El, 4,
Meguid, Esmat Abdel, 21–2, 177
Meir, Golda, 12, 17, 28, 109–10, 112, 117, 251
Memoirs of Mahmoud Riad, 117, 131, 174
Mengistu, President, 102–3
Middle East, 8, 11–13, 15, 20, 23, 28, 32–4, 38, 41, 49, 74–7, 89, 96–7, 105–6, 128, 134, 137, 154, 160, 162, 164, 175–8, 180, 193, 197, 208, 225, 255–6, 260, 262, 268, 283, 297, 299, 310, 316, 319–20, 328, 341, 361, 368, 376, 383, 385–6, 390–1, 397–8, 402–3
Misr Criminal and Public Prison, 4–5, 7, 362
Mitla Pass, 24, 116
Mobutu, President, 342
Mondale, Walter, 26, 81–3, 187–8, 203, 217, 299, 303–4, 307–8, 316, 319, 329, 337, 375
Montgomery, General, 1
Morocco, 34, 78–9, 133, 194–5, 260, 298–9, 339, 343, 381

Moses, 23, 32, 61, 321
Moyne, Lord, 7
Mubarak, Hosny, 20–2, 48–9, 58, 61, 66, 72, 159, 166, 190, 206–7, 230–1, 264
Muhammad V, 79
Muhieddin, Fuad, 295
Muslims, 52, 202, 323, 394
Mustapha, Himmat, 280–1
My Life, 109, 117

Nahas, Mustapha El, 1–3, 6
Namibia Contact Group, 101, 107
Nasser, Gamel Abdel, 8–11, 18, 28, 37, 39, 42–3, 81, 87, 118, 126, 137, 194, 349, 352–3, 367
National Assembly, Egyptian, 88
National Democratic Party, 294
National Party, 1, 294, 301
National Security Council, Egyptian, 43, 48–9, 66, 93, 124, 224–5, 272–3, 280–1, 286–7, 288–90, 293, 295, 314, 326, 328
Nazis, the, 1
Nixon, Richard, 11, 101, 120
Nobel Peace Prize, 52
Nofal, Sayid, 159, 164
Numeiry, Gaafar Mohammed, 34, 105, 140, 168–9, 170, 172, 182, 191

October magazine, 50, 60, 69
October War *see* war
Oman, 35
Organisation for Arab Unity, 20, 74, 212
Osman, Osman Ahmed, 3–6, 73, 200
Osman, Amin, 352
Othman, Ahmed, 142
Owen, David, 96

Palestine, 6–7, 8, 12, 17, 24, 28–9, 30, 32, 34, 49, 55–6, 65, 67–8, 104, 106, 125–31, 147–8, 165, 177, 197–8, 235, 275, 306, 327, 373, 383
Palestine Liberation Organisation (PLO), 7–8, 15, 20, 21, 34, 36, 55, 61, 67, 75–6, 98, 115, 120, 125–8, 132–8, 140, 148, 152, 165, 172, 231, 235, 284, 334–5, 364
Palestinians, the, 10, 15, 26–8, 33–4, 36, 38–9, 44–6, 47, 53, 55–6, 59, 63, 70, 75–6, 80, 87, 89–91, 95–6, 99, 106–7, 134, 139, 140, 152, 155–7, 161–3, 170–1, 184–6, 204–5, 210–5, 218–9, 221, 226–7, 230–3, 277, 284–5, 296–7, 304, 311, 317–9, 329–32, 344, 355, 364, 366–7, 371–2, 378, 386, 388–9, 393–4, 398–400
'Palestinian Arabs', 26–7, 56, 60, 63, 130, 213, 263
'Palestinian Jews', 26–7, 60, 130
Panama Treaty, 83
People's Assembly, Egyptian, 11, 14, 16, 118, 121, 125
Perez, Shimon, 62, 98–9, 105, 108, 188–9, 191, 193–4, 197–9, 205, 219, 252, 279, 283, 292, 309, 350
Poncet, Jean François, 295
Powell, Jody, 301

Quandt, William, 13, 110–14, 117, 188, 203, 263, 267, 299, 318, 346
Rabat Summit Conference, 26, 36, 126–7, 165, 170, 221, 231, 233, 235, 264, 365
Rabin, Yitzhak, 12, 17
Radwan, Fathy, 1
Rafah, 24, 60, 93, 104, 373, 404
Ramadan, Hafiz, 6
Ras Muhammad, 47, 202, 373, 405
Revolutionary Command Council, the, 53, 118, 121
Riad, Mahmoud, 16, 19, 117, 131, 133, 140, 159, 174
Ridi, Abdel Raouf Al, 41, 161, 165, 208, 270, 318, 320–1, 346
Rimon, Eleizer, 135
Rogers Plan, 257
Romania, 99–100, 110
Rommel, Erwin, 1
Rosen, Maier, 307
Russia, 10–12, 15, 22, 37–9, 42–3, 54, 61, 76, 98, 101–3, 106, 111, 113, 120, 129, 152–3, 242, 251, 261, 338, 341–2, 367–8

Sabbah, Sheik El, 140–1
Sabri, Ali, 9, 37, 42
Sadat, Anwar El, 2–7, 8–14, 16–27, 41–5, 48–50, 52, 55, 58–62, 65–71, 72–4, 76–87, 88–91, 93–5, 97–107, 109–16, 118–22, 124–30, 134–8, 140–4, 144–9, 150, 155, 157, 159–64, 165–71, 173, 176, 178–81, 184–9, 190–8, 199–200, 202–6, 209, 211–2, 216–7, 219, 221–5, 228, 230–2, 238, 243–5, 247–8, 250–4, 255–8, 260–9, 271–3, 279, 280–2, 284–

Index

95, 301–3, 305–10, 312–5, 320–22, 324, 326–8, 332–7, 339–43, 346–8, 349–60, 361–3, 365–9, 370–4, 376, 378–9, 385, 390, 397, 402, 405
Sadat, Jihan El, 191–2, 197–8
Said, Ahmed Khairat, 18
Salem, Mamdouh, 19–20, 22, 48, 72, 73, 124, 167, 264, 294
Salem, Salah, 8, 13, 53
Samaria, 24, 130, 148, 329, 331
  see also 'Judea and Samaria'
Saudi Arabia, 13, 29, 35–6, 41, 78, 82, 140–1, 147, 162, 164, 168, 170–4, 222, 231, 233, 237, 260, 267, 272–3, 279, 289, 299, 337, 339, 342, 365, 368
Saunders, Harold, 81, 112, 178, 180–1, 182, 184, 256–60, 263, 299, 346
Sayid, Ahmed Maher El, 20, 41, 161, 208, 228, 230, 236, 240, 270, 360
Scheel, Walter, 104
Schmidt, Helmut, 18, 72, 97, 105, 108
Security Council, U.N., 33, 43, 103, 111, 116, 139, 172, 177, 222, 247, 284, 297, 308, 373, 389, 395, 402–3, 405
Security Council Resolution:
  242, 24, 25, 44, 49, 50, 56, 80, 84–6, 91, 94, 115–6, 130, 155, 162, 165, 184, 193, 197, 210, 213, 215, 222, 227, 236, 242, 247, 251, 253, 258, 261, 263, 267, 270, 279, 283, 289, 296, 303, 311, 319, 327, 329–31, 372, 386, 390–1, 393, 397–8, 400, 402–3, 404
  255, 174
  388, 56, 111, 115–6, 197, 386, 390–1, 393, 397–8, 403
  339, 111
  340, 111
  425, 139, 177
  see also United Nations Resolution:
Setta, Ahmad Bou, 78–9
Shakir, Mohamed Ibrahim, 358–9, 382
Shamir, Yitzhat, 18
Sharm-El-Sheikh, 24, 308, 373, 404–5
Sharon, Ariel, 18, 50–1, 69, 209
Sharraf, El Sharif Abdel Hamid, 230, 236–7
Shawkat, General, 135
Sibai, Youseff El, 106–7, 124–5, 129, 177
Sinai (Peninsula), 8, 23–4, 26, 29, 31–2, 39, 44–5, 47, 50–2, 57, 60, 69, 72–3, 79, 82, 89–90, 96, 99, 110, 116, 148, 155, 167–8, 177, 188, 190, 202, 205, 214,

220–5, 235, 250, 263, 283, 285, 289, 296, 304–10, 313, 318, 326, 328, 331–3, 344, 348, 349–50, 354, 360, 364, 367, 372–3, 386, 39–2, 405
Sinai, Mount, 202–3, 205, 222–4, 292
Sirry, Hussein, 1, 6
Sisco, Joseph, 112
Socialist International, the, 98, 194, 197, 198, 279, 292,
Sorani, Gamel El, 128
South Africa, 75, 153, 175–6
South Lebanon *see* Lebanon
South Yemen *see* Yemen
Soviet Union/Soviets *see* Russia
Steadfastness Front, 34, 36, 76, 104, 127, 129, 132–3, 136–7
Sterne, Oliver, 295
Straits of Tiran, 24, 387, 404–5
Sudan, the, 34, 105, 136, 152, 168, 339
Suez Canal, 10, 297, 325, 341, 350, 388, 404–5
Sufism, 192
Sultan, Prince, 143
Syria, 10–11, 15, 17, 21, 28–9, 34–6, 42, 52, 75, 89, 113–7, 127, 132–3, 136–8, 140, 151, 169–70, 191, 202, 231–2, 237, 260, 266, 335, 386

Tallal, King, 194
Tamir, General, 59
Taraf, Nour-el-Din, 1
Tewfick, Ahmed, 3
Tewfick, Hussein, 2–6
The Battle for Peace, 40, 135, 139, 145, 207, 348, 360
The Secret Conversations of Henry Kissinger, 110, 117
The Talk of the Initiative, 93, 95
The Year of the Dove, 45, 46
Tito, President, 39, 75–6, 100
Tohamy, Hassan El, 34, 48, 79, 192–6, 199–203, 265, 285, 293, 305–7, 314–5, 321, 332–4, 334–5, 346, 353, 371, 377, 379
Tunisia, 260
Turk, Prince, 143
Turkey, 152

United Arab Emirates, 136, 140
United Kingdom *see* Britain
United Nations, 11, 20, 24, 29, 30, 33–5, 44, 68, 76, 89, 129, 137, 139, 157, 159,

413

166, 168, 176–8, 202, 216, 235, 241, 266, 285, 308, 311, 344, 372–3, 383–4, 387–8, 404–5
United Nations Charter, 33, 175–6, 253, 385, 390–1, 392, 395, 397–8, 401–2
United Nations Resolution:
  124, 278
  242, 24, 25, 33
  334, 296
  3375, 20
  see also Security Council Resolution:
United States of America *see* America
USSR *see* Russia

Vance, Cyrus, 46, 48, 50, 56–7, 59, 61–2, 64–70, 72–3, 81–2, 91, 95, 128, 155–7, 168, 177–8, 180, 182–3, 185, 200, 209–19, 220, 227, 233–4, 236–7, 239–41, 244–5, 248–9, 255–7, 259, 262–8, 271, 282, 288, 298–9, 303–5, 307–10, 314, 316, 317–8, 328–9, 334, 354–6, 360, 375–7

Wafd Party, 1–3, 6
Waldheim, Kurt, 167, 176–7, 222
Walters, Barbara, 381
War, the 1963, 15
War, the 1967, 8, 24, 29, 33, 36, 38–9, 57, 60, 74, 176, 194, 281, 310
War, the October/1973, 10, 18, 29, 31, 36–7, 42, 57, 68–9, 101, 116, 133, 194, 248, 281, 285, 287, 350, 365
War, the Six Day, 130
Weil, Van, 16, 105
Weizman, Ezer, 40, 50–2, 55, 58–9, 69, 135, 139, 142–4, 145–9, 173–4, 182, 199–205, 207, 209, 211–2, 219–20, 222–3, 225, 244–5, 249–50, 282, 292, 303, 321–2, 329, 331, 348–9, 351–9, 360
West, the, 102, 106, 167
West Bank, 8, 24, 27, 29, 33, 36, 39, 44, 48–52, 57, 59, 65, 68, 79–80, 82–3, 86, 89–92, 95–6, 99, 128–9, 147–9, 155–63, 165–6, 171, 178–82, 184, 187, 189, 193–4, 197–8, 202, 204–5, 210–7, 219–21, 223, 230–1, 233–6, 241, 246, 249, 256, 258–9, 261, 263, 268, 275, 277–8, 282–5, 288–9, 296, 302, 304–9, 311, 313, 316–20, 326, 328, 330–5, 341–5, 347, 351, 354–5, 359, 364, 366–7, 372–3, 383–4, 386–7, 391–4, 398–400
What Price Israel?, 13
World War II, 1, 58, 223

Yadin, Yigael, 62, 183, 245
Yamani, Zaki El, 168
Yariv, Aharon, 113
Yemen, 335; North, 136, 140; South, 34, 132, 136, 140
Yemen Arab Republic, 187
Yemen, People's Democratic Republic of, 187
Yost, 373
Young, Andrew, 178

Zaghloul, Saad, 7, 280–1
Zaire, 179
Zionism, 6–7, 33, 157, 162, 185, 249, 273, 288, 333, 361